Connolly

CHANGE AGENT SKILLS
IN HELPING
AND HUMAN SERVICE
SETTINGS

Other Books by Gerard Egan

Face to Face: The Small-Group Experience and Interpersonal Growth

The Skilled Helper: A Model for Systematic Helping and Interpersonal Relating
(Second Edition)

Exercises in Helping Skills: A Training Manual to Accompany the Skilled Helper
(Second Edition)

Interpersonal Living: A Skills/Contract Approach to Human-Relations Training in Groups

You and Me: The Skills of Communicating and Relating to Others

CHANGE AGENT SKILLS IN HELPING AND HUMAN SERVICE SETTINGS

GERARD EGAN
Loyola University of Chicago

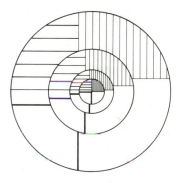

BROOKS/COLE PUBLISHING COMPANY
Monterey, California

Brooks/Cole Publishing Company
A Division of Wadsworth, Inc.

Printed in the United States of America

10 9 8 7 6 5 4 3 2 1

Library of Congress Cataloging in Publication Data

Egan, Gerard.
    Change-agent skills for the helping and human service professions.

    Bibliography: p.
    Includes index.
    1. Social work education—United States. 2. Social
service—United States—Case studies. 3. Public relations—Social service—Case studies. 4. Bureaucracy—
United States—Case studies. 5. Organizational behavior—Case studies. 6. Communication in social work—
United States—Case studies. 7. Social work administration—United States—Case studies. I. Title
HV11.E43 1985   361.3′07   84-7804
ISBN 0-534-03624-4

Sponsoring Editor: Claire Verduin
Editorial Assistant: Pat Carnahan
Production Editor: Penelope Sky
Manuscript Editor: Carol King
Permissions Editor: Carline Haga
Interior Design: Victoria Van Deventer
Cover Design: Debbie Wunsch
Art Coordinator: Judith L. Macdonald
Interior Illustration: Art by Kathie and Ralph
Typesetting: Graphic Typesetting Service, Los Angeles, California
Printing and Binding: R. R. Donnelley & Sons Company, Crawfordsville, Indiana

Preface

Human-service professionals, including counselors, social workers, welfare-agency personnel, clinical psychologists, teachers, school psychologists, nurses, ministers, and community workers, interact with specific individuals; they also intervene, directly or indirectly, in the social settings or systems in which their clients participate. Hannafin and Witt (1983) describe this kind of intervention from the viewpoint of the school psychologist, but what they say applies to all other human-service providers.

> System-level intervention (SLI) is a procedure whereby school psychological services are planned and provided in consideration of both the direct and indirect service needs in a school system *and* the influence of the school system in contributing to referral problems and solutions. SLI requires a basic understanding of the structure and mechanics of systems and a formalized plan for intervening for the purpose of modifying system failures. The intent of SLI is not to discount or eliminate direct or indirect interventions. The purpose of SLI is to effect changes where appropriate at the most fundamental sources of a system in order to preempt subsequent problems . . . [p. 130].

Hannafin and Witt do not suggest that system-level intervention should replace contacts with individuals: Both are needed.

Furthermore, helping and human-service professionals or paraprofessionals are also *managers* of systems, though they may prefer not to claim the title. They manage agencies, practices, parishes, case loads, classrooms, student service centers, departments, hospital floors, wards, and programs. They must organize, plan, set goals, make decisions, administer programs, develop subordinates—in short, they must do *all* the things that managers do, even without the label.

   The problem is that such professionals often intervene in systems and manage them without ever having been trained to do so. Consequently, the purpose of this book is to give helping and human-service workers, both in the field and in training, the working knowledge and skills necessary to managing and intervening in systems.

   I would like to thank Bill Richardson of North Texas State University and James Grayber of Northwestern University for reviewing the manuscript of *Change Agent Skills*; and the people of Brooks/Cole for producing the book.

Gerard Egan

Contents

vii

7

Goal-related Programs   123

PART **2**

PEOPLE   141

8

Human Resources   143

9

Roles and Relationships   158

10

Communication   175

11

Leadership   195

PART **3**

THE PERVASIVE VARIABLES   213

12

The Reward System   215

THE PERFORMANCE SYSTEM

There are three major parts to this book. Part 1 discusses the major elements of the system that lead to performance; that is, with the accomplishment of goals. Part 2 is about the people who do the work, the human resources of the system. Part 3 presents several pervasive variables that affect the way people do their work.

Part 1 includes the following elements:

- The skills needed in order to gather data and turn it into information (Chapter 3).
- The assessment of the generic and specific needs and wants of the members of the receiving system; that is, of the clients of the organization or institution (Chapter 4).
- The establishment of the mission and major aims of the system, based on the needs and wants of clients (Chapter 5).
- The establishment of specific goals or outcomes that meet the specific needs and wants of clients (Chapter 6).
- The creation of step-by-step programs to lead to these desired outcomes.
- How to obtain and maintain the material resources needed to implement programs (Chapter 7).

1

1

Intervening in Systems

People working in the helping and human-service professions are beginning to realize that they are more than deliverers of human services to individuals. In much of the work they do, they are managers and consultants, whether formally or informally. The time seems ripe to train future human-service professionals and paraprofessionals for these managerial and consultancy roles and to provide in-service education and training for workers who are already exercising these roles. (Caulfield and Perosa, 1983; Cochran, 1982; Conyne, 1983; Engelberg, 1980; Holahan, 1977; Leonard, 1977; *Personnel and Guidance Journal,* February and March, 1978; Rickard and Clements, 1981; Splete and Bernstein, 1981; Stum, 1982.)

The fact that you are reading this book implies an interest in managing, intervening in, or changing some kind of organization, institution, community, or subunit of any of these. However, you may well ask yourself, "How will this or any book help me? The social systems I face are unique and have their own unique problems." Let's take a look at uniqueness. If each social system—each family, each classroom, each neighborhood, each community, each institution, each project, and each program—is unique, then no book will help you. You will just have to grapple with each new situation. If you are diligent, you will become artful, but without any social *science* of system design, development, or change to help you on your way. The members of organizations, institutions, and communities love to see *their* social systems as unique. This belief justifies the problems they are experiencing and explains why needed change does not get off the ground. While each social system is a distinctive collection of human beings, however, none is absolutely unique.

Galbraith (1977) uses three overlapping circles to illustrate why a science of system design and change is possible (Figure 1-1). The *darkest* area indicates what

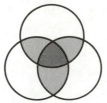

FIGURE 1-1.   Commonalities among organizations   *(The figure was suggested by John Dutton at the Kiev Seminar on Organization Design, USSR, May 29-June 2, 1972. See Jay Galbraith 1977, pp. 7–9.)*

all organizations (also institutions, and communities) have in common; the *lighter gray* areas show what some organizations have in common with certain others, and the *white*, what is unique to any given organization. Galbraith believes that 50% to 75% of the variance in organizations is accounted for by a combination of the black and the striped areas. This book, designed to help the human-service practitioner, deals with the black area, the core of any human system.

MODELS OF SYSTEMS

If you were to establish a mental health clinic, add a human resource development department to a hospital, assess the impact of a school or of an individual classroom on the human development of the students, redesign a counseling or therapy group, start a food pantry for the poor at a local church, or assess the efficiency of a social skills training program in a halfway house, you would use the models, methods, and skills outlined in this book. For the sake of simplicity, the model related to designing, redesigning, facilitating, and assessing the functioning of systems is called *Model A*. This model or framework is a "package" that includes submodels, methods, and skills all related to designing, running, and assessing a system or subsystem. It deals with what Hannafin and Witt (1983) call "the structure and mechanics" of systems.

If, on the other hand, you wanted to handle the problem situations that arise in the day-to-day operation of a system or subsystem or those that are discovered through a more formal and extensive process of assessment or diagnosis, then you would use the problem-management model (which I plan to treat in another volume). For instance, if you discovered that the school was failing to contribute to the human development of its students in various ways, if federal funds for your day-care center had been cut in half, if the clinic director's heavy drinking was getting in the way of the job, or if insurance companies were about to deny third-party payments to your mental health clinic because the clinic had not demonstrated that its interventions in the lives of its clients were both effective and cost efficient, then you would use this second model together with the methods and skills that make it work. Again for the sake of simplicity, I call this second "package" *Model B*.

Model A, then, deals with design, redesign, functioning, and assessment as they apply to any system or to any subunit of that system. It outlines the essential elements of any given system, whether school, classroom, counseling group, hospital, hospital ward, clinic, community, family, correctional facility, or any other kind of collection of people that can be called a human system, and shows how these elements fit together. Model B deals with solving problems and planning development and change. It addresses such questions as: How do we go about changing a system so that it conforms with the logic of Model A? How do we choose among the many different ways of redesigning or improving a system? Model A presents the logic underlying a well-designed and well-functioning system plus an understanding of why this logic so often goes awry, while Model B provides the logic of a step-by-step process of problem management, system development, or organizational change. Of course these two models are interrelated. A great deal of Model B is implied in the explanation and illustration of Model A found in this book.

When Galbraith (1977) talks about designing a system, he implies the need for both Model A and Model B. He points out that organization design consists of two choices: First, what kind of structure, process, and reward system should we adopt? And second, how do we get from where we are to where we want to be? What Galbraith calls structure, process, and reward system are all elements of Model A. Getting "from where we are to where we want to be" is the essence of Model B.

These two models together with the methods and skills they entail provide a framework for the working knowledge and skills change agents need to do their work. "Working knowledge" is the kind of information that enables a person to act. It is practical rather than theoretical knowledge. When the Green Bay Packers football team was winning consistently, Vince Lombardi, their coach, was asked to explain his success. He replied that he made sure the players were good at basics: They were trained to block and tackle well. Change agents could borrow this page from Lombardi's book. The methods and skills of Models A and B are the basics one needs to work with organizations, institutions, and communities as manager or consultant.

Since the term *model* will be used frequently, a few words about models and "working models" are in order.

Working models

If design and change are to take place in an orderly fashion, those involved in these processes need a clear picture of their objective. Visualizing design, assessment, and change through simple—but not oversimplified—models or frameworks can help everyone involved attain this clarity (see Lippitt, 1983).

In the sense in which the term is used here, a model is a framework or visual portrayal of how things actually work or how they might work under ideal conditions. Such a model is a kind of cognitive map that shows people how something is put together or illustrates the steps in a process, showing how one step follows from another. A *working model* is one that enables the user to achieve concrete and specific goals and to do so efficiently. Unassembled furniture, for instance, is accompanied by a set of illustrated instructions that show the buyer how to assemble it.

ιyer, then, has a "working model," a cognitive map with potential for action. king models differ from models that merely explain something. While models plain can ultimately be useful, often they can be too abstract or too compli- ----- o serve as frameworks for immediate action. Complicated models related to explaining organizations, institutions, and communities should be "translated" into more simplified working models if they are to be of service to the practitioner.

Counselors and other helpers need a working model of the helping process. The model in Figure 1-2 is a simple model or framework that counselors might use in working with their clients (see Egan, 1982a, 1982b). Both verbally and graphically, this map tells counselors what to do and the general order in which to do it. Therefore, it has immediate "delivery" potential. This framework can be shared with the client so that both counselor and client are operating from the same cognitive map.

Two criteria characterize working models: (1) they must be complex enough to account for the reality they attempt to describe and portray; (2) they must be simple enough to use. A model that meets only the first criterion is likely to be of interest only to theoreticians and researchers. A model that meets only the second criterion would tend to be simplistic rather than merely simple, and would therefore be useless as a working model. Lippitt (1983) suggests that models for *practitioners* such as managers, consultants, and other change agents need to be two-dimen- sional, linear, and basically nonmathematical. Complex and sophisticated three- dimensional, nonlinear, and highly mathematical models may be powerful instru- ments in the hands of theoreticians and researchers, but usually they do not help practitioners and clients very much—at least not until they are translated into sim- pler forms.

In summary, then, working models—as opposed to models devised primarily to explain systems—

- provide a vehicle for translating theory and research into a visualization of how things work;
- constitute a framework for action or intervention (delivery);
- suggest the methods, technologies, and skills needed to get the work done;
- are two-dimensional, linear, and nonmathematical;
- are simple without being simplistic.

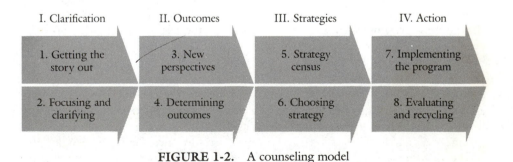

I. Clarification	II. Outcomes	III. Strategies	IV. Action
1. Getting the story out	3. New perspectives	5. Strategy census	7. Implementing the program
2. Focusing and clarifying	4. Determining outcomes	6. Choosing strategy	8. Evaluating and recycling

FIGURE 1-2.   A counseling model

Model A, which is outlined in the next chapter, is a working model with these characteristics.

Different kinds of systems

Since both *system* and *change agent* are critical terms, it is helpful to consider how they are used in these pages. Change agents deal with *human systems*—that is, organizations, institutions, and communities, together with the subunits and programs that constitute these systems. A human system, in its most general sense, is a group of regularly interacting or interdependent people forming a unified whole. Common definitions of organizations stress the *goal-directed* nature of human systems:

> [A social setting is] any instance in which two or more people come together in new relationships over a sustained period of time in order to achieve certain goals [Sarason, 1972, p. 1].

> When persons interact for individual and joint objectives, an organization exists [Hicks and Gullett, 1976, p. 34].

> Organization emerges whenever there is a shared set of beliefs about a state of affairs to be achieved and that state of affairs requires the efforts of more than a few people [Galbraith, 1977, p. 34].

Porter, Lawler, and Hackman (1975, pp. 69–71), in summarizing common definitions, list five dimensions of organizations, including goal orientation:

1. *Social entities*. Organizations are human systems; they are social entities involving people who are acting, interacting, and reacting.
2. *Goal-oriented*. Organizations are instrumental; that is, they are established to achieve specific goals.
3. *Structure*. The work necessary to achieve goals must be divided up in various ways.
4. *Coordination*. There is need to coordinate and direct the activities of people in different roles carrying out different tasks in order to accomplish the goals of the system.
5. *Continuity*. An organization is not merely an ad hoc group of people; the activities and relationships of the organization continue over time.

While these definitions deal with organizations, communities, too, have these characteristics. A family is also a system in which "persons interact for individual and joint objectives." Self-help groups such as Alcoholics Anonymous and cooperatives are social entities, are goal-directed, have structure, need coordination, and have continuity.

Let us consider some of the different kinds of human systems to which Model A applies.

Organizations. Generally organizations are human systems that manufacture products or produce services or provide a combination of products and services for individuals or other systems *outside* the organization. For instance, General Motors produces automobiles (products), and hospitals provide various forms of medical intervention (services). Sears not only sells its customers underwear and sofas but also examines their eyes, cleans their carpets, and takes care of their insurance and investment needs (products and services). These organizations are producing systems, and the consumers are members of the receiving system. The duality of producing system and receiving system is illustrated in Figure 1-3.

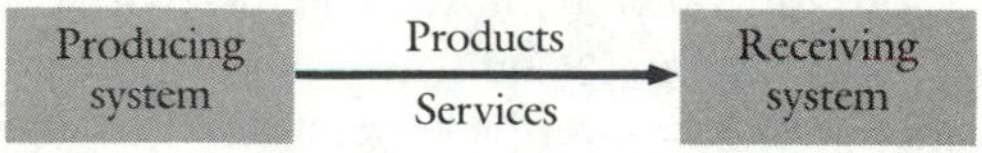

Producing system	Products —————▶ Services	Receiving system

FIGURE 1-3.   Producing and receiving systems

Community systems. These systems provide services and sometimes products for *their own* members. Figure 1-4 depicts the kind of exchange of services found in communities such as families and peer groups. The overall mission or goal is the common good or betterment, however defined, of people in the community. There are smaller communities such as families and peer groups, middle-size communities such as voluntary associations, and larger communities such as neighborhoods and church communities. Generally, such systems meet basic human needs and wants such as those for sustenance, security, belonging, companionship, intimacy, entertainment, recreation, and the like. The larger the community, the greater its need for organizational structure.

Institutions. Webster's dictionary defines an institution as "a society or corporation especially of a public character." Institutions provide services of one sort or another for society. Hasenfeld and English (1975) define human services agencies as institutions that serve the needs of individual members of society and in so doing maintain and protect the social structure.

Since in many institutions staff and members spend time together, institutions can take on some of the characteristics of a community. Since institutions differ sharply in terms of voluntariness of participation on the part of their members—

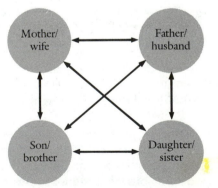

FIGURE 1-4.   The exchange of human services in a community group such as a family

consider prisons, hospitals, correctional institutions, orphanages, and graduate schools—they also differ sharply in their community characteristics.

Hybrid systems. Some systems provide services and/or products both for their own members and for others. For instance, in Western society, members of religious orders live in community but also run such organizations or institutions as schools and hospitals. On the other hand, organizations in Japan, such as large manufacturing concerns, are often places where workers recreate, meditate, and socialize. When workers develop a deep sense of loyalty to these organizations, there is a distinct community dimension.

Some voluntary associations, such as stamp-collecting and ski clubs, meet the needs of only their own members. Others try to meet the needs of their own members and of those outside the formal association. For instance, clubs devoted to the protection of the environment meet the needs of their members and also the needs of the wider community or society. Social clubs like the Elks, the Knights of Columbus, and the Masons often provide services for nonmembers, for instance, by establishing boys' clubs and hospitals and by raising funds for a variety of charitable purposes. Professional associations such as the American Medical Association and the American Psychological Association promote the professional interests of their members but they also, at least ideally, monitor the behavior of their members and therefore provide a protective service for their members' clients.

Human-service systems. Since this book is about helpers as change agents, special mention is made of human-service delivery systems—that is, organizations or institutions that provide a wide variety of human services to the members of society. Hospitals, mental health clinics, schools, orphanages, neighborhood organizations, boys clubs, churches, and a host of government agencies are included in this category. Professionals such as nurses, doctors, lawyers, social workers, counselors, psychotherapists, consultants, and ministers belong to systems that specialize in the delivery of human services.

> These organizations offer an almost infinite variety of human services for citizens, from the rich to the poor, from birth to death. They provide health care, education, material assistance, control and rehabilitation of offenders, employment advice, and family counseling. Human services agencies also make life safer, more enjoyable, and more convenient through public services such as pollution control, public transportation, recreational facilities, and information dissemination. The individual services provided by these institutions are indispensable to the survival of modern society. They socialize its members, integrate them into the social structure, and protect their general health and well-being. Most of the institutions operate on public funds, but some are supported by private endowments or by nonprofit fee schedules. Still others are profit-making businesses that operate on client fees and/or contracts with federal, state, or local governments [Gallessich, 1982, pp. 7–8].

Systems that deliver human services face special problems in terms of both effectiveness and efficiency.

Since terms such as *organizations, communities, institutions, associations, social units,* and *primary and secondary groups* all refer to human systems, their definitions tend to overlap. No attempt is made here to set up a scientific taxonomy of human systems or to develop exact definitions for different kinds of systems. Rather, the above list reminds the reader that there are many different kinds of human systems, each with its own needs and problems, and suggests that the models and principles for improving systems apply, however analogously, to *all* human systems. All human systems organize themselves, however loosely, to meet specific needs and wants. While the family and a manufacturing concern will certainly apply system-improvement principles differently, both systems are pursuing relevant need-fulfilling goals. Models that spell out the logic of system performance and system improvement have something to say to both. In this book, however, examples are drawn from the kinds of systems that are relevant to people working in human-service professions.

Producing system/receiving system

All human systems and subsystems produce something, at least if the term "produce" is used in a broad sense. They produce products or services or a combination of the two for some kind of receiving system. The members of a family produce a variety of products (meals, clean laundry) and services (affection, conversation, protection) for one another. Hospitals provide such things as diagnostic tests and operations for patients. A college counseling center produces a variety of developmental and therapeutic services for the student population. In human systems that are communities or have community dimensions, however, the distinction between producing system and receiving system is not clear cut.

Suppose you enter the hospital because you have a sharp pain in your lower right side and feel nauseated. The hospital is the producing system in that it provides such things as diagnostic tests, surgery, and other forms of medical help, and you are the receiving system, the patient. You are the receiving system in a very special sense, however, because of your intimate involvement with the process. First of all, you actually live in the hospital for a period of time. Second, you are not a mere passive recipient of products or services, even though you are called a "patient." You participate both physically and psychologically in the services provided by the hospital. If you are to get well, you must participate actively by working in a variety of ways toward your own wellness. Active participation is required by other human-service ventures such as social service, counseling, education, and church organizations. Human-service systems are cooperative ventures and therefore have a distinct community dimension—at least ideally. Hospitals and schools at times seem like factories, but not when they are at their best.

The distinction between producing and receiving system is even more blurred in such community systems as families and voluntary associations. Since the members of these systems provide services for one another, the members of the producing system are also members of the receiving system. Someone in the family cooks the meal (or it is a cooperative effort), but whoever cooks it also eats it. There is still a production and an exchange dimension to these systems, however, since services relating to sustenance, security, daily maintenance, the solution of everyday problems, companionship, and intimacy are both "produced" and "received" by the members of a family.

Input–transformation–output

The producing process involves some kind of input, some kind of transformation process, and some kind of output. If the input is dirty clothes, the transformation is laundering, and the output is clean clothes. Of course, the people who constitute the producing system use a variety of resources to do the laundering, and the clean clothes are destined for some receiving system.

> At a minimum, then, organizational rationality involves three major component activities: (1) input activities, (2) technological activities, and (3) output activities. Since these are interdependent, organizational rationality requires that they be appropriately geared to one another. The inputs acquired must be within the scope of the technology, and it must be within the capacity of the organization to dispose of the technological production [Thompson, 1967, p. 19].

The input–transformation–output process can become complex. In automobile manufacturing there is a clear distinction between the producing system, the automobile manufacturer, and the ultimate receiving system, the people who buy the cars. But in the kinds of communities or community-like systems with which or within which human-service providers work, the distinction is blurred. For instance, if a classroom is to be successful, it needs a variety of *inputs*, including physical resources such as buildings and books, the knowledge and skills of the teachers, and the knowledge and skills of the students. The transformation process involves interactive behaviors on the part of teachers and students, as illustrated in Figure 1-5.

Within the family there are tasks to be done and services to be exchanged that involve inputs, transformation, and outputs. Consider the conversations that characterize companionship: The partners take basic communication abilities (input), transform these abilities into actual conversations with each other (transformation process), and thereby provide a form of companionship for each other (output). If this analogy is pushed too far, it results in an overly mechanistic look at community. However, this input–transformation–output model, expanded and developed into Model A, is useful in analyzing any given system, whether organization, institution, or community, and discovering the kinds of improvement it needs.

AGENTS OF CHANGE

If there is any truth in the cliché that the only stable thing about systems is change, then promoting and managing change is a major task of those with leadership and managerial responsibility within the system. In these pages the word *change* refers to designing and constructing a system from the ground up or improving a system that already exists. It refers to both the fine tuning in design and functioning that takes place from day to day and to the major reorganization of a system. It refers to handling both major and minor problem situations and to making major and minor decisions that affect the system.

Who acts as an agent of change in human systems? Is it just the director or administrative officer of the system and his or her staff? Does *change agent* refer

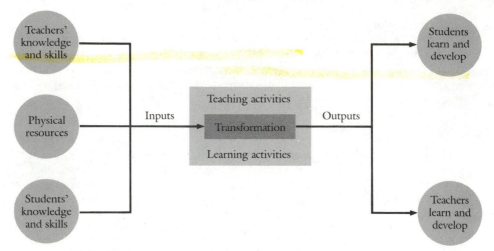

FIGURE 1-5.   Inputs, transformation, and outputs in a classroom

principally to the internal or external consultant or the systems specialist? Does it refer to the supervisors who make day-to-day decisions about the operation of the system? Or is there something of the change agent in all of us?

In its widest sense, change agent refers to anyone who plays an important part in designing, redesigning, running, renewing, or improving any system, subsystem, or program. Managerial consultants, then, are change agents, but so are the managers themselves. Educational consultants are change agents, but so are administrators and teachers. Moreover, since most change programs fail unless all the members of the system or subsystem participate in and cooperate with the change, all system members are, in their own way, agents of change. No matter who initiates change in a system or subsystem, the change process becomes the property of all who are asked to participate in it and who are affected by it. For instance, if students are asked to cooperate in educational change efforts, then they too, at least ideally, are *agents* of change and not merely *patients* or passive recipients.

Not everyone in the system is a designated leader nor does each member have the kind of authority, power, or influence that an officially designated leader has, but everyone in the system, to a greater or lesser extent, "owns" a piece of the leadership process. Failure to realize this can lead to disastrous consequences:

> The leader of a large North American diocese announced one day that there was to be a major fund drive to raise more than a hundred million dollars. For both the pastors and the people of the diocese this was a bolt from the blue. They had not been consulted in any way about the fund drive or its aims and they were angry. As a result there was a great deal of resistance to the drive even though parishioners considered many of the projects to be funded worthwhile. Ultimately, goals had to be lowered and the drive ended on a sour note. Thereafter, the climate in the diocese was never the same.

In this case a decision came down from "on high." The designated leader and his staff, to the detriment of the entire project, failed to see leadership as a process involving the members of the system.

In summary, then, change agents in the wide sense, while they may not be officially designated leaders, are people who nevertheless participate in significant ways in the leadership process. While the models and methods described in this book are of immediate interest to those explicitly entrusted with the *management* of design, functioning, and change, they speak to everyone involved in and affected by these processes.

In a more restricted sense, change agents are the managers and consultants who work in human-service settings.

Managers refers to all of those entrusted with any kind of managerial or super-visory authority within the system: leaders, administrators, supervisors, project directors, program coordinators, and the like. The term refers to anyone who is entrusted with the responsibility of designing a human system, subsystem, project, or program and of trying to make it work. If you need to get the work of a system or program done through the cooperation of others who work in the system, then you are a manager. While managers may do some of the "substantive work" of the system—for instance, the director of a mental health center may do some therapy—their special task is to facilitate the work of others. The head nurse in a hospital unit may on occasion deliver services to patients, but her or his principal task is to see to it that quality care is delivered through the nurses on the unit. This task involves managing the human resources of the nursing department and managing the interface between the nursing department and the other departments of the hospital.

Human-service workers are the professionals, paraprofessionals, or volunteers who function under the direction of the manager in a human-service system. Managers get the work of the system done through others called workers or staff or employees. While the head of nursing coordinates the work, the nurses on the floor get the work done. Human-service workers need system-related skills for the following reasons:

1. *The human-service mini-system.* The interaction between a human-service worker and his or her client is in itself a mini-system subject to the principles outlined in this book.
2. *Settings as clients.* Human-service workers often cannot do their work well without understanding and dealing with the social settings in which their clients find themselves (Egan and Cowan, 1979). For some human-service workers, the social setting *is* the client. Family therapists, school psychologists, and social workers work with units, such as families, classrooms, and neigh-borhood organizations.
3. *Human-service practitioners as consultants.* Today, helping and human-service practitioners such as psychologists, counselors, and social workers are becom-ing consultants in the more formal sense. The models, methods, and skills outlined in these pages are the essential tools of the consultant.

Consultants are people who, without taking over responsibility for a task, help others to get it done. They are facilitators. They help people see what needs to be done and encourage them to do it. External consultants do not belong to the particular organization but are called in to help in a variety of ways. Internal consultants are members of a particular organization who are assigned the task of helping leaders to do their work more effectively and efficiently. Gallessich (1982), in discussing new social roles for human-service professionals, calls consultation a *"tertiary institution* that helps secondary ones serve society" (p. 3).

Anyone with co-workers or subordinates can become a consultant by adopting a consultancy approach to managing, directing, or supervising. People who take a consultancy approach to leadership see themselves primarily as facilitators who help others develop the resources needed to get the work done. Good managers often have a significant degree of consultancy in their approach to managing because they realize how much they depend on others to accomplish the work of the system. They value in their subordinates the kind of autonomy that contributes to productivity.

Many consultants are technical experts or advisers. For instance, an expert in hospice care may be called in to give technical advice to a hospital that is starting a hospice. In this book, however, the consultant is seen from a more general perspective—that is, as one who is expert in organizational realities. Such a consultant may know relatively little about the technical side of a hospice, but since a hospice is a human-service delivery *system*, such a consultant could provide assistance to the hospice as a system. This book addresses anyone involved with or interested in the system, including the consultant. The book is about the system and what it needs to be effective and not about the process of consultation. Therefore, it is not meant to take the place of books dealing exclusively with consultants and their roles (for that see Alpert and others, 1982; Blake and Mouton, 1976; Block, 1981; Gallessich, 1982; Goodstein, 1978; O'Neill and Tricket, 1982). But since the consultant is an important agent of change and since there are consultancy dimensions to every managerial role, a model dealing with the roles in the consultancy process is in order.

THE TRIADIC CONSULTATION MODEL

The triadic consultation model depicted in Figure 1-6 is a simple framework that helps clarify different *roles* in the consultation process (Egan, 1978; Tharp, 1975; Tharp and Wetzel, 1969). The model is "triadic" because it emphasizes three basic roles: the role of the consultant or consultancy group, the role of the mediator or mediator group, and the role of the target person or target group.

These roles can be found in different kinds of systems (Figures 1-7, 1-8, and 1-9).

The consultation process roles

The target denotes the members of a system whose behavior is to be modified (changed, facilitated, supported) so that the system might meet its goals more effectively. For instance, a social worker employed by the city, working in conjunc-

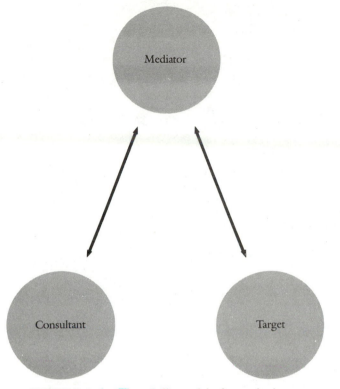

FIGURE 1-6.   The triadic model of consultation

tion with the leaders of a neighborhood organization, learns that the elderly in the area take relatively little advantage of the social services available to them. Consequently the quality of life has deteriorated among the elderly. The goals of the change effort are to assess the needs of the elderly in the neighborhood and to help them take advantage of available services. The elderly constitute the target group. In Figures 1-8 and 1-9, the students of a school and the members of a church congregation are target groups.

The target group is not merely a group of passive people to whom something is to be done. If the neighborhood change program is to be effective, the elderly will have to do something. The members of the target group must understand, participate in, cooperate with, and execute programs of change if change is to take place at all. If the members of the target group are not active in the process, then the efforts of mediators and consultants will fail.

The mediator is an individual or a group of individuals capable of influencing the behavior of the target. Tharp and Wetzel (1969) emphasize the ability of the mediator to *control* the behavior of the target group by controlling the reinforcers or rewards for which the members of the target group work. For instance, management can control the behavior of workers by incentives such as pay increases, bonuses,

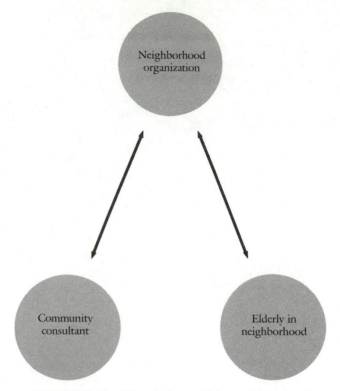

FIGURE 1-7.   The triadic model in a neighborhood

promotions, and the like, and also by exercising the power to hire and fire. However, I prefer to take a wider and perhaps more constructive view, seeing the mediator as having resources to *help* the target achieve desirable goals (see Egan, 1978). I would like to emphasize the mediator's role as *facilitator* and not as controller. Ideally, the mediator, whether individual or group, both supports and challenges the target in the latter's efforts to achieve system goals more effectively. Mediators not only challenge the members of the target group to contribute to efforts to change the system or subsystem for the better, but they also support these efforts by sharing their resources.

The mediator or mediator group may also be part of the target group; that is, they represent the interests of the target group. For instance, a small group of graduate students discussed with a faculty consultant their dissatisfactions with the clinical psychology program. Since the graduate students wanted changes both for their fellow students and for themselves, they had to be active both as mediators and as members of the target group.

The consultant is a person or a group of people with the knowledge, skills, programs, vision, and technologies needed both to help the mediator plan for system improvement and to help the mediator influence or facilitate the work of the target

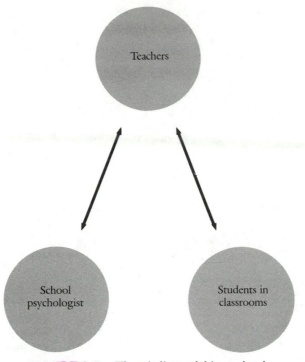

FIGURE 1-8. The triadic model in a school

group. An educational consultant might show a group of teachers how to increase
the learning potential of students by having the students in upper grades participate
in the teaching of students in lower grades. Or a managerial consultant might train
a group of managers from an organization to act as mediators in an effort to design
a change program—from diagnosis through evaluation—for the entire organization.

In the triadic model of consultation, the consultant does not ordinarily deal
directly with the target group, though he or she might observe how the mediator
interacts with the target and suggest ways of interacting more productively. In my
view of the triadic model, just as the mediator helps the target group participate as
effectively and as humanly as possible in the process of system improvement, the
consultant provides resources, including support and challenge, that enable the
mediator group to do its facilitator work more effectively.

Changing roles in consultation

As circumstances change, the same person can be target, mediator, or consultant
within a system. As illustrated in Figure 1-10, for example, a high school teacher
might find herself or himself successively in target, mediator, and consultant roles.
In each of these cases, the consultant shares resources and facilitates the work of

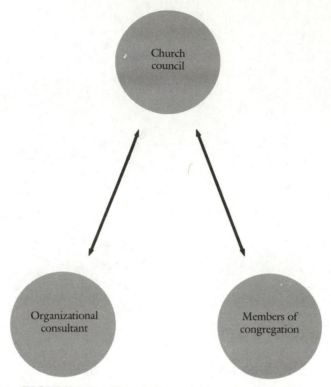

FIGURE 1-9.   The triadic model in a church setting

the mediator; and the mediator, enriched by these resources, influences the behavior of the target, enabling the target to progress actively toward the goals of the system.

The triadic model can be expanded in both directions by introducing a higher order of consultants, more mediators, or more remote target groups (Figure 1-11). The purpose of this scheme is not to establish a power hierarchy or a pecking order or to determine which roles are the most prestigious or the most important. Rather, its function is to delineate *resource* relationships, identifying who has the resources to help the next person down the line achieve desired goals. This model is certainly a social-influence model, but it works best if the process of system improvement is a cooperative venture rather than one emphasizing control.

Consultant	Mediator	Target
School psychologist	Principal	TEACHER
Principal	TEACHER	Teacher's aide
TEACHER	Teacher's aide	Students

FIGURE 1-10.   The teacher as target, mediator, and consultant

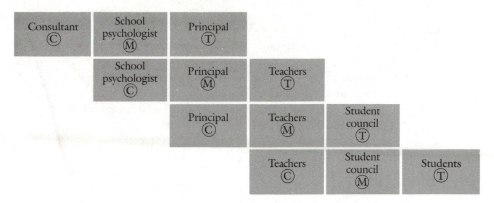

FIGURE 1-11.   Expanding the roles in the triadic consultation process

Gluckstern and Packard (1977) describe a successful project in a correctional facility that illustrates what is best in triadic consultation.

> The objective of the consultation was to move an authoritarian, repressive prison from a place where lives are trivialized to a place where inmates are given the opportunity to develop. A university consultant, who specialized in counseling, group work, and organizational development, met with a correctional officer actively interested in prison reform. The correctional officer served as the primary mediator. In a sense there were two target groups. The immediate target group was the staff of the facility; the inmates constituted the more remote target group. Without the cooperation of the staff, nothing could be accomplished. The mediator helped the consultant develop relationships with both staff and inmates.
>
> At the end of the first year of the project, the following had been accomplished: An occupational training project was on line, a self-help drug rehabilitation group was operating, a basic learning center had been set up, and a degree program affiliated with the university had been established. At the end of the second year there was a governing board composed of administrators, correctional officers, *and* inmates.

This case illustrates an important point in the triadic model: consultants, mediators, and target groups can learn a great deal from one another. The model represents learning/facilitation/action, not power.

"GIVING AWAY" SYSTEMS-INVOLVEMENT SKILLS

Change-agent skills are systems-involvement skills. All people need these skills in order to participate in, cope with, and contribute to human systems such as family,

neighborhood, work, and government (Egan and Cowan, 1979). Systems-involvement skills form one of many "packages" of *life skills* people need to pursue developmental goals and both cope with and grow through developmental crises. These
developmental events don't take place in a vacuum; they are not merely personal
events. They take place in systems—that is, in the context of the social settings of
life. Ignorance of how the principal social systems of life work and failure to develop
a certain degree of "system smarts" can impede human development and in extreme
cases contribute to social maladjustment and psychopathology. Maslow notes that
"what we call 'normal' in psychology [and in human systems] is really a psychopathology of the average, so undramatic and so widely spread that we don't even
notice it ordinarily" (p. 16).

Miller (1969, 1981) has urged social scientists to "translate" theory and research
into practical working knowledge and skills so that these can be "given away" to
ordinary people through education and training (see Chavis, Stucky, and Wandersman, 1983). This "giving away" needs to take place when professionals work
with the popular self-help movement (Gartner and Riessman, 1977; Pancoast,
Parker, and Froland, 1983). Havelock (1973), in discussing organization-development interventions in educational systems, notes that these interventions are
incomplete if the system is left without the capacity to renew itself. Egan and Cowan
(1979) have noted, however, that formal educational systems traditionally have been
hesitant to teach such essential skills as planning, problem solving, and decision
making and that professionals, perhaps fearful of working themselves out of a job,
are hesitant to give their "secrets" away. Individuals are expected to acquire these
skills somehow through experience. This book attempts to "give away" systems-
oriented working knowledge and skills, not only to those who manage systems,
but also to those who participate in them. These models, methods, and skills are
not the exclusive domain of professionals and paraprofessionals. They belong to all
who live and function in a variety of social systems. Effective helping and human-
service interventions leave clients *empowered* to act on their own behalf (Berger and
Neuhaus, 1977).

As Caplan and Nelson (1973) and Ryan (1971) note, psychological approaches
to change are biased toward seeing individuals as solely responsible for their problems and therefore as solely responsible for efforts to change. Very often, however,
systems not only cause problems, but also limit the individual's solutions—for
instance, a failing economy breeds unemployment no matter how willing people
are to work. Teachers who maintain rigidly authoritarian classrooms and teach by
monotonous reading from notes place limits on student enthusiasm.

Individuals can be taught how to see the world from a systems perspective (Kauffman, 1980, 1981). Furthermore, they can be taught to assess the ways they are
being affected by the various social settings of their lives, how to involve themselves
more creatively in these settings, how to challenge social systems responsibly, how
to contribute to system improvement, and how to cope with systems that are
affecting the quality of their lives in adverse ways. Systems, and not just individuals,
can suffer from the "psychopathology of the average."

PRODUCTIVITY AND THE QUALITY OF LIFE

In a sense this book is about two interrelated issues—productivity and quality of life. Productivity refers to effectiveness and efficiency, getting the work of the system done, accomplishing its goals, and doing so at a reasonable cost. Quality of life refers to the degree to which the legitimate needs and wants of the members who live or work in the system are satisfied. Both of these are *comprehensive* terms; that is, each includes the other even though each stresses a different vantage point. The interrelatedness of these two issues is seen most clearly perhaps in community-living systems. For instance, if there is little love or affection among the members of a family, then the quality of community life of its members suffers. If a father sexually exploits his daughter, then one family goal, security from attack, is not met and the quality of the daughter's life suffers.

Productivity and quality of life are also interrelated in businesses. If workers suffer from poor working conditions, they probably will not be as productive as they could be. If they work in a system with a country club atmosphere, then quality of life (at least one conception of it) might be high, but productivity is likely to suffer. But perhaps more to the point, workers ordinarily feel good about achieving the legitimate goals for which they are responsible. Therefore, whatever prevents them from achieving these goals can also affect how they feel about their own work—that is, the quality of their work life.

By definition, human-service practitioners deal with the quality of life. Human-service organizations, institutions, agencies, and workers are productive to the degree that they help their clients improve the quality of their lives.

2

A Model of System Design, Functioning, and Assessment

While problem-solving models abound, the human-services literature offers relatively few practical working models that deal with the design, functioning, and assessment of systems. The few that exist are not in logical step-by-step progression or are not comprehensive enough (Pascale and Athos, 1981; Kotter, 1978; Nadler and Tushman, 1977; Weisbord, 1976). Many design models refer mainly to structure, which is only one part of system design. Model A deals with the basic system elements involved in design. The elements of design can relate to an *entire* organization, institution, or community—for instance, a welfare agency, a school, or a community center—but they can also relate to any *subunit* within a larger system—for instance, the outpatient department of a hospital, the counseling center of a school, or the section of a community center that deals with the elderly. Finally, design elements can relate to the *programs* within the subunits of larger systems. The personnel department, a subunit of a large welfare organization, is responsible for training, for example, but training is best seen, not merely as one of the programs of the personnel department, but as a system in its own right. That is, training is a further subsystem within a department, which is itself a subsystem.

THE ELEMENTS OF MODEL A

This chapter presents an overview of these Model A design elements as an orientation or "advanced organizer" (Ausubel, 1968) to provide a context for considering each separate element in greater detail. A simple example will be used to illustrate the elements of Model A. We will consider the Counseling Psychology program in the psychology department of State University, though we might have discussed a welfare agency, a community organization, a classroom, a mental health center, or any other human-service system or any of the programs that a human-service center might administer.

I. The performance system

Model A is quite logical. Once it is determined by the members of a producing system that they would like to meet the needs of a receiving system, then all the elements of Model A are demanded, each giving rise to the next. Of course, the world of organizations, institutions, and communities is not as logical and as rational as the model. The first six elements of Model A relate principally to the work of the system and its accomplishments.

1. *Needs and wants*. Assessing the needs and wants of the members of the receiving system or of the community.
2. *Mission*. Determining the overall purpose of the system.
3. *Major aims*. Translating mission into the major aims or areas in which accomplishments are to be pursued.
4. *Goals*. Translating major aims into the concrete accomplishments to which the work of the system is directed.
5. *Programs*. Developing the means and step-by-step procedures to achieve these goals.
6. *Nonpeople resources*. Providing the material resources people need in order to get the work of the system done.

II. The people

The next five elements deal with the people who make the system work.

7. *Human resources*. Getting the human resources needed to implement programs—that is, to do the work of the system.
8. *Roles and responsibilities*. Dividing up the work that needs to be done and establishing job descriptions.
9. *Relationships*. Determining how both people and system subunits need to work together to accomplish the goals of the system.
10. *Communication*. Making sure that people get the information and the feedback they need to do their work well.
11. *Coordination/facilitation/authority/accountability*. Establishing leadership or managerial roles to make sure that all the elements of Model A are coordinated.

III. The pervasive variables

The next four elements "rinse through" and affect the functioning of the system. They, too, need to be managed.

12. *Reward system*. Providing the incentives and rewards for getting the work of the system done.
13. *Quality of life*. Making sure that the legitimate needs and wants of those who work in the system are taken care of.

14. *Environment*. Monitoring and managing the impact of the external environ-
    ment on the system.
15. *Politics*. Monitoring and managing the ways stakeholders in the system wield
    power, both overtly and covertly.
16. *The arational and culture*. Trying to understand and manage the impact of
    the arational, unsystematic, and nonlinear dimensions of both the system
    and its environment; coming to terms with the ways both stated and unstated
    values, assumptions, policies, and rules affect the productivity and quality
    of life of the system.

Model A does not provide the principles of organization design but rather the
logic that underlies design efforts and a checklist for engaging in actual design
efforts. To the extent that Model A provides the skeleton or outline to which design
must conform, it is a prescriptive model. It provides systematic answers to such
questions as: What are the essential elements of any system? How do these elements
fit together and interact? How does a system operate? The actual design of any
given organization relates to the particular ways in which the elements of Model A
are handled.

Model A is a working model. In this overview Model A is presented as a rational,
systematic, and linear method for designing and assessing human systems. Miller
(1978) defines a systematic method as "a method of performing an operation that
provides for order, consistency, unity of purpose, direction, and coordinated effort.
A systematic method provides a view of a total operation that enables the viewer
to see each part of an operation in relation to other parts and the whole" [p. 396].
Since the world of systems is not always rational, systematic, and linear, however,
useful ways of coming to terms with the "arationality" of systems will have to be
discussed.

Each element of Model A will now be explored and applied briefly to the design
and execution of the Counseling Psychology program at State University. The
purpose of this program, of course, is to train people to be effective helpers. Training *as a system*, and not merely as a program, is chosen because most readers will
have had ample experience with training as both trainees and trainers. The example
is purposely idealized and oversimplified in order to express clearly the elements of
Model A.

I. THE PERFORMANCE SYSTEM

The logic of a system is this: people use their knowledge and skills and physical
resources to work through step-by-step programs for accomplishing concrete and
specific goals that relate to one or more of the major aims of the system; accomplishing these goals and aims means that the organization is accomplishing its
mission; the sure sign of this is that the relevant and legitimate needs and wants of
the members of the receiving system (that is, the clients) are being met. Let us now
look at each of these elements and flesh them out through the example of the
Program in Counseling Psychology.

1. Assessing the needs and wants of members of the receiving system.   In Chapter 1 we reviewed an organizational input-transformation-output model. People in human-service organizations take inputs such as their own and their clients' working knowledge and skills and such material resources as buildings, meeting rooms, furniture, video equipment, blackboards, and the like, and in cooperation with their clients transform these resources into outputs that meet the clients' needs and wants. Social workers may use these and other resources to help clients satisfy their need for decent housing or to help in settling family disputes. The members of a community use resources for similar purposes: a family buys food and turns it into meals to satisfy both nutritional and psychological needs. As indicated in Figure 2-1, it is essential that an organization first assess the relevant needs and wants of the receiving system or of the members of the community. Models and skills related to needs assessment are important for change agents.

Since people come together in social groups in order to satisfy others, well-run systems develop the instruments needed to identify the relevant needs and wants

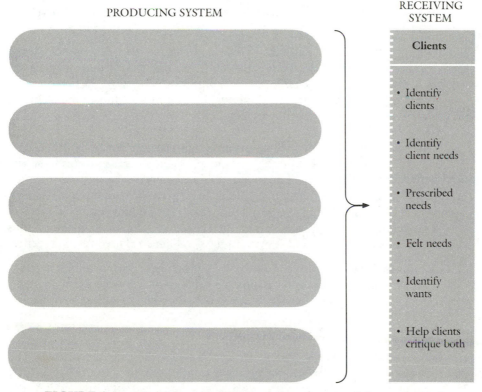

I. THE PERFORMANCE SYSTEM

PRODUCING SYSTEM

RECEIVING
SYSTEM

Clients

• Identify
  clients

• Identify
  client needs

• Prescribed
  needs

• Felt needs

• Identify
  wants

• Help clients
  critique both

FIGURE 2-1.   Model A starts with the needs and wants of the members of the *receiving* system.

of the members of the receiving system or of the community. These instruments include interviews, surveys, observation, research data, and intuition.

> The faculty of the Counseling Psychology program know from their own experience, from the experience of other such programs, and from the research literature what their trainees need to become effective helpers. From time to time, however, they also use both interviews and surveys to make sure that they are tailoring their services to the actual needs and wants of *this* student group of trainees at *this* time. The students want whatever they need to become effective helpers, but they don't know precisely what this entails. Since their needs are generic, they count on the faculty to prescribe the kinds of models, methods, and skills that will make them competent. The members of the faculty know that the bottom line of the training program is that the clients of those they are training will actually be helped. Therefore, they ask such questions as: What do clients need to know or be able to do in order to manage the problem situations of their lives more effectively? What has to happen between helper and client in order to raise the probability that the client will live more effectively? The trainees need models, methods, and skills that will help them both understand their clients in ways that serve the counseling process and help them manage the problem situations of their lives.

In this example the needs of the ultimate receiving system—the clients—help define the needs of the intermediate receiving system—the trainees themselves. Systems work best when they are driven by relevant needs. It becomes obvious that mistakes in assessing the needs and wants of the receiving system lead almost inevitably to ineffectiveness and inefficiency in delivering human services.

2. The mission of the producing system.   Mission concerns what the system is about, what its overall purpose is. Since people form groups in order to satisfy needs and wants, however, mission, as indicated in Figure 2-2, is derived from the needs and wants of the members of the receiving system or community. Through its mission a system indicates the area it will address. The administration and faculty of a high school might say they are in the human development business, thus defining the mission of the school in terms of the developmental needs of its students.

> The mission of the Counseling Psychology program at State could be stated as training effective helpers; or as supplying its graduates with the working knowledge and skills they need in order to help their clients manage problem situations effectively.

Mission is a generic statement of purpose. Ideally, it is stated in terms of the overall *accomplishments* to which the system is directed. It includes a statement of the guiding values of the system and the principal policies that flow from these values. The program at State, for example, emphasizes such things as the dignity and self-responsibility of the client. Therefore, helping should occur in ways that respect the client's dignity and encourage self-responsibility.

I. THE PERFORMANCE SYSTEM

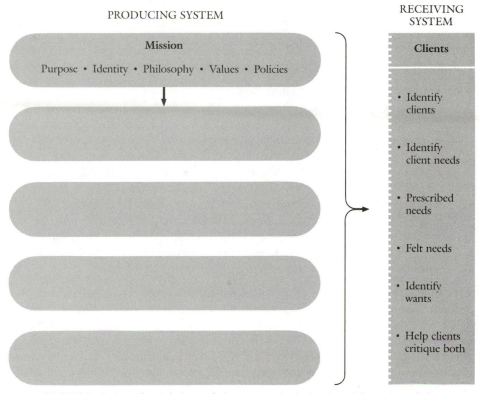

FIGURE 2-2.   The mission of the system includes the philosophy of the system.

The administrators and staff of an organization may not know what their business really is. What is the business of high schools? Teaching such things as reading, mathematics, and social sciences? Helping students become good citizens? Training them in the culture and the folkways of their society, and in communication skills and problem solving? Preparing students for a career and for life in a broader sense? Imparting values? A combination of all of these? Schools, governmental agencies, churches, and the helping professions *do* many things, but this does not prove that they understand their mission clearly or that their members agree as to what that mission is. And while people live naturally in various kinds of communities, they are often unaware of the overall purpose of the community and of its major aims. Although the community supplies valuable services, its leaders may lack the certainty of direction possible in systems where the mission is defined in terms of the needs and wants of the clients.

3. Major aims of the mission.   While the mission delineates the overall purpose of the system, mission-statement language tends to be too general to generate specific and relevant programs. Mission, as indicated in Figure 2-3, needs to be translated into major aims that relate more specifically to the needs of the client population. A high school may say that its mission is the holistic human development of its students, and then develop its major aims in terms of (1) academic competence, (2) social-emotional growth and development, and (3) values clarification and construction. These major aims carve out specific areas of student need.

> The major aims of the Counseling Psychology program at State relate to major areas of working knowledge and skills that will help trainees understand and help clients. For instance, one such area is developmental psychology. The faculty members have learned that a working knowledge of developmental psychology provides an excellent framework for understanding clients and their problems across the life span. Seeing clients from a developmental framework moderates the helper's tendency to judge clients on the basis of narrower frameworks such as abnormal psychology. A major aim of the program is therefore to see to it that graduates possess the ability to understand clients and their problem situations in terms of developmental stages, developmental tasks, and the normal developmental crises that people face as they move from life stage to life stage.

Of course, this program has other major aims, such as giving its participants the working knowledge and skill to use a problem-management model of helping (Egan, 1982), the ability to understand clients and their problems in terms of social settings of their lives, and the ability to train clients in the kinds of life skills that will help them manage their lives more effectively (Egan and Cowan, 1979). The development of major aims gives a system more specificity of direction, enabling its managers to allocate their resources to high-priority areas.

4. Setting concrete and specific goals.   As indicated in Figure 2-4, goals are derived from each major aim. As clear and specific translations of the overall purpose of the system, goals represent *accomplishments* that satisfy specific needs and wants of the members of the receiving system. Ideally, organizations state their goals as clear outcomes that are measurable or at least verifiable, realistic (not set too high), and adequate (not set too low). In complex organizations, mission and major aims must be translated into a network of goals and subgoals.

In the best organizations members understand the goals and are committed to attaining them. Achieving goal clarity is relatively easy in some systems, but more difficult in others. An automobile manufacturer is not vague about the specific goals that represent translations of the organzation's mission statement. While some lemons may roll off assembly lines, few vague automobiles do. However, in human-service organizations such as welfare agencies, schools, churches, governmental agencies, and social-service systems, where it is more difficult to state concrete goals, the goal-setting phase of the operation is sometimes bypassed; planners leap from mission and major aims to programs. This omission leads to ineffectiveness and inefficiency.

I. THE PERFORMANCE SYSTEM

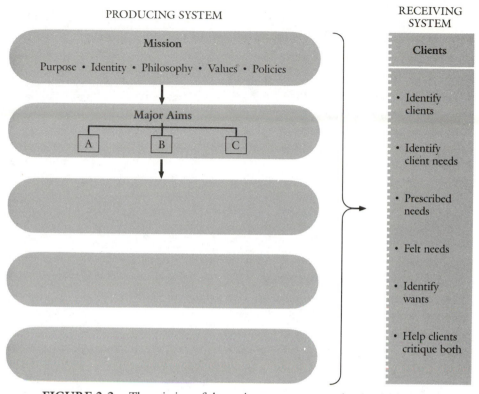

FIGURE 2-3.   The mission of the entire system or any subunit of the system needs to be translated into more specific aims, indicated by A, B, and C.

The faculty of the Counseling Psychology program at State realize that their mission is not to train people—that is an overly programmatic view of what they do—but to produce graduates with certain kinds of working knowledge, skills, and values. Since mission statements and major aims are not specific enough to give direction to program development, however, each major aim must be translated into specific accomplishments that can be called goals.

For instance, at the end of the training program in an eclectic problem-management helping model, the trainees will have a working knowledge of each of the steps of the model and be able to demonstrate their knowledge by explaining the model to others. They will have learned, practiced, and used each of the skills needed to make the model work. One of the central skills is accurate empathy. Trainees will have a cognitive understanding of this skill, a working knowledge of its uses, and experience in using it in practicum sessions to establish relationships with clients, make them feel understood, and help them explore and clarify problem situations.

A training program is actually a complex *system* in which mission must be translated into major aims, major aims must be translated into goals, and goals must be translated into a network of subgoals, which are pursued bit by bit until trainees demonstrate competence as helpers. In training programs these goals and subgoals are specific kinds of working knowledge and skills, which are acquired, practiced, and used.

The staff of a parish asked me to help them assess what they had accomplished over the year. When I asked them what they thought they had achieved, they said, "God alone knows." God alone knew because, while they had beautiful mission statements and major aims based on the scripture and tradition of the church, and while they worked hard at its many different programs, they had not established specific goals that could be verified. Although they were doing valuable work, they were at a loss to evaluate it. They might have accomplished even more with the sense of direction that comes from specificity of goals.

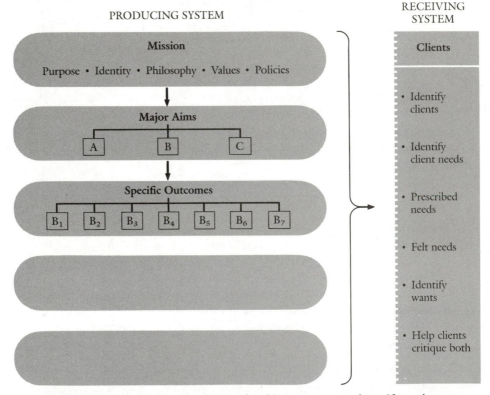

FIGURE 2-4.   Aims need to be translated into concrete and specific goals or outcomes. In this example, Aim #B is translated into Goals # 1, 2, 3, and so on. Aim #B is accomplished when these goals are accomplished.

5. Developing programs to achieve goals.   In well-designed systems well-shaped programs are developed to achieve specific goals. "Well-shaped" means that each program moves step-by-step toward the goal; no step is too complicated or too difficult; the relation of one step to the next is logical and clear; and the connection to the goal is logical and clear.

If hot-line volunteers are told, "Just be a warm, caring human being to the people who call," they are engaging in a program that is neither clear nor systematic nor clearly connected to a specific goal. Under these circumstances it is not likely that the volunteers will be of much use to the callers.

In Figure 2-5 each step of the program is indicated by a number. The letter n refers to the total number of steps required by any given program. Simple programs might involve a couple of steps, while complex programs might call for extensive linking of steps. If there are several goals, each goal will have its own program.

In complex systems with many goals, each goal may have a number of subgoals or intermediate goals leading up to it. In the production of an automobile, for

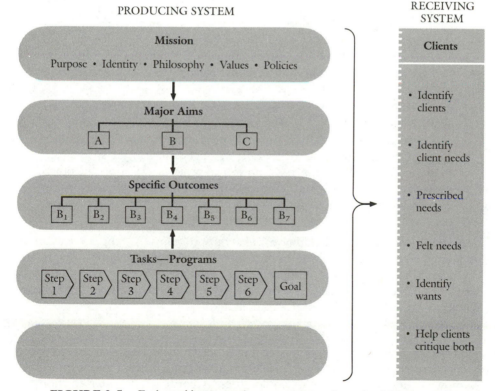

FIGURE 2-5.   Each goal has a step-by-step program through which the goal is achieved.

instance, the engine, the chassis, and the electrical system constitute major subgoals in the production process. Each of these subgoals has programs of greater or lesser complexity leading up to its accomplishment. Complex goals in any kind of system, including human-service systems, can be accomplished by dividing them into a series of subgoals each with its own program. (Some people wonder why we can shape the complex goals, subgoals, and programs that put a person on the moon but cannot manage to get eighth graders in some school districts to read at a sixth-grade level.)

The faculty members of the Counseling Psychology program set up programs for each goal. They devise a generic program for imparting skills:

1. *Cognitive understanding.* They make sure that trainees understand the skill in question. Reading and lectures are steps in this process.
2. *Clarification.* For greater clarity, trainees are given an opportunity to clear up misconceptions about a particular skill. They ask and answer questions relating to the skill.
3. *Behavioral understanding.* The trainers model the skill in question, using live participants or video.
4. *Behavioral testing.* Trainers make sure that the trainees have a behavioral, and not just a cognitive, understanding for the skill. They are helped to use the skill in brief, guided exercises, then given the opportunity to clarify what they still do not understand.
5. *Practice and feedback.* The trainees practice the skill under guidance and, after giving themselves feedback, receive feedback from fellow trainees and trainers.
6. *Practicum.* Brief practicum experiences are furnished to help trainees try their hand at the skill "live." This too is followed by feedback.

The trainers use inductive variations of this deductive training model. In doing so, they try to fit the training model to the learning style of the trainees. The faculty members set up special projects to achieve the other goals of the program. For instance, in order to develop a working knowledge of developmental stages, tasks, and crises, the trainees do a personal developmental "audit" and interview people across the life span.

A number of questions should be asked about programs. Are they derived from and designed to achieve concrete and specific goals? Are they realistic—that is, are the necessary human and physical resources available? Are they cost efficient in terms of both psychological and economic costs? Are they relatively simple step-by-step processes or are they overly complicated?

6. Managing the material resources needed to execute programs. One of the tasks of those who manage a system is to see to it that the material resources needed to execute programs are available and in working order. This area of Model A, shown in Figure 2-6, may be called "logistics." According to Webster's dictionary, *logistics* is a military term meaning "the procurement, maintenance, and transpor-

I. THE PERFORMANCE SYSTEM

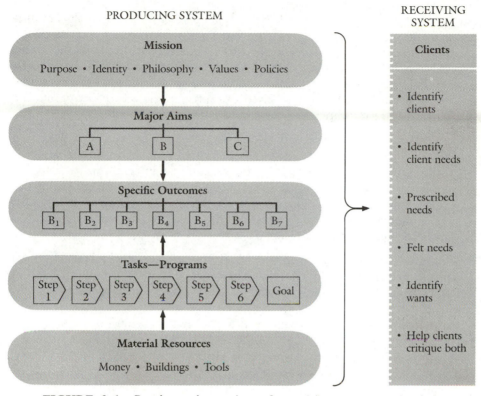

FIGURE 2-6. People need a variety of material resources to do their work.

tation of material, facilities, and personnel." In complex manufacturing organizations, logistics is a major task. Many of the subgoals and subprograms of the system relate, ensuring that material resources are there and in good working order when needed. If a small part is missing, an entire assembly line may have to be shut down. If the musical instruments do not arrive, the orchestra cannot give the concert. In no system can the care of material resources be taken for granted.

Logistics is important in human-service systems also. Schools don't operate without buildings and blackboards. Counselors need environments that do not distract them and their clients from their work. A system needs funds to buy the material resources it needs and usually to pay its workers. In larger systems an entire department is set aside to deal with finances. Fund-raising skills are important to many people in human-service systems.

Another important logistical issue is the quality of nonpeople resources. If the raw products are poor or if the tools are inadequate, then even the most enlightened and most skillful workers cannot be productive. Gilbert (1978) suggests that one of the reasons that some teachers are ineffective and some students fail to learn is that the books available are poor tools of instruction. At some time or other in their learning careers, most people have cursed the dullness or the incomprehensibility of some text. At a certain high school a teacher of advanced algebra died suddenly of a heart attack. One day the substitute who took her place asked the students to read a short chapter in the text. When they had finished, he asked: "Would those who understood what they read raise your hands?" No one did. The teacher said, "Rip it out of the book." Then, as one of the students was walking up and down the aisles collecting the rejected chapters in the wastepaper basket, the teacher said: "I read it three times, and I didn't understand it either."

> The faculty members of the Counseling Psychology program at State have their own logistical worries. New programs mean that there is less office space at the university. Because of cutbacks in funds, instructors must try to do more with less. On a more positive note, there is the opportunity of making more innovative use of the high-quality audiovisual equipment they have. There is the constant search for textbooks that meet the needs of their students.

While human-service systems are often impeded by lack of money and other material resources, they are also often wasteful of resources, especially because they fail to determine what business they are in and establish concrete goals to meet the needs of clients.

In summary, elements 1 through 6 in Model A give us an overview of what needs to be done to achieve the goals of the system and, by doing so, to satisfy the needs of the receiving system. The next five elements deal with the people who do this work and accomplish these goals.

II. THE HUMAN RESOURCES OF THE SYSTEM

When some people talk about organizational design, they mean fashioning the structure of the organization. Structure includes (a) roles and responsibilities, (b) relationships, (c) communication processes, and (d) issues related to coordination, facilitation, authority, and responsiblity.

7. **Managing the human resources.**   As indicated in Figure 2-7, the major resource of any organization, institution, or community is the people who live and work in the system. Using working knowledge, skills, and material resources, people implement the programs that lead to the accomplishments of the system. Teachers help students learn by using their own knowledge of a particular subject, instructional skills, and resources such as books, classrooms, blackboards, and audiovisual materials. Counselors using counseling models, methods, and skills, help their clients manage their lives more effectively.

Personnel functions include staff selection, training, and development. In staffing programs, care needs to be taken to choose people who already have or can learn the working knowledge and skills required to do the work of the program. Systems differ widely in terms of the competence of people who staff programs. All of us

II. THE HUMAN RESOURCES OF THE SYSTEM

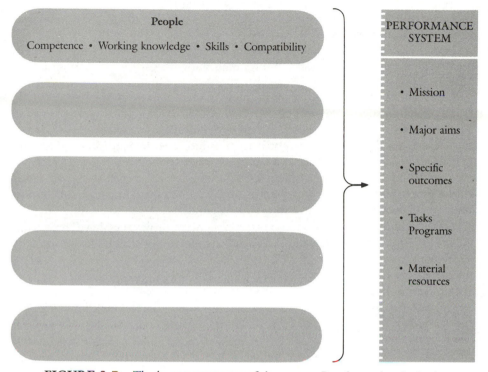

People

Competence • Working knowledge • Skills • Compatibility

PERFORMANCE
SYSTEM

• Mission

• Major aims

• Specific
  outcomes

• Tasks
  Programs

• Material
  resources

FIGURE 2-7.   The human resources of the system. People need to be both competent and compatible.

have met incompetent people in the organizations with which we deal. And incompetence is no respecter of position—that is, it can be found at both the lowest and the highest levels.

The faculty of the Counseling Psychology program must be competent in the kinds of working knowledge and skills they are trying to impart. For instance, they need a working knowledge of human development, including the human development issues facing their trainees, so that they can understand the kinds of problems their trainees are experiencing as they move through the program.

Because they are teachers and trainers, they also need teaching and training skills. The faculty members in the counseling program are committed both to their own competence and to the competence of their trainees. They continually update themselves through a variety of conferences and other professional development experiences. They remain close to the state of the art in counselor training. For instance, since many of the trainees are midcareer participants who have a great deal of human experience, faculty members spend time reviewing the principles of adult education and applying them in the classroom and in the training groups.

A legitimate complaint in some training programs is that the trainers themselves lack both training skills and the competencies they are trying to impart (Carkhuff and Berenson, 1976). In some professional programs academic and research skills are prized more than practitioner and training skills.

8. Determining roles and responsibilities.   In most systems people either choose or are assigned specific tasks. The expectation that an individual will accomplish some task or group of tasks within a system determines the person's *role*. The fact that people are defined by task-related roles as indicated in Figure 2-8. When we talk about the role of a mother in a family, we refer to the tasks she is expected to accomplish and, generally, the kinds of behavior that are expected of her. These expectations differ from culture to culture and from family to family, and may even undergo significant changes over the life of a family.

The ideal is that people choose or are assigned to roles they have the qualifications (working knowledge and skills) and the motivation to fulfill. But in many

II. THE HUMAN RESOURCES OF THE SYSTEM

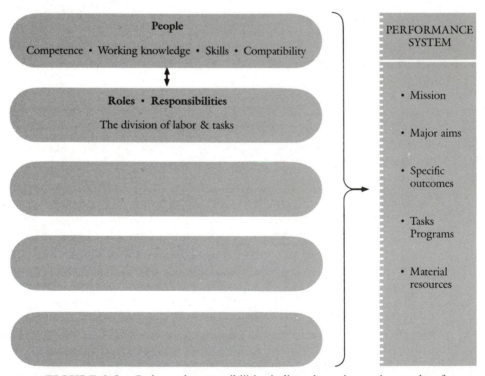

FIGURE 2-8.   Roles and responsibilities indicate how the work or tasks of the system are divided up.

organizations people are promoted to managerial positions, not because they are good at managing, but because they are good in some technical area. They like the promotion and the perquisites that come with it, but they do not like the challenges that come with authority. For instance, people get married and have families without the working knowledge and skills to carry out the responsibilities of spouse and parent.

Since the counseling program at State is an educational and training experience, it has community overtones. The members of the faculty do not constitute a pure-form producing system nor do the program participants constitute a pure-form receiving system. Together they form a teaching/learning community. Therefore, both the roles of faculty members and the roles of students must be considered.

Faculty members in the program find themselves to be, either formally or informally, teachers, trainers, advisers, counselors, program developers,

II. THE HUMAN RESOURCES OF THE SYSTEM

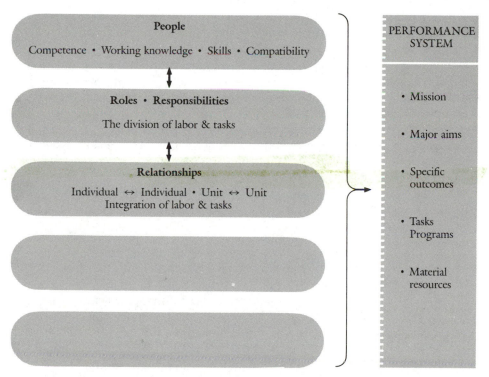

FIGURE 2-9.   People in their various roles relate to other people in order to accomplish the goals of the system. In complex organizations, the various departments or subunits also relate to one another in order to achieve the work of the system. Relationships indicate the ways in which tasks must be integrated.

theoreticians, tutors, researchers, confidants or confidantes, ombudsmen, managers, friends, leaders, and colleagues. The students, when asked, tend to see themselves somewhat flatly as learners, students, or trainees. When pushed, they realize that they participate in one way or another in many of the same roles as the members of the faculty.

Any given person may have a number of roles in a system. Ordinarily people work best when their roles are clear both to themselves and to others in the system. Roles, whether formal or informal, are functional if they contribute to the productivity and the quality of life of the system.

9. Making relationships clear.   Structure, the division of labor, leads naturally to relationships—that is, people working together to accomplish the goals of the system. Cooperative, goal-oriented relationships between and among individuals, between and among groups, and between and among departments are hallmarks of successful organizations. In more complex systems there are not only more relationships, but often more complicated relationships. For instance, an individual may report both to a head of a department and to a project director from a different department. In a well-designed system, relationships are not created lightly; that is, like roles, relationships exist primarily for the accomplishment of goals.

It is not enough that individual roles be clear; the relationships between and among roles also must be clear. Often individuals, groups, and entire departments must cooperate in order to carry out certain tasks. For instance, the planning department of a large welfare agency must get data from all departments if it is to draw up a meaningful five-year plan. All personnel should know what kind of information is needed from each department, who within the department is responsible for gathering the information, to whom it is addressed in the planning department, and when it is needed. Fuzzy relationships between individuals and departments can lead to misunderstandings and unnecessary conflict. If relationships are not clear, they will stand in the way of efficient execution of programs. On the other hand, if goals, programs, and structure are not clear, then relationships cannot be clear.

A number of different relationships among the faculty members of the counseling program at State must work if the participants are to receive quality instruction and training. The program has an interdepartmental dimension: The sociology department teaches a course called "Counseling from the Viewpoint of Applied Sociology" and the anthropology department teaches courses called "Counseling and the Culture of Individuals and Social Settings" and "Intercultural Counseling." The people who teach these courses meet with faculty members of the counseling program in order to integrate their offerings with the mission and philosophy of the program. All concerned want to avoid a hodgepodge of unrelated courses.

Formal and informal student/faculty meetings are considered important. A forum is established in which faculty members share their ongoing research and students share possible thesis and dissertation topics. Through this forum students become "apprenticed" to faculty members in ongoing research projects. Both benefit from the relationship.

In organizations, relationships exist primarily to get the work of the system done. Socializing is a secondary objective, although very important in terms of quality of work life. In communities, however, relationships exist for themselves; that is, relating is one of the major aims of the members of the community.

10. Establishing effective communication.   If relationships are to work, the parties involved must communicate clearly to one another. Communication, as indicated in Figure 2-10, is the life blood of the system and, like blood, can be contaminated. The two major forms of communication are information sharing and feedback.

Information sharing. In a well-designed system, members freely share with one another whatever information is needed to get the work of the system done. In

II. THE HUMAN RESOURCES OF THE SYSTEM

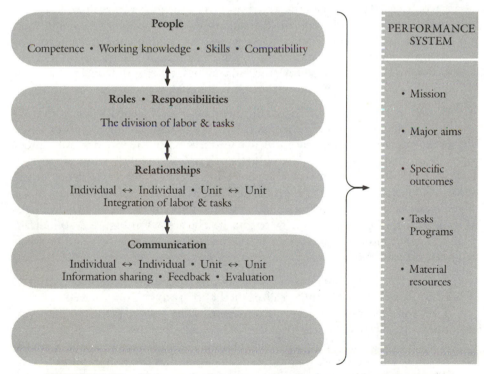

FIGURE 2-10.   If the work of the system is to be done and its goals accomplished, people need to exchange the kind of *information* that is needed to make decisions and provide direction. People also need *feedback*, both confirmatory and corrective, to keep them on course.

hierarchical systems information moves freely both horizontally and vertically. People are reinforced for sharing essential information. Withholding essential information from co-workers is a pet strategy in a system pervaded by a competitive, win-lose climate. Since each member is out for himself or herself, withholding information is enforced if it leads to personal gain.

The faculty members of the counseling program use regularly scheduled meetings to exchange the information they need. The length of the meeting is determined by the objectives they want to accomplish. If there is little information to be exchanged, the meeting is deferred. An informal intraprogram newsletter cuts down on the need for meetings. Any faculty member who has information about such things as new books and key journal articles merely lifts a phone and dictates a message to a secretary who puts it into a word processor. Then a two- or three-page newsletter is circulated with some frequency. This leaves meetings free for issues that are confidential or that call for discussion.

The faculty members also realize that their students will do better in the program itself, in each of its courses, and in each assignment if they have a clear idea of what is expected of them. Students are socialized into expecting clear information and demanding it when it is not forthcoming. And, since teaching/learning is a two-way street, students are encouraged to share information that they think will contribute to the quality of the program. Some students visit other universities, talk to students in other programs, and share whatever they find interesting or challenging.

Feedback. In a well-designed system the members receive feedback first of all from the work itself and also from others as needed, both confirmatory feedback when things are going well and timely corrective feedback when they are not. All sources of feedback are open and operative. If the work is designed well, workers can give themselves feedback, but they can also get feedback from co-workers, clients, supervisors, and managers. Many systems are deficient in this area. Good feedback is not given either because the members of the system do not know how critical feedback is or because they do not know how to give it. The arrows in Figure 2-10 indicate that communication channels are open both among team members and between teams or departments.

Both faculty and students in the counseling program benefit from feedback. However, both groups realize that the ability to give oneself feedback takes precedence over hearing it from others. Therefore, all in the program make sure they have a clear idea of what is expected of them. For instance, trainers know what competence in training looks like. They are the first to know when they are training well and when they are training poorly. The same is true for students. They know what competence in counseling models, methods, and skills looks like and they know, for the most part, when they are doing well and when they are doing poorly. However, confirmatory feedback from others is useful and rewarding. Moreover, since corrective feedback when one is off course and does not know it and directive feedback (how to get back on course) are essential, they are given carefully, but freely.

Faculty members build feedback sessions for themselves into the classes. If a problem arises, they don't wait until it is too late to do something about it. Most initiate a series of formal feedback meetings two or three weeks into the semester. Feedback in the program is not seen as invasive. It becomes a part of the culture.

Without good *ongoing* feedback, evaluation processes turn into judgments. For instance, recently I met someone who had been fired. When he asked why he was being fired, he was told that "the bottom line has not been right for the last year and a half." This was the first time he heard of management's displeasure. If frequent feedback from co-workers and supervisors is added to self-feedback, then ongoing evaluation becomes a reality that eliminates the need for traumatic end-of-the project evaluation.

II. THE HUMAN RESOURCES OF THE SYSTEM

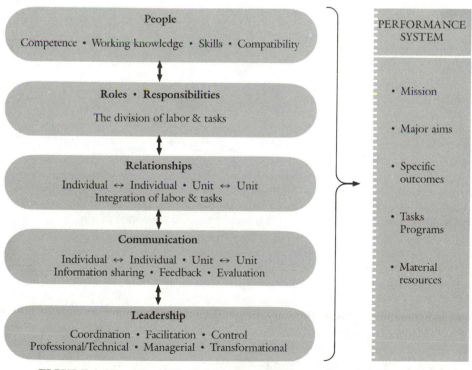

FIGURE 2-11.   The work of the system must be coordinated. This requires people in leadership roles.

11. Leadership: inspiration, coordination, and facilitation.　All systems need technical, managerial, and inspirational leadership. As a system grows more complex, there is a greater need for coordination, and the role of coordinator or manager becomes essential, as indicated in Figure 2-11. With that role comes authority, the power to make decisions and give instructions to others about matters relevant to the tasks of the system. In the best systems, managers are coordinators and facilitators rather than wielders of power. They coordinate and oversee the work of the system in a variety of ways. They make sure that: the needs of the receiving system are assessed; the system clarifies its mission and communicates it to its members; the mission is translated into major aims; each aim is translated into concrete and specific goals; programs are designed and implemented to accomplish goals; the material resources of the system are available and functioning; the human resources of the system are developed; roles and responsibilities are assigned; functional relationships are established and developed; relevant information and feedback flow through the system; and all of these functions are coordinated. In a word, managers oversee and coordinate all the elements of Model A.

Some systems are structurally *flat*—that is, there are very few managerial layers. An example of this is the classroom, where there is usually only one manager, the instructor. Other systems are *tall*; that is, there are many managerial layers. The ideal is that structure serves function: There are only as many managers or managerial layers as are needed to oversee and coordinate the work of the system. However, since promotion is such a highly prized incentive and reward, there is a tendency in some systems to establish too many managerial positions. The managerial role, however important, is still only one of the many important roles in a system.

> There are sixteen faculty members in the counseling program. Sue Undsett is the program director. She is responsible for many of the administrative duties that are part of university life, such as the scheduling of classes and the drawing up of the annual report. She manages the interface between the program and the psychology department and between the other disciplines (sociology, anthropology) involved in the program.
>
> The role of the program director has been clarified in a meeting of the entire staff. The director is not a "boss" in the usual sense. All the important decisions in the program are made by the faculty. Once faculty members have a clear idea of what the mission, aims, and goals of the program are and of its individual courses and seminars, they are given a great deal of autonomy as to how they will accomplish these goals. Since roles and relationships are clear and functional and since clear-cut information-sharing, feedback, and decision-making processes are in place, all derived from and contributing to the mission of the program, the role of director can remain mostly administrative. Problems and conflicts that arise in the program are handled in faculty meetings and referred to the psychology department only if they cannot be handled "in house."
>
> Since the students are encouraged to see and experience the program as a teaching/learning community, they have representatives at the faculty

meetings and serve on the ad hoc task forces that are set up from time to time to explore opportunities or problems. Each student has an adviser who helps the student plan and manage problems. The program is competency-based. Students are required to understand what is expected of them and to manage problems by themselves, in conjunction with fellow students, with their advisers, or in extraordinary circumstances, in a meeting of the entire faculty.

In this example the system is not overmanaged. Accomplishments, competence, coordination, self-governance, and facilitation are more important than control, power, and authority.

III. THE PERVASIVE VARIABLES

The third part of Model A deals with five sets of factors or variables that affect the way a system functions. These are the reward system, climate, the environment, system politics, and a variety of arational factors, particularly the culture of the system. These factors permeate or "rinse through" the system, affecting its day-to-day functioning for better or worse.

12. The reward system: using the principles of behavior intelligently.   The reward system includes more than just incentives and rewards. The principles of learning or behavior involving the use of reinforcement, punishment, modeling, shaping, aversive conditioning, and the like are also included, as well as how they are handled and their impact on the system. Figure 2-12 shows these principles encircling and permeating the system because they affect it in each of its functions. People in well-functioning systems have at least an implicit working knowledge of and respect for the basic principles of human behavior and the ability to apply these principles to the structure and functioning of the system (Luthans and Kreitner, 1975; Miller, 1978). Organization-development efforts that center around such issues as motivation, reward systems, job satisfaction, and job enrichment are all based on the principles of human behavior. While common sense would seem to dictate that such important principles be learned and put into practice early in life, the reality is that these principles are not learned in any explicit and direct way through ordinary educational channels. And therefore, we have cases of otherwise intelligent people unwittingly reinforcing, both in themselves and in others, behaviors they are trying to eliminate and failing to reinforce or even punishing behaviors they are trying to maintain.

A working knowledge of these basic principles has high priority because the principles remain operative whether they are known and used explicitly or not. And they profoundly affect every aspect of the working of a system. For instance, if feedback is not rewarded or experienced as something rewarding in an organization, we cannot expect the members of that organization to give good feedback, even when they have the ability to do so.

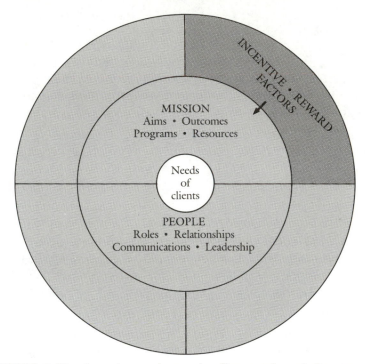

FIGURE 2-12.   Incentives and rewards affect people and the way they work.

Of course the faculty members and students of the counseling program are well aware of these principles since they form part of the curriculum. However, they are accustomed to applying these principles to individual rather than system functioning. An effort is made to introduce the principles of behavior in courses that deal with systems and the social settings of life. For instance, the family is studied from the perspective of incentives, rewards, punishment, extinction, shaping, and avoidance.

Furthermore, the counseling program itself is reviewed from the viewpoint of these principles. Students discover that, although research is mandated, it is made aversive through such things as courses in statistics that are more concerned with derivations of formulas than applications to practical research problems. Each part of the program is reviewed in terms of available incentives and possible competing disincentives.

The ability to apply the principles of behavior both to individuals and to systems should become second nature.

13. Climate and quality of life.   Those who work in organizations and live and work in institutions have needs and wants that must be satisfied if the quality of working life in those systems is to be acceptable. System members want to be

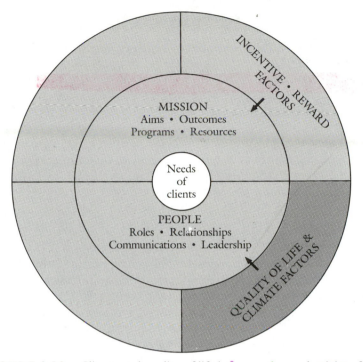

FIGURE 2-13.   Climate and quality of life influence the productivity of the system.

respected and treated fairly by their fellow workers and by those in supervisory and managerial positions. They expect decent wages and decent working conditions. They look for physical and psychological security. If their legitimate needs and wants in these and other areas are met, then it can be said that the organizational climate is good and that workers are enjoying a high quality of working life. Figure 2-13 shows the second of the five sets of factors that surround and permeate the system, affecting the way it functions.

In organizations and institutions there is often a relationship between quality of working life and productivity. For instance, if working conditions and wages are poor in a nursing home, then workers might well refuse to work up to their potential. Because they feel they are being treated unfairly, they might even engage in subtle forms of sabotage. Then the quality of life suffers for the patients also. In this case, poor quality of life affects productivity, the accomplishment of aims and goals.

On the other hand, poor productivity can affect quality of life. If a school has so many poor teachers and poor programs that students do not learn, then the failure to achieve desired outcomes is frustrating and depressing. The quality of life of both student and staff suffers because, whether they admit it or not, they see themselves belonging to a losing institution.

Good working conditions do not lead automatically to increased productivity.

And the fact that an organization is well run and productive does not automatically mean that staff morale will be high. It is dangerous to consider quality of work life outside the context of productivity and to consider productivity outside the context of quality of work life.

In communities, quality of life is synonymous with productivity. The "products" of a family—such things as security, companionship, communication, good relationships, nourishing meals, clean clothes, a sense of belonging, a clean house, the exchange of love and affection—are precisely the things that make for high quality of life. In institutions and institutional agencies, the distinction between producing system and receiving system is more clearly defined, but at least in some cases, a sense of community pervades institutional life and purposes. The "products" of a hospital—all the procedures and outcomes that constitute medical care—are not only intimately related to the quality of life of the members of the receiving system, but also very often depend on the cooperation of the patient and are best delivered in a community-like atmosphere.

> The quality of life in the counseling program at State is high for both faculty and students for a number of reasons. First, the system is productive. Faculty members and students see learning take place in terms of both research and training. Participating in the program is satisfying because it works. There is a sense of belonging to an enterprise that is headed in the right direction. Second, people respect and care about one another. Students feel that they are treated fairly. Third, a number of social needs are met in the day-to-day relating that goes on between student and student, faculty member and faculty member, and faculty member and student. Fourth, both faculty and students have a degree of autonomy in choosing how they will go about their work. The goals are clear, but there is a degree of freedom in choosing the means of achieving these goals.

In a word, the climate in the program is good; the quality of life is high.

14. Managing the environment.   No organization, institution, or community exists in a vacuum. Families live in neighborhoods, the personnel department relates to all the other departments of the company, a company has competitors, nations exist in the international community. Any given system is affected by other systems and, in turn, affects other systems. Figure 2-14 adds the notion of environment to Model A. In a sense the environment is not "out there." The effect or impact of the environment is "in here," affecting this organization or this subunit for weal or for woe.

If a system such as a hospital is seen as a whole, then the environment includes the community in which it is located, other hospitals in the area, medical and governmental accrediting and regulatory agencies, the state of medicine in the country, medical schools, unions, the state of the economy, hospital supply companies, nursing schools, insurance companies, and the like. If a subunit such as the laboratory of a hospital is considered, then the immediate environment includes all the hospital units that affect the productivity and quality of life of those in the

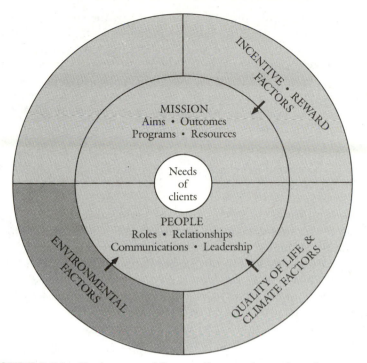

FIGURE 2-14.   Environmental factors affect people, work, and outcomes.

laboratory and all the units whose productivity and quality of life are affected by the laboratory.

In well-run systems, managers know how to protect the system from harmful environmental influences, how to utilize helpful environmental resources, and how to see to it that the system accomplishes its goals without damaging the environment. Organization change and development efforts sometimes fail, not because they are poorly conceived, but because managers fail to take into account the limitations of the environment.

> The most important unit in the immediate environment of the counseling program is the psychology department. Its policies directly affect the status and the running of the program. Care is taken to keep communication open with the chairperson of the psychology department and its various committees. However, other university departments and the university itself, in its policies and budgeting, are also part of the immediate environment.
>
> The members of the program are sensitive to the "perimeter." They see the environment as a locus of both opportunities and threats. For instance, a new program in organizational development is a threat in that it will consume scarce resources, but it is also an opportunity in that it deals with models, methods, and skills relevant to counselors but not yet avail-

able in the counseling program. The program director deals with the threat by preparing a realistic and convincing budget. She deals with the opportunity by asking members of the new program to sit down with a representative group from the counseling program to discuss ways in which they might be of service to each other. The program in organizational development calls for courses in communication and small-group skills. These are among the strong points of the Counseling Psychology program, which already has faculty members to teach these courses.

An "environmental scan" for major upcoming threats and opportunities is a major part of *strategic planning* that relates directly to determining the mission and long-term aims of the system.

15. System politics.   Even though many people dislike the fact, politics are part and parcel of organizational and institutional life. Politics deal with such realities as power, the struggle for and allocation of scarce resources, influence, decision making, and the imposition of ideology. Maintaining that politics have no place in human-service organizations and institutions does little to eliminate them. Accepting the fact that all human systems are politicized to a greater or lesser extent, and a willingness to work with political realities such as coalitions, make more sense than a "politics are dirty" approach. Figure 2-15 completes the first circle of pervasive elements by adding political factors.

> The members of the counseling psychology program were not completely pleased when two members of the psychology department pushed for the acceptance of a new program in organization development. Resources for social-science programs were already too scarce. In fact, at a meeting of the graduate faculty council, one of the members of the counseling psychology program argued that it was not the right time for the introduction of such a program. However, once the new program was approved by the Board of Trustees, the director of the counseling psychology program met with the director of the organization development program to see what kind of trade-offs they could work out. She saw possibilities in developing this new coalition.

Consultants and managers need not sacrifice deeply cherished values in order to become political. Indeed, they can work toward the humanization of politics within the system.

16. Arationality and culture.   While the fifteen elements outlined above constitute the *logic* of the design and functioning of a system, the organizational *form* of the design itself is the particular way in which these elements are configured and interrelated and *actually operate on a day-to-day basis* in any given organization, institution, or community. While all systems need to divide up the work, for example, each system can do it in a different way. While all organizations have explicit or implicit personnel policies and procedures—that is, ways of dealing with people

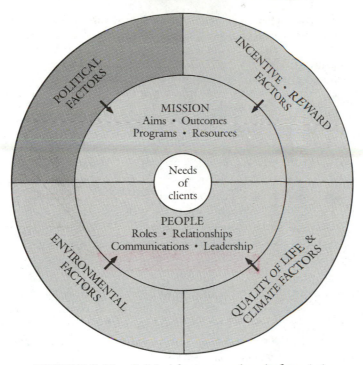

FIGURE 2-15. Political factors complete the first circle.

resources—these policies and procedures may differ greatly from organization to organization. And the process is not as rational, linear, and systematic as it has been presented here.

Earlier we considered some definitions of organizations as rational entities. However, Cohen, March, and Olsen (1972) give a definition of organizations from an *arational* rather than a rational point of view.

> An organization is a collection of choices looking for problems, issues and feelings looking for situations in which they might be aired, solutions looking for issues to which they might be an answer, and decision makers looking for work [p. 2].

In a sense the culture of a system could be called a collection of predetermined choices, issues, feelings, and solutions waiting for an opportunity to be used. *The "arational" in organizations, institutions, and communities is all that is not rational, linear, and systematic.* In most systems this is a great deal. There is a difference between a "strategic" and an "emergent" view of a system, for instance. The strategic is what is planned, while the emergent is what takes place even though it is not planned. Understanding systems from a strategic point of view is not enough. The unplanned is part of every system.

The rational dimensions of system design and functioning are emphasized in Model A. But the elements of Model A, since they are affected by various sources of arationality, need to be seen from a real rather than an idealized perspective.

Anyone who samples the literature on organizations will soon notice a term that occurs over and over again, *rationality* [Diesing, 1962]. This concept does not necessarily mean that organizational actions are logical or sensible, but rather that they are intended, thought about, planned, calculated, or designed for a purpose. . . . The fact that organizations typically exhibit a great deal of turbulence, disorder, and unpredictability does not necessarily disprove the theory that their origins were rational or that they are trying to be rational [Weick, 1979, pp. 19–20].

The elements of Model A are coupled, fitted together, or bonded *to a greater or lesser extent*. Often enough they are more "loosely coupled" (Weick, 1979, 1982) than people would care to think. Planners are not asked to stop planning or to stop devising rational frameworks such as Model A to help design, run, and assess systems. Rather, the planner is cautioned not to count on rational factors as the only determinants of the design and functioning of systems, but to watch for arational elements as well. As demonstrated in Figure 2-16, arational and cultural factors permeate the entire system, even the other pervasive variables.

Think of systems in terms of both *logic* and *literature*. The logic of a system relates to designing and planning—the conscious use of the elements of Model A. The literature of the system refers to the descriptions or *stories* of what the system is like in fact. The formal leadership of a system, the one that is written down, relates to the logic of the system. A story about how leadership actually emerges and functions relates to the literature of the system. "This is what we planned" relates to logic. "This is what actually happened" relates to literature. Many people tend to have an understanding of and approach to systems that is overbalanced on the side of logic. The *wise* leader or manager has a solid working knowledge of the rational dimensions of models such as Model A and enough experience to allow the logic of a system to be interpreted by its literature. Logic deals with the rational, systematic, and linear aspects of systems. Literature deals with the arational, unsystematic, and irregular aspects of systems.

An understanding of systems that is limited to rational models such as Model A is a two-dimensional understanding. The understanding that comes from an appreciation of the "hidden dimensions" (Hall, 1966, 1977) of systems that constitute their internal culture is a three-dimensional understanding. Smart people understand the technology of the system, including the skills and methodologies related to needs assessment, mission development, strategic planning, goal setting, program development, personnel development, structure, role development, relationships, and communication. Smart people acquire wisdom by understanding technology, models, methods, and skills against the background of sociocultural systems and the constantly shifting complexities of individuals, systems and subsystems, the environment, and the interactions among these. They understand the rational, but they also have a feeling for the arational.

The arationality of individuals. Human systems have members who are all too human; they are complex, emotional, subject to change, and sometimes in disarray. People often do not understand their own actions. They say one thing, but do another. They want to be rational, but let emotions win out over reason, even when this course is self-destructive. Churchman (1968) talks about the "antiplanning"

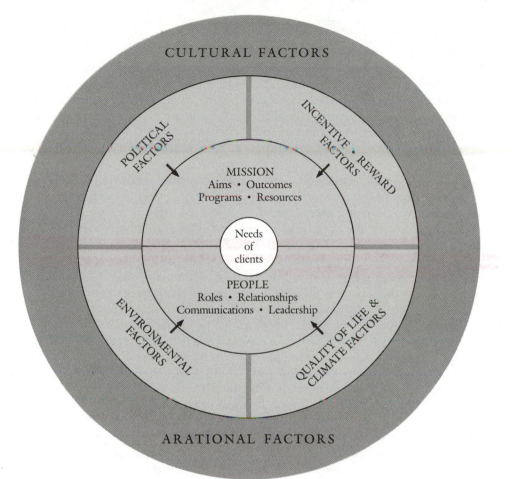

FIGURE 2-16.   Culture and other arational factors permeate the system and affect everything that happens in it.

tendencies in most people. Many people seem to be content with merely living and working within systems in a reactive rather than a proactive way.

The arationality of systems. Systems, too, are all too human—that is, complex, subject to change, and sometimes in disarray. For instance, different departments of an organization develop adversarial relationships with one another when cooperation would lead to greater productivity and improved quality of life. Nations talk about national pride and prefer to solve their differences by war instead of negotiation. Many things in systems "happen" without being planned; many things that are planned never happen.

Organizations, despite their apparent preoccupation with facts, numbers, objectivity, concreteness, and accountability, are in fact saturated with subjectivity, abstraction, guesses, making do, invention, and arbitrariness . . . just like the rest of us [Weick, 1979, p. 5].

The unpredictability of the environment. The environment, too, is complex, changing, and often turbulent. Local, national, and world politics are constantly changing. There is a conservative backlash, and senators who were considered part of the Washington landscape are thrown out of office. Multinational organizations, once considered industrial Rocks of Gibraltar, sink into the sea because of a national and international economy they cannot control or cope with. New technologies create new businesses almost overnight and new regional economies emerge. And all of this takes place with little planning or control.

As Diesing (1962) suggests, we talk a great deal about rationality and see ourselves and the system to which we belong as rational, but we talk little about arationality. We develop rational models, methods, and skills, but we do not systematically consider the "principles of arationality" that permeate every rational thing we do. We need models for understanding and strategies for dealing with the arational in ourselves, in the systems to which we belong, and in the environment that controls much of our destiny. I do not mean that rationality should "win out," as it were, over arationality—for instance, that reason should win out over emotion, that systematic data gathering should win out over intuition. Rather we need to understand how both the rational and arational are balanced and counterbalanced in our individual lives and systems. The arational, while it may be a source of ambiguity and unpredictability, is also often a source of richness and beauty in life.

The Japanese are currently riding high in the world of business and industry, and many explanations have been offered. One is that they do not overvalue reason. Pascale and Athos (1981) discuss the Japanese word *rikutsupoi* which means "too logical." They note that "the Japanese are generally suspicious of too much logic" (p. 99) and that mature managers frequently use the word *rikutsupoi* to designate younger managers who lack experience. Sometimes an overly rational, linear, and systematic approach to designing or changing a system can be too narrow and, therefore, self-defeating and irrational.

Let us return to the counseling program at State. Up to now we have considered that program in a rational, linear, and systematic fashion. It is time to take a brief look at each of the first fifteen elements of Model A through the lens or filter of the sixteenth, the arational. If we had looked at a real university-based human-service delivery program rather than the idealized one at State, we might have found one or more of the following:

Needs assessment. Some programs stay with traditional training models even though they have outlived their usefulness—that is, they do not review ongoing theory and research and update the prescribed needs of their students. Tradition or mere inertia becomes more important than accomplishments related to the more effective delivery of services.

Mission. Some programs are not sure whether they are training practitioners, academicians, theoreticians, researchers, or what I call "translators," people who develop the ability to identify the best in theory and research and "translate" the best into models, methods, and skills that help practitioners become more effective

(Egan and Cowan, 1979). There are basic disagreements among faculty members as to what business the helping and human-service training programs are in.

Major aims. In some programs instruction and training cover such a wide range that students do not know what is most important. One student, who was about to graduate with a master's degree in counseling psychology, felt that he was not very good at counseling. I asked him in what courses he had learned the actual art of counseling. He found the question difficult to answer but finally named two courses that dealt with some of the basics. It seems he was graduating from a program in which the priorities were not clear; there was no clear idea of what was essential.

Goals. Some programs do not let students know in specific terms just what kinds of competencies they are to be trained in and for which they will be accountable. Another student failed an oral examination in clinical psychology *after* he had finished a year-long internship because he had no clear idea of what his approach to therapy was—a clear-cut case of blaming the victim. Of course, the ultimate victims in such cases are the clients.

Programs. When goals in training systems are not spelled out concretely, it is difficult to determine whether the operative programs lead to valued accomplishments. Psychology programs insist that their students become conversant with the empirical method and then violate their own expectations by failing to determine empirically whether their programs achieve the desired results. Individual courses suffer from the same malady. For instance, the desired outcomes of courses in statistics are not always clear, but it is clear that the way statistics (and research methodology in general) is taught is aversive. Even though the "ideal" in clinical psychology training programs is the "researcher-practitioner," the vast majority of graduates from these programs do not engage in research once they are no longer forced to.

Physical resources. One of the greatest offenders is the textbook. Too often books are expressions of the erudition of the author, the pride of the publisher, or the accepted norms of academia rather than instruments to help both instructor and learner make sure that learning takes place. In many programs there is an underuse of video equipment. Students in the helping professions should not graduate without seeing themselves involved in the major roles they will play in their professional lives. And yet many students graduate without ever seeing themselves in action.

People resources. Faculty and training staff are often chosen to be members of a staff because of their academic background and credentials, not because they have demonstrated competence as teachers and trainers. Often schools overlook incompetence in staff members while demanding competence of students.

Roles. It is not uncommon for a faculty member to have a number of different roles, both formal and informal—theoretician, trainer, researcher, counselor, writer, adviser, practitioner, committee member, university employee, administrator—and to experience ambiguity and conflict in these roles. Some faculty members love to do research and yet hate to write.

Relationships. Helping and human-services programs in universities should be, at least to some degree, interdisciplinary. And yet the departments of these universities are often so protective of their own turf that interdisciplinary cooperation is almost impossible. One school solved this problem by starting a program in organizational development that reported directly to the dean of the graduate school and thus avoided interdepartmental rivalries.

Communication. In some programs students have difficulty finding out just what is expected of them. There is a system of faculty advisers, but it is not used. I have known cases of students finding out that their performance was unacceptable only during the year they were to graduate.

Coordination/facilitation. Faculty members are not always good managers. They do not manage programs or even classroom experiences well. They can be authoritarian even when explaining the undesirable impact of the authoritarian personality.

Principles of behavior. Although faculty members and students in most human services programs are aware of the principles of human behavior, they do not always apply them either to the program or to their own lives. Faculty members teach that distributed learning is more effective than massed learning and then give examinations based on massed learning.

Quality of life. Often quantity rather than quality of instruction is the order of the day in academic programs. The quality of life of some students suffers because of the "rat race" character of the programs they are in. The quality of life of other students suffers because they do not see themselves becoming more competent. When productivity is low, quality of life is low. The complaints of students are merely dismissed by the faculty.

Managing the environment. Courses taken by students in other disciplines or departments are viewed with suspicion. Little attention is given to assessing the quality of practicum, clerkship, internship, and field experiences. Societal changes affect the delivery of human services, and yet little attention is paid to this interface.

Culture. Like the vast majority of systems, helping and human-service programs do not examine their own overt and covert cultures, celebrating what is both individual- and system-enhancing and challenging what is individual- and system-limiting.

I am not suggesting that all academic and training programs suffer from all these forms of arationality. Nor do I mean to suggest that what is arational is necessarily negative. Emotions, intuition, and imagination are forms of arationality that can add depth and color to individuals and systems. In a later chapter culture and other sources of arationality will be discussed more fully in an attempt to see systems in three rather than in two dimensions.

THE USES OF MODEL A

Model A can be used in various ways by those who have responsibility for the design and functioning of systems. Model A provides a practical tool for designing a system or subsystem, a guide for running systems, an instrument for assessing systems, a common language for talking about systems, a cognitive map of systems, and a framework for organizing system interventions.

Designing and running a system. First of all, Model A is a kind of generic template that can be used to put a system or subsystem together "from scratch." It is a checklist that helps people design systems in an orderly way and prevents them from over-looking critical issues such as the kind of culture that is being created or the impact of the environment.

Assessing systems. A working knowledge of Model A helps the members of organizations to discover what is and what is not working. As Weisbord (1976) suggests, diagnostic frameworks such as Model A can be placed over an organization like a radar screen. The "blips" that appear on the screen are the inconsistencies, the trouble spots, the danger points, the "soft" areas needing attention and change. Model A, then, is the first step, the diagnostic or assessment step, in Model B, the step-by-step process of change. Managers at any level of an organization can use Model A as a checklist for an organizational, departmental, or program checkup. The more people in the organization, institution, or community conversant with some form of Model A, the more potential participants and contributors there are to the diagnostic process.

Talking about systems. A shared understanding of Model A helps all those involved in a system—managers, members, consultants—talk a common language and cooperate more effectively in diagnosis and change.

Mapping the organization. Model A outlines the "geography" of the organization. In the case of organization-development interventions, it makes the point or points of entry into a system visually clear. It also makes it quite clear that organization development interventions are systemic even when they relate to one specific area in the system. For instance, the assessment of the needs and wants of the receiving systems can affect every other dimension of the organization. The establishment of more effective feedback processes or the failure to establish them can profoundly affect both quality of life and productivity. Change efforts directed at any part of an organization ripple throughout the system. Model A enables people to understand the logic behind this ripple effect and even to visualize it.

Organizing interventions. Model A can be used to help identify the specific organization-development technologies that are needed to handle the problems of an organization, institution, or community. If relationships and communication are poor within a specific team, for instance, team building is called for. If students are not learning, then goal-setting and program-design skills are called for. Model A, since it is a broad-band model of design and assessment, helps prevent administrators, directors, managers, consultants, and other change agents from using pet but inappropriate technologies in addressing system problems. For instance, even though one may be an expert in team building, Model A clearly indicates that team building is ineffective when goals are not clear. All too frequently, human-service providers do whatever they do best—that is, they use the most familiar intervention strategies no matter what strategy is called for by the problem situation. Both Model A and Model B provide frameworks that can be used to organize and clarify the entire range of organization-development interventions.

3

The Data and Tools
of Needs Assessment

If Carlos Mendoza wants to set up a nurse-practitioner office in a small town in central Illinois, he must first find out if anyone wants a nurse practitioner there—he must do a needs assessment. He must also find out if the community has the resources to support his professional practice. He needs data. If Sharon Steinberger is to install a new record-keeping system in a state mental hospital, she must have a clear understanding of the needs to be met by record keeping and the deficiencies of the present system. She needs data.

People form human systems, such as communities or organizations, in order to satisfy needs and wants. People marry in order to satisfy needs and wants for companionship, security, and sexual expression. Hospitals are established to meet the medical needs of the members of a community. Automobile manufacturers stay in business because they meet the needs and wants of people for personal transportation. Pharmaceutical companies meet a wide variety of needs—a psychiatric patient's need for a tranquilizing agent, or a diabetic's need for insulin.

Three categories of needs can be found in organizations and institutions.

System as a whole. What does the system as a whole need in order to be effective and efficient? Model A answers this question. For instance, in order to be effective and efficient a social-service agency needs clear goals. The social workers themselves need certain working models, methods, and skills in order to deliver services effectively and efficiently.

The receiving system. What are the needs and wants of the members of the receiving system that relate to this organization or institution? A social-service agency in a depressed section of a large city, for instance, must find out what people's needs are if they are to provide social services intelligently.

The producing system. What do the members of the producing system need in order to enjoy a reasonably high quality of life working within the system? For instance, what do correctional officers need in order to feel good about working in a correctional facility? The needs of those who work in an organization or institution must be fulfilled to improve the quality of life.

This chapter focuses on both the gathering of data needed by the system in general and that specific kind of data gathering called needs assessment. The emphasis in this chapter is on assessing the needs of the members of the receiving system.

THE DATA-GATHERING PROCESS

All decision makers and consultants in the decision-making process need to understand the rudiments of effective data gathering and develop the skill of translating data into useful information.

Data-based decision making goes on constantly in all sorts of systems even when it is not called by that name. For instance, a family checks newspaper ads weekly and keeps in touch with a real estate agent to see if there is a house for sale in a desirable neighborhood. Political parties gather data to see if a particular candidate has a chance of winning. The incumbent administration gathers data to see how much confidence the public has in its policies and programs. Nursing supervisors gather data in order to give feedback to nurses. Businesses gather data in order to assess their economic soundness. Major league baseball teams gather data to assess their strengths and weaknesses. The examples are endless. Therefore, the techniques considered in this chapter relate to data gathering by kind of system or subsystem.

The following is an adaptation of a data-gathering process suggested by Kilburg (1978):

1. *Clear goals.* Determine what is to be accomplished through the data-gathering process; make sure the goal is concrete and clear. Avoid gathering data just for the sake of gathering data. Ask, "Why is the data being gathered? To what decision does it relate?"
2. *Clear and relevant questions.* Formulate the questions that the data-gathering process will attempt to answer.
3. *Appropriate data-gathering instruments.* Select data-gathering instruments that fit the situation.
4. *Adequate sampling.* Use the instruments either with all the members of the system in question or with a representative sample.
5. *Meaningful data analysis.* Through analysis and interpretation, turn the data into information directly related to the decisions that need to be made.
6. *Clear and relevant presentation of results.* Present the results in a form that is understandable to those who are to review the data and make the decisions.
7. *Informed decisions.* Make decisions on the basis of this reliable and valid information.

1. The goals of data gathering

Why is data being gathered in the first place? What will data gathering accomplish? Before any data gathering takes place, the reasons for it should be as clear as possible. Consider the following example:

To learn more about their parishioners, the staff of St. Bernard's parish decided to send out a survey to all the members. They considered themselves lucky because a neighboring parish had already drawn up a survey. They asked and received permission to use it. There was a good return, and the survey produced a huge amount of data. They did not know how to analyze it, however, because they had not first decided what they wanted to accomplish by gathering the data. They had not even looked upon it as a way of assessing the needs of their members.

A different approach would lead to a more favorable outcome: "We are not sure whether we are meeting the needs of our members because we do not have a clear-cut idea of what these needs are. We would like to find out what the ministry-related needs of the members of St. Bernard's are. By ministry-related needs we mean those needs that can be served through the ministry of the staff and the ministry of parishioner to parishioner. Therefore, we do not want to find out *all* the needs of our members, but only those that might be met through participation in this congregation."

The ultimate accomplishment in data-gathering processes is not only valid and reliable data, but also *relevant and useful information*. Such questions as, "What decisions need to be made? Do we have the information we need to make those decisions? What kind of information do we lack in order to make these decisions?" must be asked before data gathering begins. Data gathering is a *program* that makes sense only in terms of a clear-cut goal or set of goals. The amount of data that is gathered but unused is a striking monument to system inefficiency. It is a costly example of system arationality.

2. Accomplishment-oriented questions

The next step is the formulating of clear questions related to decision making. To learn the needs of the elderly in a neighborhood, human-services centers must ask personal, interpersonal, social, sociological, economic, and cultural questions. Answers to these questions are essential for making decisions about program development and resource allocation. The questions must be incisive enough to produce valid and reliable data.

A data-gathering *lens* is an instrument that enables a person to focus more clearly on an object. Models and frameworks are lenses or collections of lenses. Model A, for example, is a set of lenses that enables managers and consultants to ask the right questions about systems. It is up to each system to develop the sets of lenses that enable it to gather the particular kind of information it needs. To design programs that contribute to the human development of college students, planners could use a set of developmental-task lenses (see Egan and Cowan, 1979, 1980) focused on needs in the areas of competence, autonomy, value development, identity, friendship and intimacy, love/marriage/family, work and career, community and civic involvement, use of leisure, and lifestyle. Questions would relate to the developmental accomplishments expected of students during the four years of college.

The literature of systems is full of examples of poorly formulated questions or inappropriate questions borrowed from some other system. They may seem to be "good questions," but questions are good only if they relate to decision-making needs.

3. Data-gathering techniques

Once questions have been formulated clearly, it is necessary to decide how the answers will be solicited. The techniques to be considered in this section can be used to gather data for a wide variety of purposes.

The principal sources of data are interviews, surveys, observations, and documents related to the system in question (Bouchard, 1976; Nadler, 1977). Of course, any combination of these methods may be used. Interviewing, preparing and administering surveys, observing the functioning of a system, and reading the documents related to it are basic to the consultation and change process. Consultants and change agents need at least basic skills in these areas.

Interviews.   Although interviewing is a useful data-gathering technique, it is frequently overlooked.

> The diocesan directors of continuing education for priests hired a consultant to help them with their work. At their semiannual meeting the directors complained that few priests attended the "excellent" continuing education events they held. The consultants soon learned that these directors had collected little or no data regarding the continuing education needs and wants of priests. As a result, their offerings represented imaginary needs, unrelated to the felt needs and wants of the parish clergy.
>
> Since a large group of parish priests were meeting in another part of the conference center, the consultant suggested a brief experiment. Eight priests from the other group were invited to discuss their ministry-related needs and wants. These eight formed a circle and discussed their needs and wants, while the continuing education directors listened silently. Before beginning, the priests were merely instructed to talk as freely as possible and to suggest some continuing education and training programs that might help them meet their needs. After listening for twenty minutes, the directors were asked to comment. Most agreed it was clear that their offerings had flopped because they had almost no idea what the priests "out there" really needed and wanted. They were amazed by what they had learned merely by asking, "What do you think you need?"

In this case even a rather primitive form of unstructured interviewing produced rewarding results. Gilbert (1978) discusses PIPs—potential for improving performance—in organizations. When the PIPs are large, he says, even simple, common-sense interventions such as the one above can produce significant results. Nadler (1977) talks about three levels of interviewing:

- *Unstructured.* The interviewer uses general probes, such as "Tell me what you think you need to do your work better." "What are some of the problems you run into living alone?" The interviewer offers minimal guidance in order to learn what the respondent feels is important. The interviewer provides lenses with a very broad focus; it is up to the respondent to do the focusing.

- *Structured, but open-ended.* In this case the lenses are much more specific and focused by the interviewer. Predetermined questions are asked on predetermined topics. The interviewer might ask an open-ended question such as: "How do you know when you are performing well?" and then follow it up with a series of more specific probes. The respondents answer questions in their own words.
- *Structured, fixed response.* The interviewer might pose multiple-choice questions, such as "In view of your age and the fact that you are living on your own, which of the following programs do you think might help make your life more comfortable?" The respondent is asked to choose from a list of five previously selected programs. As Nadler notes, this interview is like a personally administered questionnaire or survey, but it has the advantage of allowing for immediate clarification or follow-up probing.

Interviewing can be formal (specified place, time, length) or informal; it can be done with individuals or groups, and it can deal with smaller or larger samples of the population under consideration. Different kinds of interviewing get different kinds of data from different people. If the people to be interviewed are highly defensive, then formal group interviews will probably yield little useful information because they will not want to reveal themselves before others. The consultant must ask, "What is the best way to get the data I need for making decisions?"

Planners need an understanding of the advantages and disadvantages of interviewing as a data-gathering technique in order to make judgments about usefulness and cost-effectiveness. The following list of *advantages* is drawn from Jones (1973) and Nadler (1977).

- *Rich data.* A great deal of highly relevant information can be generated and, with a skillful interviewer, in a relatively short time.
- *Consultant visibility.* The consultant is not a shadowy figure to be feared or treated with suspicion. The assumptions of both interviewer and respondent about the fact, form, and content of the interview can be checked by either.
- *Adaptability.* If the situation changes, the interviewer can immediately adapt to the change. Such adaptation is impossible with printed surveys.
- *Reinforcement.* Most people like talking about themselves and their work. They like to believe that they are helpful, and they like the opportunity to express their opinions.
- *Follow-up.* Immediate follow-up is possible. Consultants can make sure that they understand what the respondent is saying by checking the respondent's frame of reference. Responses can be expanded by soliciting examples and further explanation from the respondent.
- *Discovery.* If important new issues are uncovered during the interview, new questions and probes can be formulated on the spot.
- *Language.* Since the interview is a dialogue, the respondents reply in their own words, not the more formal or technical language of a survey. Interviews avoid literacy problems among respondents.
- *Credibility.* When the respondents participate in the generation of data, they

are more likely to believe the feedback they get after the interview data are analyzed.

- *Relationship building*. Interviewing provides an opportunity to establish rapport with respondents. It shows that the individual is important to the system. Interviewing provides an opportunity for person-to-person sharing.
- *Openness*. To encourage openness in respondents, change agents can be open about themselves and their intentions.

As Jones (1973) notes, "No strategy that has so much promise can be without drawbacks" (p. 215). Here, then, are some of the major drawbacks of interviewing as a data-gathering technique.

- *Expense*. Interviews are expensive in terms of time and personnel.
- *Bias*. Interviewers can bias the data in a variety of ways; for instance, by asking leading questions and by being selective in the data recorded. Respondents also can add their biases; for instance, by telling only what they think the interviewers want to hear.
- *The counseling trap*. Sometimes it is difficult to avoid prolonged conversations related to the personal concerns of respondents. The empathic interviewer may be seen as helper or therapist.
- *Difficult coding*. The data gathered, while rich, may be difficult to code or categorize. Analysis of the data is difficult when the data are not directly comparable to data gathered by other methods or even by other interviewers. Important data can get lost in the summarizing process.
- *Threat to respondents*. Although people like to talk about themselves and their work, circumstances may make openness seem threatening. Threat, then, becomes a source or cause of bias.
- *Inaccessibility*. Sometimes interviewers find it difficult to make appointments with key respondents. Either these respondents are resisting the process, or the organization is set up so that accessibility is difficult.
- *Overly rich data*. Sometimes the data are so rich that the interviewer feels overwhelmed when it comes to the analysis and interpretation of what has been uncovered.

Despite these disadvantages, most consultants would agree with Nadler's (1977) summary statement that interviewing "still remains perhaps the single most useful data collection tool in an organization" (p. 124). Interpersonal style and basic communication skills are directly related to skillful interviewing (Egan, 1976).

Surveys and questionnaires.   At first glance surveys seem to be the royal route to data gathering. Most people are familiar with this technique, and it is easy enough to print and distribute any number of questionnaires. However, there is more to a good survey than meets the unskilled eye. The information gleaned from a survey is only as good as the construction and execution of the survey itself.

There is an extensive literature on conducting and interpreting surveys (Alderfer and Brown, 1972; Alderfer and Holbrook, 1973; Bouchard, 1976; Bowers and

Franklin, 1972, 1976; Hausser, Pecorella, and Wissler, 1977; International Business Machines, 1974; Nadler, 1977; Neff, 1965; Taylor and Bowers, 1972; Williams, Seybolt, and Pinder, 1975). Instead of a summary of this literature here, some of the simple, practical suggestions offered by Burges (1976, 1978) provide insight into the nature of surveys.

As with any kind of data-collection technique, it is essential to determine precisely what the survey is to accomplish before constructing the questionnaire itself. Next, it is crucial to determine just what kind of information is needed to accomplish the goals decided upon. Only then can the questionnaire be prepared properly. Since the way a questionnaire is designed determines, to a great extent, the quality of the data it will provide, Burges offers the following suggestions:

- *Reasonable hunches.* The questionnaire represents the researcher's best guesses about what factors are relevant to the issue being researched. In needs assessment, those doing the research must have some good ideas about the needs of the people being studied. If key needs are overlooked in the construction of the questions, essential information will be overlooked.
- *Comprehensiveness versus length.* The questionnaire should be comprehensive without being so long that it discourages respondents.
- *The best questions.* Brainstorming can be used to generate many more questions than are needed in the questionnaire, and then through a winnowing process the best questions—that is, those most likely to produce the kind of data needed—can be chosen.
- *Easy questions first.* Difficult and threatening questions should be avoided early in the survey. Respondents should be given a chance to get a feel for the questionnaire before being asked such questions.
- *Clarity.* Since no interviewer is present to clarify questions, the questionnaire must be written and rewritten until it is as clear, concise, and understandable as possible. Questions that mean different things to different people are worthless.
- *Close-ended questions.* Questions with fixed-alternative answers should be used. These include yes/no, ranking, rating scales, multiple-choice questions, and the like. The larger the sample, the greater the need for close-ended questions. For the sake of clarity the response categories used should be exhaustive and mutually exclusive. If questions deal with earned income, for instance, one of the categories should be "no earned income." Although open-ended questions allow people to personalize a survey, they are very difficult to summarize and interpret, especially when surveys are administered without any kind of interview.

Hoffman and Pool (1979) report the use of a survey to assess the needs of the part-time faculty of a college. The voices of part-time instructors are often either not raised or raised but not heard. And yet they contribute substantially to the functioning of the college. Without part-time teachers many colleges would not remain financially viable. The survey dealt with content needs, process needs, and incentive needs.

Content needs. The survey allowed the teachers to indicate what they needed in certain major areas such as the evaluation of teaching, curriculum development, interpersonal skills, educational technology, and student services. The survey showed marked needs in such areas as counseling and advising students, managing individualized instruction, developing multimedia presentations, and the availability of student counseling and tutoring. The teachers were greatly concerned about evaluation—that is, self-evaluation, peer evaluation, and student evaluation.

Process needs. The survey also dealt with process needs, or the ways in which the content needs were to be met. The survey suggested guided discussions, intervisitations of faculty, lectures, programmed instruction, workshops, encounter groups, individualized instruction, professional meetings, role-playing, and simulations. Respondents indicated that short-term workshops and professional meetings would meet their process needs best. With respect to scheduling, the survey suggested dates immediately prior to the fall semester, various days during the semester break, Saturdays during the academic year, week nights on which the individual instructor teaches, and week nights on which the individual teacher does not teach. Most of the respondents favored time immediately preceding the beginning of the fall term. With respect to location, the survey offered as possibilities campus sites, metropolitan sites outside the campus, and retreat sites. Most of the respondents favored some on-campus site. Since their time was limited, they wanted the most convenient location.

Incentive needs. This category dealt primarily with the economics of incentives. The survey suggested that the person could be rewarded for attending these events by such things as a commendation in the instructor's personnel file, a flat monetary payment for each event attended, increased consideration for a full-time position, released time from classes with no loss in pay, and teaching hour equivalency payments. There is no indication whether the survey included a consideration of intrinsic incentives such as increased competence. Most of the instructors indicated that increased consideration for full-time vacancies would by itself serve as sufficient incentive for participation.

Nadler (1977) discusses the advantages and disadvantages of surveys. The adaptation that follows relates primarily to surveys filled out without any kind of interviewing. The *advantages* of surveys are:

- *Adequate sample size.* Surveys can be distributed easily to a large number of people simultaneously.
- *Easy analysis and feedback.* If the questions are of the fixed-response type, then analysis and feedback are relatively simple procedures. Data can be quantified and summarized easily.
- *Low cost.* Once the questionnaire has been standardized, the costs of distributing and analyzing it are low in comparison with costs of interviewing.
- *Wide scope.* It is easy to amass a large amount of data on a wide range of topics.
- *Control by researchers.* Right from the start, the data collectors decide what kind of information they are going to receive and how it is going to be analyzed.

There is something "neat and clean" about survey research that is well done.

Surveys also have a number of disadvantages, some of which are counterparts to the advantages:

- *Lack of empathy*. Although questions may be written in the language of the respondents, surveys cannot be personalized. Respondents often approach surveys with an indifferent attitude.
- *Lack of adaptability*. If the questionnaire itself or any individual question proves inappropriate to the situation, or if some important question is left out, nothing can be done about it. For instance, if some important need area had been omitted from the survey of part-time instructors, it would have been necessary to put out a separate survey for that area. The advantage of high control leads to the disadvantage of lack of adaptability.
- *Unanswered questions*. Respondents are free to ignore questions even though the survey begins with an exhortation to answer all.
- *Difficult interpretation*. Data that are easy to quantify are not necessarily easy to interpret. Sometimes the ease of quantification leads to a false assumption about easy interpretation.
- *Self-report bias*. Respondents may get bored or tired, answer a whole set of questions the same way, try to guess what the researchers are looking for, and introduce other forms of bias.
- *Excessive data*. Such a wealth of data can be collected that researchers are overwhelmed when attempting to interpret it.
- *Deceptive simplicity*. Since surveys seem so easy to construct, administer, and analyze, there is a tendency to rush into them without adequate preparation.

This brief summary of issues related to surveys shows that it is imperative to develop a working knowledge of this data-gathering technique and some skill in its use before using it in change projects.

Some authors contend that tight control is unnecessary. Sherwood (1981) agrees it is important to elicit data that are relevant to system-oriented decisions, but believes that in many cases the needed information can be obtained through standard questionnaires. Most organizations, institutions, and communities face the same kinds of problems, and many of the problems are recurring ones. Standard questionnaires suffice, especially if a few questions are added that relate to the specific problems this particular system is facing.

Sherwood makes two important suggestions. First, interview people before formulating the questionnaire to find out what questions they think should be asked. Very often the questions they suggest are the very questions included in standard surveys. Since the respondents were asked, however, they now "own" the survey in a more substantial way. Interviewing should include people who "march to a different drummer" in the organization. "Include the office crank," is Sherwood's suggestion.

Second, Sherwood recommends adding an open-ended question or two asking what the individual needs in order to do his job better. "Better," of course, relates to both productivity and quality of life. Standard organizational questionnaires cover most of the topics related to both work effectiveness and quality of life.

However, ending the questionnaire with an open-ended question helps the respondent to personalize the task.

Sherwood in no way suggests that data gathering be a sloppy process. He is merely pointing out that it is inefficient to use a micrometer when a yardstick will do just as well. The issue is *useful information*, not sophistication of technique. He is more concerned with what systems do with the valid information they have gathered. He suggests that most systems go astray, not because their information is unreliable, but because they fail to use it or use it poorly.

Observation.   One way to collect data is by watching what is happening in a group, a community, or an organization and recording these observations. Like interviewing, observation may be formal or informal. A neighborhood organizer once said to me, "I try to walk through the neighborhood I'm working in at least once every day or so. I have no particular agenda. I don't necessarily talk to anyone. I just want to see what's going on. I'm open to whatever strikes me." This is a highly informal and unstructured approach to observation. Others document a more systematic approach to this data-gathering technique (Bouchard, 1976; Burges, 1976a, 1976b, 1978; Jenkins, Nadler, Lawler, and Cammann, 1975; McCall and Simmons, 1969; Nadler, 1977; Schatzman and Strauss, 1972; Spradley, 1980; Whyte, 1955).

Of course, observation must first be related to some purpose or goal. As Nadler (1977) notes, it is obvious that "simply entering an organization and observing things as they happen is significantly different from planned, systematic observation, be it structured, semistructured, or unstructured" (p. 136).

Second, lenses are useful for both observing behavior and recording data. Since total observation of a system of any size is impossible, models and lenses are needed to tell observers what to observe, when to observe it, and what to record. Nadler divides planned observation into these types:

Structured observation calls for specific lenses or guidelines for watching behavior and precise categories or instruments for recording observations. In human relations training groups, for instance, it is possible to see whether such skills as empathy, confrontation, and immediacy are learned and with what degree of assertiveness they are used. The training model itself (see Egan, 1976, 1977) provides guidelines for both observing and recording behavior. Through observation it is possible to develop an "interaction profile" on each member. This profile indicates strengths and weaknesses in such categories as self-disclosure, empathic responding, challenging, and group-specific skills.

Spradley (1980) provides a number of different frameworks or lenses to help focus the observation process. He divides observations into descriptive, focused, and selective types:

It is useful to think of the three kinds of observation as a funnel. The broad rim of the funnel consists of *descriptive observations* in which you want to catch everything that goes on. These are the foundation of all ethnographic research and will continue throughout your entire project. Moving down from the mouth to the rim, the funnel narrows sharply. *Focused observations* require that you narrow the scope of what you are looking for. But when you start this more focused type of investigation, you know what you are looking for—the categories. . . . At the bottom of a funnel there is an extremely narrow, restricted opening. *Selective observations* represent the smallest focus through which you will make observations. They involve going to your social situation and looking for differences among specific . . . categories [p. 128].

Spradley presents a Descriptive Question Matrix as a comprehensive framework or lens for observing.

Semistructured observation does not require specific lenses for observing behavior, but after a period of watching, the observer fills out a form with specific categories. For instance, Jenkins and associates (1975) used semistructured observation to study psychological characteristics of job performance. Observers watched people work for an hour and then filled out a 15-page form that organized the observations.

Unstructured observation, according to Nadler, is not unplanned and unsystematic because what to observe, how to observe, and when and where to observe are planned. But there are no *formal* lenses or guidelines for observing and no specific categories or instruments for recording what has been observed. There is only a general and implicit structure for both observing and recording. Unstructured observation works best in the hands of relative experts working with small groups. For instance, a consultant is asked to attend a meeting of a work team, watch how the members work together, and give them feedback on their performance. In observing and giving feedback, the consultant uses implicit models or guidelines relating to effective teamwork.

Good observers know why they are collecting data, develop trusting relationships with those to be observed lest they be seen as "snoopers," use at least implicit models of observing, search for clues, follow leads, develop working hypotheses, discard or recast hypotheses when the data demand it, and record their observations carefully.

The following lists of advantages and disadvantages of observation are drawn principally from Burges (1976a, 1976b, 1978) and Nadler (1977).

Some of the *advantages* of observation as a data-gathering technique are:

- *The skilled observer*. The observer, if skilled and sensitive, becomes a highly flexible instrument for gathering data.
- *Direct contact*. In interviewing, people report on behaviors; in observing, behaviors and their results are the focus.
- *Functions and methods*. Observing reveals not just *what* is done but also *how* it is done. Sometimes the "how" is even more important than the "what."
- *Adaptability*. The observer can seek out clues, follow leads, make and remake hypotheses. The observer can see important things that are not usually measured.
- *Elimination of bias*. Since observing bypasses the kind of self-reporting involved in interviews and surveys, it also bypasses the kinds of bias that affect the reliability and validity of self-reporting.
- *Validity checks*. After interviewing or surveying, observation can be used to check the validity of self-reporting.
- *Behavior in process*. Observing deals with the here and now, while interviewing and surveying ordinarily take a retrospective view.

Some of the *disadvantages* of observing are:

- *The unskilled observer*. If the observer is not skilled and perceptive, observation is time wasted. Observer bias is always possible. For instance, an observer prejudiced against a class of people will see their behavior through this prejudice.
- *Limited access*. Observers might not have easy access to the situations to be observed. If they must demand access, they put the people to be observed on guard. If they do not let people know they are being observed, they may be in for reprisals.
- *Bias*. If people know they are being observed, they may engage in behaviors that are awkward and atypical.
- *Difficulty of coding*. Observations are not easy to code and quantify and therefore not easy to analyze and interpret.
- *Lack of systematic methodology*. It is difficult to prepare lenses or guidelines for observing and instruments for recording.

Because of its many limitations, observation should not be the sole data-collection technique in any given project. It can be a very powerful technique, however, when used in combination with an interview or a survey.

Reading relevant documents.   Use of documents is a much underused data-gathering technique. Reading is called an "unobtrusive measure" since, if the documents are public or easily accessible, data can be gathered quietly without threatening others (although the *use* of the data may threaten people).

> A hard-working faculty member of a large urban university served on a number of university committees. Whenever he was asked to serve on a committee or to attend a meeting, he would first read whatever documents he could find that related to the functioning of the committee or the purpose of the meeting. He would read all the minutes of previous meetings, for instance, or find out what other universities had done with respect to the issue at hand. As a result, he came to meetings better prepared than others. He had a much clearer idea of the needs being addressed, how they had been addressed before, what actions had been taken or programs developed, and what the outcomes had been. Because he knew the complete *history* of the issue, he was not likely to repeat mistakes that had been made in the past. As might be expected, many of his colleagues were annoyed, though some admired his ability to become so fully prepared and knowledgeable. This faculty member's preparation for meetings was unobtrusive, but his participation in the meetings themselves was open and direct.

A variety of documents supply the kinds of information that help change agents work with systems.

Mission related documents. Often a variety of documents indicate the overall purposes and policies of a system and even the purposes and policies of a subsystem within the organization. These documents include constitutions, charters, bylaws, statements of purpose, guidelines, and rules and regulations. A consultant was called in to mediate a dispute between a director of a large mental hospital and some members of his staff. To prepare herself for the conflict-management sessions, she read the charter and mission of the hospital, the documents dealing with relationships between director and staff, and the minutes of meetings in which the issues in question had been discussed.

Archives. Many systems store important data about themselves and their operations. The totality of these documents is called the archives, a word that suggests musty vaults. In modern organizations and institutions, however, the archives may be primarily computer storage banks. Archives can include statistical summaries, records, annual reports, financial reports, correspondence, minutes of meetings, memoranda, press releases, histories, and descriptions of programs. Since combing through the archives of a system may prove to be drudgery, the change agent must decide whether the information to be obtained is worth the effort.

Good community organizers are people who "know their territory." Before observing a community or interviewing anyone in it, organizers can find out a great deal about it. For instance, by reading the pertinent documents they can discover the racial and possibly the ethnic composition of the neighborhood, its crime rate, the density of population, the range of incomes, the average income, the number of people unemployed or on welfare, the number of taverns, the kinds of businesses and their size, the number of people in different age groups, the applicable zoning laws, the frequency of police patrols, the number of parks and their sizes, the number of automobiles, the number of automobile accidents and major danger spots, numbers and types of schools and churches, number and location of hospitals and where their patients come from, and so on. Good organizers are well informed when they go into communities. A great deal of their power lies in what they know.

> The residents of a neighborhood in a large midwestern city expressed a great deal of fear about the value of their homes when a nearby neighborhood began to "change." Living in an all-white neighborhood, they worried about the consequences of blacks moving in. They were not necessarily prejudiced, but prejudiced or not, they lived in fear.
>
> A sociology instructor from a local community college was a member of the community organization for that area of the city. He wanted to help the home owners allay some of their fears by developing a realistic working knowledge of real estate in the area, including patterns of buying and selling. With the help of local real estate firms, he conducted a series of workshops designed to raise the real estate consciousness of those who owned property in the neighborhood.
>
> In the first workshop he helped people understand the present sociological picture of the neighborhood. In the second workshop he focused on real estate, including such topics as the kinds of housing available in the neighborhood, the range of values, average value, the number of renters, the length of time the average renter stayed in the community, the

range of rents, the number of absentee landlords, the degree of appreciation of property over the last five years, the number of homes bought
and sold in the last three years and the prices paid, the state of repair of
buildings in the area and the number of building code violations, the
number of violations still in court, and so forth. In a third workshop he
dealt with the prognosis for real estate in the area. He examined changing
real estate patterns in adjacent neighborhoods and tried to predict what
kinds of sociological change might take place over the next five years and
the impact these changes would have on real estate. In a final workshop
he indicated possible responses to the changes taking place, especially
insofar as these changes related to real estate.

The percentage of home and business owners who attended these
workshops was extremely high. They used the meetings as a forum to air
their fears and hopes. And most people not only attended all four workshops, but also indicated that they were interested in periodic follow-up
meetings. The faculty member, when promised some volunteer help, agreed
to publish a real estate newsletter that would update the information shared
in the workshop and to chair two or three meetings on the same subject
per year.

These meetings did not automatically allay fears, solve problems, or stem the tide
of sociological change in the city and its neighborhoods. But the workshops turned
out informed citizens who could talk together more intelligently about the city, the
neighborhood, and its real estate. Both individually and collectively, the home
owners could respond more intelligently to the problems of urban living. No magic
here, but rather the power that comes from relevant information translated into
decision making and action.

4. Adequate sampling

Sampling is an important issue in the data-gathering process. If the techniques just
described cannot be used with all the members of the system because the system is
too large, it is more feasible to tap a representative sample. The key word, of course,
is *representative*. Earlier this century a telephone poll was conducted during a pres-
idential campaign to predict the winner. The poll showed conclusively that Thomas
E. Dewey would be the winner, but Harry S Truman actually won. The problem
was sampling. At the time of the campaign the *average* family did not have a
telephone. Therefore, a telephone poll automatically introduced bias into the data.

In gathering data you should include both representative and key people in the
sample, as the following example shows:

A consultant interviewed the administrator of a large hospital and his
executive staff individually. Then they all met together to plan the next
step in an action-research project. At the beginning of the meeting the
consultant asked, "Is everyone here who should be here?" Everybody

looked around, and finally a staff member said, "Where's Jane?" "Who is Jane?" the consultant asked. The administrator said, "She's my secretary." Everybody agreed that she should be there. She was privy to most of the confidential information at the top of the organization, she knew all the staff, she arranged meetings between staff members and the administrator, and she facilitated the communication of important information among members of the entire team. After the meeting the consultant interviewed her just as he had interviewed the others.

The administrator's secretary was a key person even though she was not a member of the staff itself.

Who are these key people? If you are a consultant to the organization, you can easily find out who they are because most insiders know. Simply say, "I'm going to interview a number of people in the organization. I can't interview everyone, but I don't want to leave out anyone it would be important to hear. Who should be included?" If you address this question to a number of people from different areas of the organization, you will soon find out who is key.

Key people are those who see the system and its functioning from some important vantage point. The administrator's secretary had a unique vantage point. Sometimes you will hear something like this: "You had better include Ed. He's been complaining about things around here for years. You won't know the underside of the organization until you've talked to him. He's an expert in it." Not all the key people are found on the organizational chart. Most systems, especially larger systems, have both formal and informal structures. Representatives from the informal system can be as important as representatives from the formal system.

Any standard textbook in statistics will provide guidelines to help you avoid sampling errors. You will also discover that it is impossible to avoid all error. When reading about sampling guidelines and sampling error, however, beware of becoming a victim of the "micrometer versus yardstick" trap. In most data-gathering projects you will probably not need highly refined statistical tools. Most organizations are probably too "loosely coupled" for extensive use of refined statistical analysis (Weick, 1979). Such tools are meaningful in the hands of the specialists who conduct research into organizations, institutions, and communities. But among managers, data gathering for practical decision making is less demanding than data gathering for research.

5. Using data to make decisions

Next the data must be analyzed and interpreted. In this important step the data are turned into *relevant information*, which is essential to decision making. If the purpose of data gathering is clear and if meaningful questions have been formulated and asked of both key and representative people, then the task of interpretation may be relatively easy. The statistics should yield answers to the questions you have asked. These answers will have greater or lesser degrees of probability—that is, the data will yield both conclusive and probable answers.

Do not gather data and then ask, "What are we going to do with it?" Knowing how you are going to analyze and interpret the data—that is, knowing how you are going to turn it into relevant information—is part of the overall data-gathering plan. The overall plan should be clear from the beginning.

6. Clear presentation of results

Present the results in an easily understandable form to those who are to make the decisions. *Everyone who contributes to the data-gathering process should get feedback on the results.* For instance, in large organizations a cascading approach to feedback can be used. The president receives the results first and handles the feedback meeting with senior officers. Then each officer handles the feedback meeting for the people who report to him or her. This process continues all the way down the line, with supervisors handling feedback meetings with line workers.

The chief executive officer should not get privileged information and then decide what *part* of the results the others are to get. Sherwood (1981) suggests that such a process contributes to maintaining adversarial relationships and a climate of distrust. The top person might say to the consultant, "I can't share this with everyone!" In this case the consultant should help him or her to see the benefits of sharing the results with everyone and the costs of not doing so. The chief executive should understand that data gathering has both productivity and quality-of-life implications. The consultant acts as a kind of counselor, helping the chief executive officer deal with any disquieting emotions associated with this kind of openness.

Like the president, others will have misgivings about these feedback meetings. Supervisors may need some training if they are to give the people they supervise a clear picture of the survey results and the implications of these results.

7. Informed decisions

The payoff or "bottom line" for data gathering is, of course, system-enhancing decisions based on reliable and valid data. Some systems collect valid data, turn it into useful information, and then fail to use it.

> A consultant was invited to work with the board of directors of a hospital. During her first visit, she got the feeling that they had gone through this process before. Toward the end of the first meeting she asked them if there had been any previous studies of the hospital. The administrator opened a desk drawer and pulled out a rather hefty tome. It was the report of a consulting team who had visited the hospital two years earlier. No action had been taken on it. After a second meeting this consultant decided not to work with this hospital because staff members were not ready for change (see Pfeiffer and Jones, 1978, on organizational development readiness).

Failure to take action on data gathered breeds cynicism in organizations and institutions.

ARATIONALITY AND DATA GATHERING

Managers need to be aware of the arational dimensions of the data-gathering process:

- *Lack of overall purpose*. People sometimes gather data without knowing why they are doing so. Data gathering becomes an end in itself rather than merely instrumental in making decisions.
- *Poor questions*. Questions are often poorly formulated and not related to some overall purpose. The investigators don't know what they want to learn and why. Some questions are omitted because the data gatherers don't want to upset people. Or the data gatherers themselves, without being fully aware of or admitting it, want to avoid potential conflicts.
- *Unsuitable data-gathering techniques*. When people don't know which techniques would be most useful, they choose the most familiar techniques rather than the most suitable. They choose instruments without considering the advantages and disadvantages of each in relation to the overall purpose of the data-gathering project. They lack the skills needed to use techniques well. They devise surveys poorly, for instance, or they interview without first developing interviewing skills.
- *Sampling errors*. Samples are not always representative, and investigators may overlook key people. Often samples are too small for valid results or unnecessarily large and therefore cost-inefficient.
- *Lack of analysis and interpretation*. Data is collected, but not analyzed or interpreted. People think that it will speak for itself even when it does not. Or people don't know how to mine relevant information out of the data gathered. Or they use sophisticated statistical techniques when simple inspection would suffice. After information has been gathered, people ask, "Now what should we do with it?"
- *Inadequate presentation of results*. The information found in the data is not always communicated to those who need to know. Rather it is hoarded and used as a political tool. People who contributed to the process are not told of the results, or they are given watered-down versions that suit the purposes of management. If the people who conduct feedback meetings lack the skills to do so, others are not helped to see how the results relate to productivity and quality of life.
- *Uninformed decision making*. With respect to decision making there are at least three common forms of arationality. First, decisions are made without gathering the data needed to make an informed decision. Second, data are gathered, but are not relevant to the impending decisions. Third, relevant data are gathered but not used.

Of course, data gathering is not always a formal or rational process. As human beings we are constantly gathering and processing data and making decisions based on it. We develop hunches based both on behavioral cues and on intuition. The very complexity of data makes data gathering an arational process even when it is formal.

4

Understanding Needs and Wants

Assessing needs and wants is one of the most critical parts of designing any kind of human system. Logically, assessment of needs and wants is the *first* step. Moreover, if a system already exists, it cannot be understood without understanding the needs and wants it was designed to satisfy. If the needs and wants of the members of the receiving system have never been defined, then the system will suffer from a great deal of ambiguity. If needs are not clear, then goals will be unclear or unrelated to needs and wants. Some human-service systems try to engage in well-defined programs, hoping to clarify needs along the way. But ambiguity, however disguised, persists because programs are not clearly related to goals and goals are not clearly related to needs and wants.

> Terry Nixon suggests to some of his friends that they should meet once a week to discuss what is happening in their lives. He calls this a "personal-growth group." This sounds like a good idea, so seven friends join the group. At the meetings they talk about a wide variety of things, ranging from how they feel about the local professional sports teams to misgivings about the values they are pursuing. After a few weeks some of the members begin to drop out. Within a couple of months they decide to call their discussions off because they don't seem to be getting anywhere. Terry still thinks it is a good idea, and he does not know what has gone wrong.

A group is bound to run into trouble when the members decide on a *program*—having meetings—before they consider what needs and wants will be satisfied through these meetings. Vague expectations are raised, but members drift away because they cannot tolerate such vagueness for long.

Too often those in charge of systems take a "stones instead of bread" approach to needs and wants. People who need bread are given stones instead. For instance,

73

inmates of correctional institutions need some kind of rehabilitation. Some get it, but many do not. (Of course, not all prisoners *want* rehabilitation.) Rape victims need support and justice; instead they often receive suspicion and the runaround. Counseling and psychotherapy clients need to manage their problems and their anxiety more effectively; instead of help they may receive not much more than a deeper understanding of the theories of their helpers. If staff members want to participate more substantially in the decision-making process of a social-service agency, then offering them more training or better fringe benefits is not going to satisfy their need. If interns at a mental health clinic are dissatisfied with the quality of supervision they are receiving, giving them time off for lectures is not going to fill their need. Insensitivity to needs and wants is a bit of arationality that is part of the "literature" of many systems.

DISTINGUISHING NEEDS FROM WANTS

Needs are dynamic; that is, they are incentives for action. People strive for those things they believe they lack; they work to remove states of deprivation. Webster's dictionary defines need as "a condition requiring supply or relief" and also as "the lack of anything requisite, desired, or useful." Need ordinarily denotes some kind of deficiency, deprivation, or discrepancy.

- *Deficiency*. A person with scurvy has a vitamin C *deficiency* and needs this substance for physical health or wholeness. People without problem-solving skills have a deficiency. They need these skills to manage the problem situations of their lives more effectively.
- *Deprivation*. A starving person is *deprived* of food and needs to eat and drink in order to maintain life. A person in solitary confinement is deprived of the company of other human beings as a form of punishment, on the assumption that people need and want company.
- *Discrepancy*. For a person living in a squalid house without proper sanitation facilities, there is a *discrepancy* between what is and what ought to be, or between the actual and the ideal. This person needs better housing.

Even in these few examples it is clear that there is a hierarchy of needs. The person deprived of food and drink will die if this need is not met. On the other hand, people living in squalor may be exposed to health hazards but will not die for lack of better housing. Therefore, food is an *absolute* need and better housing is a *relative* need.

Absolute needs refer to whatever is needed to sustain life or continue the species. People have an absolute need for food and water. If everybody in the world were denied cross-sex companionship, then the human race itself would die out. Therefore, with respect to the continued existence of the human race, cross-sex companionship (or artificial insemination) is an absolute need.

Relative needs refer to what is needed to improve the quality of life. A person can survive without cross-sex companionship, but this deprivation affects the quality of life.

Scriven and Roth (1978) offer a definition of need that is based on *adequacy* rather than discrepancy and helps distinguish needs from wants. They say that the statement "Jane needs *x*" means that without *x* Jane is in an unsatisfactory condition. For instance, without confirmatory and corrective feedback about the quality of her work, Jane is in an unsatisfactory condition. She feels confused and frustrated. If Jane gets feedback, she benefits significantly in terms of both productivity and quality of life.

If *x* represents need rather than want, then having *x* enables the person to achieve, *but not surpass*, a satisfactory condition. The statement "Andrea needs food" means that she is in an unsatisfactory condition with respect to food—she is hungry, suffering from malnutrition, or even starving to death. She benefits significantly by eating; that is, she appeases her hunger, begins to recover from malnutrition, or is saved from starvation. However, Andrea's life can be sustained by very moderate amounts of inferior food. By eating nutritional food, Andrea moves from an unsatisfactory to a satisfactory condition. Moderate amounts of quite ordinary food will move her to a state of adequacy, thus satisfying her need. By eating larger amounts of food or more appetizing foods, she would surpass a satisfactory condition with respect to food. She would move beyond needs to wants. As Scriven and Roth note, "Need stops and wants begin at the level of adequacy" (p. 3). The millionaire with a broken arm needs treatment for the arm, not a second million.

To locate the dividing line between needs and wants, consider the O'Briens, a family of four with an income of $12,000 at a time when a government agency has set the poverty level at $12,500. Such a family is in an unsatisfactory condition with respect to the ability to pay for such necessities as food, clothing, medical services, and housing. If the O'Briens were to receive $500 more per year, at least theoretically, they could meet their basic needs in North American society. But notice that some agency has defined for them what is adequate and what is less than adequate—an estimation that may or may not be correct. Defining what is adequate in such a case is not just an economic act; it is also a political and cultural act.

Needs can be related to goals through the use of an "if-then" formula: "If I want to stay alive, then I need to eat." "If I want to become a licensed doctor in North America, then I need to go to medical school." "If I want to swim every day, I need a house with a swimming pool." The "needs" here refer to the programs or means that are essential to the goals desired. The goals themselves, however, may be absolute—staying alive—and therefore refer to absolute needs or they may be relative—studying medicine—and therefore refer to the quality of life. They may deal with superfluity rather than adequacy—a house with a swimming pool—and therefore refer to wants rather than needs. Becoming a doctor is a want rather than a need with respect to career.

Some degree of relativism is inherent in the distinction between needs and wants. The far ends of the scale are easy enough to identify. Shelter is a need for everyone, but a mansion is a want. Scriven and Roth point out that the middle ground is somewhat murky:

> Needs are . . . normally relativized to whatever standards of feasibility the time acknowledges as well as the standards of living we currently recognize. What we call a necessity

in the United States would be a luxury in Pakistan. . . . Need is . . . largely a context-dependent word like "large"; there are no absolute standards for it [Scriven and Roth, 1978, p. 9].

As Scriven and Roth suggest, wisdom in needs assessment requires the ability to adapt the definition to specific situations.

A visitor from Tanzania asked me to show him some of the slums of Chicago. I drove him to an area of the city identified as a slum by all social indicators. As we drove through this area, he asked me when we were going to reach the slums. I replied that we were in the middle of one of Chicago's worst slums. He looked reflectively at the brick buildings, the automobiles lining the streets, and the television antennas that sprouted almost everywhere and said quietly, "The rich in my country do not live this well."

A quality-of-life approach

The human-services professions help people with their quality-of-life needs and wants. The American Institutes for Research (Flanagan, 1978), in a major research effort toward improving the quality of life of people in the United States, began by defining empirically what people mean by quality of life. Through nationwide interviews of people in all socioeconomic classes, they collected 6,500 critical incidents. Through a process of refinement, the incidents yielded 15 quality-of-life categories based on the experiences of this varied group of people:

1. Physical and Material Well-Being

A. *Material well-being and financial security.* Having good food, home, possessions, comforts, and expectations of these for the future. Money and financial security are typically important factors. For most people, filling these needs is primarily related to their efforts or those of their spouse.

B. *Health and personal safety.* Enjoying freedom from sickness, possessing physical and mental fitness, avoiding accidents and other health hazards. Problems related to alcohol, drugs, death, and aging are also included. Effective treatment of health problems is a large component.

2. Relations with Other People

C. *Relations with spouse (girlfriend or boyfriend).* Being married or having a girlfriend or boyfriend. The relationship involves love, companionship, sexual satisfaction, understanding, communication, appreciation, devotion, and contentment.

D. *Having and raising children.* Having children and becoming a parent. This relationship involves watching their development, spending time with them and enjoying them. Also included are things like molding, guiding, helping, appreciating, and learning from them and with them.

E. *Relations with parents, siblings, or other relatives.* Having parents, siblings, or other relatives. In these relationships, one experiences communicating with or doing things with them, visiting, enjoying, sharing, understanding, being helped, and helping them. The feelings of belonging and having someone to discuss things with is a large component.

F. *Relations with friends.* Having close friends. In these relationships one shares activities, interests, and views. Important aspects of these relationships involve being accepted, visiting, giving and receiving help, love, trust, support, and guidance.

3. Social, Community, and Civic Activities

G. *Activities related to helping or encouraging other people.* Helping or encouraging adults or children (other than relatives or close friends). This can be done through one's efforts as an individual or as a member of some organization, such as a church, club, or volunteer group, that works for the benefit of other people.

H. *Activities relating to local and national governments.* Keeping informed through the media; participating by voting and other communications; having and appreciating one's political, social, and religious freedom. One component of this includes having living conditions affected by regulations, laws, procedures, and policies of governing agencies and the individuals and groups that influence and operate them.

4. Personal Development and Fulfillment

I. *Intellectual development.* Learning, attending school, acquiring desired knowledge and mental abilities, graduating, and problem solving. Other aspects involve improving understanding, comprehension, or appreciation in an intellectual area through activities in or out of school.

J. *Personal understanding and planning.* Developing and gaining orientation, purpose, and guiding principles for one's life. This may involve becoming more mature, gaining insight into and acceptance of one's assets and limitations, experiencing and awareness of personal growth and development, and realizing the ability to influence the course of one's life significantly. It also includes making decisions and planning life activities and roles. For some people, a major component arises from religious or spiritual experiences or activities.

K. *Occupational role (job).* Having interesting, challenging, rewarding, worthwhile work in a job or home. This includes doing well, using one's abilities, learning and producing, obtaining recognition, and accomplishing on the job.

L. *Creativity and personal expression.* Showing ingenuity, originality, imagination in music, art, writing, handicrafts, drama, photography, practical or scientific matters, or everyday activities. This also includes expressing oneself through a collection, a personal project, or an accomplishment or achievement.

5. Recreation

M. *Socializing.* Entertaining at home or elsewhere, attending parties or other social gatherings, meeting new people, interacting with others. It may include participation in social organizations and clubs.

N. *Passive and observational recreational activities.* Participating in various kinds of passive recreation, such as watching television, listening to music, reading, going to the movies, and going to entertainment or sports events. It also involves appreciating the art and beauty in many aspects of life.

O. *Active and participatory recreational activities.* Participating in various kinds of active recreation, such as sports, hunting, fishing, boating, camping, vacation travel, sightseeing, etc. This may also involve playing sedentary or active games, singing, playing an instrument, dancing, acting, etc. [Flanagan, 1978, pp. 139–140].

These needs and wants define the quality of life desired by people in the United States. Obviously the categories are not equally important to all people. And the relative importance of any given category can change over the life span. Most of the needs and wants expressed on this list are goals that are achieved by participation in or interactions with various organizations (workplaces, stores, banks), institutions (government agencies, churches, hospitals), and communities (families, neighborhoods, voluntary associations). These are the client needs and wants that human-service systems address. Clients may be the individuals or the settings in which individuals attempt to meet these needs and wants.

General versus specific needs

Needs and wants can be compared as either general or specific:

General needs. People have general needs and wants in the area of medical care, education, religion, and family life. If a soldier is wounded on the battlefield, it is obvious that he needs medical care even though it is not yet clear what specific kind of medical care he needs. Flanagan's discussion of the quality of life lists categories of generic needs, such as "relations with friends," followed by specific examples like "being accepted, visiting," and so on. General needs are related to the *mission* and the *major aims* of the system.

Specific needs. If there are many casualties on a battlefield but medical personnel are few, a kind of needs assessment called *triage* may take place. The wounded are sorted into three groups: The first group includes those who will die with or without medical attention. This group is left unattended. The second group includes those who will survive with or without immediate medical attention. This group, too, is left unattended. The third group includes those for whom immediate medical attention means the difference between life and death. This group receives immediate attention. Diagnostic procedures and exploratory surgery identify specific needs. The process moves from the generic ("He needs immediate medical attention") to the specific ("He needs his spleen removed, his stomach repaired, and antibiotics to guard against peritonitis").

Specific needs are related to the *goals* of the system—that is, they are specific indications of what the goals should be. As Scriven and Roth (1978) point out, "As needs assessment becomes more precise, specific, and useful, it does come very close to goal setting" (p. 9). If needs are clear and specific, then goals are merely their "flip side." If "spleen damaged beyond repair" is the finding of the exploratory operation, then "spleen removed" becomes the goal.

Organizations, institutions, and communities frequently make mistakes in translating from generic to specific needs. No kind of system is exempt from this common form of arationality. The Ford Motor Company once spent a great deal of money designing, manufacturing, and marketing an automobile called the Edsel. Few people wanted the Edsel, however, and it became a multimillion dollar marketing mistake. Medical misdiagnoses lead to concrete and specific but inappropriate medical interventions. Churches often translate soul-stirring mission statements into trivial goals and programs. In all these cases there is a failure to translate generic needs into the specific needs that lead to the setting of concrete and specific goals.

Felt, expressed, prescribed, and comparative needs

Bradshaw (1972), in discussing the delivery of social services to people in need, distinguishes four different kinds of need: felt, expressed, normative or prescribed, and comparative.

Felt needs. A felt need is any need perceived by the person with the need. It can be an absolute need ("I need food and water"), a need related to the quality-of-life ("I need someone I can talk to"), or a want ("I need a long vacation in the Caribbean").

All of these statements could be recast in an "if-then" format: "If I am to stay alive, then I need food and water." "If I am to straighten out my life and get rid of my anxiety, then I need someone to talk to."

If felt needs exist, then by implication so do *unfelt* needs. For instance, people need vitamin C even though they are not aware of it. People need dental work or medical care without realizing it. Freire (1970) developed a process of helping oppressed and exploited workers who were unaware of their oppression get in touch with needs related to the quality of human life. He did not tell these workers what they needed—that is, he did not prescribe their needs for them—but he helped them raise their consciousness with respect to quality-of-life issues so that they could determine for themselves what they needed.

Expressed needs. Expressed need is felt need translated into a request or demand for some product or service. Needs that are felt are not automatically expressed. Some people feel the need for better housing, for instance, but they may not express the need for a variety of reasons: they don't even think of expressing it, they are afraid of the consequences of expressing it, or they think that expressing it would be a waste of time. On the other hand, many people express felt needs—that is, they make demands—even though others consider their demands unreasonable. John wants Jane to spend more time with him even though Jane thinks that she spends too much time with him already.

Prescribed needs. A prescribed need, which Bradshaw (1972) calls a "normative need," is what the expert or professional perceives to be needed in a given situation. Prescribing implies that one person or group is "more knowing" than another about some aspect of human living. These "less knowing" people are not in touch with their needs, or lack the understanding that leads to need-satisfying action, or are faint-hearted in pursuing their needs and therefore need to be challenged to do so. Those who prescribe needs hope the "less knowing" will eventually realize that these prescriptions reflect actual needs, or that they will at least accept the prescriptions on the authority of the prescriber.

All sorts of communities, organizations, and institutions engage in prescribing needs. For instance, churches make prescriptions about the spiritual needs of their members: "You need to believe this creed." "You need to pray." "You need to go to church on the sabbath." "You need to care about your neighbor." Educational experts and schools prescribe needs for learners: "You need to learn the multiplication tables." "You need to attend gym class." "You need to know something about American literature." "You need to be able to write coherent sentences and paragraphs."

In a counselor training program—or in the language of Model A, in a counselor training *system*—most of the needs are prescribed needs. Trainees usually enter the system with some generic felt needs: "I need to learn whatever is necessary to make me a good counselor." "I need to learn the helping models, methods, and skills that will make me a skilled helper." Trainees want to become competent and they assume that the professionals who run counselor-training departments, because of their research and experience in helping people, know what these models, methods, and skills are.

In everyday life we run into an endless array of prescribed needs. The surgeon general has determined that people need to be warned about the hazards of smoking. The vast advertising industry floods the public with all sorts of prescriptions implying that wants are really needs. Advertising is not merely a process of informing; its purpose is to *create* wants and needs.

Comparative needs. Bradshaw defines comparative need in a social-service context. As the name suggests, comparative need is determined by comparing one person to another, one group of persons to another, or one area to another. If one person, group of persons, or area is currently receiving some social service that a second person, group, or area *with characteristics similar to the first* is not, then the second person, group of persons, or area is in comparative need. For instance, if one area of a city with a high degree of pathology has a mental health clinic while a second area with a similar degree of pathology does not, then the second area is in comparative need of a clinic. The people in the second area may or may not feel the need for it.

By using plus and minus signs for each of the four needs, Bradshaw establishes a kind of need taxonomy for the delivery of social services. The order of needs he follows is: normative or prescribed, felt, expressed, and comparative. In any given case each may be present (+) or absent (−). Some of the possibilities follow:

+ + + + . This code would indicate that the need is prescribed, felt, demanded, and comparative. For example, the people in one area of a city are being considered for federal assistance for housing rehabilitation. Experts have determined that their housing is substandard; the people feel ill-housed and have demanded help; and people with similar housing in another area of the city are already receiving assistance.

+ − − − . In this case experts see a need, but those who are considered in need do not feel it and therefore do not demand it; assistance is not supplied to others in similar circumstances. For instance, experts believe that training in problem solving and decision making should be a part of the curriculum of schools from primary through higher education. Both students and parents are unaware of this need, however, so they do not demand it, and generally it is not supplied in other school systems. In a case such as this, helping parents and students become aware of the need would be an initial strategy.

+ + − + . In this case, although individuals are needy by all definitions of a need, they do not want or are not able to request or demand satisfaction.

> Demand is limited by difficulties of access to a service. . . . Difficulties of access may be due to a stigma attached to receipt of a service; geographical distances that make it difficult to claim . . . administrative procedures that deter claimants, or merely ignorance about the availability of a service [Bradshaw, 1972, p. 642].

For instance, a college student is in need of counseling, which is available at her school, but fails to request it because she feels that she will be stigmatized by her classmates for taking advantage of the service.

It is obvious that other combinations of needs are possible. Bradshaw's taxonomy provides a kind of shorthand for reviewing needs. Thayer (1973), however, cautions that relativism of need is still an issue in these categories.

> It should be recognized that these are only categories of need or criteria. The extent of measured need within each category will vary. Normative need will vary according to the particular criteria adopted. Felt need may vary according to the observer's sub-jective assessment of intensity of feeling while the various channels through which demand can be expressed will give different estimates of expressed need. Comparative need will vary according to the areas which are considered and the particular social, demographic, or environmental characteristics which are taken into account [p. 92].

Comparative housing needs in Cairo, Illinois, for instance, will differ radically from comparative housing needs in Cairo, Egypt.

The ability to distinguish between prescribed and felt needs is an essential part of the decision-making process with respect to program development. Consider an example: The directors of a graduate department in psychology want to set up a continuing education program for professionals engaged in clinical practice. Since they do not want to offer mindless programs that people mindlessly attend, they must determine the needs and wants of those working in the field. Ideally the data-gathering process will tell them, with a reasonable degree of probability, what kinds of courses and workshops would meet a balance between the felt needs of clinicians and the prescribed needs generated by the faculty.

The directors might suspect that clinical workers would flock to workshops designed to update their knowledge and skills in psychological testing (felt needs). They doubt that clinical workers will demonstrate the same kind of interest in workshops designed to give them skills in assessing the impact of systems such as families, peer groups, school, neighborhoods, churches, and voluntary associations on human growth and development, even though the directors think that these skills will make people in the field better clinicians (prescribed needs). In a word, the faculty mem-bers have hunches that have to be substantiated. They have to identify the felt needs of these practitioners and learn whether prescribed needs can be transformed into felt needs.

THE CRITIQUE OF NEEDS AND WANTS

Ideally, program planners and consultants distinguish between needs and wants, assess the intensity of needs, and establish priorities among conflicting needs. Scho-lastic philosophers long ago urged people "to do necessary things first, then those things that are useful, and finally, if time and resources remain, to do what is pleasing."

In view of the relativism of needs and the difficulty of separating needs from wants, some writers (James, 1956; Monette, 1977, 1979) suggest that what ordi-narily takes place under the rubric of need assessment—the discovery of felt needs, on the one hand, and the prescription of needs, on the other—is often inadequate because it is done *uncritically*. It is certainly important to discover what people say their needs are (felt needs), and it is also important to discover the needs that individuals and organizations, institutions, and communities prescribe for others. However, it is just as important to understand the *basis*—what Freire (1970) calls *causes*—of both felt and prescribed needs and to be able to evaluate these bases. In short, needs assessment is not and cannot be value-free because the process is not only technical but also ethical, cultural, and political. Monette (1979) advocates using Freire's (1970) approach in assessing educational needs. He says that although Freire

> begins with the felt needs of the learner, he does not simply cater to them. . . . Freire's contention is that oppression comes from within the individual as well as from without; and hence that felt needs must be . . . questioned as to their causes if people are to be freed from blind adherence to their own world views as well as to the world views of others which they have uncritically internalized. Freire attends to the contradictions in the perspectives informing felt needs and he guides the learners in exploration of world views which may possibly be more adequate to their situation. If, for example, someone comes to Freire demanding a course in cattle fattening, Freire first assists that person in examining the causes of the felt need for such instruction and he provides relevant help only when the contradictions inherent in the demand of the person have been examined and the felt need has been rediagnosed. In the above case, probing into causes might lead the participant to the conclusion that action is needed not on the level of cattle care according to his initial perception, but on the level of marketing practice [p. 89]

Note that Freire does not prescribe what is needed, but asks the clients to take a critical look at what they think they need.

What is said of felt needs also may be said of prescribed needs—neither is absolute. For instance, medical regulatory agencies have found evidence that some surgeons perform unnecessary operations. Therefore, patients are urged to get "second opinions," rather than submit to surgery upon the advice of one doctor. Some writers (Bledstein, 1976; Haskell, 1977) suggest that professionals tend to prescribe too many needs without revealing the bases of their prescriptions and encouraging public discussion and criticism.

Assessing needs critically involves discovering their causes, identifying the assumptions and values on which they are based, assessing the cost/benefit ratio in satisfying them, establishing priorities among competing needs, and making sure that needs are related to goals.

Needs assessment is one form of data gathering and therefore the seven steps of the data-gathering process apply.

Purpose. In organizations and institutions the purpose of needs assessment is to discover the relevant prescribed and felt needs and the wants of the members of the receiving system. Since needs and wants change, this process is necessarily ongoing. Some organizations and institutions go out of business because they fail to keep in touch with the needs and wants of the people they serve. Since the generic needs and wants of the members of the receiving system relate to the mission of the organization or institution, and since their specific needs and wants relate to its goals, staying in touch with their needs and wants is necessary for the reassessment and fine-tuning of both mission and goals. A failure to understand the dynamic interplay between needs and wants and mission and goals can lead to confused and misdirected action within the producing system and frustration and disaffection within the receiving system.

Relevant questions. In systems such as clothing and automobile manufacture that cater to the ever-changing felt needs and wants of the receiving system, marketing and advertising questions are central. In human-service systems that emphasize prescribed needs, such as schools and hospitals, questions related to research and its translation to need-serving programs are central. For instance, doctors ask themselves such questions as: Given the present state of research and the kinds of interventions that have been established to remedy this patient's disorder, which intervention is best? Moreover, the felt needs of patients cannot be overlooked. Given the possible side effects and cost of treatment, would the patient be willing to submit to it?

Meaningful sampling. Once relevant questions have been formulated, researchers need to select samples that are representative of target populations. Is a curriculum that "works" in a middle-class school in a Chicago suburb going to "work" in an inner-city school in Chicago? How similar are the prescribed needs and wants of the students in these two areas?

Useful data-gathering techniques. Which data-gathering techniques will enable us to get essential information and make reasonable decisions most effectively and efficiently? In the case of prescribed needs, what kind of research is most relevant to the needs and wants of the target population? What kind of "engineering" is needed to translate that research into the technology that will serve the needs and wants of the members of the target population?

Data analysis. How can we be sure that we are getting needs-related information from the data we have gathered? In the case of systems that manufacture products, there is a danger of skewing the data so that it fits the needs of the producing system instead of reflecting the needs and wants of the receiving system. "We have this great new program and we are sure it will succeed!" Enthusiastic statements like this one should be examined carefully. "Let's continue to teach the same curriculum in the same way; after all, it has withstood the test of time." Statements such as these are heard in the halls of self-serving rather than client-serving systems.

Data feedback. Data on needs and wants is useless until it reaches the right hands. The education enterprise, for example, is one of the most creatively self-critical systems in the United States. The literature on education is filled with insights into what is going wrong and how to right it. But somehow this information does not seem to reach those who can do something about it. At times it seems that critics talk mainly to critics and not to students, parents, school boards, superintendents, principals, and teachers.

Decisions based on valid data. The ideal approach to decision making would state, "Our ongoing needs assessment has indicated significant changes in the needs and wants of the members of the receiving system. In light of this information, what kinds of changes, if any, would we like to see in our mission, major aims, and goals?" Some systems would want to know precisely what the current fads are since their business depends on fads; other systems would want to avoid mere fads. Graduate departments in counseling psychology, for instance, would not want to introduce significant changes in their curriculum every time a new approach to counseling was formulated and a new book published.

5

Mission, Major Aims, and Strategic Plans

The word *mission* comes from the Latin verb *mittere* meaning "to send." Missionaries, then, are people sent out to preach the religious message and engage in religious behavior, however these may be defined in a specific religion. What they are to accomplish constitutes their mission. Although traditionally the word *mission* has been used in a religious context, more recently it has been used more generally to define the broad purposes and values of all sorts of organizations, institutions, and communities. The mission of a university deals with education and service to the community. The mission of an automobile manufacturer deals with private transportation. The mission of a community organization deals with the quality of life of the neighborhood. Mission indicates the "business" of the organization or institution.

STATING THE MISSION

Mission in its fullest sense includes the elements depicted in Figure 5-1, which shows that mission flows from the needs of the members of the receiving system. Many systems do not make explicit statements about these elements or even consider them explicitly. The following statements relate mission to the needs and wants of the receiving systems:

- "Our organization deals with hunger in underdeveloped countries."
- "We deal with the needs of elderly shut-ins."
- "We deal with the needs of people newly released from mental hospitals."
- "Our halfway house deals with the needs of people newly released from prison."

A more complete mission statement would include these dimensions:
Overall purpose: an indication of the major thrust of the system.

I. THE PERFORMANCE SYSTEM

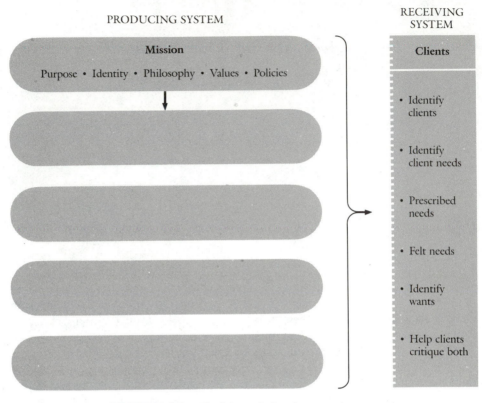

FIGURE 5-1.   Deriving mission from needs

Identity: an indication of the kind of organization, institution, or community the system sees itself to be.

Values: a statement of the philosophy and values for which the system stands.

Major policies: a statement of the policies that stem from the values the system espouses. Policies indicate the ways in which the system pursues its goals.

Like the entire organization, institution, or community, each subunit has a mission. A high school has an overall mission, and the subunits, such as the biology and athletic departments, have their missions, too. A city council has its overall mission, but each agency, such as the building inspection department, has its mission.

The missions of the subunits relate to the needs of other units within the system. The hospital laundry's mission, for example, relates to the surgery unit's need for clean linen. Sometimes a subunit is not quite sure whose needs or which wants it is meant to satisfy. When a large university established an organizational development department, its members were not sure whether they should plan programs or wait to be asked to act as internal consultants. A consultant helped them set up a university-wide needs-assessment program related to organizational development. They discovered that members of the university community needed to find out what organizational development is.

Overall purpose

A statement of the overall purpose of the system answers such questions as: "What business are we in? What products are we to produce? What services are we to provide? What is our principal thrust?" Answers to such questions assume that the system is aware of the generic needs and wants it is trying to satisfy. The statement of overall purpose should be broad enough to cover or include all significant outcomes and activities of the system.

Common sense dictates that the members of any organization, especially those with leadership positions, should know what the overall purpose of the system is and that there should be consensus among them. But common sense does not always prevail in all systems.

> A consultant was asked to facilitate a meeting of a government human-service agency. Those attending the meeting included the administrator of the agency and the regional directors, about fifteen people altogether. The consultant began the meeting by asking each person to write out what he or she thought was the mission of the agency. The administrator objected. He said that this task would be a waste of time since he and the directors certainly knew what the overall purpose of the unit was. The consultant suggested that nevertheless it might be a good way to start since they would begin with an experience of consensus. After each person had written out what he or she thought was the mission of the agency, the consultant read these statements aloud. There was practically no agreement among the directors of the agency with respect to its mission. There was no consensus about what "business" they were in.

Such ambiguity is common in service-oriented systems, including the service-oriented subunits of larger organizations. And if the leaders are not sure what business they are in, how can ordinary members be expected to know? So that everyone has a clear idea of the overall purpose of the system, it is useful to put the purpose in writing. The written statement can be shared by everyone and updated as the system itself and environmental conditions change.

The organizational development department of the university had to forge its overall purpose in meetings with the higher managers who had decided to create the new department. The initial statement follows:

> Our purpose is to help all the units of the university promote organizational effectiveness. A university or any of its subunits is effective (1) if it is productive—that is, if it achieves its goals and does so with a reasonable degree of efficiency—and (2) if at the same time it promotes

the quality of life of those who work and learn in it. Our aim is to help any unit of the university to become effective in this sense. We are a service department; we place our resources at the service of any unit that wishes to make use of them.

This statement of overall purpose indicates in a very general way the needs of the departments of the university, needs related to both productivity and quality of life.

An organization dedicated to helping the hungry indicated its overall purpose as follows:

This organization deals with hunger in third- and fourth-world countries. Our purpose is to provide information on the needs and wants of those nations to all U.S. organizations involved in providing food directly or indirectly to other countries. Our purpose is also to influence Congressional legislation that relates to hunger in those countries. We provide information and we lobby.

Identity

Just as individuals need and profit by a sense of personal identity, so organizations, institutions, and communities need and profit by a sense of corporate identity. The very name of the system and often its logo serve to proclaim this identity. The Counseling Services Department of a college, in changing its name to the Department of Student Development, made the following statement:

We are now called the Department of Student Development. Of course, we still provide counseling services, but we have changed our name because we do much more than that. Our services are not limited to people who are trying to manage social-emotional problems more effectively. We have a variety of programs to help students meet the challenges of the developmental tasks of life. These include career testing, life-planning workshops, training in communication skills, training in problem-management skills, personal-growth groups, and the like. We are helpers when you are in trouble, but we are also consultants to your growth and development.

This is a "who-we-are" statement, one that indicates what makes this particular system distinctive.

Identity deals with two factors, one inward and one outward. From the inside view, how does the staff see the system? Do the workers know its roots and history, take pride in its accomplishments, and evaluate its potency or capabilities realistically? If so, the identity statement will reflect their pride:

The Rehabilitation Institute has served this community for almost half a century. We provide quality service. We are on the cutting edge in research and the development of technology at the service of rehabilitation. Our staff members are proud to work here.

Many communities—and even families—lack identity. A person in a family therapy group said, "Living at home is like living in a hotel. People come and go as they will. There is little interaction and little feeling for the family as a unit. In many ways we are just a geographical unit. We all live in the same place." She was describing a family with little cohesiveness and little sense of identity.

Identity also describes how people on the outside see the system. Talking about her family, a woman said, "I think people see us as caring. People like to drop in on us. There are seven kids in the house, but when the local parish needs a place for a kid to stay during a crisis, they tend to come to us. They like the way we interact with one another." The members of this family see themselves appraised as a cohesive, caring unit.

On the other hand, the counseling staff of a large corporation experienced an identity crisis in terms of the way other workers saw them: "People come here only if it's the last resort. Even then, they come as secretively as possible and present all sorts of concerns about confidentiality. Coming here is an admission of failure." Staff members felt they needed to project a "healthy and upbeat" image to those who worked in the organization. They sought the services of a consultant to help improve their outward identity.

Holiday Inns, Inc. spells out its mission in terms of its identity and corporate philosophy.

We are
a forward-looking, innovative industry leader
with clearly defined goals,
producing superior products, services and
consistently high return for
our shareholders.
We will
maintain integrity in both our internal and
external relationships, fostering respect for
the individual and open two-way
communications.
We will
promote a climate of enthusiasm, teamwork
and challenge which attracts, motivates
and retains superior personnel and rewards
superior performance.

One of the messages of the book *In Search of Excellence* (Peters and Waterman, 1982) is that successful organizations have a strong sense of identity. Workers know who they are and where they are going. This is true not only of businesses, but also of human-service organizations.

In the case of a subunit of a larger organization, the mission statement should indicate the relationship between the unit and the rest of the organization and the distinctive contribution each unit is to make. Consider the mission statement of the building-inspection unit of a local community council.

Since the quality of housing stock is one of the most important factors in any community and the members of the community have the right to expect that code violations will be handled promptly, the Central Community Council will maintain a building inspection unit. The building inspection unit reports directly to the Council Director. It is responsible for checking on building code violations in all buildings, both residential and commercial, located in the area served by this community council. The inspection unit will check on code violations that are reported to the council by members of the community, and it will also systematically canvas the central neighborhood building by building in order to discover unreported violations. This work will be carried out by a volunteer team under the direction of a former city building inspector, now retired, but working part-time for the council. It is the responsibility of the director and the members of the council board to follow up on violations that are discovered.

This statement identifies the subunit, relates it to the larger unit, indicates its overall purpose, states the needs that require such a unit, points out its distinctive contribution, notes the groups to be served, and indicates the geographical area where it will work.

Philosophy and values

While many organizations do not state publicly or even discuss privately the principal assumptions and values from which they operate, a full statement of mission includes a clear statement of both central beliefs and cardinal values. The philosophy of a system includes its assumptions about people and about conducting the work of the system. These assumptions are ladened with values: "The people who work here are our most important resource," or "People have a right to grow and develop both at work and outside of work." In a full statement of mission, the system spells out its major beliefs and the values they are based on.

The Johnson & Johnson corporation has elaborated its "credo" in terms of its responsibilities. This credo of a profit-making business is largely applicable to non-profit human-service organizations:

We Believe

that our first responsibility is to our customers.
Our products must always be good, and
we must strive to make them better at lower costs.
Our orders must be promptly and accurately filled.
Our dealers must make a fair profit.

Our second responsibility is to those who work with us—
the men and women in our factories and offices.
They must have a sense of security in their jobs.
Wages must be fair and adequate,
management just, hours short, and
working conditions clean and orderly.
Workers should have an organized system for
suggestions and complaints.
Foreman and department heads must be qualified and fair minded.
There must be an opportunity for advancement—for those

qualified—and each person must be considered an
individual standing on his own dignity and merit.

Our third responsibility is to our management.
Our executives must be persons of talent, education, experience
and ability.
They must be persons of common sense and
full understanding.

Our fourth responsibility is to the communities in which we live.
We must be good citizens—support good works and charity,
and bear our fair share of taxes.
We must maintain in good order the property we are
privileged to use.
We must participate in promotion of civic improvement,
health, education and good government,
and acquaint the community with our activities.

Our fifth and last responsibility is to our stockholders.
Business must make a sound profit.
Reserves must be created, research must be carried on,
adventurous programs developed, and mistakes
made and paid for.
Bad times must be provided for, high taxes paid, new machines
purchased, new factories built, new products launched,
and new sales plans developed.
We must experiment with new ideas.
When these things have been done the stockholders
should receive a fair return.
We are determined, with the help of God's grace, to fulfill
these obligations to the best of our ability.

In a chapter entitled "Hands-On, Values-Driven," Peters and Waterman (1982) discuss how an explicit values orientation contributes to the success of organizations.

> Let us suppose that we were asked for one all-purpose bit of advice for management, one truth that we were able to distill from the excellent companies' research. We might be tempted to reply, "Figure out your value system. Decide what your company *stands for*. Put yourself out ten or twenty years in the future: what would you look back on with greatest pride?"
> We call the fifth attribute of the excellent companies, "hands-on, values-driven." We are struck by the explicit attention they pay to values, and by the way in which their leaders have created exciting environments through personal attention, persistence, and direct intervention—far down the line [p. 279].

As Argyris (1983) points out, espoused values are not always the values-in-use in any given system. A system should state these values explicitly, however, so that the members of the system and those it affects will have criteria for the accountability of the system. Then the system can be challenged from within and from without to live up to the values it espouses.

Major policies

Webster's dictionary defines policy as "a definite course or method of action selected to guide and determine present and future decisions." While goals deal with the outcomes of a system—that is, its achievements—policies deal with the ways the system functions. Policies stem from values, either explicit or implicit; they are norms that guide the system as it goes about its work. The managers of an institution might say: "We believe that we have the broadest vision and the best information and that we, therefore, are in the best position to make decisions." In such an organization it is obvious that participative management and participative decision making are not values. Therefore, in such a system the policy is to send information "up" to management and to wait for decisions to come back down.

The Scott Bader Company, a multimillion-dollar chemicals manufacturing firm in England, explicitly states its values and some of the policies that stem from these values in its "Code of Practice for Members," which is part of its 1972 constitution.

We recognize that we are first a working community and that it is our basic attitude to our work and to our fellow workers that gives life and meaning to the commonwealth.

We have agreed that as a community our work involves four tasks, economic, technical, social, and political, neglect of any one of which will in the long term diminish the commonwealth. We feel that the practical working of a balance between the four tasks is a continuing study for the membership as a whole.

We are conscious of a common responsibility to share our work among ourselves in such a way that it becomes a meaningful and creative part of our lives rather than merely as a means to an end.

We recognize that there are some members in a position of authority. Such members have a greater opportunity and hence a special responsibility to facilitate the building of jobs which are capable of fulfilling us as people; to act as "catalysts of common effort" and not as authoritarian "bosses."

We recognize that since management by consent rather than coercion is an appropriate style for the company, a corresponding effort to accept responsibility is required from us all. This will show in a desire to attend meetings and to participate in the affairs of our community; it will show in increased communication between persons and between groups and departments . . . above all, it will be seen as a genuine willingness to learn, to develop and grow.

We try to be open and frank in our relationships with our fellow workers, to face difficulties rather than avoid them and to solve problems by discussion and agreement rather than through reference to a third party.

We agree that in event of a downturn in trade we will share all remaining work rather than expect any of our fellow members to be deprived of employment, even if this requires a reduction in earnings by all.

We recognize that we have a responsibility to the society in which we live. . . .We agree that . . . our social responsibility extends to:

• Limiting the products of our labour to those beneficial to the community, in particular excluding any products for the specific purpose of manufacturing weapons of war.

- Reducing any harmful effect of our work on the natural environment by rigorously avoiding the negligent discharge of pollutants. Questioning constantly whether any of our activities are unnecessarily wasteful of the earth's natural resources.

Scott Bader is a profit-making company, but this statement can serve as an example for human-service systems. It mentions values and also spells out the *policy* implications of these values—that is, the ways the company will go about achieving its goals. A value: peace and sacredness of human lives. A policy: refusal to make the instruments of war. The point here is not whether one agrees or disagrees with either the values or the policies; it is rather that a complete statement of mission includes explicit references both to values and to the major policies that flow from these values. But few organizations are like Scott Bader in terms of explicit espousal of values and policies: "[R]ecognition of an organization's role in serving higher-order human values still awaits full-scale acceptance" [Pascale and Athos, 1981, p. 192].

IDENTIFYING MAJOR AIMS

The overall mission or purpose of a system is so broad that it needs further definition if it is to lead to the establishment of specific, achievable goals. When the purpose of the entire system and the purpose of each subunit have been translated into more specific aims, as indicated in Figure 5-2, these aims can be translated into concrete goals. Aims are links between mission and goals. Honda's mission, for example, deals with providing motorized transportation for individuals. This mission is made more specific when Honda says that it will produce motorcycles, standard automobiles, and small trucks. These aims are eventually embedded in concrete goals. In the case of Honda, this means such tangible products as Accords, Civics, different kinds of pick-up trucks, and different-sized motorcycles.

The following mission statement includes a brief description of the major aims of a neighborhood mental health clinic.

> The mission of the Southtown Mental Health Clinic is to provide a broad range of mental health services to people in the immediate area. These services include counseling and psychotherapy, both preventive and rehabilitative drug abuse programs, programs for battered women, programs for victims of rape, and programs for the unemployed.

The aims of the clinic are stated in terms of available programs that address general areas of community need.

Cherniss (1977) describes an effort to help a mental health center expand its mission to include not only direct remedial services but also prevention and consultation. Figure 5-3 shows the major aims of the expansion.

Each major aim category could be subdivided. Goodstein (1978) discusses four types of mental-health consultation: "(1) client-centered case consultation, (2) consultee-centered case consultation, (3) program-centered administrative [system] consultation, and (4) consultee-centered administrative [system] consultation" (p. 24). In order to expand its services, the center's personnel have to ask some serious

I. THE PERFORMANCE SYSTEM

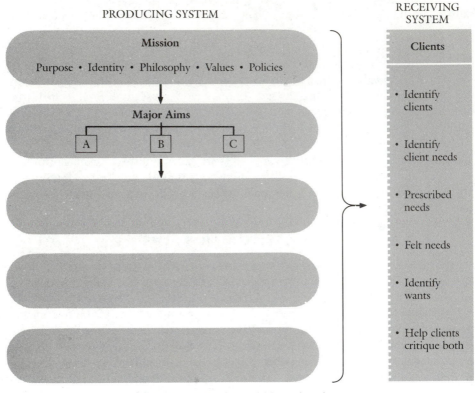

FIGURE 5-2.   Identifying major aims

questions: "Do we have the competence to provide new services? Do we have the resources to do this? Do we have the will to do this—that is, do we believe in it?"

Sometimes organizations serve the needs and wants of their clients more effectively by expanding their services, but not every organization is capable of managing unfamiliar activities. Peters and Waterman (1982) found that the best-run busi-

FIGURE 5-3.   Aims of a mental health center

nesses in the United States had in common the fact that they did not branch out into businesses they did not know how to run. Therefore, a mental health center should offer a variety of consultation services only if the expansion meets needs and wants and only after its counselors have learned how to offer consultation effectively.

The family is an example of a small community with a broad mission or purpose and limited resources. The overall mission of a family is to meet the human needs and wants of its members and to help its members achieve a decent quality of life. This purpose is translated into major aims that include physical sustenance, love and affection, education and training, and security. Admittedly, few families reflect this explicitly on their mission and major aims, but there is no reason why they should not.

A rape crisis center wanted to expand its function within the community. Previously it had engaged almost exclusively in direct services to actual rape victims. Now many of the workers wanted to combat rape as a social problem. While they believed that the direct-service work they were doing was invaluable, they wanted to expand into education and advocacy. Figure 5-4 indicates how they translated their new mission, helping both actual and *potential* victims of rape, into further aims. A statement of major aims answers such questions as: "What are the major thrusts of this system? Where are we going to put our energies? How are we going to allocate our scarce resources?" *Major aims are the major accomplishment-oriented priorities of the system.*

Aims are more specific than statements of mission, but still not specific enough to stimulate action. Consider the following aims established at the beginning of the academic year by the president of a large, religious, urban university with a medical school and hospital:

1. To improve the quality of the attention we give to each student, to each patient, and to each co-worker.
2. To grasp better what we know and what we believe, and how they are related; then to assist students and patients to integrate their knowledge and their faith.
3. To acknowledge the family as the basic unit of society, and to promote our students' desire and knowledge about becoming responsible spouses and parents.
4. To institutionalize values and ethics in every department and program.
5. To amend our communication with one another, enhancing the quality and reducing the costs.
6. To improve our methods of helping our most talented students develop themselves [Baumhart, 1981, p. 1].

While such statements are more concrete than the general mission of the university, they still lack the specificity of goals. These aims do not spell out concrete outcomes or accomplishments. For instance, we can ask such questions as: Precisely what does it mean "to improve the quality of attention" given to students, patients, and co-workers? What precisely does it mean "to institutionalize values and ethics" in the departments and programs of the university? These aims provide direction, but if they are to be pursued and accomplished, they must be translated into specific goals and objectives.

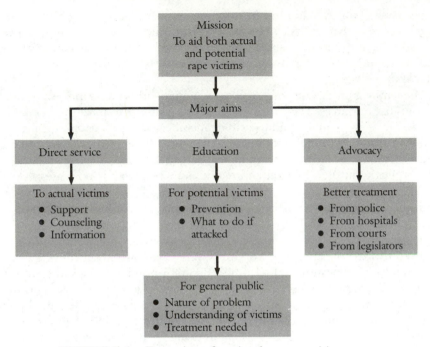

FIGURE 5-4.   Expansion of services by a rape crisis center

The ideal is that everyone associated with the system know and understand the mission and major aims that act as driving forces within the system. Part of the arationality of systems, however, is the fact that even when mission and major aims are clear to the managers, they usually are not communicated clearly to everyone within the system.

> In a study I conducted many years ago, we found that the majority of officers in an air force division were unfamiliar with the mission of their own unit as set down in the organization's manual. The majority of enlisted men could not identify their own jobs and had only an approximate idea of their own duties. . . .The commanding general of the division, an officer famous for his solid achievements and his flamboyant style, found these results incredible. "They couldn't not know their own squadron commanders," he objected, "any more than not know me." The next survey of the division's personnel asked them to identify their commanding general; a sizable percentage had never heard his name [Caplow, 1976].

Research shows that top administrators believe about 80% or 90% of the people in the organization know its mission, while at the line level, only about 15% actually do. In the best organizations, the mission is electric and energizes everyone from top to bottom.

STRATEGIC PLANNING

To be productive, an organization needs to engage in at least three different kinds of planning: (1) long-term or strategic planning, (2) yearly or operational planning, and (3) immediate, day-to-day, or tactical planning. The kind of planning that relates specifically to mission and major aims is called *strategic planning*. This long-range planning deals with the overall purpose and direction of the organization, institution, or community rather than with its yearly or day-to-day operations. Clifford (1981) describes strategic planning as

> the capacity of an organization to deal with the long-term, fundamental requirements of the institution and its constituent businesses and to maintain a balance of these strategic considerations with inevitably intense pressure for short-term performance [p. 1].

Nicholls (1981) defines strategic planning as

> the analytical and creative process whereby strategies are developed to cope with . . . competitive [environmental] forces or shape them to our advantage. It involves no more than thinking creatively about the business, the competition, and the forces of change at work in the environment to identify emerging opportunities and threats [p. 3].

Nicholls adds that strategic planning is useless without strategic management, "the ability to translate [plans] into realistic programs and objectives that can be implemented by all levels of the organization" (p. 5).

While these writers refer specifically to businesses, what they say, with some adaptation, applies not only to profit-making organizations but also to nonprofit institutions and communities. In the case of nonprofit systems, competition may not be critical but other environmental forces such as the economy and government are. While strategic planning is a powerful tool for all systems, it is generally unused or underused even by the business community. For instance, national, state, and local governments and their various agencies badly need strategic planning, but since profit is not an incentive and since politics rules the day, it ordinarily does not take place in any comprehensive way.

Strategic planning attempts to answer questions about the future: "What does the future hold? How do we best respond to an uncertain future? What long-term threats exist in the environment? What opportunities lie down the road? What resources are needed to cope with the future? Do we have these resources? If we don't have them, how can we get them?" Too many systems live from day to day, and then one day, much to their surprise, find out they are no longer viable.

> The superior of a large order of nuns asked a consultant to facilitate one of their annual meetings. There were more than 1500 nuns in a midwest province that covered two states. The consultant asked the superior for certain actuarial data—data that she seemed somewhat reluctant to give. He discovered that more than 50% of the nuns in that province were retired, that the average age of the nuns was 65, and that the province had only two novices. He asked the superior if these were the issues that she wanted to deal with at the meeting. She said no and went on to outline certain operational issues that were bothering her. The consultant sat back amazed since, actuarially, the province was no longer viable and no one

seemed to want to take a hard look at what could be done about the future of the order.

The crush of day-to-day concerns can mask both threats and opportunities.

Strategic planning is based on quantitative and qualitative information and not merely on assumptions and speculation. It is not an exercise in musing and dreaming, though musing and dreaming can play a part in it. Hard facts and informed assumptions and predictions lead to hard decisions about the allocation of the system's resources. The distinction between facts—what is known for sure or can be known for sure—informed assumptions, and dreams must be clear. Honesty about what is known and what is not known is essential. The facts needed for planning are not always easy to come by. People must dig, search, open their eyes, drop defenses and prejudices, open windows, and permit data to challenge cherished assumptions and hypotheses. As Argyris (1982) suggests, undiscussable issues must be ferreted out and their undiscussability challenged. There is a difference between solid information and overly precise and detailed information. Strategic planning does not require the same kind of precision as operational or tactical planning.

Once the facts are known, they can be shared with workers throughout the organization. In the Matsushita Corporation, potential managers start at the bottom and rotate through a wide variety of jobs. When they finally reach managerial positions, they know experientially what it feels like to be a line worker, a clerk, or a salesperson. Since few organizations follow this procedure, however, consciousness raising is the first step in the strategic planning process. In the discussion that follows, a private urban university will be used as a concrete example of an organization moving through the strategic-planning steps.

Current strategic position

Consciousness raising. Help the members of the system learn what the system is like. Many people who live or work in a system do not know enough about how it works, how it interacts with the environment, what the current trends are, what changes are expected in the future, its goals, and how the individual contributes to its mission. Most people in organizations, institutions, and communities need to know more about the strategic-planning concept, how the process affects them, and how they might participate in it.

Faculty members have a large stake in keeping the university viable, meaningful, and relevant. Through faculty senates and councils they can learn a great deal about how the system works. The problem is that faculty members, because of the freedom they enjoy, have a way of carving out little kingdoms, or at least duchies, within the institution and paying little attention to what is happening to the system as a whole. This tendency may be reinforced by administrators who are not adequately aware of and engaged in strategic planning or simply prefer to be left alone.

Participation. Decide who is to participate in the strategic planning process and how. Staff people are planners by trade and, since they are not involved directly in operations on a day-to-day basis, they have a wide perspective and a degree of objectivity that is understandably lacking in their line managers, whose primary concerns revolve around day-to-day operations. On the other hand, line managers have a realism about operations that is understandably lacking in staff people. Since it is line people who translate strategic plans into reality, however, they need to be involved in the strategic-planning process. Without the commitment of line managers, strategic plans are not going to work (Ellin, 1981).

The future of a university should be guided not only by a board of trustees and administrators such as presidents, vice-presidents, and deans, but also by the collective wisdom of its faculty, who are line managers involved in day-to-day operations. Strategies should be developed to tap into the resources of the faculty and to involve them in strategic decision making. Line managers are privy to quantitative and qualitative data that is essential to the decision-making process.

Line managers do not automatically think in strategic terms. They need to be instructed in the concepts of strategic planning and encouraged to think in both strategic and operational terms. When line managers do participate in strategic planning, they need to be encouraged to express creativity *within guidelines*. The chief executive officer of the system must make these guidelines clear. If the president of the university has decided that a variety of satellite minicampuses is not a feasible way of attracting students, then planning committees should know of this decision. If the president believes that the university can create "new educational businesses," then this belief should be clear.

Finally, participation must be real and not just token. Even when line managers act only as a consultative group, their consultation must be taken seriously. Put simply, if you want meaningful participation, you must be willing to share some real power.

Review of mission. Review the current mission and strategy of the system in terms of identity, overall purpose, and major aims. It may be that no one is fully aware of the current long-term strategy. If this is the case, strategy will have to be inferred from what the system is actually doing and from the actual trends and changes over the last five or ten years.

- Identity questions include: "Who are we? How do we differ from what we were ten years ago?"
- Overall purpose questions include: "How do we, *in practice*, currently define the business we are in? How does our current business differ, if it does differ, from the business we were in ten years ago?"
- Major aims questions include: "What, currently, are our major aims? How do these differ from those of ten years ago? What are our major accomplishments? Are these accomplishments the same as our stated aims?"

If espoused major aims and accomplishments differ from actual major aims and accomplishments, these differences should be noted as clearly as possible, in quantitative and qualitative terms. If quality teaching at the undergraduate level is an espoused major aim of a university, it must be determined in quantitative and qualitative ways whether this aim is being translated into significant accomplishments or whether it has suffered from competition with other aims, such as research.

Allocation of resources. Review the major ways in which the resources of the system are currently allocated. Are resources allocated in support of the stated major aims of the system or does the allocation of resources reflect "rearranged" priorities? For instance, a university that states that quality undergraduate instruction is one of its major aims might discover that excellent teachers are not rewarded by recognition, promotion, tenure, and salary increases in the same way as faculty members who do research and publish. Note again that quantitative and qualitative answers are required by questions such as "Where do we currently allocate our resources?"

It helps to diagram the principal findings of the mission and aims review (for instance, a diagram with arrows showing principal environmental influences). Visualizing the system through a kind of strategic "map" helps dramatize findings, provides a way of communicating complex problems to people, and makes long-term planning more concrete.

Internal strengths and weaknesses. Use Model A as a tool to assess internal strengths and weaknesses with respect to goals, programs, personnel, material resources, financial resources, and the like. Again, quantitative and qualitative data are important. Important questions here are: "Do we have the internal resources to fulfill our mission as currently defined? Are we making the best use of these resources? What resources do we lack? What resources are inadequate? What internal resources do we fail to use?"

If the university is to engage in strategic planning, its planners must assess its use of resources realistically. They cannot do this unless wider aims have been translated into verifiable goals. To some this may seem such a herculean task as to preclude meaningful strategic planning.

External strengths and weaknesses. Scan the environment to see how the system is currently interacting with it. An environmental "scan" should include all factors that are relevant to *your* system: the current state of the economy, political realities, direct competitors, demographics, new technology, government regulations, market demands, the kinds of people that make up the receiving system and their needs and wants, and the trends in the helping or human-service "industry" to which your system belongs. Important questions are: "Are we failing to take advantage of opportunities? Are we ignoring any threats?" Many systems overlook the global picture.

Desired strategic position

The organization or institution now considers its *desired strategic position*. When the environment is turbulent and uncertain, planners may apply the "Law of the Situation."

> The *Law of the Situation* is a term coined in 1904 by Mary Parker Follett, the first management consultant in the United States. She had a window-shade company as a client and persuaded its owners they were really in the light-control business. That realization expanded their opportunities enormously. The Law of the Situation asks the question "What business are you really in?" [Naisbitt, 1982, p. 85].

Naisbitt gives examples of how progress depends on reconceptualizing the mission and major aims of the system. The case of the railroads is one of the most dramatic. If during most of this century you had asked railroaders what business they were in, they would probably have said "railroading." Suppose they had said they were in the transportation business, "moving goods and people." Today we would have the Pennsylvania Airlines and the Chesapeake and Ohio Motor Company. But railroaders found it impossible to reconceptualize what business they were in. In turbulent environments human-service organizations and institutions, too, need to reconceptualize what business they are in or might be in. It is fascinating to speculate what creative answer might be given.

Environmental scanning. Scan the environment with a view to identifying critical variables that are going to affect the system in the future. In order to draw up strategic plans, it is necessary to ask: "What trends does current research in our 'industry' indicate? Where will our services be needed? How many new professionals and paraprofessionals will be coming into the field? Will there be places for all of them? What different kinds of work will open up for human-service professionals? What population shifts are taking place and how will they affect us? Is full employment a thing of the past? In what direction is the economy headed? What threats will be the most serious in the next five years?"

Sometimes the environment is relatively placid, sometimes it is turbulent. When the environment is turbulent, the need for strategic planning increases. Paradoxically, however, turbulent environments make strategic planning more difficult because change, and often sudden and unpredictable change, rather than stability is the order of the day.

The university faces an environment that includes fewer students, older students, diminishing government aid for both students and programs, students who have been poorly prepared in primary and secondary schools, increased competition, minority populations with inadequate financial resources and significant cultural variations, changing views about the need for college education, new technologies such as those related to microprocessors, people who are overeducated for the jobs that are available, greater demand for vocational education, too many tenured faculty, and too many faculty members in disciplines no longer in demand. Most administrators could extend this list without much effort. The turbulent environment increases the need for strategic planning but makes it more difficult, especially for universities in which strategic planning has not heretofore played a role.

Scenario writing. To visualize the future, planners can practice scenario writing. This technique is especially helpful when the environment is causing disorder within the system itself. In human services, scenario writing deals especially with uncontrollable variables that are likely to affect the functioning of the system: competition for clients, changing demographics, political shifts, economic swings, changing governmental regulations, insurance companies' demands for proof that a person has been helped, law suits against human-service systems for failure to fulfill expressed or implied contracts.

Although these variables are uncontrollable and therefore unpredictable, it is possible to determine a range of uncertainty for each relevant variable. A university cannot predict how many students will seek its services in the future, but its planners can envision several plausible scenarios. Planners can draw up a "downside" or pessimistic scenario in which changing attitudes, a stagnant economy, technological innovations, and the like lead to a serious and sustained drop in the number of people seeking admission to *this* university. They can also draw up an "upside" or optimistic scenario in which an improved economy, increased leisure, and technological innovations will lead more people, especially adults, to seek admission to the university. After an upside and a downside scenario have been elaborated, then the "most probable" scenario can be drawn up as the basis for decision making. Scenario writing can be a kind of common-sense armchair exercise or, with the use of computers, a sophisticated technique dealing with the possible interactions of many variables. Obviously the usefulness and not the sophistication of the scenario is the critical issue. (A more complete discussion of environmental effects can be found in Chapter 14.)

Values. Values provide the guides, norms, and standards for strategic plans. Planners need to compare espoused values with values-in-use and settle on a realistic set of values. Discrepancies between espoused values and values-in-use constitute one of the most common forms of arationality found in both systems and individuals. There is little use in opting for values that are no more than window dressing. If optimization of return on capital is an important value, then it should be so stated. Quality-of-life values should be stated explicitly. The place of risk in the system also should be spelled out. A recruiter in a large tertiary-care facility, in describing the job and the institution, wrote: "The Organizational Development Specialist will design and implement organizational and departmental interventions and develop and conduct major seminars and training programs for management personnel and medical staff. Our is a collegial, unstructured environment, where risk-taking, tolerance for ambiguity, and professional growth are qualities valued."

The time-honored values that universities incorporate into their mission statements are not necessarily their values-in-use. Strategic planning calls for clarifying these values and then linking them with the institution's major aims so that it is clear in what accomplishments these values will be embedded.

Formulation of plans

Formulation of strategic plans. Strategic plans reset the long-term course of the system, but the course should not be set in cement. It should include strategic alternatives. Draw up alternative strategies in light of all the information gathered; then choose what seems to be the best alternative, and use other alternatives as contingency plans.

> Create, analyze, and ultimately choose from several distinctly different yet attractive strategies for the company [or institution or community] in order to provide strategic direction to the major operating units for detailed evaluation and planning of development tactics [Nicholls, 1981, p. 24].

"Present strategic position" provides a base or reference point against which other strategies can be compared. Alternatives are based on what the system has the resources to do in light of uncontrollable environmental variables and in light of the level of risk and cost that is acceptable to the system. Balancing risk with opportunity is not an easy task, especially when the environment is turbulent.

The new strategy—that is, the "desired strategic position"—might involve changes in the mission of the system. In the light of the information gathered and the scenarios written, the mission of the system should be restated. Determine what is primary, what is secondary, and what is nonessential. Over time all systems acquire excess baggage. Practices become outmoded and drain valuable resources. Often it is hard to drop these practices because they have become part of the culture of the organization. Therefore, strategic planning may involve various forms of retrenchment. The university, for instance, might redefine its mission to include different kinds of adult education involving various forms of "outreach" into the surrounding communities or even beyond these communities. This redefinition may mean retrenching graduate programs that have outlived their usefulness. "Managing decline" is a skill that, for obvious reasons, is not often taught in schools or pursued in organizations, institutions, or communities (see Hirschhorn, 1983). Retrenchment is a way of helping the system become lean and flexible again in the pursuit of realistic aims.

The new strategy must be realistic—that is, within the physical and psychological resources of the system and in tune with expected environmental realities. If the plan is not realistic, it will end up on the shelf with other unused reports.

Strategic versus operational issues. Separate strategic or long-term issues from operational or short-term issues. The tactical issues are best left in the hands of line managers. However, both upper and middle managers should consider together the impact of strategic decisions on current operations, especially when these decisions involve new ways of doing business. For instance, if the university makes the decision to get into the business of adult education in a major way, policies of the admissions office may change radically. It may become the admissions/recruiting/marketing office. Once the admissions personnel realize they are to market adult education, they can redesign their own system and formulate the strategies needed to fulfill this new function.

Communication. Communicate the revised strategy to the members of the system through line managers. Make sure that the members of the system see the practical implications of the strategy and elicit their feedback. Then set about the task of linking strategy to operations. Newly formulated long-range strategy does not produce results unless it is linked specifically to operations. Without the commitment of line managers and personnel the strategy will fail. Linking means that the strategy must be translated into aims, goals, objectives, and programs. Resources must be allocated: at all levels and in all departments, with involvement and commitment of line managers, with a clear indication of where the resources—including financial resources—are going to come from, with incentives clearly stated, and with accountability. Budgeting and other forms of short-term resource allocation are critical. If adult education is to become one of the principal aims of the university, for instance, then funds for pilot projects in adult education—their development, marketing, and evaluation—must be made available. There should be a clear timetable for getting projects on line.

Monitoring. Monitor the implementation of the strategy. Watch especially the environmental variables over which control is low, such as changes in government policy and shifts in the economy. Measure results and reward performance, especially the achievement of interim objectives. Strategic planning is an iterative process. It is not done every five, ten, or twenty years and then evaluated at the end of this time span. There should be an annual strategy-management cycle, a 1985–1990 plan followed by a 1986–1991 plan. Mechanisms should be developed for updating and fine tuning the strategy. Early-course, mid-course, and late-course adjustments should be made as required. If there is little response to adult education programs sponsored by the university, for instance, contingency strategies should be considered.

Advantages and disadvantages of strategic planning

This kind of long-range planning has both advantages and disadvantages (see Ellin, 1981; Quinn, 1980, 1981). Among its *advantages*, strategic planning

- helps to give the system a stronger sense of identity
- helps managers see what they are doing in wider frameworks, especially frameworks drawn from the external environment
- helps managers feel more comfortable about the future, because the future in some way is being "tended to"
- helps managers make today's decisions in light of the future
- requires rigorous communication about mission, major aims, goals, and resource allocation
- creates a network of information
- forces the system to take stock of all resources, both internal and external
- stimulates and gives direction to long-term specialized studies that contribute, down the road, to strategic decisions
- provides a forum for constructive conflict and criticism in which the contributions of devil's advocates are welcomed
- provides a matrix of alternative directions in which the system may move. The degrees of freedom (or lack thereof) the system enjoys or can create become clear.

Because it is an iterative process, strategic planning takes a great deal of time. People who do not ordinarily talk to each other must do so now. The process may raise suspicions, give rise to individual and interdepartmental conflicts, create competition, and disrupt established relationships. People—especially those concerned with day-to-day operations—may see it as a waste of time. Workers need additional support after the planning process has been implemented.

Among its disadvantages, strategic planning

- requires more information than the system possesses
- causes hard work that is not rewarded immediately
- uncovers realities, such as declining resources, that are unpleasant to face
- produces data that are difficult to analyze
- provokes resistance by challenging the culture of the system

- causes frustration by generating good ideas when the resources are not adequate to translate them into action.

Arationality in strategic planning

The process described in the preceding pages is systematic, rational, and linear. Quinn (1980, 1981) tempers this view by pointing out the arational and nonlinear nature of the planning process in practice. He points to three disturbing trends in formal planning:

> Planning in large enterprises often becomes a rigid, costly, paper shuffling exercise divorced from actual decision processes. Instead of stimulating creative options, innovation, and entrepreneurship, such planning often merely expands the controllership function, extending formal performance measures ever farther into activity areas.
>
> Most important strategic decisions seem to be made outside the formal planning structure. This tendency is especially marked in highly entrepreneurial or smaller enterprises. But it is also prevalent in successful large organizations with well-accepted planning cultures.
>
> Much of the management literature seems bent on developing ever more sophisticated models and organization forms for a system that is not operating the way the model builders think it is—or should be—operating [1981, p. 1].

Quinn and others stress some important arational learnings about both formal and informal planning. Formal planning is only part of a system's overall development of strategy. A great deal of informal planning underlines any formal strategy. In addition, strategic planning in practice seldom looks as it does in the books. It is carried out by processes that are "typically fragmented, evolutionary, and largely intuitive" (Quinn, 1981, p. 2). Lindblom's remarks (1959) about the "science of muddling through" are relevant here. Further, strategy is not evolved globally and written down in one place; rather, it is an evolving process. The plan need not be a formal scheme at all; it can be a set of flexible guidelines within which specific strategic decisions or plans for different parts of the system—innovation, diversification, major reorganization, retrenchment, or relationships with critical environmental systems such as government—are allowed to emerge and mature incrementally. Quinn calls such strategic plans "living" or "evergreen" (p. 16), and suggests that managers use these guidelines continually to study the actions of their organizations and guide them proactively and "incrementally toward strategies embodying many of the structural principles of elegant formal strategies" (p. 2).

Rapid and unexpected changes in the environment call for *piecemeal* strategic decisions, changes that are not foreseen by formal planning processes but which call for strategic decision making. Since in all systems there are always areas of ambiguity, most managers remain open to information, from operations or the environment, that will influence the system's strategic thrust. Information that signals the need of a change in strategic posture does not often come from formal environmental scanning. Rather, managers "feel" that something is "not right" or that some opportunity is being missed. Pursuing these hunches is part of the informal and incremental nature of planning. Some parts of strategic plans need to be "floated" in the system for a while in order to gain acceptance. During the "float," valuable information can come from within the system to help fine-tune a decision. Allowing ideas to float is contrary to the demands of rigid planning timetables. It does take political realities, the system, and potential rigidities in the culture into consideration. Partial solutions to strategic problems can be tried before an entirely new posture is adopted—Quinn talks about "trial balloons" and "systematic waiting" (1981, p. 25). All this helps develop a consensus within an organization or institution before formal commitment to a new strategic posture takes place.

6

Clear and Realistic Goals

To function competently, every system needs clear, valuable, and measurable goals or outcomes. Concrete goals are especially important in systems that provide services rather than products—schools, mental health delivery systems, churches, governmental agencies, and the like—and in subsystems that provide services in product-oriented organizations. The training division of an automobile manufacturing concern, for instance, is more likely to have hazy goals than the production department. A manager's goals are usually hazier than a typist's goals.

People chosen for leadership functions in systems frequently are not competent in goal-setting skills. Perhaps organizations assume that most people pick up these skills automatically through the ordinary experiences of life. There is little evidence, however, that this happens. Most people pick up enough of the rudiments of goal setting to "get by," but people who have responsibility for the functioning of systems need more than survival skills if these systems are to be effective and efficient.

Various authors use different terminology to describe both goals and the goal-setting process. To avoid confusion and ambiguity, it is necessary to define as clearly as possible the goal-related terminology used in this book:

Mission relates to the identity and broad purposes of the organization, institution, or community. The mission identifies the "business" the system or subsystem is in.

Major aims are more concrete than mission, but still fall short of the specificity needed by goals. Figure 6-1 shows that major aims are links between the overall mission and the goals.

Goals are the specific outcomes or *accomplishments* toward which the energies of the system are directed. Goals deal with *results* and therefore cannot be stated with the generality associated with mission or aims. Goals are the specific accomplishments that satisfy the specific needs of the members of the receiving system.

A complex goal is one that can be divided into a variety of subgoals. For instance,

I. THE PERFORMANCE SYSTEM

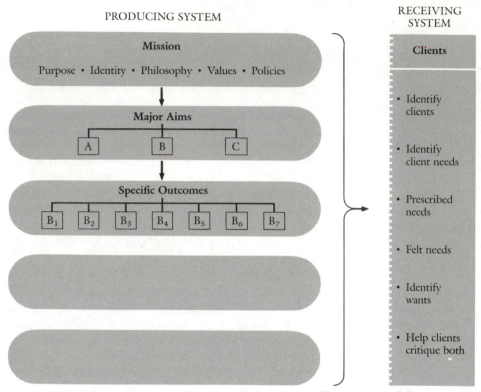

FIGURE 6-1.   Aims translated into goals—the specific outcomes of the system in terms of products or services.

automobiles or jet airplanes, productive counseling sessions, successful consultations, and good marriages are examples of complex goals.

Objectives are the major steps in a program designed to achieve a goal. Objectives, then, are *subgoals* and require the same specificity as goals. If the goal is complex, for instance, a successful intervention into a family by a social worker, the programs developed to achieve it are complicated. Complexity is handled by a hierarchy of intermediate goals: goals can be broken down into subgoals, and any given subgoal can be broken down into even further subgoals.

It is not only the *total* organization, institution, or community that has a mission, aims, goals, and objectives. Each *subunit*—the typing pool, each college course, each area of a mental health clinic, the teen club of a church—should have its own mission, mission statements, aims, goals, and objectives.

Goal setting is the process of *shaping*—becoming more and more concrete about the outcomes or accomplishments of a system or subunit. A goal exists when a mission or aim has been: translated into an *accomplishment* that is *clear and specific* enough to be measured or verified, delineated by measurable *criteria, realistic* or capable of being achieved, *adequate* to satisfy some need or want, consonant with the *values* of the system and its members, set in a reasonable *time frame*, clearly *communicated* to and understood by whoever is responsible for achieving the goal. In well-functioning systems, the system as a whole and each subunit of the system have goals with these characteristics.

To summarize, then, goal-setting skills deal with *shaping*; they enable individuals to move from mission, through major aims, to goals that have the characteristics outlined above.

GOALS AS ACCOMPLISHMENTS

People too often confuse programs with goals, behavior with accomplishments, work with outcomes. A goal is something that *will be* achieved in the future, and consequently goals give direction to behavior, work, and programs. An accomplishment is a goal that *has been achieved*. Gilbert (1978) suggests using "accomplishment language" to clarify aims and goals. He uses past participles to distinguish accomplishments from the programs and behaviors that lead to their achievement: appendix successfully *removed*; communication skills *learned and used*; marital problem *managed*; term paper *written and turned in*; letter *typed, signed, and mailed*; reading skills *improved*; a specific behavior pattern *practiced*.

A great deal of activity may occur and people may work hard without really achieving goals that relate to the overall mission of the system. A consultant might say, "I really think I helped my client" without appraising the outcome in terms of clear and specific accomplishments. If a management consultant is called in, then "problem *managed* more effectively" or "managerial skills *improved*" is the aim of the consultation. Once aims are stated in accomplishment language, it is easier to determine whether they have been accomplished.

Without clear and specific goals, systems are plagued with the "tyranny of programs." In lieu of clear and specific goals, people elaborate clear and specific programs and then *trust* that they are accomplishing something. When a director of a state welfare system heard the term "the tyranny of programs" at a workshop on change-agent skills, she exclaimed, "That's precisely what we do. We adopt every new and flashy program that comes down the pike, especially the federal pike, and then eventually discard it when it doesn't work. While we may have a fairly clear idea of our mission and some of our aims, we do not have a clear idea of what people need, and we certainly do not have clear and specific goals. But we do have lots of programs and lots of people engaged in them."

Goals need to be clearly distinguished from the programs through which they are achieved. Programs are the step-by-step processes that lead to the accomplishment of goals. If programs deal with behavior—specific behavior or action that leads to the accomplishment of a goal—then the goal is the accomplishment itself. If one of the major aims of a correctional facility is rehabilitation, then "recidivism *reduced*" is a goal. The rehabilitation programs lead to this outcome. People leave the correctional facility and do not return or they stay out longer. Since "recidivism *reduced*" is a complex goal, it is achieved through behavior arranged in interlocking programs with subgoals (subaccomplishments).

In product-oriented organizations it is relatively easy to identify both the subaccomplishments (the engines manufactured) and the overall accomplishments (automobiles rolling off the assembly line). When the accomplishments of organizations, institutions, or communities are services rather than products, however, there is a tendency to confuse programs (behavior, work) with accomplishments (goals). For instance, people come to mental health centers because they have problems they are not managing well. If the help they receive is useful, the outcome is some new pattern of behavior or a condition that did not exist upon the client's arrival. The accomplishment is: clients are now managing problems more effectively. Help, whether it is called counseling, psychotherapy, social service, ministry, or something else, is a program—that is, behavior that is justified only if it leads to a valued accomplishment. Being in therapy is not in itself a valued accomplishment, but managing one's life more effectively *is*. The former is a means; the latter is a goal. If therapy is successful, new, more constructive patterns of behavior are now in place (see Egan, 1982). Ideally, counseling or therapy is the collaborative process (the program, the set of behaviors) through which clients are helped to develop these new patterns of behavior. Currently the British police are being asked to transform themselves from an activities-based to an outcome-based organization. For instance, patrols are *activities* and merely listing the number of patrols engaged in tells us little. The real question is: to what valued outcomes (for example, fewer burglaries or traffic jams) do the patrols contribute? And how can patrols be arranged to contribute to such outcomes?

Even in most product-oriented organizations, some members provide services for other members rather than products. Managers, internal consultants, and trainers, among others, fall into this category. When assembly line workers are installing an engine their behaviors contribute in obvious ways to the ultimate goal of manufacturing an automobile, but the contributions of managers, staff, consultants, and trainers are not always that clear. It is not as easy to establish goals for service-oriented work, but it still can and must be done. If one task of the manager is to coordinate work so that time is not lost (one worker is not idle while another worker finishes a task), then this objective must be stated and open to verification. "Coordination" is a managerial aim that must be translated into identifiable accomplishments.

Church workers often say that "only God" knows the value of the work they are doing. While this statement may be true in some ultimate theological sense, it does not excuse church workers from establishing goals in terms of accomplishments. One minister told a consultant that his goal was to help his parishoners become "more spiritual." Since the word *spiritual* is abstract, the consultant asked the pastor to identify a subgroup of parishoners that he would like to help become more spiritual. The pastor suggested the teenagers. The consultant then asked a question that often helps turn an abstract term into a concrete one: "What does a spiritual teenager do that a nonspiritual teenager does not do?" Another way of putting this question is, "What do spiritual teenagers accomplish that nonspiritual teenagers do not?" If the answer is that only God knows, then perhaps it would be better to turn the task of the spiritualization of teenagers over to Him. In this case the pastor suggested that part of being spiritual in the church community was loving others with the kind of substantial love that includes helping people in need. This suggestion was further translated into providing services for elderly members of the congregation who needed help to accomplish the ordinary tasks of life. "Services provided for the elderly" became one possible aim in the cause of teenage spirituality. This aim was translated into such accomplishments as "floors swept, windows washed, errands run, papers read to those with failing eyesight, transportation provided," and so forth.

Accomplishments that are internal rather than external are accomplishments nonetheless. For instance, part of teenage spirituality revolved around prayer. "Prayer engaged in" or a "pattern of praying *in place* in the life of the teenager" is an accomplishment even though it cannot be seen by others. In counseling, goals often revolve around such "inner" accomplishments. For instance, some people get into psychological trouble because they fail to control self-destructive thoughts. "Self-defeating thoughts *reduced*" or "thoughts in which the client puts himself down *controlled or eliminated*" are accomplishments to which the helping process addresses itself. They are inner accomplishments that relate to managing the client's problem situations and therefore to improving the quality of the client's life.

CLARITY AND SPECIFICITY OF GOALS

Mission statements and aims can be translated into accomplishment language—"spirituality of the community *developed*," "motivation *improved*," "working conditions *improved*," "communication *improved*"—and still lack the clarity and especially the specificity of goals. Abstract terms such as *spirituality, motivation,* and *communication* must be defined behaviorally if mission statements and aims are to be translated into concrete goals. "Incentives improved" is better than "motivation improved," but still it is necessary to make clear what is meant by *incentives* and what is meant by *improved.* In the example of "teenage spirituality," it was necessary to determine what patterns of both internal and external behavior constituted spirituality before it was possible to translate such an abstract term into clear and specific language.

A corporate vice-president wanted me to facilitate a day-long meeting between the company's training and organizational development teams. I asked him what he wanted to exist at the end of the day that would not exist at the beginning—that is, what accomplishments he expected. He said that was a good question. I said I would not come until we had worked out a satisfactory answer. The director of training was leaving and the vice-president had to decide whether to merge these two divisions or keep them separate. If they were to remain separate, the functions of each and the interrelationships between the two had to be spelled out more clearly and a new director of training chosen. The people in the training division thought their work was being questioned because their director, a person who commanded their loyalty, was being let go. It was clear to me that all of these issues could not be handled in a day. Therefore, if my intervention was to lead to some meaningful accomplishment, I had to know precisely what that accomplishment would be. The vice-president suggested a meeting in which the members of both divisions could express their feelings about their work, about the relationships between the two divisions, and about a possible merger.

The vice-president was talking about a program. And since "facilitating" refers to various forms of behavior that become meaningful only through accomplishment, I needed clarity about the goal before I could undertake the program. A consultant could go to the meeting, try to be helpful, and see what would happen—many consultants seem to do this—but as a one-person consulting system, I wanted to identify the needs and expectations of the receiving system. Once it was clear that "thoughts and feelings about the relationships of the divisions, the quality of work, and a possible merger *explored and clarified*" was one of the goals for the day, I realized that I could help to achieve this goal. These workers certainly had the skills to explore thoughts, attitudes, and feelings and, as far as I could determine, the incentives to do so.

Goals in a skills-training program

Most people in helping and human-service professions have had some training in communications skills. Suppose a human-service agency would like to establish a training *system* (not a program) in communication skills. The needs have been assessed and the general *mission* of the training—communication skills *improved*—has been established. The needs assessment has indicated that therapists need the following "packages" of communication skills:

Exploratory skills to help clients "tell their stories"—that is, to recount and explore problem situations.
Challenging skills to help clients to develop new perspectives on their problem situations. Clients can then break old frames and reframe their perspectives so that problems are more amenable to solutions.
Feedback skills to give clients both confirmatory and corrective responses as they implement strategies to manage problem situations.
Conflict-management skills to help clients understand and manage conflicts with the significant others of their lives. Negotiation skills are a part of this "package."

These skills (and certain others) are the *major aims* of the communication skills training system. Major aims, however, are not the specific outcomes of the training process. Some of the specific skills that make up the exploratory package are:

Active listening: the ability to listen to and understand clients' verbal and non-verbal messages and to understand the clients' point of view.
Empathic responding: the ability to communicate to clients that the therapist has understood both the experience and behavior discussed and the feelings expressed.
Probes: the ability to use statements and direct or indirect questions to stimulate and provide direction for clients as they explore their problem situations.

Once the specific skills have been clearly defined and described in behavioral terms, they become the concrete *goals* of the training process. They are the desired outcomes, the valued accomplishments, the expected results of training. The valued outcome of learning accurate empathic responding can be stated like this: the skill of accurate empathic responding *learned, practiced, and transferred* to interactions with clients. Each skill in each major-aim package should be described carefully in behavioral terms. The whole process, from establishing a mission to setting specific goals, is summarized in Figure 6-2.

VERIFIABLE AND MEASURABLE GOALS

In product-oriented systems, it is clear that the product has been produced: the car rolls off the assembly line. But in systems that deliver services rather than products, verifying the achievement of goals is more difficult. Change agents need measurable goals based on established requirements or criteria. Kellog and Burstiner (1979) suggest the following checklist for measuring goals:

- What will be measured?
- How will you measure it?
- How frequently will you measure it?
- Will it give you objective, preferably numerical, data about quality, quantity, and time?
- What number or range is considered about right?
- What number or range indicates that attention is needed?
- Does the information obtained pinpoint what aspects of work need attention (p. 185)?

Goals must have some usefulness or value and they must be cost effective. An

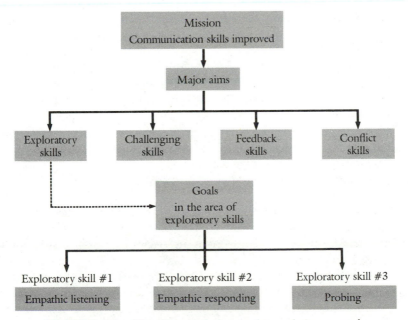

FIGURE 6-2. Translating mission to aims and aims to goals

accomplishment, in Gilbert's view, is "worthy" if it is valued by someone and if its value outweighs the cost of achieving it. If a company spends $50,000 to produce an automobile, and no one will offer more than $40,000 for it, then its cost outweighs its value and the goal is simply not worthy. If, on the other hand, parents pay $100,000 for a series of operations that save their daughter's life, they see this accomplishment as worthy because, in their eyes, the life of their daughter is beyond price.

Therefore, discovering whether a goal is worthy involves determining the *value* or *usefulness* of the accomplishment, determining its *cost*, and determining whether the *ratio* is favorable—that is, determining the *cost effectiveness* of the accomplishment. If the accomplishment has little or no value or the cost is out of proportion, the goal is not worthy. Effective systems pursue goals that are both useful and cost effective.

Systems need goals that are prized because the accomplishment of these goals will satisfy needs, wants, or both. It is not enough for training departments to produce events that help members of the system improve their skills. These skills must be useful—that is, they must enable people to do their work more effectively and efficiently. It is not enough for a church to present just any liturgy as an act of communal worship. The liturgy should be one that captures the minds and hearts of the congregation so that they feel renewed in their desire to commit themselves to the mission of the church in their private lives and in the community.

The criteria that specify the value of a goal are based on quantity and quality.

Quantity and quality of outcomes

Quantity includes such measures as volume, rate, and timeliness. If a new program will reduce recidivism in the state reformatory by only 2%, the goal might not justify the expense of the program.

If the president of a university is trying to influence a board of trustees that numbers 23 people, then "a few board members persuaded" is meaningless, but "12 board members persuaded" is significant. If therapy helps a patient reduce her free-floating anxiety so that she is able to resume her daily tasks, the goal is valuable enough to warrant the time and effort of patient and therapist alike.

Timeliness also can be essential. If a client is seriously considering suicide, stress should be reduced immediately. Training people in life skills, so that they can manage interactions with themselves and others before they run into serious trouble, makes more sense than waiting to help them after they are already in trouble (see Egan and Cowan, 1979).

Rate of production is a third measure of quantity. When human-service professionals are expected to see too many clients per day, the number of interventions should be considered versus the quality of interventions. Creative ways are needed to increase the number of interventions without damaging, and perhaps even improving, the quality of service. Group approaches, instead of individual counseling, may improve rather than damage the quality of the outcome for each participant.

Criteria that relate to quality include accuracy, novelty, "class," and various combinations of these. The quality of a watch that is accurate to within ten seconds per month is higher than that of a watch that is accurate within ten minutes per month.

People in the helping and human-service professions can see that the quality of their clients' lives suffers in innumerable ways. A prison inmate suffers when the prison focuses on security and punishment and neglects rehabilitation. When two people are living hopelessly in a marriage that has died, a marriage therapist is concerned with improving the quality of their lives, not just preserving the marriage.

> A family therapist realized that if she helped the Millers "rescue" their marriage merely by encouraging them to stay together, the quality of their lives would not improve. The Millers needed to reduce the number and the viciousness of their conflicts. Conversations in which neither spouse tried to trick, manipulate, punish, demean, test, give orders to, or merely endure the other became one of the goals of therapy. She helped them to experience the rewards of "quality" interaction, conversations in which they respected and supported each other. The therapist helped the couple to see that patterns of "quality" behavior had to replace their habitual conflicts.

A mental health clinic helps clients manage problem situations more effectively. The process includes helping clients clarify their problems, develop new perspectives on them, establish problem-managing goals, develop programs, and implement and evaluate these programs. "Problem situation managed more effectively" is the valued outcome of this process. The quality of this outcome suffers if other people act *for* the client. Higher degrees of self-responsibility in problem management increase the quality of the outcome. The quality increases further when clients have learned the *skills of problem management*.

At one time, many large cities constructed high-rise apartment buildings for low-income housing. In many cases these projects proved to be disasters. Quantitative goals, "housing units constructed," were achieved, but little attention was paid to quality-of-life issues. No one asked, "Are people ready to make the transition to high-rise living?" Recently, two different cities dynamited many of these buildings, which had proved to be woefully inadequate to the needs and wants of the poor.

Service organizations and communities have to struggle with the quantity and quality criteria that are meaningful for the outcomes they are in business to achieve. Quality control is just as important in these systems as it is in product-oriented organizations.

Cost effectiveness

An organization is effective if it actually accomplishes its goals; it is efficient only if the benefits/cost ratio is favorable. The benefit must outweigh the costs.

Service-oriented systems sometimes fail to determine what it costs to achieve their goals. For instance, a large Catholic diocese in the United States maintains two high-school seminaries, one college seminary, and one graduate seminary. The principal goal of this elaborate system is "priests ordained." Since quite a few young men drop out of the seminary system along the way, however, the actual cost of ordaining a man to the priesthood is extremely high. Church members are reminded, especially at seminary collection times, that maintaining a seminary system is costly. If they were told the actual cost of moving a person through the educational funnel to the priesthood, even the most loyal members of the diocese might cry out that there must be a less costly way of educating and training priests. Church administrators say that the seminary system provides other benefits besides just "men ordained." But usually these benefits are not outlined in accomplishment terms and neither their cost nor their cost effectiveness is measured.

Similar situations arise in all the helping and human-services professions. Are the outcomes worth the money that is spent? Often enough the actual monetary cost is not even known.

Cost can refer also to the psychological wear and tear that people experience in the pursuit of goals: exhaustion, worry, conflict, and other forms of stress. The psychological cost of the accomplishment of human-service goals is often excessive. If surgery and drugs help cancer patients to prolong life and suffering, the quality of life so prolonged should be considered.

Costs can be measured also in terms of physical or psychological damage to individuals and damage to the environment. While worry and stress are considered ordinary psychological expense, a "nervous breakdown" would be considered a form of psychological damage. An abortion is not a *valued* accomplishment for the client if the religious and psychological traumas associated with it are too costly.

Every accomplishment should be valuable enough to warrant the costs that go into achieving it. If monetary costs are too high, a product-oriented company loses money and eventually goes out of business. A business failure can be due to a depressed economy, overwhelming competition, changing needs and wants on the part of consumers, or poor management. Poor coordination keeps some workers idle and increases the labor costs; quality control is poor and products are returned; poor supervision leads to excessive turnover and higher training costs; workers are trained in skills that do not contribute to productivity; accounts receivable are not managed well, cash flow is affected, and the organization must borrow money at high interest rates. An extended recession catches the company with high inventories and labor contracts that call for periodic cost-of-living increases.

Churches, governmental agencies, educational institutions, and other human-service organizations and institutions, to a greater or lesser extent, have some built-in protection. Since their services are seen as essential, they continue to be funded whether they are efficient or not. If the question of efficiency arises, emotional arguments are used to persuade people that cost should be a secondary issue. And since the goals of these systems are seldom articulated clearly, it is almost impossible to determine whether these agencies are efficient. These systems sponsor many programs, but in the absence of clear goals it cannot be determined whether a program is efficient. Even when a goal is clear, its sponsors may consider it valuable without identifying specific ways in which the goal contributes to the quality of life of the people they serve. For instance, "highways built" may be seen as a value beyond dispute. With powerful lobbies operating in federal corridors, state capitols, and city halls, questions related to the environment, higher taxes, future maintenance, and specific needs are often brushed aside.

Ideology is often a factor in determining the ratio. If the benefit is defined as absolute, for personal or ideological reasons, then the cost is dismissed as immaterial. For example, the cost of finding a kidnapped child is immaterial to the child's parents. The mission, aims, and goals of military preparedness can be stated in such absolute terms that the cost of national defense is not open to question. If people argue that channeling so much money into an arms buildup decreases the quality of life for many citizens, their common sense or even their patriotism is challenged: "What would 'quality of life' mean after an enemy nuclear attack?"

Even when the goal is not considered absolute, there is resistance to the idea of measuring goals. In service-related systems or subsystems, some people see measurement as "inhuman." Or they say that many human accomplishments cannot be measured. Negative reaction to measurement comes from a number of sources:

A *fear of overcontrol*. If measurement becomes in practice a goal in itself rather than an instrument of quality control, it will meet with resistance. Ideally, goal measurement should be in the hands of the person responsible for accomplishing the goal, whether manager or staff worker.

A *fear of accountability*. Measuring goals introduces accountability into systems that are accustomed to running without it. When this is the case, the issue of accountability should be examined openly. Creative ways of dealing with accountability in helping and human-service organizations and institutions are desperately needed.

A *fear of the mechanization of human life*. Some people plead, "Let life happen; don't burden it with unnecessary technology." However, just "letting life happen" probably contributes as much to human misery as overcontrolling and overtechnologizing life. If goal measurement can contribute to the quality of human life in organizations, institutions, and communities, it should be done. Let it be done in as humane a way as possible.

REALISTIC GOALS

One of the most difficult aspects of goal setting is determining whether a goal is too high or too low. It is possible for both individuals and systems to set goals that are beyond their reach or inadequate to meet their needs. In designing a system, therefore, attention must be paid to the system's resources, obstacles that must be overcome, and limitations or allocations of time.

Resources.   Resources must be either available or developed through a subprogram. If a group of people band together to buy an apartment building to turn it into relatively low-cost condominiums for themselves, they need not only money, but also a working knowledge of the real estate market, condominium conversion procedures, mortgages, building rehabilitation, and condominium management— not to mention the ability to work and live together. The buyers involved have to consider whether enough resources are available to pursue the goal "building purchased and turned into condominium units." If the resources are not available for such a serious step, they might consider preliminary goals such as educating themselves about both real estate and condominium conversion.

Before workers within the system are asked to accomplish goals, their leaders must ask, "Do these individuals have the resources they need?"

Mrs. Clark was admitted to a hospital for minor surgery. After the rituals at the admissions desk were over, the woman at the desk said: "Mr. M., a volunteer here at the hospital, will now show you to your room." Mrs. Clark turned around and there was Mr. M. Without a word he turned and walked toward the elevator. In the elevator he stared straight ahead and said nothing. He led Mrs. Clark to her room, gave her a couple of pamphlets on hospital routine, and said that the resident would be in later.

"Patient's initial anxiety reduced" could be one of the goals of the hospital volunteers. Erik Erikson (1964) suggested that a person's first hour in an institution such as a hospital can set the tone for the person's entire stay. Volunteers can allay the patient's initial anxiety by adding a note of warmth at the beginning. Mr. M., however generous, did little to allay Mrs. Clark's anxiety.

Control.   People cannot be held responsible for goals over which they have no control. In human services, the point of delivery is ordinarily in interactions with clients. Those who work in human services try to persuade clients to act on their own behalf and help them develop the resources needed to do so. Goals cannot be reached without the collaboration of the client. A counselor can mount a training program that increases the probability that clients will acquire certain skills, but he or she cannot acquire skills for them.

Consultants cannot be held responsible for changes within the system with which they are consulting, because they do not have control over the change process. Consultants, however, can help managers become more effective agents of change in a variety of ways. They can help managers use Model A to assess the system or any given subunit. They can help managers assess needs, clarify goals, redesign jobs, create training programs, change the structure of the system, clarify roles and relationships, design feedback systems, and manage conflicts. But it is the managers in conjunction with the members of the system who actually do these things. If the system is riddled by conflict, the consultant's aim is not "conflict managed," but "manager helped to manage conflict between department A and department B."

Obstacles.   For goals to be realistic, no major environmental obstacles beyond the control of the system establishing the goal must exist. If the city council has passed a moratorium on condominium conversion, it constitutes a major environmental obstacle to developers. People working in human services need to develop a working sociology, a working anthropology, a working political science, and a working economics of the social systems that have an impact on their organization or institution (see Egan and Cowan, 1979).

The environment for any given unit in a multiunit system includes all other units in the system. When the director of admissions wanted to institute a new hospital-wide computerized information system, she ran into trouble with some of the other departments. For instance, nursing and admissions had always played a game, the latter always looking for empty beds, the former delaying information about the availability of beds in order to catch up on necessary work. The new computer system would make the number of empty beds immediately available. Nursing wanted to delay the system until they had found new ways to allow breathing room at peak work periods.

ADEQUATE GOALS

Goals are adequate if they are substantially related to the mission of the system and if they actually meet the needs of the members of the receiving system or community.

The mission deals with the overall purpose of the system, the business it is in, the reason for its existence. Goals are adequate if, in some reasonably substantial way, they further the mission of the system. For instance, if the purpose of the system is to provide cheap, reliable personal transportation for people in third-world countries, then a rugged, low-cost bicycle, motorbike, or automobile may well be a substantial translation of this mission.

Some service-oriented systems, such as churches, government agencies, educational institutions, and the helping professions have beautiful mission statements that are not translated into adequate goals. College catalogues are filled with courses that have fine mission statements but no specific goals. Sometimes the missions and major aims of these courses are translated into concrete and specific learning goals through the syllabi of individual instructors or through objectives outlined at the beginning of each course. But often course mission statements promise more than is delivered and no concrete goals or objectives are provided.

In the customer-service departments of some stores, customers suspect that "complaints discouraged" is the aim, rather than "complaints handled to the customer's satisfaction." In many church communities, members have not spent the time and effort needed to translate mission into adequate goals and subgoals.

Goals are adequate only if they respond to the specific needs of the members of the receiving system or the community. If the needs-assessment task has been ignored or has been perfunctory, it is impossible to determine whether goals fulfill this requirement. A heart patient may need not only a bypass operation, but also help in changing the lifestyle that contributed to the heart problem in the first place.

GOALS CONSONANT WITH VALUES

After her promotion to a managerial position, Mrs. Thomas was assigned the task of arranging for disposal of the company's toxic waste. She was told to get rid of the waste "in whatever way she could," and little money had been allocated for the task. Mrs. Thomas felt she was being tested. Those who promoted her wanted to see how "flexible" she was and how loyal to the company's interest. She finally left the company because she felt she was under pressure to adopt methods that were contrary to her personal values. Getting rid of toxic waste is obviously necessary, and Mrs. Thomas felt that it could be done in a way that would not damage the environment. Her superiors, however, had other criteria in mind: "Do it at a very low cost, as quietly as possible, with no legal recriminations."

Human service systems have to be sensitive to the values of their clients, especially when these values conflict with institutional values. If clients do not want to solve or manage their problems through divorce, sterilization, welfare, or chemotherapy, they should not be pressured to do so.

TIME

Both individuals and systems need adequate time in which to accomplish their work. A change program in a state correctional facility failed when too much was expected too soon. Since deadlines were not met, the leaders assumed that people were not really interested. The truth is that the deadlines were not realistic.

At the other extreme, workers are unlikely to reach their goals if no deadlines are set:

> A consultant was involved in an extensive organizational development effort with a large social-service organization. One of the problems discovered during the assessment stage was that the director of family services and the director of community consultation services seldom talked together even though both of them were dissatisfied with the relationship between the two departments. Both told the consultant that the relationship needed to be restructured, and one of the decisions they made at an action-planning meeting was to meet and start this process. When the consultant returned six months later, he discovered that the meeting had never taken place. Although they had agreed to meet, they never set a time for the meeting. The consultant asked them when they were going to meet. When they answered, "Next week," he asked them "When next week?" When they finally agreed on a specific day and time, the consultant asked them where they were going to meet. The consultant increased the probability that the meeting would actually take place by making the specifics of the meeting more and more concrete.

Realistic deadlines help people place realistic demands on themselves.

In sum, one of the most critical questions managers and supervisors can ask themselves is, "Do staff members know precisely what is expected of them in terms of accomplishments, and do they understand the criteria by which accomplishments are to be measured?"

> In a state mental hospital, psychology interns were assigned to routine testing of patients. Beyond that they were allowed to interact with patients on both open and closed wards, but were never told what was expected from these interactions. Nor were any specific outcomes indicated with respect to their own education and training. As a result, a number of the interns did a great deal of reading during working hours. Since they did not know what was expected of them, they did what people fresh from years of academic training do best—they tried to learn from books. Not only did their development suffer, but they were a grossly underutilized resource in the hopsital.

Lack of clear goals constitutes one of the principal forms of the "psychopathology of the average" of organizations and institutions.

THE ARATIONAL DIMENSIONS OF GOALS
AND GOAL SETTING

We have discussed a number of the arational dimensions of goals and goal setting in human-service systems. For instance, goals are passed over in favor of programs, so there is a leap between major aims and programs, and programs are mistaken for goals. Or goals lack one or more of the characteristics discussed in this chapter—for instance, they are stated in programmatic language rather than in terms of accomplishments or without any indication of time frame.

Another form of arationality emerges when care is not taken to match complex problem situations with complex goals. People look for the "quick fix" and fail to engage in goal shaping. Planners seek simplistic responses or solutions for such complex problems as deteriorating marriages, poor-quality education, deteriorating neighborhoods, or poverty, instead of painstakingly matching these problem situations with a well-shaped hierarchy of interrelated goals and subgoals.

The use of imagination. On the other hand, there are positive forms of arationality. Let us say that concerned people want to improve living conditions in a deteriorating housing project. Some goals are quite obvious—security increased, elevators repaired, grounds cleaned, complaints solicited and managed, transience reduced, and the like. But sometimes the severest problems also offer the most room for inventive solutions. For instance, tenants who contribute in specific ways to the quality of life of the housing project are given points and can earn the right to move into the better apartments as they become vacant. Or instead of merely setting up a tenants' association or encouraging tenants to become more involved, the apartments are given to those who live in them. They are allowed to fix them up, and sell them when they need to move.

There is a great deal of room for the use of imagination in devising goals in human-service systems. With client needs so great and resources so few, imagination becomes the critical arational resource. It is reasonable to fund and staff productive social-service projects; it is wasteful to throw money and people at a social problem without making some attempt to assess the creativity of the solution.

The emergence of goals. People sometimes ask, "Is it always necessary to establish goals directly and specifically? Is it not possible to let mission, major aims, and goals emerge as the system or subsystem moves along?" These questions are asked by people who feel restricted by the explicit processes of mission development and goal setting. After all, it is impossible to throw things together on an assembly line and see what might "emerge," but it *is* possible to devise a helping or human-service program and "see what happens."

If these questions mean, "Is it possible to run the system [for instance, a school, a welfare agency, a mental health clinic, a managerial training department, a church group, a social club, a psychotherapy group] with some general ideas of mission and goals and gradually formulate both mission and goals more explicitly in the light of our experience?"—then the answer seems to be "yes." Mission development and goal setting are not processes that are accomplished and then set in stone. Mission development and goal setting are both inductive and deductive processes.

The system is open to environmental influences, and aware that imagination, intu-ition, risk taking, and discovery are important processes in helping and human-service organizations. In any given system, mission and goal definition are some-times implicit rather than explicit processes.

However, if these questions imply that clear-cut mission, mission statements, major aims, and goals are not required in service-oriented systems, then the answer is that "emergence" in this second sense is dysfunctional. If imagination, risk taking, intuition, and discovery lead to the emergence of goals, then they should be iden-tified as goals and become part of the overt performance system. I do not agree with those who claim that human-service work is all art and intuition. Programs without missions and goals lead to the "tyranny of programs" because behavior becomes more important than accomplishment.

7

Goal-related Programs

Programs are the means for accomplishing goals—that is, the strategy or plan of action to be followed in order to achieve a specified goal. Programs constitute the *work* of the system. Each person in the system—administrator, director, staff member, accountant, maintenance engineer, and so forth—in his or her roles pursues programs in order to accomplish his or her share of the goals and subgoals of the system. When this work is well done and well orchestrated, the interrelated goals, the major aims, and the mission of the system are accomplished. Effective programs, then, lead in a cost-effective way to the accomplishments specified by the mission and goals of the system.

Ideally, programs are clear, concise, and efficient step-by-step processes that lead from Point A to Point B. Point A is where the system is—let us say it is the point where a social worker is about to enter a family in crisis—and Point B is the accomplishment toward which the system is directing its resources—in accomplishment terms, "crisis *managed*." The program is the route between A and B. Program planners ask themselves: What are the major things we have to do to get from Point A to Point B? Figure 7-1 indicates that each goal is achieved through a program that calls for a number of steps.

This chapter deals with the final elements of Part 1 of Model A: (1) the programs required to accomplish each goal, (2) the material resources required to implement each program, and (3) operational planning.

STEP-BY-STEP PROGRAM PLANNING

The term *program*, as it is used here, refers to a particular part of a system, the activities that lead to goals. Sometimes people say that they want to establish a

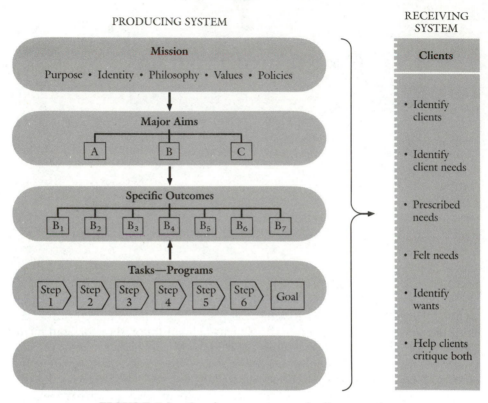

FIGURE 7-1.   Step-by-step programs leading to goals

program when they actually want to establish a *system*. For instance, people may say that they want to set up a training *program* when they mean, at least in the language of Model A, that they want to establish a training-delivery *system*. The problem is more than semantic. Since programs deal directly with behavior and only indirectly with the accomplishments toward which this behavior is directed, establishing a training program rather than a training system may lead to a great deal of activity (behavior) and few accomplishments (valued goals that are actually achieved). Establishing a training system (as a part of a larger system) entails identifying the needs and wants of those being trained, developing mission statements, turning these into specific goals, establishing step-by-step programs for the accomplishment of these goals, and so forth. Model A is a blueprint for designing a training subsystem (program) as part of a larger system.

A training example

Let us continue the example of a communication-skills training system set up for paraprofessionals in a social-service center. The specific skills, such as empathy and confrontation, have been established as the valued outcomes. The training *program* might include the following steps:

Step 1: Cognitive understanding.   *Outcome*: This step is accomplished when the trainees have a basic cognitive understanding of the skill. *Program behaviors*: Reading, reviewing written examples, discussion, and question and answer sessions related to the skill in question.

The trainees demonstrate that they possess cognitive understanding if they can explain the skill to someone who has never heard of it. At the end of this step the trainee can say, "I know what this skill is about. I know its essential features and I can explain them clearly to others."

Step 2: A behavioral understanding.   *Outcome*: This step is accomplished if the trainees have, in addition to an intellectual grasp of the skill, a working knowledge of the skill as it is actually used in a human-service situation. *Program behaviors*: Live or video demonstration of the skill.

At the end of this step the trainee can say, "I know what this skill looks like in action. I understand how it is used in an actual human-service situation."

Step 3: Initial know-how.   *Outcome*: This step is accomplished when the trainees know how it feels to use the skill with another person. *Program behaviors*: The trainer "walks the trainee through" the use of the skill, providing needed guidance and feedback.

At the end of this step the trainee can say: "I have a feeling for how the skill is used in helping a client."

Step 4: Mastery through practice.   *Outcome*: This step is accomplished when the trainee begins to use the skill correctly and with some facility. *Program behaviors*: Trainees practice the skill with their peers and receive feedback, both confirmatory and corrective, from themselves, their peers, and their trainers.

At the end of this step the trainee can say, "I can now actually use this skill accurately and with some facility in my interactions with others."

Step 5: Actual interactions with clients.   *Outcome*: At the end of this step the trainees have transferred this skill to actual interactions with clients and are using it appropriately to achieve the goals of the helping process. *Program behaviors*: Actual use of the skill with clients, review of audiotapes or videotapes of their sessions, feedback from self and from supervisors.

At the end of this step the trainee can say, "I am using this skill accurately in my sessions with my clients. I feel more and more comfortable in using this skill and it enables me to help my clients manage the problem situations of their lives more effectively." In other words, the overall goal of the training system, "relevant skills learned and transferred," has been accomplished.

The substeps of a program.   The ways in which these objectives are to be accomplished have been elaborated only in a general way. However, for each of these steps there are substeps leading to the accomplishment of the objective. In Step 1, for example, the desired outcome, or objective, is "the elements of the communication skill of accurate empathy grasped cognitively by the trainee." This outcome is accomplished through these substeps: First, the trainees read an explanation of the skill together with some examples. Second, the trainees listen to a brief description and discussion of the skill by the instructor. Third, the trainees are urged to discuss the skill with their fellow trainees and to ask questions of the instructor. Fourth, the instructor asks questions of the trainees to make sure that they understand the elements of the skill.

Large systems have complex networks of interrelated goals and subgoals. This complexity is handled by: setting clear goals, spelling out the relationship among goals, designing clear step-by-step programs for the accomplishment of each goal, and specifying clear substeps leading to the accomplishment of each subgoal. This is the way automobiles are put together on assembly lines. Complexity in any system or subsystem demands coordination and attention to detail.

Principles of programming

The following principles can be used as an outline, guide, or checklist for the task of program development.

Link programs clearly to goals. If you are having trouble establishing programs, consider the possibility that your goals are not clear enough, or that they are really general aims or mission statements. If "listening skills improved" is the training goal, then it is probably clear and you can begin to develop programs to implement it. But a broad statement like "social-work skills improved" must be clarified before training programs in social-work skills can be established.

A group of people led by the director of behavioral medicine at a large medical school persuaded the faculty to mandate a course in human-relations skills for first-year medical students. At the end of the first year a consultant was called in because the program had failed. The medical students hated it. The consultant discovered that the faculty had chosen a "community" model of human-relations training. The students were asked to reveal information about themselves to one another and to practice such skills as accurate empathy as they did so. The students thought the course had little or nothing to do with medicine.

The consultant suggested a different model, one more intimately related to the mission, major aims, and goals of a medical school. He suggested that empathy skills could also relate to a medical "problem-management" model. The faculty members agreed that medical interventions could be conceived of as forms of problem management. Diagnoses were made, medical interventions were determined and implemented, and the results were evaluated. Traditionally diagnosis was done by testing, by "hands-on" approaches, and by *listening to the patient* ("If you listen carefully to the patient, he or she will tell you what's wrong").

The students could listen to patients better if they had the kinds of communication skills that were taught by the members of the team, and once these skills were taught in the context of a medical model, students found them more relevant. The team members could make the same demands for excellence in this area as other faculty members were making in other areas.

Examine a variety of ways to accomplish goals. Do not make the mistake of establishing the first program that comes to mind. Keeping an open mind about different paths to goals can contribute to the effectiveness and the efficiency of your programs. Remember that imagination is a system-enhancing form of arationality.

Spend some time brainstorming program possibilities. If a task is ordinarily done in a specific way, ask yourself whether there are other, perhaps better, ways of doing it. There is no need to pursue innovation for its own sake, but neither should it be avoided if it can contribute to the efficacy and efficiency of the enterprise. In designing programs, do not ignore the history of the system with which you are working—what past programs have been successful and what current programs are working for us?—but do not remain tied to history. "We have always done it this way" is often a sign of stagnation rather than stability.

In the example of training paraprofessionals in communication skills, the training program outlined above is only one possible approach. It might not be the best. The program outlined is systematic and *deductive*, but an *inductive* or a combination inductive-deductive program might be more successful. For instance, the instructor might begin this way:

> "I'm about to demonstrate a dialogue with a client, and I'm going to do it in two different ways. I'll stop and tell you when I'm going to change the approach. As you listen to me, I want you to identify the principal differences between the first and second approaches and ask yourself which way you would prefer if *you* were the client."

The instructor then engages in an interaction with a confederate. At first her style includes many questions and attempts to influence the client but few attempts to listen and understand the client's needs. After she stops and tells the trainees that she is now going to do it differently, she listens well and uses a few probes and a great deal of empathy to learn the client's view of his problem situation. After the two dialogues are over, the trainees point out the differences between the first and second approaches, and the instructor writes these on the blackboard. Then she asks the trainees to discuss how they would have felt if they had been the client in each of the two dialogues.

Note that this is an *inductive* way of achieving Steps 1 and 2 of the training program outlined earlier. The major subgoals remain the same, but the substeps used to achieve them are quite different. Inductive approaches to training are often "messier" since it is harder to control them, but they are usually more dramatic and more involving. The question is, What kinds of programs or subprograms will help me achieve goals and subgoals most effectively and efficiently? Or, What kind of program is best linked to the goal?

Look for exemplars. An exemplar is a person or a system that achieves goals quickly and at lowest cost. Exemplars are the people or systems that "do it best." Looking for exemplars is another way of searching for the most suitable program instead of settling for the first one that comes along. Whatever the task might be, ask yourself, "Who else is doing this? Who is doing it best in terms of quality and cost effectiveness? Who is developing new, better, and more efficient technologies?"

Many human-service systems, including the service-oriented subunits of organizations and industries, are inefficient because they fail to look for innovative "technologies" that enable human services to be delivered effectively and efficiently. Clergy, for example, might suppress their initial and usually quite laudable tendencies to meet needs through their own personal efforts. Consider the following example:

> The ministers of a particular religious denomination were asked to make contributions from their own pockets to a fund to help the hungry in third-world countries. This venture proved quite successful. From time to time the denominational newsletter carried letters from grateful ministers in foreign lands with accounts of how the money had been spent.
>
> But at a monthly meeting one minister asked what the goal of the program was. He said the goal of the program seemed to be twofold: to raise funds for the indigent and to encourage ministers to make a sacrifice for a good cause. After all, many ministers were contributing to the hunger fund not from excessive wealth, but rather from their own "first-world" indigence. Consequently, the entire project was limited. If the primary goal was to provide funds for self-help projects in third-world countries, more money could be raised in a more flexible program. Some ministers might want to give money, while others might want to contribute their services as fundraisers or influence members of their congregation to join such organizations as Bread for the World. Still others might want to do all three.
>
> And so the program was changed. Quite a few of the ministers became fundraisers in their own congregations and in the business community or became advocates for one or another organization dealing with world hunger. The amount of money sent to fund the self-help projects increased greatly and many more parishioners became active in the hunger movement. The expanded aim became: "Hungry people in the third world *helped* through the resources of the ministers of this denomination." But now the "resources" included their abilities as fundraisers and organizers as well as their money.

Invent programs, evaluate them, choose the most promising program, and reserve alternate programs in case your first choice is unsuccessful. Programs tend to be better if they are chosen from a number of possibilities. Contingency programs can be substituted if the first-choice program proves to be flawed. The criteria for choosing programs are effectiveness, efficiency, and quality of life in the system.

Effectiveness. Will this program, if implemented, actually achieve the goal? And to what degree (in terms of quantity and quality)? For instance, showing a variety of movies to trainees in communication skills might stimulate and entertain them— "I really enjoyed the movies"—without improving their communication skills. The aim of the training program is "skills *improved*," not "trainees *entertained*." Effectiveness is the essential criterion. It makes little difference if paraprofessionals improve their communication skills if these skills do not contribute directly or indirectly to their work with clients.

In helping and human-service organizations, the issue is "quality" services. However, quality refers not just to the models, methods, skills, and programs used by practitioners, but to *outcomes*. A service program is good to the extent that it leads to goals, to outcomes valued by clients and society. Sometimes I hear such statements as, "It's amazing to see her work!" referring to social workers, counselors, group leaders, and other human-service workers. If this comment refers to an entertaining virtuoso performance such as might be expected from a violinist, it may or may not lead to valued outcomes.

Efficiency. Which program is most efficient in terms of time, money, and effort? That is, which program makes the best use of the resources of the system? The instructor training paraprofessionals in communication skills realizes that an inductive approach is more costly in terms of time, effort, and money. She needs an assistant, whose salary adds to the cost. The instructor is more tired at the end of the day when she uses inductive training approaches. Her research indicates, however, that the trainees are more highly motivated when she uses inductive approaches; they learn the skills better, retain them better, and actually use the skills more frequently in dialogues with clients. She ultimately chooses a program that is partly inductive and partly deductive. This choice cuts down on the cost and is almost as effective as a totally inductive approach.

Quality of life. If two programs are equally effective, the more efficient of the two is not automatically the best. The legitimate needs and wants of those who must implement the program must be taken into consideration. The most efficient form of an assembly line might mean that the tasks of the line workers are backbreaking, boring, and dangerous. If this is the case, then efficiency conflicts with quality-of-life considerations.

> A psychologist in a VA hospital, putting most of his time into direct service to patients, was approaching "burn out." After returning from a workshop on the use of training in mental hospitals, he began to spend more time training his aides in problem-management skills. He taught them how to run goal-oriented group sessions with patients. From then on he spent more time supervising the aides, who carried out programs with the patients. In this case both productivity and quality of life improved because of the new program.

Shaping the program: Systematically elaborate the major steps and the substeps. Once you have decided which program to pursue, map out the practical details. After the communications skills instructor had decided that her training program would use a combination of inductive and deductive approaches, she designed a program that would lead to the essential communications skills. It is useful to map out or diagram the entire program. A diagram or flow chart of what needs to be done to get from Point A to Point B can be relatively simple or quite complicated. The more complicated it is, the more the need for the diagram. Some kind of visual representation of the program will help you see the interrelationships more clearly, arrange the parts more effectively, and understand problem areas more thoroughly. Major steps and their subgoals stand out more clearly. With a map in front of you, you can ask yourself what is right about the program and what problems may arise in its execution. When complicated programs are broken down into subgoals and subprograms, they can be achieved, if the time frame is realistic.

Make sure that all subgoals have the characteristics of goals. Subgoals are really intermediate goals. Therefore subgoals must be:

- stated as clear, specific, behavioral *accomplishments*
- *related* clearly both to the next subgoal and to the major goal toward which they are directed
- capable of being *measured or verified* in terms of quantity, quality, and cost
- *realistic*—that is, within the resources, capabilities, and control of those working on the program
- consonant with the *values* of the system and its members
- clearly *communicated* to whoever is responsible for achieving any particular subgoal
- assigned a reasonable *time frame* for completion

In arranging steps and substeps, consider the order in which steps are taken. Which step needs to be done first, which second, and so forth? For the sake of economy, which steps can be taken concomitantly? What would happen if the order of steps were reversed?

A large university dormitory system chooses resident assistants (RAs) from among juniors and seniors. I was consulted on how the RAs might be trained in problem solving and peer counseling. The logic seemed to be: (1) select RAs, (2) train them. I suggested that the process be reversed. Each semester and every summer, the university would offer a course in the essentials of counseling with a problem-solving framework. RAs would be chosen from those who successfully completed this course. In this way the best prospects could be chosen, already trained in the elements of counseling.

Schedule the work to be completed within a reasonable time. Scheduling becomes especially critical in complex systems. In everyday situations, scheduling affects all of us. Recently I walked into a doctor's office with a two o'clock appointment and was seen promptly at two o'clock. My surprise grew as the same thing happened two more times. Finally, I asked the receptionist what was happening, since this prompt service was beyond my ordinary experience. She said, "It's two things: one is scheduling and the other is not making the dollar the ultimate criterion." Doctors are notorious for filling waiting rooms with patients. In some places, however, there is currently a glut of doctors. I have helped a hospital grapple with a significant drop in the number of patients at the ambulatory patient center. Patients don't like to be kept waiting. They were becoming impatient and choosing another hospital. The problem was difficult to manage because of medical culture: Everyone waits for doctors and doctors wait for no one.

Implementation of programs

A practical concept in the bridge between the planning and implementation of programs is what Anthony, Pierce, and Cohen (1979) call "check" or "think" steps.

Check steps are actually "questions steps." That is, they indicate to clients what they should be asking themselves during the implementation stage. Check steps are used to guide clients'... performance. There are three types of check steps: "before" check steps; "during" check steps; and "after" check steps. As the names suggest, before check steps indicate what clients should think about before performing a certain behavior; during check steps indicate what clients should think about while performing the steps; after check steps indicate what clients should think about after performing the step [Anthony, Pierce, and Cohen, 1979, p. 53].

The last step before implementation of a program or subprogram is to draw up a list of practical check steps. The following questions are asked before anyone begins to implement the program:

- What is needed before this step can begin?
- Which steps need more care and attention than the others because they are more important or more difficult?
- Is the division of labor clear to everyone, especially those who must cooperate to complete the program?
- Does each person know what is expected of him or her?
- Does each person have the working knowledge and skills needed to execute this program?
- Does each person have whatever program guidelines might be useful?
- Have we obtained the agreement and cooperation of key superiors for this program? Are all systems "go"?
- What obstacles can be expected as we move through this program and how can they be overcome?

Force-field analysis

Force-field analysis (Lewin, 1969; Spier, 1973) addresses the question of obstacles and assesses resources in the implementation of programs. Despite its rather sophisticated name, force-field analysis is a relatively simple way of developing "during" (that is, during the implementation) check steps. Through force-field analysis, program developers anticipate what forces will prevent people from implementing programs (restraining forces) and what forces will help them (facilitating forces). The first step, then, is the identification of both restraining forces and facilitating forces. this process is illustrated in Figure 7-2.

Identify restraining forces. The identification of possible obstacles helps "forewarn" those who are implementing programs so that they will be prepared to solve any problems they encounter. Two consultants used force-field analysis to help high school teachers identify the possible restraining forces associated with the development of a curriculum-evaluation program. They uncovered such problems as fear of the changes that might be demanded by the evaluation process and unwillingness to spend the extra time and do the extra work entailed by the program.

Restraining forces can come from within those who are implementing programs, from others, and from the environment. Sometimes programs go awry because people fail to consider environmental factors. Robert Carkhuff's book *Cry Twice!*

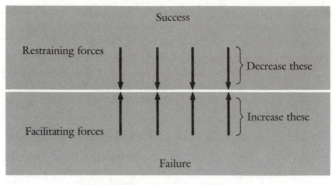

FIGURE 7-2.   Force-field analysis

(1974) is the bittersweet story of a highly successful change program in a correctional facility that was eventually subverted because political realities were not identified early enough as significant restraining forces.

Identify facilitating forces. In a more positive vein, force-field analysis can be used to identify important *resources* to be used in implementing programs. These are the "facilitating" forces. Facilitating forces, like restraining forces, can be persons, places, or conditions. Facilitating forces for the teachers mentioned above were the teacher-to-teacher communication demanded by the evaluation program and awareness that the school would soon be evaluated by the regional accrediting body. Sometimes simply being aware of a pitfall is enough to help people mobilize their resources to handle it. The consultants helped the teachers to give themselves "permission" to air their fears about an increased work load and a more demanding curriculum. A simple airing of these fears greatly reduced their impact.

Implementation tactics

In the implementation phase the focus shifts from strategy to *tactics* and *logistics*. Tactics is the art of adapting a plan (program) to the immediate situation. Adaptation includes the ability to change the plan on the spot in response to unforeseen complications. Logistics is the art of providing resources *when they are needed*.

All of us have experienced problems in trying to implement programs. We make plans and they seem realistic to us. We undertake the initial steps of a program with a good deal of enthusiasm. Soon, however, we run into tedium, obstacles, and complications. What seemed so easy in the planning stage seems quite difficult in the implementation stage. Entropy, the tendency of a system to decline over time, is a common form of arationality. Stein (1980) suggests that we need program "rachets," organizational strategies and tactics designed to prop up and revitalize programs when they begin to flag.

When the fifteen-week semester begins, students and instructor are quite enthusiastic. Around the eleventh or twelfth week, however, the bloom is off the rose. But there are program rachets. For instance, instructors can save the most engaging material of the course for the last four weeks of the semester. This material can be presented through various forms of experiential learning so that the students are highly involved. Recently, I have presented the problem of the "flagging program" to the students at the beginning of the semester as a problematic form of arationality that we must all manage together.

Programs work best when they are well "shaped." Shaping involves providing models for program participation, not demanding too much (or too little) too soon, providing enough incentives to stimulate program participation, minimizing the punitive side effects of program participation, and making sure that avoidance is not rewarded. Avoidance mechanisms are potent restraining forces in the implementation of programs. Avoidance will take place if the rewards for *not* doing something are stronger than the rewards for doing it. Avoidance is usually not a sign of ill will. Program avoidance is more likely a sign of a poorly designed and managed program, and therefore a managerial rather than a participatory problem. In the helping and human-service professions we are sometimes too quick to blame our clients for lack of progress. We should first ask ourselves whether we are managing our part of the human-service delivery system well. Is our own house in order? If not, we are likely to continue a long but dysfunctional tradition of "blaming the victim" (Ryan, 1971).

Good tacticians possess the ability to change behavior to address new conditions. Programs deal with how to get goals accomplished. Whenever possible, the details of the "how-to" should be left to those responsible for carrying out the program. Activities are often performed more effectively and more efficiently by an individual who participates in planning them. In bureaucratic systems job descriptions are usually so detailed that even minor steps in programs are spelled out in detail. While this detail insures a great deal of control and predictability in the system, it can eliminate creativity. In program execution, creativity coupled with accountability would seem to contribute more to both productivity and quality of work life. If people can achieve goals effectively and efficiently—that is, according to predetermined criteria—by doing work their own way, there is little reason to insist that it be done the "company" way.

MATERIAL RESOURCES

To accomplish productivity-related tasks, people need money, equipment, buildings, tools, rooms, uniforms, furniture, vehicles, books, and the like. Human-service practitioners use buildings, automobiles, flip charts, blackboards, desks, chairs, and other material resources in order to implement programs. The task of managing nonpeople resources is often a formidable one. Figure 7-3 indicates the relationship of material resources to programs.

Financing. Money is a critical resource, and finance-related programs are essential. Nevertheless, a great deal of emotion surrounds money. The word *money* has a whole range of emotional connotations from "evil" and "degrading" to "noble" and "exciting." But rational decisions in human-service organizations, as in all other organizations, institutions, and communities, are based on the economics of the system as they relate to the larger economy. The fact that members of some human-service systems remain or are kept financially naive is a cause for concern. To remain

I. THE PERFORMANCE SYSTEM

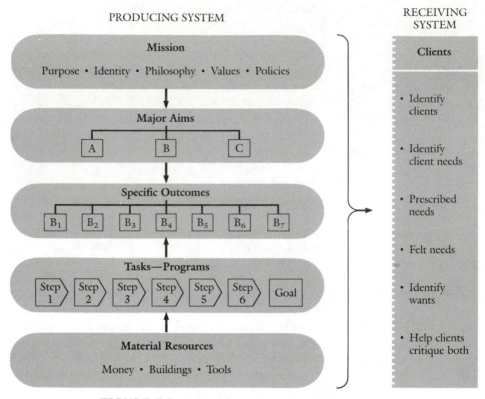

FIGURE 7-3.   Material resources needed for programs

financially and economically innocent is to court both manipulation and fiscal disaster. All human-service practitioners need to become informed about such concepts as funding, budgeting, accounting, overhead, cash flow, compensation, fringe benefits, taxes, and inflation, even if they are not members of a finance-related department such as strategic financial planning, budgeting, or accounting. Figure 7-4 indicates some of the programs (work) related to money and its management.

Materials and Tools. Productivity is also related to the choice of materials and tools. Instead of hiring a second secretary, for instance, a health clinic might want to consider buying or leasing a word processor. Depending on the kind of work the secretary does, this equipment may double his or her productivity. The cost of the machine is much less than the cost of maintaining another secretary.

Books are important tools in educational settings. Gilbert (1978) suggests that teachers are hampered by the textbooks that are currently available. Texts, he says, generally satisfy the interests of authors and publishers rather than teachers and students. Often people are accused of incompetence when the real problem is that they are saddled with ineffective materials and tools or have not been trained to use them effectively.

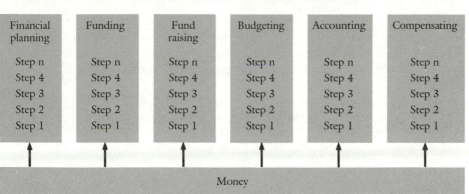

Financial planning	Funding	Fund raising	Budgeting	Accounting	Compensating
Step n	Step n	Step n	Step n	Step n	Step n
Step 4	Step 4	Step 4	Step 4	Step 4	Step 4
Step 3	Step 3	Step 3	Step 3	Step 3	Step 3
Step 2	Step 2	Step 2	Step 2	Step 2	Step 2
Step 1	Step 1	Step 1	Step 1	Step 1	Step 1

Money

FIGURE 7-4. Programs relating to money management

It is critical to link nonpeople resources to valued accomplishments. Failure to determine specific student- and teacher-related accomplishments has resulted in unused television cameras and tape recorders. Before ordering such equipment, potential users need to ask themselves accomplishment-oriented questions. One wonders how many unused or underused computers will be found in human-service systems over the next decade.

OPERATIONAL OR PERFORMANCE PLANNING

Strategic planning covers the longer term and includes goals and major aims. Operational or performance planning usually covers one year at a time and includes goals, programs, and resources, both human and material. Performance planning ties together many of the elements that have been considered so far and enables an organization or any given subunit of the organization to

- ensure *clarity* of organizational and unit goals and programs on an annual basis
- provide the basis for the *individual performance plans* of the members of the organization or unit
- help managers *allocate resources* on an annual basis more effectively
- provide agreement on performance objectives between staff members and supervisors, which can be used as a basis for *performance appraisal*

The development of unit performance plans is the responsibility of each unit manager. The plan, once developed, can be used by all individuals working in the unit to develop their own individual performance plans. In the example that follows, the training unit of a large mental health center will be described to make the unit performance plan concrete. The five elements of the plan are: (1) linkage, (2) performance areas, (3) key performance areas, (4) priority performance objectives, and (5) performance indicators.

Step 1: Establish essential linkages. It is essential to *link* the unit plan to the overall objectives of the organization or institution. The plans of the training unit need to be linked to the mission, the strategic plans, and the operational plans of the mental health center itself and to the training unit's own mission. These missions and plans, together with the work programs and budget of the unit, become the data base for the elaboration of the training unit's operational plans.

Step 2: List all performance areas.   List all the tasks for which the unit is responsible. For instance, some performance areas for which the training unit is responsible are:

- operational planning for the unit
- providing competent staff for the training unit
- ongoing feedback and performance appraisal for staff
- assessing the training needs of staff members
- assessing training needs of clients
- designing training programs for staff
- designing and presenting training programs for clients
- writing training manuals and preparing handouts
- implementing training programs for staff
- providing consultancy services for staff members who are implementing training programs with clients
- developing and testing new training programs
- reviewing programs developed by other centers
- looking for outreach opportunities for training in the community
- establishing liaisons with the training units of other human-service organizations
- preparing training materials for publication

Each of these performance areas will have its own specific goals and programs.

Step 3: Identify key performance areas.   Key performance areas are those that deserve priority attention during the coming year if the unit is to contribute in significant ways to the overall work of the organization. What areas are in decline and need special attention? What areas, if further developed, will help us do our work more effectively and efficiently? What areas need special attention because of the changed overall priorities of the organization? Usually no more than four or five areas will be designated. If too many areas are designated as "key," the word loses its significance. Using the questions in this paragraph, the training unit chooses the following as key performance areas:

- *Ongoing feedback and performance appraisal for staff*: The center is adopting a new performance planning and appraisal system, and therefore it is essential that it be applied to the members of the training staff.
- *Designing and presenting training programs for clients*: Since there is a new emphasis on prevention, the center needs new training programs for a wider clientele.
- *Developing and testing new training programs*: Some of the training programs for both staff and clients are outdated.
- *Reviewing programs developed by other centers*: A search for exemplar programs is one of the steps in developing new programs.

- *Preparing training materials for publication*: Some of the center's more innovative programs merit publication, which will help establish a dialogue with other centers.

These, then, are the areas in which significant change is planned. They relate both to the development of the training unit and the development of the mental health center as a whole.

Step 4: Set priority unit objectives.   When key performance areas have been selected, two or three major performance *objectives* should be set in each area. Objectives are the actual outcomes that will be accomplished and will contribute significantly to unit and organizational effectiveness. Under the key performance area "designing and presenting training programs for clients," for example, the following objectives are set:

A workshop called "Making It as a Single Parent" will be developed and offered at three different sites in the community at three different times during the week. Since many of the clients who come to the center are single parents, prevention in this area seems to be especially needed.

A workshop called "Finding and Using Social Services" will be developed and offered in each of the housing projects in the community. The social workers and counselors often find people who do not realize that social services are available. They also deal with people who do not know how to work their way through the maze of social service offerings.

A workshop called "Networks: Finding People That Care" will be developed and piloted through three of the churches in the community.

These three workshops will considerably enhance the prevention aim of the center.

Step 5: Develop performance indicators.   Performance indicators are ways of determining whether an objective has been wholly or partially realized. Since the objectives outlined in Step 4 are goals, they must fulfill the requirements for goals— that is, they must be stated as clear and specific accomplishments and linked to major aims; objectives must constitute significant contributions to the achievement of major aims, be verifiable, be realistic, and have a clear time frame. Performance indicators must be clear enough to enable managers, supervisors, and staff members to reach conclusions independently about full or partial fulfillment of each objective. *Interim* indicators are used throughout the year for ongoing feedback, and *final* indicators are used for year-end review.

Consider the third objective in Step 4, "A workshop called 'Networks: Finding People That Care' will be developed and piloted through three of the churches in the community." Both interim and final indicators are needed to determine whether this objective has been achieved:

Interim indicators. Jane S. will be in charge of initial design. A tentative workshop design will be circulated to John B. and Odette Y. by February 15. Their written comments will be on Jane's desk by March 1. The final design will be in print by March 15. By March 1, John B. will have the written permission of three pastors to conduct this workshop on their premises. Jane S. and John B. will have met with these three pastors and discussed the details of the workshop with them by April 1. Also by April 1, the dates for the presentation of the workshops will have been agreed upon by Jane S., John B., Odette Y, and the pastors.

Final indicators. By the end of June, six workshops, two at each site, will have been presented, two each by Jane S., John B., and Odette Y. By the end of July, follow-up questionnaires will have been mailed to the participants in order to see what behavioral changes have taken place. Sample interviews with 30% of the participants will have been conducted by Jane S., John B., and Odette Y. by September 15. A final report on the workshop and its outcomes with recommendations, prepared by Jane S., John B., and Odette Y., will be ready for discussion with the entire staff at the mid-October meeting of the training unit.

In keeping with the principles outlined earlier in this chapter, these three members of the training unit will meet at the beginning of the program to discuss some of the normative arational dimensions of the project. For instance, they will discuss inertia, the various forms of initial resistance in themselves and others, and entropy, the various ways in which the project might droop toward a whimper rather than head for a bang. They will see to it that enough initiatives exist to handle the inertia and enough program "rachets" are in place to handle the entropy.

Figure 7-5 diagrams the five steps of unit performance planning.

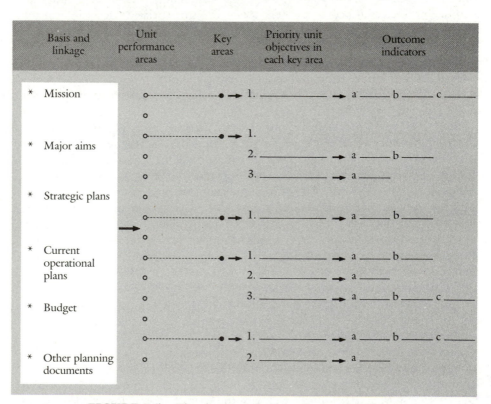

FIGURE 7-5. The elements of unit performance planning

PROGRAMS AND ARATIONALITY

Here are some of the common forms of arationality associated with programs:

Awkward beginnings. Egan's dictum states: "Expect beginnings to be messy." No matter how hard we try to start an enterprise on the right foot and in the right direction, something usually goes wrong. There is a brittleness about beginnings that makes people nervous. They are not themselves. Novice consultants meet with a group of teachers and come back saying how awful the meeting was. The teachers were suspicious, they refused to own the project, and the consultants felt inept. Or everything seems to go wrong during the first meeting of the training group. People don't like the group they are in, nobody wants to cooperate, the training design cannot be implemented—the list could go on and on. And yet there is hope. The second half of Egan's dictum states: "After messy beginnings, things get better." The same consultants come back from the second meeting saying that the teachers now seem to have their act together. The members of the training group settle down and begin to like the group they are in.

There is a difference between messy beginnings and incompetent and poorly planned beginnings. When people are competent and enterprises are well planned, the leaders can reduce stress by understanding the nature of beginnings and having the patience to tolerate some ups and downs until the system is running smoothly.

The tyranny of programs. In human-service systems, people often expect program development and execution to take the place of concrete and specific goals. They say, "Let's do a survey" or "Let's put on a workshop," without linking the survey or the workshop to mission, major aims, and goals.

One reason that training programs can be so notoriously cost-ineffective is, as Gilbert (1978) points out, the "tyranny of programs." Parkinson's (1958) law—"work expands so as to fill the time available for its completion" (p. 2)—rules the day. This "law" can be modified to read: "Programs expand to fill the void left by inadequate or poorly defined goals." People in the military and in human-service professions such as the ministry often say that they work such long hours that their marriages are in jeopardy or that the quality of family life is suffering. Perhaps they like their work, find it rewarding, and therefore put in long hours even though there are some unpleasant side effects. Or they may be victims of the tyranny of programs. If "working hard" is a cultural value within a system that does not specify *outcome* effectively, the probability of long, unproductive working hours increases.

Tsongas (1981), in discussing mistakes made by liberal politicians, presents a different kind of tyranny.

> [M]any liberals failed to make a distinction between values [as part of mission] and programs. A liberal program devised in pursuit of a given value was held to be sacro-sanct, even if it was inappropriate, ineffective, or abused; the program itself became the object of loyalty, not the value it was intended to serve. Thus, when CETA was used as a source of patronage by many of the nation's mayors and county officials, the value [mission] was not being served. Liberals hurt themselves and ultimately their own values by not being willing to recognize the abuse of CETA and moving rapidly and convincingly to correct it. Instead, CETA was defended pretty much as is, and the electorate rebelled [p. 243].

Inertia. At the beginnings of programs, inertia is usually best handled by incentives rather than by harangues, threats, and prods. On the other hand, harangues, threats, and prods sometimes work without leaving the kinds of dysfunctional residue often associated with punishment. A prudent judgment should be made by the project manager.

Entropy. Programs tend to decay over time. The timely application of program rachets, which are often mid-program incentives, is much more useful than trying to find out who is to blame when things fall apart.

Contingency programming. When the well-planned program does not work, a good tactician knows it is time to move to Plan B. Often people are reluctant to throw in the towel on Plan A and move to Plan B or C. For instance, during the second workshop, Jane S. realizes that things are not going well. What worked at Church A is not working as well at Church B. However, she persists in using Program A, even though she has made contingency plans. Mid-program corrections are a sign of wisdom rather than of failure.

The best organizations have "a bias toward action" (Peters and Waterman, 1982). They employ creativity to try new methods and identify new and better ways of reaching goals. Naisbitt attributes progressive methods to "intrapreneurs," the entrepreneurs who work *within* organizations (1982, p. 195). The innovator knows when and how to test new programs without falling into the tyranny of programs and losing sight of the goal.

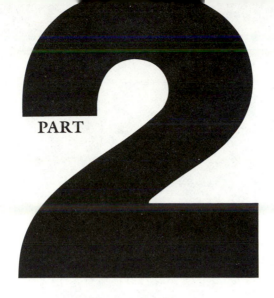

PART

PEOPLE

Every human system is a social system with a variety of social needs and arrangements. People assess the needs of clients and client organizations; people formulate mission and major aims. People set goals, gather needed resources, and execute the programs that do the work of the system. In organizations, institutions, and communities, and in the subunits, projects, and programs they encompass:

- People bring with them or develop the competencies they need in order to accomplish the work of the system (Chapter 8).
- People assume a variety of formal and informal roles related to the tasks outlined in the programs of the system (Chapter 9).
- People are involved in a variety of formal and informal relationships, cooperating and collaborating with one another to accomplish the work of the system (Chapter 9).
- In their relationships, people communicate with one another in a variety of formal and informal ways in order to accomplish their tasks (Chapter 10).
- Some people have the task of coordinating and facilitating the work of others at the service of the overall goals of the system (Chapter 11).

The sum total of roles, relationships, communication processes, and lines of leadership and authority constitute the structure of the system. Ideally, structure serves function—that is, the accomplishment of the goals of the system.

8

Human Resources

Though most organizations pay lip service to the importance of people, only the best organizations believe in and act on that premise. Peters and Waterman (1982) point out, "The excellent companies treat the rank and file as the root source of quality and productivity gain" (p. 15). The people who work in the system are important stakeholders. In organizations and institutions people can be viewed from two interrelated perspectives: (1) as those responsible for the work, and (2) as human beings with legitimate needs and wants related to the quality of work life (see Chapter 13).

People are not only the most valuable resource of a system; they are also its most costly resource. Since human resources are both valuable and expensive, the values and skills needed to shepherd this resource are of paramount importance. Figure 8-1 adds the human resources to Model A.

HUMAN RESOURCE PLANNING

If the organization is large, it will have a separate department or unit to handle personnel issues. The director of "management resources" of a large company remarked that the personnel department used to be "the dumping ground for people who couldn't make it in operations" (Kleinfield, 1982, p. 4). But today more and more personnel departments are changing their name, their function, and their status in organizations. In keeping with upgraded functions, the department is now called "department of human resources." While in some companies personnel departments stick to such narrow functions as dispensing checks and monitoring health and pension plans, in others such as Matsushita and ITT, human-resource management departments are responsible for such tasks as screening all entry-level employees, training them, schooling employees in the values of the company, training and

II. THE HUMAN RESOURCES OF THE SYSTEM

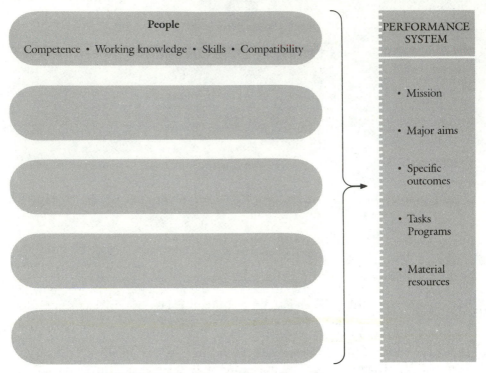

FIGURE 8-1. People: The major system resource

developing managers, evaluating employees and determining their bonuses, and screening candidates for higher managerial positions (Pascale and Athos, 1981). Human-resource development is now recognized as one of the most important functions of organizations and institutions, and the complexities of human-resource management are now appreciated.

1. Human resources are not the only resources that have to be managed in the total process of creating an effective organization. They have to be meshed with other resources such as money, technology, space, information, and so on.

2. Human resources are not passive or stable. People react to supervision, and they change over time. Supervision that works for a young subordinate may not work for that same person in midlife.

3. Human resources can make the difference between organizational failure and success. If workers have the wrong jobs or if they work below their potential or fail to learn new skills as organizational needs change, the organization is less likely to be effective in achieving its goals.

4. In most organizations the complexity of the task requires a wide variety of people to get the job done. No one approach to human-resource management can

be applied to everyone. People's needs vary, requiring managers to develop more flexible approaches to the development and management of their various categories of subordinates (Schein, 1978b, p. 293).

The overall strategic plan has important implications for the human resources of the system. If the plan calls for reducing the size and functions of the organization— for instance, the retrenchment that has taken place over the past years in psychiatric hospitals—the "management of decline" is a critical aspect. Outplacement, recasting roles and relationships, and reviewing compensation processes are issues that greatly affect morale. Especially in turbulent environments, future personnel needs and resources should be weighed against current needs and resources. Planners need to ask:

- Precisely what kinds of human resources are called for by the overall strategic plan? The plan needs to detail the kinds of jobs that will be created, the number of people needed to fill them, and the qualifications these people should possess.
- Do we presently have the human resources to implement this plan, and if not, can we get the people we need and train them? Some years ago, the human-service professions were crying out for help. Professionals with doctorates were in a sellers' market. But those fat years have been followed by lean.
- What impact would the plan have on present personnel? If the plan calls for retrenchment, it should be clear what jobs would be phased out. If extensive retraining would be required, the extent and the cost should be noted together with a timetable. Quality-of-life considerations are important. How will worker security be affected? What values will be operative if retrenchment is necessary? Will the same amount of work remain to be done even though there are fewer employees?

Both for-profit and not-for-profit organizations and institutions fail to engage in the strategic planning process in either a systematic and rational way or in the combination rational-intuitive-incremental way suggested by Quinn (1980, 1981). Even when a human-service organization does engage in strategic planning, Schein (1978b) implies that all too frequently the human-resource questions are not asked.

More dialogue is needed between human-service agencies and the professional schools that educate and train personnel for these agencies. The sole link between the school and the agency is often the intern, who may be bewildered by the discontinuities between these two systems.

Schein suggests the following steps in a full human-resources planning and development program:

Strategic planning. Decide on the major thrust of the organization. Determine what the major aims of the system will be five, ten, and fifteen years from now and beyond. Keep in mind, however, that this is an emergent process. Strategic plans should be recast year by year.

Human resource planning. Given an understanding of the direction in which the organization is moving and of the major aims that are emerging, determine the critical issues that relate to staffing. What kind of people do we need to staff this emerging organization?

Major performance appraisal. Determine present strengths and weaknesses in terms of skills, abilities, talents, potential, performance levels, the career stages and career needs of members, and the like.

Predicting future needs. Relate present resources to future needs in order to determine major personnel development needs. What skills that will be needed are lacking? What is the likelihood of growth or retrenchment? Where are we overstaffed? Where are we understaffed? What kind of retraining is needed? What more needs to be done in the area of career development? What do we do with incompetent people who have never been challenged?

Human resource development. Devise and implement the strategies needed to develop the required human resources in terms of attracting and recruiting new personnel and retraining and developing or deselecting present personnel.

MANAGING HUMAN RESOURCES

The personnel or human-resources function is a subsystem of the larger organization and a system in its own right. It assesses needs, develops its own mission and major aims, establishes goals, and elaborates programs to accomplish these goals. Once the long- and short-term needs of the system are known, they must be operationalized. The human-resource department helps managers carry out the following tasks:

Staffing includes: attracting promising prospects, assessing their ability to contribute to the work of the system, and selecting the most promising candidates and orienting them to the system.

Development includes: initial education and training, overseeing the proper utilization of human resources, offering ongoing career-development opportunities.

Appraisal includes: introducing staff members to the performance planning and appraisal system, providing ongoing feedback, carrying out collaborative appraisals.

Staffing and development will be treated in this chapter. Appraisal, since it is an important kind of communication between practitioners and their supervisors (or between the practitioner and himself or herself), will be considered in Chapter 10.

Staffing the system

Every organization and institution would like to recruit the best people it can. And yet some systems do little to attract the best people. The goal of this step is "best prospects *attracted*" or "a pool of good prospects *formed* from which the best can be chosen." Recruiters should ask, "What can we say about ourselves that will catch the eyes of the kind of people we want to recruit?"

This step calls for imagination. A magazine ad urging people to join the Peace Corps showed a picture of a South American village before the arrival of Peace Corps workers. On the following page there was a picture of the same village a year after the Peace Corps arrived. It was the very same picture. After cautioning prospective workers not to expect miracles, the ad explained that the Peace Corps members themselves would be challenged and changed for the better by working abroad.

Since most employees are recruited by word of mouth, an organization should ask itself, "How many emissaries do we have out there letting others know how good we are?" The personnel board of a large diocese was shocked to learn from a study that many priests tended to *discourage* young men from following in their footsteps. An organization probably gets the kinds of emissaries it deserves. Winners tend to attract winners; losers tend to attract losers. In a sense, the fundamental issue is not "Can we get good people?" but "Are we the kind of organization that good people would like to join?"

Assessing prospects. Many institutions hire problems. They select either incompetent people or competent people who do not fit into the system.

> The director of a mental health clinic hired a man to direct the alcoholic unit. He was certainly qualified in terms of both credentials and references. But two months after she hired him, she asked a consultant how she could legally fire him. Although the new director was competent, he was causing chaos: He was arrogant and politicized almost everything he did. Behind the scenes he tried to sabotage the "clinical ladder" career-development program the director of the clinic was promoting. As the quality of life deteriorated, productivity decreased. The director, blinded by the testimonials to this person's competence, had not read between the lines in the letters of recommendation, had made no further efforts to learn about his employment background, and afterwards admitted that her interview with him had been a social event, superficial and grossly inadequate.

Assessment procedures are important not just for recruiting but also for classifying, promoting, transferring, demoting, and terminating employees. The aim of this process is clear—"the requisite working knowledge, skills, and other qualities of prospective system members *determined*." The critical issue is knowing what to look for—knowing exactly what "requisite" means.

> Few would argue with a policy statement to the effect that it is nice to have employees who are productive, are likely to stay, will show up regularly for work, and will not steal. . . . Unfortunately, however, one cannot describe or measure job performance before it occurs. Therefore, one must assume, and if possible demonstrate, that the characteristics described prior to employment are in fact related to subsequent characteristics of performance on the job [Guion, 1976, p. 778].

Therefore, meaningful appraisal of prospects depends on clarity of mission, goals, programs, roles, tasks, and responsibilities. If the elements of Model A are not in order in the organization or institution, then relevant assessment procedures will not be in order.

The purpose of an assessment is to determine whether the prospect: has the working knowledge needed for the job; has the skills needed for the job; has the capacity and the will to be trained, if he or she does not have the requisite working knowledge and skills; is attracted to the organization and interested in the job; will contribute to, or at least not detract from, the quality of life of those who work in the system.

The following forms of system-limiting arationality are often at work in the assessment and selection process:

- The assessment process focuses on qualities and skills that have little or nothing to do with productivity or quality of life.
- People are chosen because they are good looking, because they know somebody, or because they are aggressive—not because they are competent.
- People are chosen because they fit the culture of the system and not because they will be especially productive or contribute to the quality of life. For instance, a social worker is chosen for a mental health center because she seems to have a conservative life style. Employers can unconsciously look for irrelevant qualities in applicants.

Assessment instruments such as references, questionnaires, interviews, and background investigations develop personal history or "biodata." Hastily constructed or overly general questionnaires are little help in the assessment process. The use of personal history is based on the premise that the best predictor of future performance is present and past performance (Carkhuff, 1969, 1971; Owens, 1976). And yet most of us know people—perhaps even ourselves—who did not work very hard in undergraduate days but have since had a change of heart. Bright, well-motivated people have had difficulty getting into graduate school because the specter of a low undergraduate grade point average continues to haunt them.

Interviewing is the most widely used method of assessing the qualifications of a prospect, but it is ordinarily carried out in a way that makes it neither reliable nor valid (Guion, 1976; Dunnette and Borman, 1979).

> There is not much in the research of the last half dozen years to bolster the confidence of a personnel interviewer concerned with the reliability and validity of his decisions. There is a good deal of evidence concerning the influence of variables which may make his decision less reliable and valid [Schmitt, 1976, p. 97].

If interviewers make efforts to control the principal sources of bias, however, and if they use instruments that yield accurate and relevant data, then interviewing can make a substantial contribution to the assessment process. It would probably pay the average personnel interviewer to improve his or her interviewing skills and to learn how to integrate interviewing with other sources of data, since most employers will not hire people without seeing them first. Concerning a prospective clinical psychology student, one of my colleagues said, "On paper this candidate seemed outstanding. Without an interview I would have chosen him instantly. But a 15-minute interview made it absolutely clear that this person would not make what we consider to be a good clinical psychologist."

Sampling actual performance is one of the most promising, but most expensive, forms of assessment. Many people, including myself, resist the present push toward certification of human-service providers. State certification is no proof of competence. The kinds of testing procedures presently used (such instruments as multiple choice tests) do not assess the competence of the practitioner in the actual delivery of services. Peer reviews of analogues of actual human-service delivery behavior make sense but they are expensive and are considered countercultural, since professionals are seldom assessed.

A relatively recent arrival on the assessment scene is the "assessment center." In these centers, primarily serving business and industry, a number of different people use a variety of instruments, including work analogues, to carry out the assessment process. In view of the expense, these centers are used principally in the selection of key personnel. Research (Bray, Campbell, and Grant, 1974; Huck, 1977) has shown that these centers, properly constituted and used, provide reliable data for selection decisions. As their number increases, however, so do problems, and consequently standards have been established for the proper design and use of these centers (Task Force on Assessment Center Standards, 1979; Task Force on Development of Assessment Centers, 1977). Assessment centers provide services that can benefit not only business and industry but human-service delivery systems as well. Cost must be weighed against benefits.

Selection and orientation.   Choosing personnel is a two-way street—the system is choosing the employee and the employee is choosing the system. Such choices represent various degrees of enthusiasm. The organization might well be the employee's third choice, or the employee might be the organization's third choice. People "choose" to belong to various human-service or community systems—for instance, a marriage, a day-care center, a correctional facility—for a variety of reasons. Wise managers do not equate choice with enthusiasm.

Orientation, the way a person is introduced into a system, can set the tone for the way he or she will participate. If admission procedures in a psychiatric hospital are inhospitable, as they sometimes are, the patient's stay in the hospital may be unsuccessful. And the same can be said of staff. When a person's introduction into the system is left to chance, both productivity and quality of life suffer. The aim is "new person *welcomed* and *integrated* into the system."

To assess orientation, ask these questions:

- What presently happens to a new member of this system? What happens that we do not want to happen? What fails to happen that we do want to happen?
- What, concretely, does "initial integration" into this system mean? What are the needs of the system with respect to the newcomer? What are the needs of the newcomer with respect to the system? What outcomes or accomplishments constitute initial integration?
- What programs can be developed to help the new person become both productive and at home as quickly as possible?

Orientation sessions are often dull, "canned" programs that perhaps meet some bureaucratic need, but fail to meet the needs of newcomers. Wanous (1975, 1977, 1980) has written extensively about "organizational entry" and has developed methods and tools such as the "realistic job preview" (1975) to help newcomers manage the initial stress of entry into the organization. A realistic job preview provides information about the positive and negative aspects of a job. Wanous's (1977) research showed that such previews can help newcomers develop more realistic job expectations and can lead to a lower turnover rate.

Developing human resources

If people do not have the working knowledge and skills to participate effectively and efficiently in the programs of the system, they need to be educated, or trained. (While it could be said that education leads to working knowledge and training leads to the acquisition of skills, in this book the term "training" covers both meanings.)

A great deal of money is misspent on training. As Goldstein (1980) points out, training in and of itself does not automatically result in better job performance and increased productivity. Organizations seldom find out whether any given training program actually contributes to productivity. Training programs and tools are meaningless unless training needs have been assessed and training goals specified.

> Training analysts are unique in their treatment of needs assessment techniques. For some reason, they have focused on instructional *techniques* rather than on *needs*. Thus . . . the training field is dominated by a fads approach. . . . This fads approach places a heavy emphasis on the development of techniques, without needs assessment followed by a matching of the technique to the needs [Goldstein, 1980a, p. 421].

The aim of training is not "to train people" nor even "people *trained*" (see Gilbert, 1978). Rather it is "relevant or performance-related working knowledge and skills *acquired* or *improved*." Consider the grid in Figure 8-2. Since training is expensive, it should take place only if a "yes" answer can be given to *both* questions: (1) "Are the skills relevant to productivity and/or quality of life?" and (2) "Does this particular employee lack this set of skills?" Many programs teach skills that are either irrelevant or already possessed by the trainee. These trainees would benefit more, at a lower price, from accurate information about what they are expected to do on the job. The following hard-nosed questions must be asked about training:

1. Has training been installed to meet a proven and measured performance need?
2. Are there performance measures to show that training is working?
3. Are the measures taken independently, or do we have only our training staff's word that training works?
4. Is exemplary performance the standard for training? (Exemplary performance is the performance of the best worker, with the proper incentives, working "smart" rather than hard.) And does the trainee reach the standard?
5. Are the people in charge of training competent, or is training relegated to those who just aren't good at other jobs?
6. How long is our training, formal or OJT [on the job training]? How long does it take a trainee to become a top performer on the job? If it takes more than, say, a month or two, we are probably missing great opportunities.
7. What are the true costs of our training, formal or OJT? There is little excuse not to know.
8. Are training costs budgeted?

9. What is an estimate of the value we are getting for our training?
10. Are our course lengths arbitrary or are they determined only by the time required for training?
11. Do we have access to really expert training development skills?
12. Do our training people know how to conduct a performance audit (Gilbert, 1978, pp. 238-239)?

When training suffers from the tyranny of programs, clear and specific goals are not established, but training is merely "thrown" at trainees in the hope that it will do some good. The training department takes on a kind of functional autonomy that militates against the interests of the total organization.

On the other hand, as Peters and Waterman (1982) point out, the best organizations provide ample opportunities for training and development. They do not ask members to undertake tasks for which they are not prepared.

In the human services, preparation for careers is often highly academic rather than professional. Many students graduate knowing a great deal about theory and research but without the working knowledge and skills they need. Therefore, on-the-job training is very important for the human-service provider. Too often supervisors assume that the new practitioner already has the requisite service-delivery skills. When these skills are missing, and no training is provided, clients become guinea pigs. Extensive literature suggests that when competence is lacking, such human services as counseling and psychotherapy can be of doubtful use and can even harm clients (see Egan, 1982). Educators should make sure that human-service providers have the working knowledge and skills needed to help clients manage their lives more effectively.

Training programs should be evaluated in terms of outcomes or accomplishments related to the provision of human services. But evaluation is often subjective. After the training program, when trainees are asked to evaluate what they have learned, the following comments are typical:

• "It was an exciting program. I really liked it." This comment tells us that the

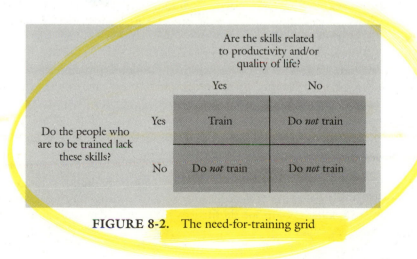

FIGURE 8-2.   The need-for-training grid

trainee was entertained, but not whether he or she acquired performance-related knowledge and skills.

- "I picked up one or two things that should be very helpful." The implication here is that training was not related to clearly understood performance needs.
- "They gave us things I already knew, but it was good to review them." The implication is that training did not apply to any working knowledge or skill deficiency.
- "I learned a lot, but I'm not sure how I'm going to use it back on the job." The training was not related to any specific performance need.

Catalanello and Kirkpatrick (1977) asked 154 companies how they assess the effectiveness of training. Most (77%) said they use reactions of trainees rather than posttests or on-the-job performance. *The cultural tendency to see training as good in and of itself* is another form of arationality that is extremely difficult to manage.

Human-service providers can use training as a way of empowering the clients with whom they work (Egan and Cowan, 1979; Larson, 1984; Marshall and Kurtz, 1982). Clients are unable to manage their own lives as effectively as they might because they lack task-related knowledge and skills. As important as problem-solving skills may be, they are not ordinarily part of the curriculum in our schools, nor are they taught in church, family, or neighborhood. While most of us pick up enough of these skills to "get by," just "getting by" is probably synonymous with the "psychopathology of the average." Training clients is not a magic solution to individual and social problems, but it can greatly enrich many human-service programs. It is an area wide open to imagination and creativity.

Human-resource development does not end with the initial training program. It is—or ought to be—an ongoing process, especially in fields where technology changes rapidly. It is heartening to see up-to-date magazines in the dentist's waiting room, but even more encouraging to see dog-eared professional journals in the inner office. Workers who read journals and attend professional conferences are taking responsibility for their own development.

In human-service settings, it is not unusual to meet practitioners who know very little about recent developments in their profession. I am not referring to fads. There is obviously a big difference between following fads and keeping abreast of serious developments in any human-service field.

Hackman and Oldham (1980) point out that staff development programs should be tailored to the needs of the organization or institution and to individual needs. They consider three different kinds of staff members: the "overstretched" staff person, the "fulfilled" staff person, and the "growing" staff person. Different approaches to development are needed for each of these. When individual differences are ignored, certain mistakes are common. The effort to "enrich" overstretched workers causes them to feel even more harried. Managers either ignore the fulfilled staff members or assume that they want to move to some higher position. Growing staff members are given too few opportunities and considered overly ambitious. Hackman and Oldham point out alternatives to these system- and individual-limiting forms of arationality.

Utilizing human resources

Once people have been trained to do the work that helps the system achieve its goals, the manager needs to consider how these people can be retained and utilized. It is a mistake to take workers for granted once they have settled into the system.

Retaining system members. In a positive sense, personnel turnover can mean that new blood is coming into the organization. These newcomers may be people with fresh hopes, new ideas, contagious enthusiasm, and refreshing vigor. Turnover can mean also that selection mistakes are being remedied. However, turnover is more frequently seen as a negative factor, indicating that good or at least adequate people are opting out of the system. Turnover can be costly in a variety of ways. New personnel need to be trained, and there may be some confusion as new people learn the ropes. High turnover can affect morale; that is, people can begin asking themselves what's wrong with a system that cannot retain its members.

How does an organization keep its good members? The answer is simple: People tend to stay in a system until the incentives to leave outweigh the incentives to stay. For instance, a worker will stay in a job until he or she receives a more attractive offer from another organization. The new job may be more attractive for a variety of reasons: The worker may be attracted to a job that offers more managerial challenge rather than one that offers greater financial security. On the negative side, a worker will stay in a distasteful job until its punitive dimensions outweigh the agony of searching for and changing to a new job.

Asking a person to leave a system—discharging, firing, dismissing, furloughing, deselecting—is just the final act of what should be a longer, more humane process. There are two extremes in firing. Many organizations fire employees without any warning. Others tolerate ineffective workers and at best try to make sure they do little harm; for instance, by relegating them to unimportant positions. Their managers hope to maintain a tranquil system and avoid the legal expense that sometimes results from firing people. This form of personnel arationality is especially destructive when joined to the arationality of hiring people who cause productivity or quality-of-life problems. To avoid both kinds of personnel arationality:

- Do not select members if you doubt that they can succeed in the organization. Being charitable at selection time is a disservice to workers and to the organization.
- Make sure that all system members have the working knowledge, skills, tools, information, and incentives to do well.
- Make sure that system members receive *ongoing* feedback, both confirmatory and corrective.
- Build periodic performance appraisals into the system. Don't avoid them to escape from unpleasant realities.
- If a system member is doing poorly, discover how much the system itself is contributing to poor performance. Perhaps goals are not clear. Perhaps supervision or the quality of life is poor. Blaming workers for a poorly managed system is another example of what Ryan (1971) calls "blaming the

victim." Provide a grievance procedure through which the member can return corrective feedback to the system.

- Give workers the challenge and support they need to act on corrective feedback, but make it clear from the beginning what the consequences of continued poor performance are. Set reasonable time limits for reaching required performance and make sure that system members know these limits.
- Finally, if someone is to be dismissed, do it assertively rather than aggressively. Provide an exit interview and, if possible, some kind of outplacement service.

Assessing skills. Underutilization of human resources is usually a managerial problem rather than an individual problem. Many human-service systems could be much more imaginative in the utilization of human resources. Lippitt (1979) describes human resource utilization as "putting the right heads together, at the right time, for the right task, with the right support to get a particular job done" (p. 309). Lippitt believes that the first step in using human resources intelligently is identifying just what these resources are. Just because someone is hired or chosen to do one task does not mean that he or she does not have the capability of doing others. He suggests the compiling of a "human resource directory" in which individuals are listed alphabetically with a checklist of their abilities, and abilities are listed alphabetically with a checklist of those who possess them.

One director of nursing in a large psychiatric hospital has a list on her wall of more than three dozen key nurses and aides. On the other dimension of the matrix she lists all skills and resources needed in the department and places checks after each nurse or aide to indicate their abilities and skills. Then when she needs people for a special assignment or wants to put together a task force, she merely glances at the chart on the wall. She finds that many of the people working in the department want to use their talents as fully as possible.

Such a human-resource directory must be kept up to date. When workers receive further education or training, either formal or on-the-job, care should be taken to list these new aptitudes.

Lippitt suggests that in some, if not most, systems, there is a cultural taboo against asking for help—that is, calling others in as consultants or co-workers on a project. He describes one company in which all staff members have a resource directory of their colleagues, and periodically they review how they have used each other during the past month. The administrator rewards and recognizes those who ask for help.

Recognizing competence

Carkhuff (1983) has drawn up five categories that are useful in organizing one's thinking about people in human-service settings. The categories are: (1) detractor/laggard, (2) observer/player, (3) participant/performer, (4) contributor/model, and (5) leader/exemplar. What follows is my own interpretation of these categories.

1. *Detractors (laggards).* A detractor actively subverts the purpose of the system.

Intentionally or unintentionally, detractors not only fail to accomplish the goals of the organization, institution, or community, but also prevent others from doing so. In a training group, for instance, a person who constantly makes clever cynical remarks is a detractor. In terms of quality of life, detractors make life miserable for others. The cynic in the training groups, then, is a detractor in terms of both productivity and quality of life. The laggard, who may be just lazy, is a person who performs, if at all, far below standards.

2. *Observers (players)*. Observers are people who sit back and watch. They don't prevent others from accomplishing goals or directly interfere with the quality of life of others. Indirectly, however, observers can interfere with both goal accomplishment and quality of life.

> Mark was in a human-relations training group. He was silent most of the time, saying little about himself and giving little feedback to others. As a result, the group would often try to deal with his passivity and he, however unwilling, became the center of the group's attention. When there was a lull in group interaction, someone would turn to Mark and say something like, "Well, what's happening with you?" And then the group would focus on Mark once more. This ritual had little effect on Mark's behavior.

In many social settings, observers like Mark eventually become detractors because they do not contribute their share to the effort of the group and they distract others from getting on with goal-related behavior. Preoccupation with a reluctant member does not improve the quality of life of the group. When I challenged one observer in a human-relations training group, he said he was *learning* in the group and *doing* outside the group. He eventually understood that without doing in the group there was little learning. Observers may also be called players, because they are "on the team," but they are substandard members in terms of productivity and quality of life.

3. *Participants (performers)*. Participants are people who, when asked or challenged, readily engage in goal-related behavior. While they usually have good will, they lack initiative. Participants ordinarily require a fair amount of supervision.

> Carmel was a member of skills training group in a counselor training program. She was usually passive, but when asked to talk about herself in relation to the goals of the group, she did so readily. When someone asked her for feedback, she gave it and the quality of her feedback was excellent. She was obviously attentive to and interested in the interaction of the group despite her lack of initiative.

At first participants require a fair amount of supervision, but they are capable of moving up to the next degree of participation. Participants may be called performers because, especially when urged or directed to do so, they can and do meet standards.

4. *Contributors (models)*. Contributors are people who, without being asked, engage in behavior that is related to both productivity and quality of life. These self-starters need little supervision. Contributors (a) quickly develop an understanding of the

goals and priorities of the group, (b) have or quickly develop the skills needed to pursue these goals, and (c) act on their own initiative. In a counselor training program, I spell out clearly what a contributor looks like and then point out that in order to move to the second phase of the training program, the trainee has to manifest consistent contributor behavior. When a trainee wants to move on to the second phase, I ask, "Are you a consistent contributor in your training group?" If the answer is "No, but," I reiterate my belief that human-service providers need to be assertive. A "participant" approach to helping is not enough. Contributors by definition are models. Their performance exceeds standards.

5. *Leaders (exemplars)*. These two highly positive terms have different connotations. Exemplars are leaders who *set* standards. As Gilbert (1978) notes, they work smarter, not harder. Exemplars exude *competence*, which is an upbeat rational term that can be described and charted. Leaders demonstrate *spirit*, which is an upbeat arational term. Spirit, while immediately understandable, is not as easily described and charted.

Leaders are contributors who help the organization, institution, community, or group increase its productivity and improve its quality of life. They provide new direction, help the system reconceptualize its mission, identify more effective programs, and discover new resources. Leaders in the sense described here may or may not hold managerial positions. Often they are not managers, but they embody system-enhancing forms of arationality.

Leaders are the "champions" of the system, according to Peters and Waterman (1982). Excercising a great deal of autonomy and working through the informal rather than the formal system, they serve many functions. They are the system-enhancing dreamers, mavericks, "wild ducks" (an Ibsen term), innovators, exemplars, intrapreneurs, gadflies, searchers, risk-takers, pioneers, heroes/heroines, or "movers." Without being fanatics, they are possessed by the mission of the organization or institution; they have "spirit." They move beyond competence to commitment. They create and move beyond creativity to innovation by helping the system translate good ideas into action. In human-service settings, leaders have passionate interest in the needs of the client and the quality of services delivered. Like contributors, they are competent in the delivery of human services, but they are never satisfied because they always believe they could do better. They challenge themselves and, directly or indirectly, they challenge others and the system.

Charles Garfield, psychologist and president of the Peak Performance Center in Berkeley, California, has identified ten patterns of behavior that are characteristic of peak performers or exemplars:

- They have a purpose in life. A person with a cause moves more quickly and persistently to goal-related action.
- They formulate plans and accomplish their goals, instead of letting life just happen.
- They don't let themselves get trapped in a comfortable "plateau" very long.
- They take risks, but they first determine, as best they can, the consequences of the risks.

- They base their self-confidence on the history of past successes that were due in large part to their skills and persistence.
- They would rather solve problems than place blame.
- They rehearse future events mentally—always with a positive outcome.
- They like to take control. If there is a leadership vacuum, they move in.
- They are concerned with quality performance, not just quantity.
- They train and utilize those around them.

Garfield points out that these are not obscure traits but skilled patterns of behavior in which people can be trained.

Peters and Waterman suggest that leaders or "champions" will emerge under certain conditions. Leaders need to be supported. If their behavior seems deviant, it should be tolerated or ignored. The system must tolerate or even encourage failures—not the kinds of failures detractors and observers are involved in, but failures indicating that mission-oriented, system-enhancing risks are being taken.

These five categories—detractor (laggard), observer (player), participant (performer), contributor (model), and leader (exemplar)—emphasize persistent *patterns* of behavior. No one is 100 percent consistent. Anyone, even an exemplar or a leader, can at times be an observer or even a detractor. After patterns of competence and incompetence have been identified, the following questions should be asked: Are the patterns of behavior we would like to minimize or eliminate (detractors, laggards) spawned by the system itself and perhaps even rewarded? Are people performing below standard (observers, players) being challenged and encouraged? Does our system reward mediocrity? Does the system provide development programs to help those who meet standards (participants, performers) develop further competency and initiative? Who are our contributors and models and how well do we support them? Does our organizational culture support exemplars and leaders? What dimensions of our culture militate against the development and emergence of exemplars and leaders?

9

Roles and Relationships

Mental health centers, schools, university counseling centers, correctional facilities, neighborhoods, self-help groups, psychiatric hospitals, church communities, classrooms, peer groups, families, boys clubs, neighborhood organizations, hospitals, and day-care centers are social systems. The members of these systems exchange a variety of services. *Structure* refers to their roles, relationships, responsibilities, communication processes, and leadership and coordination mechanisms.

ROLES AND RESPONSIBILITIES

In complex organizations, each unit has its mission, major aims, goals, and programs. Programs involve a variety of *tasks*, which represent the work of the system. In a counseling session both counselor and client have tasks to do if the client is to manage the problem situations of life more effectively. Clients tell their stories, choose problem areas for special consideration, respond to probes from helpers, make decisions, set goals, develop action programs, and implement these programs. Counselors provide structure, listen, respond with empathy, probe, and challenge as they move with clients through the counseling process. Roles, considered from one perspective, involve the *group of tasks* that any individual must do in order to accomplish goals. Figure 9-1 adds roles and responsibilities to Model A.

Seen from a different perspective, a role is a set of *expectations* that you have of yourself or that others have of you as to how you will behave or perform. People teaching in a counseling psychology program at a university may be expected to teach, do research, counsel in the Center for Student Development, and serve on both departmental and university committees. Each of these roles encompasses a group of goal-related tasks.

II. THE HUMAN RESOURCES OF THE SYSTEM

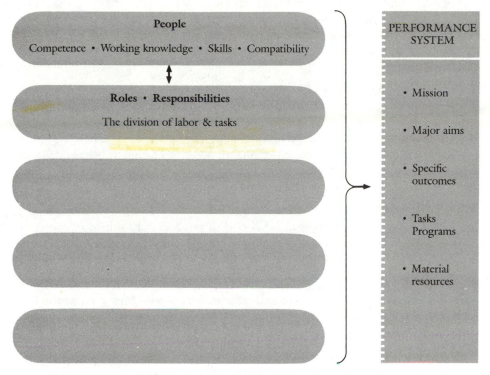

People

Competence • Working knowledge • Skills • Compatibility

Roles • Responsibilities

The division of labor & tasks

PERFORMANCE SYSTEM

• Mission

• Major aims

• Specific outcomes

• Tasks Programs

• Material resources

FIGURE 9-1.   Roles and responsibilities indicate how the work or tasks of the system are divided.

Role and style

Often the way in which a role is exercised affects both productivity and quality of life. A counselor may exercise his or her role in such an authoritarian way that the client rebels against the whole helping process (a loss of productivity) or feels uncomfortable in the counseling sessions (poor quality of life). Fuehrer and Keys (1978) describe how changing the way in which a role is exercised can help both providers and clients.

In the courtrooms of Cook County, Illinois, deputy sheriffs have the task of maintaining order and supervising prisoners and jurors. The deputies studied valued three things: (1) a good public image, (2) the ability to take decisive action in a crisis, and (3) masculine toughness. Sometimes the third value interfered with the first.

An interpersonal skills training program was conducted in which flexibility in managing courtroom situations, listening skills, the recognition of one's own emotions and those of others, feedback, and teamwork were stressed. The deputies learned that they had to concentrate more on the needs of others and become less aggressive and dominant if they were to respond effectively to emotional situations.

After the workshop the participants rated themselves and the ideal deputy lower than they had before in masculine toughness. It was still important, but they had learned that it could make them less effective in carrying out their tasks.

Emotions and other arational factors such as caring and commitment can pervade roles and greatly affect the way they are exercised. In human-service settings, style can be as important as the role itself.

Style can be considered also in terms of role-appropriate behavior. Human-service providers are tempted at times, for personal reasons, to engage in behavior that is inappropriate to the role. Some may be tempted to become sexually involved with their clients. Shellow (1965) describes a case in which role-appropriate behavior was extremely important.

> Consultants from a community field station of the National Institute of Mental Health were asked to help the civil disturbance unit of a county's police force prepare themselves psychologically for the huge civil rights march on Washington in the summer of 1963. Few of the officers felt that blacks had legitimate grievances and there was a small group of confirmed segregationists. The consultants had only six hours in which to work with the unit. They concentrated their efforts, not on changing attitudes and prejudices, but on role-appropriate behavior. It was pointed out that times of crisis, confusion, and lack of structure gave police an opportunity to resolve issues in a non-violent manner because they were seen as visible authority. The consultants encouraged strong identification with the civil disturbance unit as a way of resolving the conflict between group norms and personal prejudices in favor of group norms.
>
> There were no incidents during the rights march. Later in the year when some members of the Congress of Racial Equality (CORE) picketed two housing projects, the police unit acted so professionally that an official of CORE wrote a letter of appreciation to the police department.

In this case the consultants were wise in foregoing the luxury of trying to change deep-seated attitudes.

Role clarity

A clear statement of the roles a person is to play and tasks he or she is to perform is called a *job description*. Kellog and Burstiner (1979) suggest that the following elements should be included in a job description:

1. Mission or purpose of the employee's job in broad terms.
2. A list of specific responsibilities.
3. Reservations of authority (such as committing the organization's funds or completing contractual arrangements with outside organizations).
4. Description of working relationships with other positions.
5. Specific objective measures or standards for the work.
6. The assets, contacts, and specialized experience this individual brings to the

job and is expected to maintain and develop. These represent the individual's personal investment in the organization.

7. The salary range of the position and the way in which both the individual and organization accomplishment will be judged in determining it.
8. A statement of personal liability in the event of individual or organizational failure, including the effect on salary, employment, and probable future allocation of human and physical resources (p. 86).

Often one or more of these elements are left out of the job description. When systems fail to provide even rudimentary job descriptions, individuals and units are not sure what is expected of them. Consider the case of the following individual.

> A mental health center was glad to accept volunteers but made little effort to coordinate their work. Mrs. Cowan, a volunteer, found herself at times overwhelmed by requests for help and at other times searching for something to do. The tasks varied from trivial to traumatic. At one moment she delivered messages or made coffee for staff members, and at the next she comforted the mother of a boy who had been arrested for shoplifting. At times Mrs. Cowan felt exhilarated by the work, but at other times she became depressed. Her requests for more structure and direction proved futile. She finally left, a bit disillusioned about the role of the volunteer.

This woman was a victim of a poorly organized service center. Being socialized into the system meant being socialized into its disorder. Part of the socialization process should include clarity of role expectations. The opposite of role clarity is *role ambiguity*, which is the lack of information needed to understand and carry out the tasks of a position in an organization or institution.

A correlative to job description is *person specification*. While a job description indicates the tasks to be undertaken and the accomplishments that will be expected, person specification outlines the abilities and qualities needed by the individual who is to fulfill a particular role. For instance, the person-specification demands for a counselor working in a suburban high school may be quite different from those for a counselor doing street work in the inner city. The person-specification demands for someone who will work with a team differ from those for a person who is to work alone. The issue here is job *compatibility*.

Role conflict

Role conflict occurs when an individual is identified with two or more individuals or groups that have different and incompatible objectives and values (Dessler, 1976). Expectations do not coincide. For instance, I was hired once to teach one semester in an overseas program of an American university. When I arrived there the tasks outlined went, in my estimation, beyond the tasks discussed with me during contract negotiations. For instance, I found out that I was expected to listen to student tapes and evaluate long papers as part of a comprehensive examination system. Had I known that such tasks were to be part of the job, I would have had second thoughts about accepting the position.

A person can experience role conflict when two or more people to whom he or she relates have different expectations of him or her. For instance, a nurse at times has to choose between the authority of her supervisor and the authority of the doctor. This uncertainty can lead to stress, dissatisfaction, and lower productivity. Zawacki (1963) found that role conflict results from the dual hierarchy of hospitals. Those affected respond with hostility to physicians and with passive resistance to formal rules.

A high school teacher relates to both students and parents, whose goals and values conflict at times. Students are looking for greater freedom, while parents are looking for greater supervision and control. A high school counselor has to deal with student needs, which may differ from the expectations of parents, teachers, and administrators.

Role overload, too, can be a source of conflict. A high school principal deals with the expectations of students, parents, teachers, staff, coaches, alumni, district school officials, and community leaders, not to mention groups and individuals in his or her private life. J.M., a high school principal and a member of a religious order, did a simple exercise to illustrate role conflict and overload. He put his initials in the center of a sheet of paper and then drew spokes from the center to individuals or groups who had expectations of him either at work or outside (Figure 9-2). Then he listed the main expectations each person or group had of him. Finally, he was able to point out the main role conflicts he was experiencing. At the end of the task he said, "Now I know why I feel frustrated. First of all, there are too many expectations. And second, I'm constantly struggling with conflicting expectations." This exercise did not solve his problems, but it helped him see them more clearly. Research (Fisher and Gitelson, 1983) shows that both role conflict and role ambiguity can lead to such negative effects as lack of commitment and involvement and dissatisfaction with co-workers, pay, and supervision.

Flexibility in roles

People can get locked into a single role or set of roles even when the organization would benefit from greater flexibility. At the opposite extreme, Vaill (1980) points out, people often play multiple roles even though they have not been assigned these roles explicitly. And these are not the only forms of arationality related to roles.

Premature roles. People often play roles they are not prepared for. For instance, clinical psychology interns often act as therapists before they are ready. Couples have children without being ready for the role of parents.

Loose boundaries. People perform functions outside the stated boundaries of their role. Aides in psychiatric hospitals engage in functions such as listening to patients' problems and giving advice, functions formally relegated to counselors and psychotherapists.

Role creation. People get involved in activities for which no role definition exists. Staff members in a mental health clinic may become internal consultants even though there is no formal role of internal consultant in the system.

Assumption of authority. Sometimes flexibility means that the members of a system have to risk taking more responsibility than they have authority for.

> The opportunity to accept more responsibility than matching authority has always existed, but in the modern organization increasingly *the work will not get done* if one is not willing to function with less clear authority than one might like [Vaill, 1980, p. 26].

This "work-not-done" may well be work on which the very survival of the systems depends. At legal risk, nurses perform services that are supposed to be performed only by doctors. Hannafin and Witt (1983) enter a plea for an expanded role for school psychologists. They catalogue the kinds of system failures that plague schools because of "work-not-done" and suggest that system-level interventions (SLI) are a natural complement to their individual-level interventions with students and staff. Their research shows that many school psychologists would like to move beyond traditional tester-diagnostician and counselor-therapist roles.

Vaill claims that the best people in organizations, institutions, and communities are role-creative, that is, "endlessly intrigued, challenged, and amused to explore the mutuality, the interplay, and the evolution of self and role" (p. 26). The danger that role creativity might lead to role-inappropriate behavior is one of the tensions

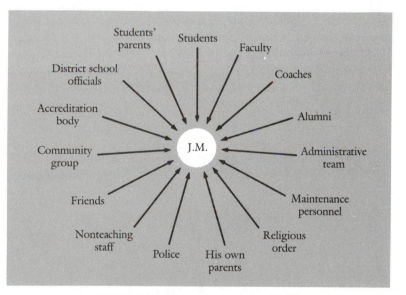

FIGURE 9-2.   Sources of role conflict

in the life of the role-creative person. At its best, role flexibility is another instance of the fact that informal dimensions of a system can be both individual- and system-enhancing. The arational ideal—informal role flexibility—differs from the rational ideal, formally defined roles that are clear and precise.

Reconceptualizing roles.   With imagination, roles can be made more flexible in human-service settings. In Figure 9-3, the two roles found in the classroom can be broken down into subroles for both teacher and student. Under *teacher* students tend to write such labels as *coordinator, appraiser,* and *disciplinarian.* Under *student* there is the traditional role of *learner.* I ask my students to suggest some more creative and even some "wild" roles in this exercise. The results usually challenge the ways classrooms are ordinarily structured.

One student in an organizational development course put *convener* under *student.* He said, "Usually teachers are the only ones allowed to convene the class. However, this class deals with quality of work life and I am the quality-of-work-life director for my district. Therefore, there seems to be no reason why I could not 'convene' the group or part of it around my experience and expertise." No reason in the world. In reconceptualizing the roles within an organization or institution, imagination can be a system- and individual-enhancing form of arationality.

Unit roles

In larger and more complex systems, various units, or groups of individuals, have roles to play. As indicated in Figure 9-4, the Rape Crisis Center has four major aims—direct service to and support of rape victims, preventive educational services for women, consciousness-raising activities in the community, and advocacy activities with police and legal system. These four areas constitute the major roles of the center. Each role entails a number of programs. Like individuals, organizational units can experience role ambiguity, role conflict, and role overload. On the other hand, the members of effective organizational units engage in role creativity related to satisfying the needs of clients and of the other units in the system.

RELATIONSHIPS

Organizations and institutions of any size develop different kinds of cooperative and collaborative relationships between individuals and groups in order to implement the programs of the system. Cooperation involves a sharing of the work, while collaboration involves a sharing of power or authority. Roles deal with the division of goal-related tasks; relationships are concerned with the integration of

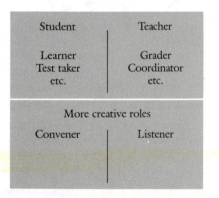

Student	Teacher
Learner	Grader
Test taker	Coordinator
etc.	etc.
More creative roles	
Convener	Listener

FIGURE 9-3. Role reconceptualization exercise

FIGURE 9-4. The unit roles of a rape crisis center

these tasks. Human-service providers must deal with a number of different kinds of relationships:

- *Individual to individual*: Counselors collaborate with individual clients in helping them manage their problems in living.
- *Individual to group*: A social worker facilitates a social skills training group in a mental health center.
- *Individual to organization*: A school psychologist acts as an internal consultant to the principal and her team.
- *Group to individuals*: The pastoral care department of a large hospital serves the needs of staff, including doctors and nurses, patients, and the relatives and friends of patients.
- *Group to group*: The nursing unit of a psychiatric hospital collaborates with the milieu therapy unit in the care and rehabilitation of patients.
- *Group to organization*: The organization–development group of a large mental health center helps the center reconceptualize its mission and major aims.

Figure 9-5 adds individual and unit relationships to Model A.

Relationship clarity

Each person (or unit) that must accomplish goals through cooperation or collaboration with another person (or unit) needs a clear understanding of the division of responsibility. The important questions are: To whom must I (we) relate in order to do the work of the system? In what ways must I (we) cooperate/collaborate with other individuals or other units in order to do the work? How is our work to be coordinated? When expectations between individual and individual, between individual and unit, or between unit and unit with respect to the integration of work do not coincide, relationship conflict results. Structure must include more than roles, responsibilities, and relationships. It must also include the authority and decision-making power needed to coordinate and integrate roles and relationships. (Leadership and coordination are discussed in Chapter 11.)

The "resource collaborator" role

Tyler, Pargament, and Gatz (1983) review the paradox associated with helping and human-service relationships, which tend to be *unidirectional*: "Within the context

II. THE HUMAN RESOURCES OF THE SYSTEM

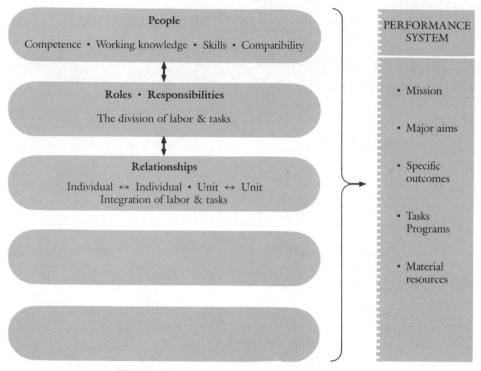

FIGURE 9-5. Individual and unit relationships

of consultative relationships, that paradox involves the incongruity between the consultant's presentation of self as expert and the consultant's goal of establishing a collaborative relationship with the 'consultee' " (p. 388) and, one might add, with the goal of helping clients become functional, competent, and independent. Rappaport (1981) criticizes the unidirectional, professional-expert model and opts for an empowerment model. But, he notes, "empowerment suggests collaborators" (p. 24), in that to empower clients is to help them develop the resources they need to manage their lives effectively. The resource-collaborator model

> makes the assumption that both parties are "origins." That is, both are the central active agents and experts in organizing, conducting, and evaluating their own lives. Both parties have equal status in defining the terms of their own reality, and each has unique perspective to offer the other. . . . The professional may have special skills and expertise with regard to some of the client's concerns. The client may have expertise with regard to his or her other concerns and also with regard to some of the professional's perspectives and world view. In fact, professionals may be unable to bring their perspectives to bear until they understand their clients' perspectives.

> The new learning by a professional may be quite substantial. If the client is a community, the new learning may involve gaining an understanding of how a unique

community functions. . . . In short, both the professional and the client have resources and limits that must be understood and respected [p. 391].

For some human-service providers, the notion that they are enriched and "empowered" by the client might well be countercultural. The best providers are learners, and their clients—whether individuals or systems—are the sources of some of their richest learnings. For many, "I learn from my clients" is not just a cliché. But is this learning the same as seeing clients as sources of empowerment? The resource-collaborator model challenges human-service providers to ask themselves just how democratic they think the helping process is and just how democratic they want it to be.

The "pinch-crunch" model

Sherwood and Glidewell (1973) have developed a model for identifying what goes wrong in relationships and identifying both helpful and unhelpful strategies for handling disruptions. What follows is an adaptation of their model.

The initial contract.   Ideally, in the beginning of a relationship the parties share all information that is pertinent to the functioning of the relationship, negotiate mutual expectations, and then formalize this mutual decision-making process in a contract, whether written or verbal. This interaction leads to role clarity and mutual commitment. The relationship may be between two people about to get married, between the director of a mental health clinic and the staff members, between a nurse working on a unit and the doctors or nursing supervisors, or between inter-relating units. The parties in the relationship could say something like this: "In terms of the variables that constitute and affect our relationships such as goal setting, program development, lines of authority, division of labor, division of resources, and the like, we know what the other group expects of us and they know what we expect of them. Our contract is clear and above board." *The rational theory is that mutually agreed on expectations lead to role clarity and to stability in the relationship.*

O'Neill and Trickett (1982) take exception to this rational ideal in their discussion of consultants negotiating relationships with clients in community settings:

> Our approach to these issues differs significantly from earlier theories of consultation. The difference can be drawn sharply by contrasting our view with the influential model of psychiatrist Gerald Caplan (1964, 1970). He tells consultants to negotiate formal contracts with specific people, to be responsible only to those people, and to quit when faced with a clash of values. In our view, obtaining formal contracts is sometimes impossible or even undesirable, the consultant's responsibilities are always ambiguous, and value clashes are hard to recognize in the entry phase [p. 105].

They adopt what might be called an "emergent" view of relationships. Relationships develop over time, often in unpredictable ways.

The arational contract.   Because of the arationality of both people and systems, no relationship is ideal. It is impossible to gather and share all the information that might be relevant to the expressed or implied contract. Even when the contract is above board, the parties tend to have somewhat different interpretations of its provisions from the very beginning, and these differences, of course, are not shared. The parties may even mentally make exceptions to the stated contract, little "side contracts" with themselves. A nurse might say, "Of course, I'll abide by the doctor's orders (unless they seriously interfere with the well-being of the patient)."

The parties change over time, often in unpredictable ways. Feelings change, tastes change, interests change, values change, commitments change. A relationship does not exist in a vacuum but in an ever-changing environment. Changes in the environment put pressure for change on the relationship. When a downturn in the economy affects the private practice of a group of psychologists, for example, tensions in their relationships to one another begin to mount. The parties to contracts often develop blind spots. They don't notice or they refuse to notice the changes that are affecting the relationship. These factors are even more likely to cause trouble if *periodic planned renegotiation* is not part of the original contract. In most contracts it is not. Of course, over the course of time, sometimes without even noticing it, the parties reinterpret the contract to suit their own changing needs, but the reinterpretations on the part of one party are not communicated to the other party. These private reinterpretations do not take the place of planned renegotiation.

Entropic pinches.   When entropy sets in, almost inevitably one or both parties experience "pinches"—that is, relatively modest and manageable disruptions of the shared expectations that formed the basis of the original contract. A licensed psychologist and a psychiatrist establish a private practice in a large midwestern city "as equals." Over the first few months, the psychologist notices that the psychiatrist makes some unilateral decisions in relatively small matters. But she says nothing. The psychiatrist has some reservations about the way the psychologist is handling a couple of cases. She, too, says nothing. While the pinches they both experience may be unsettling, they are normal and need not disrupt the relationship. Ideally, pinches are opportunities for reassessment of the relationship and for planned renegotiation of the contract.

Pinches constitute opportunities in relationships. There are many reasons why parties in a relationship fail to take the opportunity offered by pinches to address the changes in the relationship:

- *Avoidance*. Since dealing directly with pinches is emotionally demanding, many people put it off. Both parties feel pinches, but there is a silent conspiracy not to discuss them—which is easy since everyone is busy.
- *Lack of skills*. People often lack both the assertiveness and the communication skills needed to deal with pinches constructively. They may want to but at the same time feel unable to.
- *Fear of feeling foolish*. There is the tendency to say, "Maybe it's just me. And after all, it's really just a small thing. I may appear rather petty if I make an issue out of this. I'll wait until there is something more substantial to discuss."
- *Fear of renegotiation*. Sometimes present ills are seen as more endurable than the unseen ills that might come from renegotiation. What many people fear

most is that renegotiation will lead to the death—or worse, the living death—of a relationship. And so renegotiation is judged, however subconsciously, to be too risky.
- *Ignorance of the cumulative effect of pinches.* People do not see where unmanaged pinches are leading. They try to ignore the resentment and anger that are building up inside.
- *Uncreative approaches to handling pinches.* "I'm too proud to make something out of nothing, but at the same time I'm going to be a little less cooperative with him from now on." People often deal with pinches in resentful ways.

The crunch.   Pinches that are not handled lead to two kinds of crunches. The first, *explosion,* refers to open and often highly emotional crises caused by ongoing and unmanaged disruption of shared expectations. The dam breaks and the pent-up resentment and anger comes pouring out in less than useful ways. In the psychiatric hospital, nursing blows up at admissions. In their private practice, the psychiatrist and the psychologist explode at each other. In a marriage, spouse blows up at spouse. They could overlook the pinches, but they are not free to overlook the crunch.

The second, *implosion,* refers to serious conflicts that are not shared openly. Emotions are turned inward. "I'll get even with him in my own time and in my own way." "I've had it with her; from now on she'll get my minimum cooperation, and that's it." "I'll keep my creative ideas to myself, develop them, and then take them with me when I move on, which won't be long."

Since emotions are not only high but also visible in the explosive crunch, people are not in the best frame of mind to handle the crisis—but handle it they must, however unconstructively. Here are some ways in which crunches are handled:

Resentful termination. One possible way of handling a crunch or a series of crunches is an angry and resentful termination of the relationship. In this case one or both parties feel that things have gone too far, that the disintegration of the relationship is irreversible. In marriage this would mean separation or divorce. In the workplace one or more persons would quit: "I can't work with him [them] anymore" or "I've had it; this is a lousy place to work." Resentful termination is not so much a solution as a decision not to seek a solution.

Smoothing things over. Another inadequate approach to handling crunches is merely to try to smooth things over after emotions have settled down. This conspiratorial approach is very common. The parties apologize, they agree to let bygones be bygones, *but* they do not deal with the underlying issues that are causing the trouble. They set themselves up for another crunch.

Forced renegotiation. A third way of handling a crunch is to face the issues that divide the parties. Because emotions still run high, forced renegotiation is much more difficult than planned renegotiation. At this stage a mediator is often needed. In marriage, it may be a marriage counselor; in the workplace, it may be an arbitrator or negotiator. Like planned renegotiation, forced renegotiation might lead to a decision to terminate the relationship. Often fear of termination pushes the parties into the "smoothing things over" conspiracy.

Letting the relationship die. Relationships can die without being dissolved. Perhaps all of us know of marriages that have died without dissolving. It is possible to handle implosive crunches by letting the relationship die little by little. At first the spark disappears; eventually people are caught in painful, lifeless relationships both at home and at work. Implosion is more likely to take place in relationships that must continue to exist—for instance, the relationship between admissions and nursing in the hospital, between the husband and wife who do not believe in divorce, or between parent and child.

Managing conflicts

People or groups in important relationships not only need to have a good working understanding of the relationship and the expressed or implied contract from the very beginning, but they also need to establish times for review and renegotiation. It helps if people understand that entropic processes are normal and are not a sign of ill will. People can develop the assertiveness and communication skills to deal with pinches when they see renegotiation as normal rather than exceptional, and understand that renegotiation does not necessarily destroy stability in a relationship. Renegotiation that leads to termination—for instance, the psychologist and the psychiatrist decide to terminate their practice together, or a nurse transfers to a different unit in the psychiatric hospital—is not necessarily a sign of failure. It may simply be a willingness to face interpersonal or intergroup realities.

INDIVIDUAL PERFORMANCE PLANS

The purpose of the unit plan, such as the training plan of a large mental health center discussed in Chapter 7, is to review areas in which performance or accomplishments are expected of the unit and *to establish priorities*. The individual performance plan helps each person in the unit to answer two questions: (1) "What am *I* expected to do in order to see to it that the unit performance plan is executed?" (2) "Against the background of all the tasks that constitute my role in the unit, what are *my* priorities this year?"

To develop the individual plan, the staff member needs a clear understanding of the unit plan and priorities and a clear idea of his or her roles and relationships (the job description). The steps in the plan are then quite similar to the steps in the unit plan in Chapter 7.

Step 1: Establish essential linkages.   It is essential to *link* the individual plan to the overall goals and priorities of the unit, just as the unit plan—in this case, the plan of the training unit—is linked to the overall mission, strategic plans, and major aims of the organization. In other words, the unit plan and priorities constitute the data base for individual plans.

Step 2: List all personal performance areas.   List all the tasks for which you, personally, are responsible either alone or in conjunction with others. Carmen, one of the members of the training unit, is responsible for

- Designing and participating in weekly training-staff feedback meetings
- Assessing the training needs of clients
- Designing some of the training programs for clients
- Preparing reports on client-trainees for other staff members who are working with the same clients
- Acting as a consultant to counselors in the center who are doing training as part of their work with clients
- Training clients in problem-management skills
- Reviewing training models in problem-management skills developed by other centers with a view to updating the center's model
- Reviewing the current literature on problem management and problem-management training programs
- Working on a team that prepares training material for publication
- Updating training skills

Notice that each of these performance areas will have its own goals and programs. For instance, Carmen knows what kinds of skills constitute the problem-management package and the step-by-step programs needed to equip clients with these skills.

Step 3: Identify key personal performance areas.   Key personal performance areas are those that deserve Carmen's specific attention during the coming year if she is to be a "contributor" to her unit. What areas are in decline and need refurbishing? What areas, if further developed, will help her become a more effective contributor? Usually no more than four or five areas will be designated as key. Carmen chose the following areas for special attention:

Designing and participating in weekly training-staff feedback meetings. She feels that these meetings could be more useful and that she could be more assertive in giving feedback and discussing her creative ideas.

Acting as a consultant to counselors who are doing training with clients. Many of the counselors are convinced that training should be part of the services they deliver to clients, but some of the counselors need help to integrate training into the counseling process.

Reviewing training models in problem-management skills developed by other centers with a view to updating the center's model. At a professional meeting, casual conversations led Carmen to believe that new creative approaches have been developed at other centers. She believes it is time to review the offerings of other centers systematically and incorporate useful innovations into her center's approach.

She chooses these priority areas because she believes they will contribute significantly to her own personal development, to the development of the center, and to the delivery of services to clients.

Step 4: Set priority individual objectives in each key performance area.   When key personal performance areas have been selected, one to three major performance *objectives* should be set in each area. These are the actual outcomes, the critical accomplishments in each key area. For instance, to review training models in problem-management skills developed by other centers, Carmen sets the following objectives:

- Mental health centers and universities having innovative problem-management training programs will be identified and their programs obtained.
- The major innovative dimensions of their programs will be organized and presented to the training staff for review.
- The most promising innovations will be incorporated in the problem-management training programs.

Step 5: Develop personal performance indicators.   To determine whether an objective has been wholly or partially realized by the individual, performance indicators must be clear enough to enable the individual, fellow staff members, and supervisors to reach a conclusion independently about full or partial fulfillment of each objective. *Interim* indicators are used throughout the year for ongoing feedback, and *final* indicators are used for year-end review. Carmen writes a schedule for her first performance area:

Interim indicators. By January 15 a survey asking about use of problem-management training programs will have been prepared and mailed to other centers and selected universities. By March 1 the organizations that reply affirmatively will be contacted and asked for copies of their programs. The organizations will be asked to highlight what they see as innovative in their programs.

Final indicators. By April 1 the programs of the organizations that reply will be assembled and ready for study. A preliminary list of the areas highlighted will have been prepared.

Carmen writes a schedule for each objective in each performance area. This process is summarized in Figure 9-6. This rational planning approach is meant to stimulate the members of the staff and help them provide direction for themselves. It is a flexible framework that can be altered to meet changes over the year. It should be tailored to the needs and style of each member so that it will not stifle creativity. The staff member and his or her supervisor have an agreed-upon document that spells out mutual expectations—a document that may be renegotiated. This document is essential if meaningful performance appraisals are to take place.

What is outlined here can serve as a guide for setting up a personal performance planning system. The final form of the system must reflect the needs of both the human-service organization and its staff.

TEAM BUILDING

One of the most popular forms of consultant and participant intervention in organizations is team building (Dyer, 1977)—even though the evidence that team building increases productivity is meager (DeMeuse and Liebowitz, 1981; Woodman and Sherwood, 1980). Perhaps it is popular because it enhances the quality of life among those working together as teams. Defined in terms of Model A, team building illustrates the interdependence between productivity and quality of life.

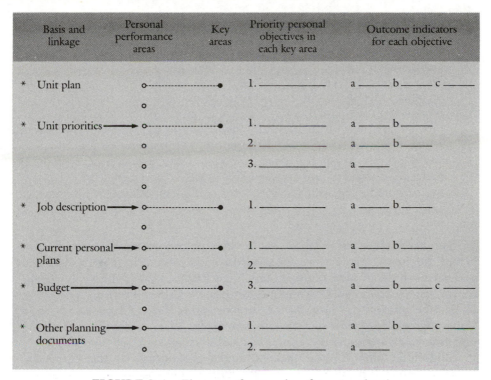

FIGURE 9-6.   Elements of personal performance planning

Teams or groups are constituted in order to accomplish goals that cannot be achieved through individual effort alone. A number of different teams may be at work in a large psychiatric hospital. The administrator of the hospital and some of the department heads constitute the administrative team. They work together to address the strategic issues and problems the hospital faces. A counseling group of eight clients co-led by two group counselors is another kind of "team" or group at work in the hospital.

The counseling group has a *mission* (helping the members manage the problem situations of their lives more effectively), *goals* (outcomes chosen by each member of the group), and *programs* (group and individual activities that lead to the accomplishment of these goals). These individuals use team building to mold themselves into a cohesive work group *at the service of mission and goals.* Team building involves clarification:

- *Tasks, roles, and responsibilities.* What is the work of the counseling group and how is it to be divided up?
- *Relationships.* How will members of the group relate to one another? What kinds of cooperative effort are needed if the group is to be successful?
- *Communication.* What kinds of communication will they engage in and how will conflicts be handled? What kind of information sharing, feedback, and appraisal are needed to accomplish goals?

- *The leadership process.* What are the roles of the formal leaders of the group? How do the members of the group participate in the leadership process? What needs to be done in terms of standards, rules, and regulations to assure quality outcomes?
- *Quality of group life.* Do the members treat one another with respect? Are the members friendly to one another? Are they learning to trust one another more and more? Have they devised reasonable procedures for handling conflict and are these procedures being used? Do the people with power use it at the service of group goals? If manipulation takes place, is it challenged? Are the rights of members being respected? Is cohesiveness developing? If there are "outsiders," how are they being helped to develop a sense of belonging? Is emotional expression encouraged? Is emotional self-indulgence challenged?

Group development or team building molds the "people" variables of Model A so that they serve the "performance" needs of the system. If the group is not productive—if the members of the counseling group do not learn how to manage their lives more effectively—then morale or quality of life will suffer.

Since the mission of human-service organizations and institutions is to help clients improve the quality of their lives, the quality of life within human-service systems themselves should reflect this mission. A nursing home with unhappy workers will do little to improve the quality of life of its residents. On the other hand, a hospice with staff members who are committed to its mission and belong to a caring and enthusiastic team will do a great deal to improve the quality of life of the terminally ill. As human-service providers learn to improve the quality of life of their own organizations and the helping relationship itself, they become better prepared to be both helpers to individuals and quality-of-life consultants to systems.

10

Communication

Communication breathes life into relationships in organizations, institutions, and communities. The exchange of messages between individuals and units creates common understandings. Figure 10-1 adds this element to Model A.

A staff member in a mental health clinic, for instance, tells the director she is so overloaded with cases that she is not able to provide quality services to her clients. If the message gets through, she and the director have a common understanding that relates to the functioning of the clinic. Communication need not be verbal. Sometimes the way a staff member looks during meetings gives the director a cue that something is wrong. Or a wife's glance to her husband at a party tells him she would like to go home. Figure 10-2 indicates the need for common understandings between people in a psychiatric hospital. Units also need common understandings in order to operate effectively (Figure 10-3).

Since human-service providers deal daily with clients with communication problems, they could become consultants to organizations, institutions, and communities troubled with ineffective communication and incapacitated by communication breakdowns.

Communication involves (1) sharing goal-related information and (2) providing feedback. Information sharing provides systems members with the working knowledge they need to pursue goals. Confirmatory and corrective feedback keeps the members of the system on their accomplishment-directed course. The quality of the communication is important. Gilbert (1978) stresses clear goals and the importance of data that is clear, accurate, and timely.

Improved information has more potential than anything else I can think of for creating more competence in the day-to-day management of performance. But, as the behavior engineering model . . . points out, we can improve information in two general ways:

II. THE HUMAN RESOURCES OF THE SYSTEM

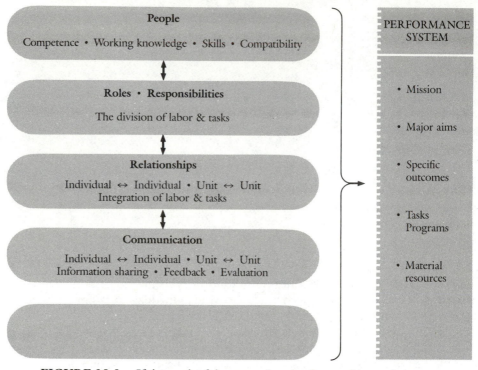

FIGURE 10-1.   If the work of the system is to be done and its goals accomplished, people need to exchange the kind of *information* that is needed to make decisions and provide direction. People also need *feedback*, both confirmatory and corrective, to keep them on course.

1. We can improve the clarity, relevance, and timeliness of the data designed to inform people.
2. We can improve people's ability to use the existing data.

Training is an attempt to create a permanent change in people's repertoires—most often, in their ability to process difficult data. As an alternative, we can work on the *data*—to try to make them simpler and clearer, thus easier to understand without extensive training. . . . [I]n my experience, one stratagem tends to pay off more often—and pay off dramatically: to improve the data designed to support performance [p. 175].

Data in the form of information that system members can easily translate into working knowledge—that is the ideal. Poor communication is one of the major sources of ineffectiveness and inefficiency in organizations and institutions.

A therapist in a VA hospital felt that he had been making progress with a marine who had been wounded in the Middle East. The marine's depression was beginning to abate and some meaningful discussions about his

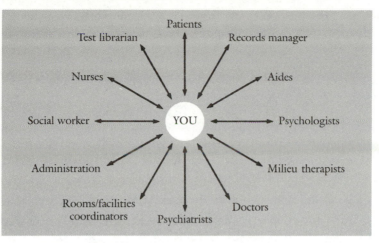

FIGURE 10-2.   Communication in a psychiatric hospital

future had taken place. Then the marine missed a therapy session. When he finally came, he seemed listless and uncommunicative. After some investigation, the therapist discovered that the marine's younger brother had been shot and wounded in a tavern, and the marine himself was about to undergo surgery. Neither the social service department nor the medical department had communicated this information so that the therapist could help the marine manage the crisis.

Communication in a system can be about any element in Model A:

• *Needs assessment*. "Half the residents in this district need some kind of psychological or social aid."

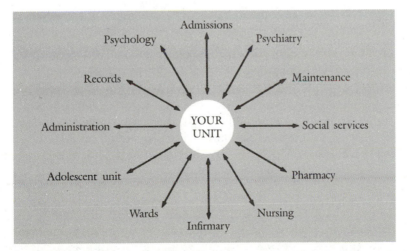

FIGURE 10-3.   Communication among units in a psychiatric hospital

- *Mission.* "The mission of this mental health center is too narrow. It is time to broaden the mission to include preventive services."
- *Goals.* "In this training group I am learning about empathy, but I'm not learning how to convey it."
- *Programs.* "He has come up with an excellent four-step method for teaching staff members how to set personal goals."
- *Nonpeople resources.* "The rooms we use for counseling are so dingy and depressing that we start with one count against us."
- *People resources.* "He is competent both as a counselor and as a manager."
- *Roles and responsibilities.* "I have been assigned the responsibility for scheduling patients in the outpatient clinic."

Examples dealing with the other elements of Model A could be added to this list. Of course, each information-sharing incident may deal with more than one element of Model A. Trainees in a counseling program might say to their instructor, "During any given group session we are not sure precisely what we are supposed to learn. And then we feel demoralized because it seems we are getting nowhere." The issues here are goal clarity and quality of life. Model A provides a framework for understanding and analyzing the communication that takes place in a system.

EFFECTIVE INFORMATION SHARING

Information can either serve or stand in the way of the purposes of the organization, institution, or community. Important information variables are relevancy, clarity, accuracy, quantity, availability, and timeliness.

Relevancy. People need information in order to make decisions. Often workers receive too much or too little information. Or they do not receive the information they need in order to make a decision, but they receive too much irrelevant information.

As an intern at a state psychiatric hospital, I participated in staffing meetings. When it was my turn to speak, I read the results of an extensive battery of tests I had given the patient together with my interpretations. It was quite a ritual. Heads were bowed during the "reading," there were a few moments of silence at the end, and then the ceremony continued. In retrospect, I have grave doubts about the relevancy of my report (and often those of others) to the actual treatment of the patient. People need information that is immediately pertinent to decision making, and enough *contextual* information to understand a patient or the work of a unit in relationship to the other units and to the system as a whole.

Clarity. Needed information should be clear. Too often senders and receivers pass and receive information that seems ambiguous to them without asking for clarification. Clients, who often do not understand what their helpers say, rarely take the initiative to clarify the message.

Accuracy. An inaccurate message may be worse than an ambiguous message. For instance, a woman opposed to contraceptive devices on religious grounds was taught the "rhythm" method and became pregnant.

Quantity. Sometimes the conscientious communicator tries to convey too much information. "Lean" organizations are called lean, in part, because they control the quantity of irrelevant information flowing through the system. Ten-page memos are distilled into one-page memos. In psychiatric hospitals, in-take personnel, psychiatrists, psychologists, social workers, nurses, and various other specialists all collect information on patients. Staffing sessions become problematic because of the amount of information available. Sheer quantity can obscure relevancy.

Availability. Relevant information should flow easily wherever it is needed in the organization—up, down, sideways, between persons, between units, between producing system and receiving system, and between the system and its environment. Unfortunately, information is a source of power and therefore one of the key tools in the political games that are played in organizations, institutions, and communities. People often hoard information and share it only when it serves their individual purposes rather than the common good of the system.

If relevant information is to be shared freely, there must be *incentives* to do so.

> The aides in a psychiatric hospital were asked to engage in a behavior modification program on one of the units. They were asked to do extensive observation of patients and fill out lengthy forms. A few weeks into the project the researchers complained to the nursing supervisor that the aides were failing to turn in the reports or doing sloppy work. A consultant who happened to be working in the same area of the hospital pointed out that there were practically no incentives for the aides to gather and share the information accurately. They saw it as added unnecessary work.

People should understand that freely sharing relevant information raises the probability that they, too, will receive the information they need to do their work. But even when incentives are provided and sharing information is rewarded, the tension between self-interest and the common good still remains.

Timeliness. All of us have received notices asking us to attend events that have already taken place. Sometimes timeliness means that information should be shared as quickly as possible. But if information is shared too soon, it may be lost or forgotten. Information should be shared when it is most likely to make the kind of impact desired by the sender.

PERFORMANCE APPRAISAL

Effective communication in organizations, institutions, and communities includes feedback and evaluation. Ideally, evaluation deals with performance—that is, goal accomplishment—in terms of both productivity and quality of life. As indicated in Figure 10-4, there are three important meetings in the performance appraisal process. The kind of communication that takes place in each is critical.

Performance planning

Much of the value of planning and setting priorities lies in the kind of communication it promotes among both individuals and organizational units. At the planning stage, discussions clarify *direction*—that is, outcomes, standards, and relationships.

Outcomes. Planning should provide clear information about what needs to be

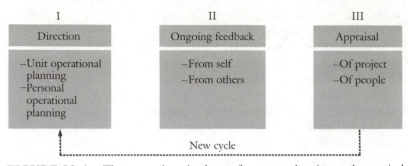

FIGURE 10-4.   Three meetings in the performance planning and appraisal process

accomplished. Goals, subgoals, results, outcomes, objectives, tasks, and responsi-bilities can be made clear. For instance, instead of telling a teenager to "do some work around the house after school," the parent tells her or him to shovel snow or clean the bathroom.

If the goals and the objectives of the system are not clear, clear communication about them is impossible. Therefore, good communication starts with clarity in goal setting and program development. Without this kind of clarity, it is impossible to give feedback and engage in meaningful evaluation. If goals are not clear at the beginning of the project, but are expected to "emerge" as the project moves forward, then at least the emergent nature of the project should be clear. Once goals begin to emerge, they should be discussed by relevant parties or stakeholders. In a grad-uate training institute, for example, the director and staff of the program, the dean of special graduate programs and institutes, the director of the institute, and the students are all stakeholders.

Standards. The criteria by which results are to be evaluated also need to be clear. The worker who is expected to "do a good job" must know what a "good job" means. A good job of shoveling snow may mean that the snow is to be removed from all the walks front and back, from the front and back porches, and from the driveway, that patches of ice under the snow also are to be removed, and that the task is to be completed before supper. Criteria for "bathroom cleaned" should be established to avoid dialogues such as the following:

Parent: "I thought I told you to clean the bathroom."
Teen: "I cleaned it."
Parent: "Well, the shower certainly doesn't look clean to me."
Teen: "I didn't know you wanted the shower cleaned."

This response is not just a teenage independence ritual. In more sophisticated language, similar conversations take place daily among adults in organizations, insti-tutions, and communities throughout the world. Gilbert (1978) suggests that in some professions, including the human-service professions, people are not accus-tomed to spelling out goals and criteria, but when pushed, they can do it. Coun-selors and therapists are much more concrete about treatment outcomes when forced to be specific as a condition for third-party payment. But clarity is a relative term. The kind of goal clarity that characterizes manufacturing concerns is not to be expected in human-service professions. But there is a type of outcome clarity that is appropriate for human-service providers.

Giving and receiving feedback

Both human-service providers and their clients need feedback to stay on course. Feedback is not an end in itself, however, though it is often discussed as if it were. Rather it is a tool related to both productivity and quality of life. Feedback is a means of getting usable information.

Two basic kinds of feedback can be exchanged in a system. *Confirmatory feedback* is feedback indicating that goals have been accomplished and that they are acceptable in terms of quantity, quality, timeliness, and cost. For instance, the director of a mental health clinic can say to herself, "I had three positions to fill this year and I have filled them with caring and competent people. I'm very satisfied with this part of my work." Confirmatory feedback may deal also with acceptable progress toward a goal or subgoal.

Corrective feedback indicates that a goal has not been reached, that it is imperfect as to quantity, quality, timeliness, or cost, or that satisfactory progress toward a goal has not been made. A supervisor might say to a staff member, "This report on John Jones is in on time, it is generally good, but it lacks some essential information." The supervisor then goes on to point out precisely what is good about the report, for instance, its suggestions about treatment, and what he or she means by "essential information."

In many systems there is an overemphasis on corrective feedback. If the only kind of feedback staff members receive from a manager or supervisor is corrective, then feedback and feedback meetings will be seen as punitive and staff members will tend to avoid them. The problem with corrective feedback is not only that it is negative—what the other person is doing wrong or is failing to do—but that it might also come as a surprise, if not a shock, to the person hearing it. The issue then is, how can the manager or supervisor be "soft" on the person while being "hard" on the problem? Research shows that even corrective feedback can be experienced as positive reinforcement by those who receive it when they see it as a way of helping them to do a good job. For many people, doing a good job is an important intrinsic reward.

Preconditions for effective feedback. Ideally feedback in an organization, institution, or community comes first from the work itself. If people have a clear understanding of both the performance and quality-of-life goals for which they are responsible and the standards by which they are to be evaluated, then *they should be capable of giving themselves feedback.* If social-work and psychology interns do not know whether they are successful until they have conferences with their supervisors, there is something wrong with the system. If people can get feedback from the work itself, they will not become overly dependent on others. For instance, if a parent, in the heat of emotion, deals unfairly with a child, after the emotion subsides, the parent should be able to give himself or herself feedback: "Now that I've come to my senses, I can see that I was unfair to Sue."

When people understand goals and standards, they are capable of giving themselves feedback and becoming partners with others in the feedback process. If people see feedback as something that happens *to* them, however, they may have to be coached to take responsibility for discussing their own performance.

> Counselor trainees in a university-based program learned the skills of counseling through group process. There were six training groups. Each group had six trainees and two trainers drawn from the second-year students in the program. There was a supervisor for every two groups. The supervisors were advanced clinical psychology students with extensive training in both counseling and group process. Finally, two instructors supervised the entire experience. Both the skills-development goals and standards of proficiency were made very clear to the trainees. Feedback was an essential part of each session. As the sessions moved along, trainees were expected to manage their own feedback. Since they understood both goals and standards, they were expected to give themselves feedback and to get whatever feedback was necessary from fellow trainees, supervisors, and instructors. Of course, feedback could be given by any of these even though it had not been requested.

Both asking for feedback and giving unsolicited feedback is often countercultural in organizations, institutions, and communities. Preventive and corrective feedback are deferred until the situation becomes intolerable or some crisis develops. Then, instead of feedback, there are often harsh judgments and negative emotions.

Rules for feedback from others.   Ideally, the rules for feedback from others should be clear to all concerned.

Legitimization. It should be clear to both parties—parents and children, husband and wife, staff members and supervisors, ministers and congregations, counselors and clients—that giving and receiving feedback is an important part of the system and that feedback is not merely permitted but encouraged. Legitimization of feedback should be one of the major overt policies of the system.

Source. In any given system there may be many different sources of feedback. In the training example, trainees could count on themselves, their peers, the trainers, supervisors, and instructors. In a human-service delivery system, practitioners can receive feedback from themselves, from peers, from supervisors, from managers, and from clients. Students can receive feedback from themselves, parents, teachers, peers, counselors, and those who direct their extracurricular activities.

Direction. In some systems the culture decrees that feedback can move only in certain directions, usually from superior to subordinate, not from subordinate to superior or even from peer to peer. If feedback is expected to move in nontraditional directions in the system, this expectation needs to be stated, clarified, and reinforced. In the best systems, communication moves in all directions—down, up, laterally—

at the service of productivity and quality of life. Peters and Waterman (1982) found that informal peer reviews are common in the "excellent" companies.

Formal peer-review systems are being developed in human-service settings (Claiborn, Biskin, and Friedman, 1982; Sechrest and Hoffman, 1982; Shueman, 1982). In a program described by Cohen, treatment reports are submitted to three peers at certain predetermined checkpoints. These reports document the client's problems, the treatment goals, the treatment programs, and the progress achieved. Acting independently, peers read and give feedback on these reports. In informal peer reviews, the goals are usually innovation, quality, and productivity. In formal peer-review systems, the goals may be "cost containment, utilization review, policing, education, and quality assurance" (Cohen, 1983, p. 362).

Frequency. Feedback from others should not be so plentiful that it takes the place of feedback from self nor so scarce that people are afraid to ask for or give it. Too frequent feedback can lead to pettiness. In training groups this takes the form of an ounce of practice followed by a pound of feedback. I prefer to see a pound of practice followed by an ounce of humane and accurate feedback. Feedback is a means, not an end. On the other hand, Peters and Waterman suggest that in the best organizations there is a great deal of ongoing, informal feedback. People in these systems feel free both to ask for it and to give it unasked.

Timeliness. When people have decided to give feedback, they can still ask themselves, "Should I give feedback right now? How critical and time-sensitive is the feedback I want to give? How receptive to corrective feedback is the other person right now?" Try to strike a balance between productivity and quality-of-life issues.

Content. Feedback meetings are first about *goals* or accomplishments and secondarily about the *behavior* or programs that lead up to the goal. If a human-service provider wears strange clothes and works at a cluttered desk, this is behavior. This same person may provide excellent services. His or her clients learn to manage their lives more effectively, and this is *performance*—that is, goal accomplishment. A discussion of behavior—what a person does or does not do—is meaningful only in the context of the accomplishment or nonaccomplishment of goals. In extreme cases, however, a person may accomplish goals through behavior that is so unorthodox as to disrupt the organization or interfere with the quality of life of other members.

While all corrective feedback may have some unintended punitive side effects, effective feedback is not intended to punish, put people in their place, or create distance. Feedback needs to be given in a way that maintains or even enhances quality of work or community life. If you are in a punitive mood, you may want to delay the feedback meeting. If delay is not possible, ask yourself, "Given my mood, how can I be soft on the person but hard on the problem?"

Making a prudential decision to defer feedback is not the same as avoiding it. Researchers have dubbed the reluctance all of us feel to be the bearer of bad news the "mum effect" (Rosen and Tesser, 1970, 1971; Tesser and Rosen, 1972; Tesser, Rosen, and Batchelor, 1972; Tesser, Rosen, and Tesser, 1971). They discovered that people tend not to give corrective feedback even when the recipient is explicitly open to it. While potential givers of corrective feedback let themselves think that they are being sensitive to the feelings of others, it is often their own feelings they are concerned about.

Giving feedback is a way of getting involved with another person. While in the work place involvement is obviously not comparable to marital intimacy, it could be called "work intimacy." Since giving feedback can feel like unwarranted intrusion into the life of another person, some managers and supervisors shrink from feedback and performance evaluation. They avoid work-related intimacy because sometimes it means spending more time with the person and dealing with emotions.

Performance appraisal meetings. Many organizations hold performance appraisal meetings semiannually, annually, or at the end of a project. In the best organizations and institutions, appraisal meetings are not deadly events but further opportunities for communication. Yet other organizations fail to hold appraisal meetings or merely provide a pro forma evaluation with little meaning for the individual or the employer. Often the problem can be traced to the manager's inability to deal with conflict surrounding transferring or terminating an employee.

> Managers in a large corporation were complaining to a consultant about the performance appraisal system. They complained that they could not say anything negative in the written report for a variety of reasons. One of the principal reasons was the fact that if they did, they could not get anybody else in the organization to take the marginal worker. As a result, marginal workers "floated" through the organization. It seems that the organization did not know how to let anyone go. Appraisal meetings tended to be *pro forma* events that left both supervisors and staff members unsatisfied.

The success of the feedback meeting depends on the quality of performance planning and feedback. Ideally, the appraisal meeting completes the feedback process and leads into a new round of performance planning. The manager deals with strengths as well as weaknesses and encourages the subordinate to be active in the appraisal process. Implications of the appraisal are explained, and objectives are set for the next time period.

MANAGING CONFLICT

One of the most important types of communication in organizations, institutions, and communities is the management of conflict. For a review of the models, methods, and skills of conflict management, see Filley, 1975; Fisher and Ury, 1981; Robbins, 1974; Robert, 1982; Thomas, 1976, 1979; Walton, 1969.

Conflict is interwoven with the warp and woof of being human. It needs little definition but demands a great deal of attention. Thomas and Schmidt (1976) found that middle managers spent more than 25% of their time managing some sort of conflict. People can be in conflict with themselves as well as with others. The focus here, however, is on conflict in which the needs, wants, concerns, or interests of two or more parties seem to be incompatible. Thomas (1976) defines conflict as "the process which begins when one party perceives that the other has frustrated, or is about to frustrate, some concern of his or hers" (p. 891).

While conflict is usually associated with disturbed relationships and emotional turmoil, it can also be seen as an opportunity. The word *crisis* comes from a Greek word meaning to divide or to decide. As a form of crisis, conflict is a time for deciding, a choice point. Ideally it is a time to review available options and to make choices that will lead to constructive outcomes. Conflict is not just inevitable, it is also potentially useful. Energy need not be poured into preventing it since avoiding conflict is tantamount to avoiding an opportunity for growth. Robbins (1974) emphasizes the value of conflict in organizations and even suggests techniques for stimulating it.

The process of conflict

Conflict can take place between individuals (for instance, between supervisors and staff members), between groups or departments (for example, between the admissions and nursing departments of a psychiatric hospital), or between an organization and system in the environment (for instance, between a community organization and the city government). Thomas (1976), building upon the work of Pondy (1967) and Walton (1969), has developed a model of the basic events in the conflict process. These events are (1) experiencing *frustration*, (2) the *conceptualization* of the conflict situation on the part of those involved, (3) *behaviors* aimed at handling the conflict, (4) the *reactions* of one party to the other's behavior, and (5) the *outcomes* to which these behaviors lead.

Frustration.   The conflict process begins when one or more parties experience frustration. A social worker feels frustrated because overscheduling prevents her or him from accomplishing a desired goal. Frustration may arise from any element of Model A—structure, goals, work design, access to and use of resources, system policies, reward system, the elements of culture such as beliefs and assumptions, quality-of-life concerns, or anything else that individuals or groups care about. The parties may feel frustration and the anxiety, anger, and depression that frustration spawns before they identify its source.

Conceptualization of the conflict.   Frustration leads the parties concerned to identify what is bothering them—that is, what the conflict is about. "I'm really angry," the social worker says to himself. "The director has scheduled me for more cases than I can handle this month."

Conceptualizations are usually quite subjective. There is probably no such thing as a completely objective conceptualization of the conflict issue. Parties tend to conceptualize issues in terms of their own interests and concerns. They seldom make an attempt to understand the concerns of the other party, especially early in the conflict process. The parties may have different conceptions of the "size" or the importance of the issue. People in conflict frequently attribute negatively valanced motives to each other, often without the facts to back up the attributions: "The director is really thoughtless. He knows the kind of load I already have. He sees me as his patsy."

Conceptualizations are extremely important, because no matter how distorted, they form the basis of each party's attempt to cope with the conflict.

Conflict-managing behavior.   People base their strategies for handling conflict on their perception of the conflict itself and on what they want to get or avoid in the conflict situation. For instance, the social worker thinks that the director is giving him too many cases as a way of testing him. However, he does not think the issue is "big" enough to take a stand and ends up by giving in: "I'll do it this month, but this is the last time he's getting away with this." Note, however, that he is still frustrated and experiences other negative emotions. His residual frustration raises the probability that Episode 1 in the conflict process will lead to Episode 2.

The reaction of others.   Obviously, behavior in conflict situations does not take place in a vacuum. Strategies used by one party evoke responses in the other party.

> It is often misleading to talk about a conflict party's behavior in terms of a single conflict-handling mode. Once interaction with another party begins, each party may make adjustments to attempt to cope with the behavior of the other party, who must in turn adjust to that change, and so on. The interaction between the parties is commonly a dynamic sequence of tactical and strategic adjustments (Thomas, 1979, p. 100).

Once the parties in a conflict define the situation as a win-lose event, there is a tendency to escalate, to use more extreme and thus more dangerous tactics. Thomas lists the following indicators of escalation: stronger demands, righteousness, refusal to listen to each other, the spread of competition to other issues, the enlistment of other parties as allies, attacks on personalities, threats, attempts to punish each other, and the violation of social norms.

In the heat of the fray the parties very often do not even realize how dysfunctional their behavior has become. They fail to consider behaviors that help reverse the escalation process—including empathic listening and responding, probing to discover the other party's point of view, being sensitive about the other's feelings, making tactical concessions and other gestures of goodwill, admitting one's own contributions to the process of escalation, indications of willingness to bargain in good faith, and explicit references to the lose-lose spiral both parties have allowed themselves to get into.

Fisher and Ury (1981) have some extremely useful suggestions for negotiating win-win solutions to conflict. They urge the parties to:

- Separate the stakes or *interests* in the conflict situation from the *positions* they are taking. The social worker asks himself, "What are my interests, stakes, and concerns?" instead of saying that he will no longer work overtime under any condition.
- Separate the issues from the people. If the director hints that their relationship depends on adopting her or his position, the social worker says that the issue is not the relationship but what is fair.

- Take time to explore one's own interests and the interests of the other party. For instance, the social worker may realize that in view of the fact that two people have left the agency in the last two months and that no replacements have been forthcoming because of budget cutbacks, the director is in a bind. He begins to explore the interests behind the demands that he take on more cases.
- Develop a range of possible solutions that take into consideration the interests of both parties without committing oneself to any specific solution. Instead of giving the director ultimatums, the social worker develops a range of solutions and asks the director to do the same.

The Fisher and Ury model has been used successfully in a wide range of conflict situations, from political and cultural impasses in the Middle East to renegotiating the lease for an apartment.

Outcomes.   A conflict can be said to be *resolved* when the parties in question are fully satisfied with an outcome. This means that there is no residual frustration or at least not enough to precipitate future "episodes." Like most human problems, however, conflict is not solved or resolved but *managed*. The fact that today's frustration is managed more or less is no guarantee that tomorrow will not spawn its own. When two parties emerge from a conflict, the "bottom-line" questions deal with productivity and quality of life.

- Did they come up with a decision that they both can live with, at least for now?
- Does this decision in some way favor, or at least not stand in the way of, the productivity of the system?
- Is the relationship between the two parties still intact and workable?
- Does the decision help improve, or at least not stand in the way of, the quality of life of the other members?
- Does the quality of the decision merit its financial and psychological costs? If not, what has been learned that can contribute to making conflict management in this system more cost effective in the future?
- Has this conflict situation helped the parties reflect on and clarify personal values, system values, and the interaction between the two?

Communication in conflict situations

O'Brien (1982) reviews the many different ways in which authors have used a grid to visualize the common communication styles people use in managing conflict. The styles depicted by the grid in Figure 10-5 are basically combinations of degrees of *assertiveness* (concern with one's own needs and wants or what one sees as the needs and wants of the organization or institution) with degrees of *responsiveness* (sensitivity to the needs and wants of the other party in the conflict). If a person combines a high degree of assertiveness with a low degree of responsiveness, for instance, he or she will tend to compete, command, fight, order, or demand that his or her solution to the conflict be adopted. On the other hand, if a person combines a low degree of assertiveness with a high degree of responsiveness, he or she might simply give in to the other party's solution.

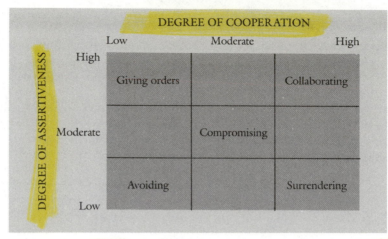

FIGURE 10-5.   A range of interactional possibilities with staff persons

There is no one best way of dealing with conflict. Different situations call for different ways of handling it. People often discover that in conflict situations they have a tendency to prefer one style (for instance, compromising) over others. After reviewing the advantages and disadvantages of each mode, however, they often prefer to increase their repertory of responses to conflict. The following list of conflict-managing behaviors is adapted from the assertiveness/responsiveness grid formulated by Thomas and Kilmann (1977):

Commanding (high assertiveness, low responsiveness). In this mode you are assertive, perhaps even aggressive in your action. You give orders, command, argue, demand, or compete. This approach may be useful: in crises and emergencies when quick, decisive action is called for; when unpopular courses of action need to be taken for the sake of the system and its members; when the issue is important and you are certain that you are right; to protect an overly accommodating self against aggressive people.

There is a price to be paid if high-assertiveness/low-responsiveness behaviors are used too frequently. You may surround yourself with people who don't think for themselves. The other members of the system may come to fear or dislike you and therefore not approach you to ask for or give information critical to the system. People may get back at you for your aggressiveness in a variety of subtle (or not too subtle) ways. You may begin to make authoritarian and self-serving rather than system-sensitive decisions.

Avoiding (low assertiveness, low responsiveness). In this mode you try not to engage the other party at all. You wish that they would get their work done on their own, not bother you, and let you get about your own work. This approach can be useful: when an issue is not important or at least is low on your list of priorities; when being able to say "It's not important" gives you breathing room. You may choose to avoid conflict when you see that you're not going to get what you want anyway;

when fighting for your position is only going to make things worse; when you need more time to gather information; when your relationship with the other party is tense and you want time to let things settle down; when the issue is merely a symptom of some more serious issue.

There is a price to be paid if the strategy of avoiding is used too frequently. If you are seen as weak and indecisive, people may begin making decisions for you, or decisions will be made by default. The organization may suffer because you are providing less input than is needed. You may let your own needs to avoid conflict become more important than the well-being of the system.

Giving in or accommodating (low assertiveness, high responsiveness). In this mode you engage the other party, but then surrender. You accommodate yourself to his or her decision. This style is useful: when you realize you have been wrong; when the issue is not critical and when it is more important to the other party than to you; when you are outmatched and losing and need time to regroup; when the relationship with the other party is more important for the moment than the issue; when you decide to help members of the system to develop responsibility by giving them opportunities to make mistakes and to learn from them.

If this strategy is used excessively, you may be seen as weak and ineffectual and begin to run into discipline problems. Your own good ideas will not get a hearing. If many wrong decisions are made, both productivity and quality of life will begin to suffer. There is no follow-up to help the other party learn from his or her mistakes. The reason for the concession—learning for you and for the other party—does not take place.

Compromising (moderate assertiveness, moderate responsiveness). In this mode the objective is to find some mutually acceptable solution that partially satisfies both parties. This strategy can be used: when the issues are moderately important but not worthy of stronger measures such as giving orders or full collaboration; when you are negotiating with a strong opponent committed to some goal other than yours; when you want to settle an issue temporarily or when time is critical; when you need a backup strategy after commanding or collaborating has failed.

On the other hand, you may lose sight of principles, long-term goals, the common good of the organization and of the people it serves. If you begin to approach everything with a sense of compromise, people will know that you are vulnerable, and the quality of decisions will suffer. A kind of lowest-common-denominatorism takes over.

Collaborating (high assertiveness, high responsiveness). Collaborating involves an attempt to work with the other person to find some solution that fully satisfies the concerns or interests of both persons. This mode is useful: when the stakes are high for both parties; when learning—testing your own assumptions, understanding the views of others—is important; when a solution of a problem will be richer because of merged insights. You may choose collaboration to gain commitment from the other party, work through negative feelings that interfere with a work relationship, or minimize risk by spreading responsibility.

Since this strategy can be time consuming, you must decide if this time is wasted.

Sometimes trivial issues get in-depth discussion and optimal solutions. If you are continually in a collaborative mode, you may miss cues signaling that the other person is not.

Although these modes or styles are helpful for reviewing your own behavior and that of others, they probably don't exist in a pure-form state. An interaction that is primarily collaborative may incorporate elements of the other modes. To complicate the picture further, McMahon (1983) suggests that the way in which conflicts are managed is influenced by such variables as the emotional intensity brought to the conflict by the parties, their conflict-related skills, how clear they are on goals or outcomes, the status of their interpersonal relationships, their attitudes toward power and authority, their concern for formalities, their concern for norms and traditions, their self-concept differences, and the degree to which they fear punishment or coercion.

In conflict situations the parties display different degrees of conflict-management "maturity" at different times. For instance, a social worker might have an adequate self-concept in dealings with peers and use collaboration most of the time with them, but have a poor self-concept with respect to people in authority and use avoidance and accommodation most of the time with superiors. While models of conflict styles may be useful in assessing one's own and others' approaches to conflict situations, care should be taken not to oversimplify complex human transactions. The models are most useful not in predicting what will happen in a conflict situation, but in helping oneself and others expand the range of approaches to managing conflict.

COMMUNICATION MICROSKILLS

If people in systems are to collaborate in such things as planning, problem solving, decision making, feedback and appraisal meetings, conflict management, and negotiation, they need the basic communication microskills presupposed by these processes. A wide variety of training programs in these skills have been developed (Egan, 1976, 1977, 1982).

The skills of listening and responding include:

Active listening—the ability to break through personal, interpersonal, system, and cultural obstacles and hear what others are saying and to hear it from their point of view.

Accurate empathic responding—the ability to communicate to others an understanding of what they have said and what they are feeling without distorting their messages and without patronizing them.

Probing—the ability to help others clarify their messages so that both you and they understand the messages better and to do so without demeaning others.

The skills of challenging, helping others manage blind spots, include:

Information giving—the ability to give others information that helps them develop a new and more useful perspective on the issue at hand.

Summarizing—the ability to bring together a number of points that the other has made so that he or she might come to understand both the connections and the import or meaning of the connections.

Advanced empathy—the ability to help a person understand the fuller import of what he or she is only half stating or hinting at.

Confrontation—the ability to help others see the discrepancies in their communications, discrepancies between what they feel and what they say, between conflicting messages, between what they say and what they do, between conflicting actions, and so forth.

Self-disclosure—the ability to share one's own experience when it might help another person develop a new and more useful perspective without diverting attention from his or her concerns.

Immediacy—the ability to engage in and to invite another person to engage in a discussion of what is happening in your relationship with him or her, especially at times when what is happening is preventing effective pursuit of some mutual agenda.

As important as these skills are as tools of both "conviviality" (in its root sense) and collaboration, there are relatively few forums in life where they are learned formally. Faculty members of a school of nursing considered a possible training program in communication skills as an addition to their curriculum. They fully believed that the ability of nurses to deliver medical services effectively was affected by their ability to communicate. Their problem was that the curriculum was already overloaded and they did not know how to fit a new offering in. The dilemma they faced has deeper roots. Ideally, prospective nurses should arrive on the doorstep of nursing school *already equipped with these basic communication skills*. In nursing school and practicum experiences these skills could be honed to fit medical settings by effective modeling and adept supervision. Since these skills are ordinarily not taught in the family or in primary or secondary school, however, prospective employees often arrive without these basics.

Some claim that no formal training is needed because through everyday experience people pick up enough of these skills to "get by." But the skills needed "to get by" are not the same as those needed to provide human services. Educators have the same complaint as the nursing school faculty—there is no room in the curriculum for formal instruction in planning, problem solving, decision making, negotiation, peer helping, and the communication skills demanded by these processes. Their plight is understandable, but the fact that there is no place in our curricula for what Gazda (1984) calls "life skills" is one of the more puzzling forms of arationality in our educational systems.

Indeed, many programs training human-service practitioners do not find room for these skills in their curricula. A graduate student in a master's degree program in counseling psychology said that he was involved in a practicum experience in counseling, his last course, but he realized that he didn't know how to counsel. I asked him in what courses he had studied the counseling process. After stopping to think, he replied, "We had one course called 'The basics of counseling' or something like that, but we didn't do much counseling." I would like to think that his experience was the exception.

ARATIONALITY IN COMMUNICATION

Communication is both the glory and the shame of human beings. It can bring us together around common purposes, and it can be used as one of the weapons of war. In the social settings of life it can be both enhancing and limiting.

Communication as limiting. The individual- and system-limiting arational factors that can influence communication in organizations, institutions, and communities seem endless.

- The communication process is almost hopelessly complex. So much happens within both sender and receiver, so much can be lost between sender and receiver, and so much "noise" both within and outside the system can affect communication processes that distortions are bound to occur.
- People hoard and distort information for political purposes; vested interests greatly influence what is and what is not communicated.
- People's communication is influenced by mood, physical condition, prejudices, grudges, likes, self-doubt, dislikes, and a host of other ill-defined internal states.
- People can be communication-lazy, sloppy in both giving and receiving information.
- People can be willing but unskilled communicators, poor at collaborative planning, problem solving, decision making, appraisal, conflict management, negotiation, and at the communication microskills needed for all of these.
- The culture of the system can limit communication in a host of ways. For instance, the culture may reward the political uses of communication, limit the use of confirmatory feedback, discourage collaborative processes, encourage hidden agendas, reinforce communication-distorting attitudes and prejudices, and condone sloppy communication.

As Caplow (1976) notes, the "communication network of every organization, large or small, has a seamy underside" (p. 75) that includes such things as spying, spreading rumors, gossiping, talebearing, and taking on the role of stool pigeon. There is always the "grapevine" at work passing along both enhancing and limiting forms of communication.

> A grapevine is capable of transmitting a variety of messages on a variety of topics. What it actually transmits during a given period seems to depend on the supply of and demand for particular kinds of information. The grapevine is most active when information is scarce and the demand for it is high; it is least active when the information is plentiful and the demand for it is low. If an organization's future plans are kept secret, there will be many rumors about future plans. If they are widely publicized, there will be few such rumors and perhaps none at all. Some sorts of information, like scandalous gossip, are always in demand and usually in short supply. When information in this category becomes available, the grapevine transmits it far and wide [Caplow, 1976, p. 77].

The grapevine, as part of the informal system, is beyond the control of both managers and staff members.

Effective communication in some systems is actually punished. Creative students with creative responses are put down by teachers. Useful ideas coming from staff members are ignored by supervisors and managers. These communication problems and others plague all organizations, institutions, and communities and tend to mock the ideals outlined earlier in this chapter. Like poverty and crime, they seem to be or actually are intractable.

Communication as enhancing. In spite of such adversarial conditions, there are arational dimensions that enhance communication. As Van Kaam (1966) has demonstrated, people have a basic drive to be understood. Since being understood is rewarding, this drive can became a force on the enhancing side of the communication ledger. For many people *work intimacy*—the kind of communication exchanged in getting a job done—is extremely rewarding. And the best systems are filled with this kind of intimacy. People in key positions enjoy and model open communication. They are nondefensive; what they say is open to disconfirmation. Their easy style encourages open communication in others. When people find open communication intrinsically rewarding, they do not have to be bribed to communicate well. In the best systems, people are eager to share, to let others know, to be informed, to offer suggestions, to be asked their opinion, to be offered suggestions. Peer reviews are informal and frequent. Peters and Waterman (1982) call this "intense communication" (pp. 218ff).

In the best systems, confirmatory feedback is not seen as a scarce resource but is given freely. Corrective feedback, though it might hurt a little, is welcomed by many people because they want to do a good job.

In many systems good communication is almost an article of faith; people *believe* in it. For instance, a large multinational corporation has developed a seminar on listening for all members of their staffs. They consider listening so important and yet so neglected that they have used magazine advertisements to let the general public know what they are doing. These advertisements point out that good listeners think more broadly—because they hear and understand more facts and points of view. They make better innovators. Because listeners look at problems with fresh eyes, and combine what they learn in more unlikely ways, they are more apt to hit upon truly startling ideas. Ultimately, good listeners attune themselves more closely to where the world is going—and the products, talents, and techniques it needs to get there.

The corporation claims that helping the members of their organization become more effective listeners has improved the quality of working life, helped to increase productivity, and helped the members of the organization become more creative. Here listening is far more than the rational process of registering accurately what the other person has said; it is a tool of creativity. Belief in listening can be extended to belief in other communication skills and processes.

Wise managers realize the complexity of human communication and all the "slings and arrows" to which it is exposed. Since they know that it will never be perfect, they have learned how to manage breakdowns in communication. They make sure that they have communication skills and know how to engage in collaborative planning, problem solving, and conflict management. They may even mandate these for others through recruitment procedures and training programs. Wise managers are humble enough to realize that actions on their part sometimes cause communication difficulties for others. Because they are wise, they look beyond individuals to the system itself as the culprit in communications breakdowns.

> Digging a little deeper, the manager will discover that in addition to their supposed incompatibilty, the people who refuse to communicate have substantial differences of interest imposed upon them by their positions in the organizational structure, so that at least one of them cannot interact freely with the other without jeopardizing his own interests or those of a faction he represents [Caplow, 1976, p. 80].

In psychiatric hospitals, for example, nurses and aides have withheld information from supervisors in order to protect patients.

But more than all of this, wise managers know how to develop and encourage *system cultures* that support the ideals of good communication. Training in communication skills and processes will not succeed unless it is an expression of the culture of the system. If a system operates on a strong but covert win-lose value system, for instance, communication will always be highly (rather than slightly) politicized. The "excellent companies" described by Peters and Waterman are subject to the same forms of system-limiting arationality as others. Their strong upbeat cultures, while not eliminating communication problems, serve as a shield against communication inertia and entropy.

11

Leadership

There are many theories and more than a hundred definitions of leadership.

Burns' (1978) monumental work, filled with amazing vignettes, is a descriptive essay rather than a theory of leadership. He concedes that leadership is "one of the most observed and least understood phenomena on earth" (p. 2). (See Bass, 1981; Burns, 1978; Fiedler and Chemers, 1974; Hollander, 1978; *Journal of Applied Behavioral Science,* 1982; Lassey and Sashkin, 1983; Stogdill, 1974; Yukl, 1981.) But in spite of its complexity, it is impossible to discuss change-agent skills without discussing leadership. In the context of Model A, leadership is about both style and outcomes, and is related to both productivity and quality-of-life accomplishments. In this sense, it is possible to distinguish between system and individual leadership. Figure 11-1 adds leadership to Model A.

Leadership can be predicated of the *system* itself if goals are accomplished, the major aims and mission of the system are fulfilled, and the specified needs and wants of the members of the receiving system are met. A counseling agency exercises leadership only if the clients actually manage the problem situations of their lives more effectively.

Anyone who contributes in any way to the accomplishment of the goals of the system participates in system-oriented individual leadership. The director of the counseling agency who hires competent staff, the counselors who use their skills, the secretaries who manage scheduling and reports, the maintenance personnel who provide a suitable place to work, and the clients themselves who translate the work in the counseling sessions into problem-managing action all contribute to the valued outcomes of the system. Pascale and Athos (1981), in their study of Japanese leadership, note that for every action on the stage, there are many people working behind the scenes: "The Japanese simply can't imagine giving sole credit to the person in the spotlight" (p. 145). This kind of interdependence is more deeply

II. THE HUMAN RESOURCES OF THE SYSTEM

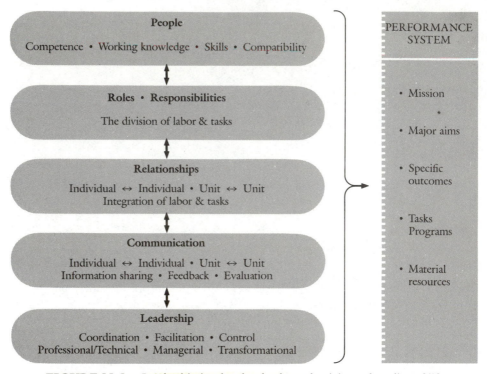

FIGURE 11-1. Leadership is related to both productivity and quality-of-life accomplishments.

ingrained in organizations and institutions than many highly independent leaders would like to admit.

THE LEADERSHIP PROCESS

In the first half of this century leadership research focused on the *traits* of leaders. Since different researchers identified different sets of leadership traits, it was difficult to relate traits to actual outcomes (Hollander and Julian, 1969). Jay (1971) notes that "any list of qualities that meant anything at all would be bound to exclude someone who had succeeded in leadership and include many who had failed" (p. 63). In the second half of this century research has focused on leadership as an interactive process in which the *leader* is but one of the elements. The other two elements, as indicated in the leadership process triangle in Figure 11-2, are the *people* who are led or influenced, and the *situation* in which influence is exercised. As the arrows indicate, influence is bidirectional among all the elements of the process. That is, both leaders and those led influence and shape one another and

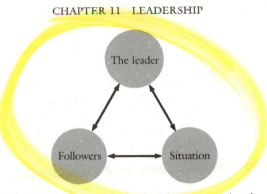

FIGURE 11-2.   The leadership process triangle

both shape and are shaped by the situation in which mutual influence is exercised. Because it involves influence—often emotionally charged—and because it is complex, leadership is subject to many different forms of arationality. The myths about leaders and leadership are endless.

The leader is usually someone designated by appointment, election, emergence, or some other means, and recognized as the superior. The designation or recognition allows the person to influence other members of the system in a variety of ways. At the same time it opens him or her up to being influenced. Wise leaders understand that leadership is a transactional process—they give and they get. Simplistic, nonprocess approaches to leadership almost inevitably lead to trouble in terms of lowered productivity, impaired quality of life, or both.

Followers. This term can be a misnomer since, as already noted, so-called followers also exercise influence on the leader. The patients of a psychiatric hospital can exercise a great deal of influence on decisions taken by administration and staff. In the health-care field highly educated, cost-conscious, and sophisticated patients are placing more and more demands on doctors. A sense of self-efficacy is on the rise among many clients (Bandura, 1977, 1980, 1982). Human-service providers may take the lead in the helping process, but ideally they empower their clients to take on leadership functions themselves, at least with respect to their own lives.

Anyone who has played the role of helper or human-service provider knows the agony of counseling reluctant and resistant clients (Egan, 1982). This is one of the major ways in which "followers" affect leaders. The wise practitioner is not surprised by reluctance and resistance, examines his or her own role in causing it, faces it squarely, does not take it personally, challenges the client to face it, and tries to collaborate with the client in inventing ways to manage it. Of course, reluctance and resistance are not attributes of clients alone. Ask the director of any human-service agency.

The situation includes a wide variety of factors such as the history of the group in question, the mission, purpose, goals, programs, resources, and structure of the system, the climate, the culture of the system, events in the environment that are impinging on the system, the timing of events, critical incidents, crises, and so forth. Different situations call for different leadership approaches. In large urban centers, there are said to be more doctors and hospital beds than are needed; government regulations and economic factors are shortening the time the average patient spends in the hospital, and day hospitals are competing with traditional ones for patients. The health-care *situation* has changed. Administrative and managerial styles are affected or should be affected by these changes.

The interactions among these three elements add up to a very complex process. Wise leaders have a feeling for this complexity and refrain from a simplistic "do what I tell you to do" approach to leading and managing. At some level of consciousness, they instinctively ask themselves: How am I being influenced by the members of this group and by the situation we find ourselves in? What changes are taking place among the membership and in the situation? What are the limits to the ways in which I can influence the membership and the situation? What leadership style is the best option, given *this* membership and *this* situation? Am I capable of carrying out the best option? In human-service settings it is possible to identify three kinds of leadership: (1) professional-technical, (2) managerial, and (3) transformational (Burns, 1978).

Professional-technical leadership

Professional-technical leaders not only have work-related skills, but they also tend to be exemplars in their areas of competence. Human-service providers in this category would not only provide excellent services for their clients but also be innovators in the delivery of these services. Such people would be "translators"— people who are capable of delivering services well, stay in touch with the best in theory and research, and turn relevant theory and research into frameworks, models, methods, and skills that benefit practitioners (Egan and Cowan, 1979). In industry these leaders might be called "product champions"—people who are restless in their search for a better product or at least a better form of the same product (Peters and Waterman, 1982).

Like product champions, some human-service-delivery "champions" march to a different drummer, bending the rules of the agency perhaps, but at the service of clients rather than of their own egos. The best organizations, institutions, and agencies, while annoyed at times by the license such leaders may occasionally take, have room for them—and sometimes *prize* them and protect them from the pettiness of the bureaucracy. But many human-service agencies have cultures of mediocrity that are much too narrow for human-service-delivery champions, especially when they deviate in any way.

Professional-technical leadership can be seen in the development of a food cooperative in an inner-city neighborhood.

> Melanie R., a former employee of the Office of Community Services in a large Midwestern city, is working with a group of people in a low-income area to establish a food cooperative. She knows a great deal about cooperatives because when she was with the Office of Community Services,

she helped other neighborhoods set them up. In doing so, she stepped on some political toes. The agency she was working for let her go because of "cutbacks." Actually, the director of the agency thought she did not "fit in." Melanie does seem to march to a different drummer, but the manager of the cooperative finds her assistance invaluable.

Melanie is not the moving force behind the cooperative nor is she the kind of person that would be chosen to run it; but through the use of her expertise, she exercises technical-professional leadership.

One very common form of system-limiting arationality is to reward professional-technical leaders with managerial positions which they are ill prepared for or do not want. The person might want the benefits that go with the promotion, but not the position itself. If the person does not have the managerial competencies needed to carry out the tasks of the position, then he or she and the organization become victims of the "Peter principle," advancement to one's level of incompetence (Peter and Hull, 1970). The social worker who is excellent in the field may or may not be good at running an agency. Yet organizations and institutions often fail to separate professional-technical capabilities from managerial capabilities and to appreciate the former in their own right.

Managerial leadership

Managerial leadership answers the question: Who is going to coordinate all the elements of Model A—in the organization, subunit, project, or program—to see that these elements mesh well enough to serve both productivity and quality-of-life goals? The traditional response, of course, is the administrator, director, manager, or supervisor who is responsible for planning, organizing, staffing, directing, controlling, and facilitating.

Planning means setting the yearly direction for the system or a subunit. Operational planning, involving major aims, goals, programs, and resources, is usually seen as a managerial task. Weick (1969) cautions against excessive planning. Planning, he says, involves putting rationality and order into one's own or others' experience. If a system is light on experience, planning may be an orderly but empty process. Weick suggests that chaotic action is sometimes better than orderly inactivity. The wise manager sees planning as much more than a rational exercise.

Organizing means structuring the work: establishing roles, relationships among individuals, relationships among organizational units, and communication processes. Organizing also means establishing the managerial and supervisory roles in the "chain of command."

Staffing means recruiting the right people and then orienting, training, and developing them. Robert Carkhuff was once challenged by someone who said, "Your programs work because you choose the best people." He answered, "Precisely."

A nurse volunteered for a human-service program offered by her church. During her discussion with the priest in charge of these programs, she said, "I feel like I'm being interviewed." The priest said, "You are. We take our programs seriously, as seriously as you take your work in the hospital. We want to make sure that the volunteer is capable and that she or he will fit into the program." She said she had thought that people would be eager to have her under any conditions. But on reflection, she thought that interviewing volunteers was a good idea.

Coordinating and directing means getting work done through the efforts of others. Since organizations are more "loosely coupled" than rational models indicate, managers must become adept at the "art of coordinating" goals with mission, programs with goals, people and resources with programs, people and organizational units with one another, and the organization itself with the environment. They make sure that goals are clear. If times change and programs no longer fit goals, they make sure that new programs come on line. To make certain that plans are realized, managers provide incentives to do the work, delegate authority and responsibility to others, manage conflicts, and encourage innovation and creativity. These functions call for exceptional communication skills.

The chairman of the psychology department asked one of the members of the department to meet with him. The issue was the way the professor "chewed up" secretaries and graduate assistants, the very people he depended on to get the work done. The latest crisis was that the best secretary in the department was about to move to another department because she could no longer tolerate his behavior. The professor in question, while admitting that he could be "difficult" at times, said that this was the first time *anyone* had brought it to his attention. The chairman realized how reluctant he was to talk to the members of the department about such issues.

Both the professor and the chairman depended on others for outcomes, but each in his own way failed to establish the kinds of relationships that facilitate these outcomes.

Controlling means making sure that progress toward goals takes place and that the quality of outcomes is assured. Managers do this by developing and enforcing performance standards, making sure that they and others pass along critical information, giving both confirmatory and corrective feedback and making sure that others do so, taking corrective action such as coaching, counseling, transferring, and firing when necessary, appraising results, appraising the performance of the members of the system, and making sure that system members are rewarded for achieving goals.

Facilitating means supporting the work of others. Effective managers do not spend a great deal of time controlling, but begin with the assumption that people know how to control their own work. Staff members usually want to do a good job. Therefore, while it is the function of a manager to make sure that standards are clear and that everyone knows what they are, there is no need for a manager to enforce standards in most cases. If a number of people fail to meet standards, this is an organizational and managerial, not a personnel, problem.

> The director of clinical services in a large psychiatric hospital knew the various ways in which "burnout" among direct service providers can take place. He tried to anticipate burnout and get staff members to do so rather than deal with it when it happened. At staff meetings he discussed innovative ways of managing burnout both personally and organizationally. He encouraged a great deal of dialogue among staff members so that no one felt isolated in their work. He had conferences conducted by experts in various disciplines. He promoted an interdisciplinary approach to patient care. Innovation in the delivery of services was immediately recognized and rewarded. Mini-sabbaticals were established for short conferences outside the hospital. Contracts were set up so that some staff members could work both in the hospital and in the community. He spoke to the members of his staff frequently and stayed in touch with their needs. He set up a long-range career development service that included an outplacement program. When a staff person felt the need for a change, he or she was helped to find another position. A sense of community and fellowship developed in the hospital. All this did not eliminate burnout entirely, but it did a great deal to lessen it.

Even in business settings, management itself is a *human-service* profession. In this sense effective human-service providers should make good managers. For instance, good human-service providers prize and work toward developing self-responsibility in their clients. And they have the kinds of communication, counseling, and coaching skills to do so. The same can be said of good managers. The role of "resource-collaborator" applies not only to human-service practitioners, but also to managers.

> Mark J., formerly in charge of the shipping department of a small local manufacturing company that relocated in the Sunbelt, is chosen to manage a food cooperative in an inner-city neighborhood. He proves to be very competent at planning and at coordinating whatever needs to be done to get the cooperative off the ground and into operation. People like to work with him because he gets things done without acting like a "boss." He has a special talent for tapping the abilities of volunteers.

Mark exercises managerial leadership. He is not an expert in cooperatives, but he knows how to make things run and how to work with people.

Peters and Waterman (1982) summarize some of these functions in a less rational way than they are described above.

> Leadership is many things. It is patient, usually boring coalition building. It is the purposeful seeding of the cabals that one hopes will result in the appropriate ferment in the bowels of the organization. It is meticulously shifting the attention of the insti-

tution through the mundane language of management systems. It is altering agendas so that new priorities get enough attention. It is being visible when things go awry, and invisible when they are working well. It's building up a loyal team at the top that speaks more or less with one voice. It's listening carefully much of the time, frequently speaking with encouragement, and reinforcing words with believable action. It's being tough when necessary, and it's the occasional use of naked power—or the "subtle accumulation of nuances, a hundred things done a little better," as Henry Kissinger once put it [p. 82].

Staff participation.   There are many ways to exercise managerial functions. Managers can assist, oversee, monitor, command, threaten, order, tell, model, invite, stimulate, motivate, see, explain, wait, collaborate, delegate, participate, and so forth. Hersey, Blanchard, and Hambleton (1978) suggest that managers and supervisors can profitably contract with staff members for leadership style.

> In most MBO [management by objectives, operational planning] programs, an effort is made only for managers and their subordinates to reach agreement on performance goals; little attention is given to developing "contracts" between managers and their subordinates regarding the role of managers in helping their subordinates accomplish the negotiated objectives [p. 215].

To develop their individual operational plans, staff members sit down with managers or supervisors, discuss organizational and individual priorities, and develop a mutually acceptable plan. At this point, a related contract can be developed that deals with the manager's style of facilitation. The staff person would say something like this: "Given this mutually agreed upon individual plan and the variety of tasks it involves, here is what I need from you in order to meet expectations." The manager would say something like this: "Given this mutually agreed upon plan and how I see you in terms of ability and motivation, here is how I intend to relate to you throughout the period of the plan." These two viewpoints would be reconciled and a contract developed concerning the role of the manager in helping staff members accomplish objectives.

A person need not be in any formal leadership role in order to exercise many of these managerial-leadership functions. In the best systems informal peer reviews go on all the time; for example, when two staff members in a mental health clinic discuss their cases with each other. Feedback is not considered an exclusively managerial function. *In the best systems, there are relatively few managers but there is a great deal of managerial leadership.* Relatively few managers are needed because the managerial functions are spread throughout the staff in informal ways. Put somewhat differently, just as staff members participate in system leadership by contributing to productivity, they participate in managerial leadership by exercising managerial functions through delegation and in many different informal ways.

Most of the problems in organizations and institutions are managerial problems. For instance, managers hire the wrong people and then blame them and others when they fail to produce. Managers fail to provide realistic planning, feedback, and appraisal systems and then wonder why productivity is low. The director of aides in a psychiatric hospital fails to make their responsibilities clear and then is angry when they don't "do what they should." When people fail to produce, good managers expect and encourage the individuals themselves to find out what they did wrong while they examine their own consciences in terms of managerial functions and seek out the organizational defects underlying the failure.

Tactical planning.   In the light of both strategic planning and the priorities developed through operational planning, managers and staff members need to organize each week and each day. Tactical planning means (a) time management and (b) day-to-day problem solving.

Time-management. Careful operational planning can be seriously hampered by lack of day-to-day organizing. Time management refers to setting priorities for the week and for the day and seeing to it that they are accomplished. Many managers handle the same piece of paper—for instance, a letter that needs to be answered—literally a hundred times before it is finally taken care of.

Day-to-day problem solving. If there are no operational plans, management-by-wondering-what-will-happen-next or management-by-crisis fills the void. But even when effective planning has taken place, day-to-day problems arise. Therefore, managers need to be able to face relatively small problems efficiently in order to prevent them from becoming large ones. Good managers anticipate problems, determine which ones need attention, analyze these problems quickly, and decide who should solve them—the manager, another worker, or a team. The manager knows how to develop a solution, pedestrian or imaginative as the case requires, work out a program to get it done quickly, then act and evaluate. The pieces of paper that are picked up and set aside over and over again tend to be the ones that represent small problems, not needing attention right now, but in the end devouring much too much of the manager's time.

Transformational leadership

The transformational leader communicates the ideals, values, and purpose of the system to the members in such a way that they are moved to pursue them. Such leaders usually have a larger vision of things than the other members of the organization, institution, or community and the ability to communicate this vision to others and move them to action. This kind of leadership might also be called inspirational or charismatic leadership—though Burns rejects the latter terms as so overburdened with meanings as to "collapse under close analysis."

In the case of the cooperative, Caroline D. exercises transformational leadership.

The idea for the food cooperative started with Caroline D., a social worker in a small community mental health center in the area. She discovered and publicized the fact that food prices in the local stores were much higher than they were in middle-income areas of the city. Her commitment to the neighborhood and her enthusiasm for the project are the sparks that keep the project alive. She sees the community as a whole, she understands the social, economic, and political forces at work both in the community and in the city surrounding it, and she defines problems and solutions in terms of these wider perspectives. She stirs the imagination of other members of the community and moves them to join forces. She makes sure that the mission of the cooperative is clear and clearly understood by those who have a stake in it.

Caroline may also be a fine manager and a highly qualified provider of human services, but in the case of the cooperative and in the neighborhood as a whole, her major contribution is in terms of transformational leadership.

Such leadership is essentially arational, and thus it can be abused. The examples of those who have used their charisma to damage or destroy both individuals and social settings (the "Jonestown" phenomenon) are legion. However, such self-serving and destructive use of power is not leadership since the term *leadership* has a positive connotation.

Transformational leaders are shapers of values, creators, interpreters of institutional purpose, exemplars, makers of meanings, pathfinders, and molders of organizational culture. They are persistent and consistent. Their vision is so compelling that they know what they want from every interaction. Their visions don't blind others, but empower them. Such leaders have a deep sense of the purpose of the system and a long-range strategic sense, and these provide a sense of overall direction. They also know what kind of *culture,* in terms of beliefs, values, and norms, the system must develop if it is to achieve that purpose. By stimulating, modeling, advocating, innovating, and motivating, they mold this culture, to the degree that this is possible, to meet both internal and environmental needs.

William C. Norris (1983), a leader in the business world, provides an example that appeals to human-service providers. The founder and chairman of Control Data Corporation, he provides an example of transformational leadership not only within his own company but in the business community itself. His thesis is that social needs are not a threat to business; rather they provide opportunities for business.

> When a business becomes conscious of its social responsibilities and willing to do something about them, it starts looking for ways to maximize its positive effects on its non-shareholder constituencies. Usually the business turns to such policies and programs as equal job opportunities for employees, improved career counseling for the disadvantaged, counseling for chemically dependent workers, community involvement, heightened product safety, pollution reduction, energy conservation, charitable contributions, and the like [pp. 52–53[. . . . But even though these efforts are all highly laudable, their end results tend to be narrow in scope and small in scale. Meanwhile, major societal needs are left relatively unattended. And these are the needs that underlie and are interrelated with inflation, unemployment, underemployment, and similar woes.
>
> That these problems persist only serves to underscore the fact that corporations must effect fundamental changes in their strategy. They must begin turning unmet social and economic needs into profitable business opportunities, with the costs being shared between themselves and government [p. 53].

All three forms of leadership allow degrees: degrees of professional expertise, of managerial skill, of transformational leadership. Others besides formal leaders can participate in ad hoc ways and to a greater or lesser extent in all three forms of leadership. For instance, the secretaries in the medical department of a large corporation provide a significant amount of informal counseling for other employees. In many organizations, a great deal of the coaching and counseling one might expect to come from managers comes from peers.

FOLLOWERS: SITUATIONAL LEADERSHIP AND MATURITY

Since followers constitute one of the angles in the triangular process of leadership, their differences lead to differences in leadership style. One lens that can be used to judge differences among followers is maturity. For Hersey and Blanchard (1982; Hersey, Blanchard, and Hambleton, 1978), follower maturity is a key factor in what they call "situational" leadership. The concept of situational leadership

> is based on the amount of direction . . . and the amount of socio-emotional support . . . a leader must provide, given the situation and the "level of maturity" of a subordinate [Hersey, Blanchard, and Hambleton, 1978, p. 217].

Situational management

Maturity in an organizational sense relates to both the ability (job maturity) and the willingness (psychological maturity) of a staff person to direct his or her own behavior with respect to any given task. According to Moore (1976), maturity includes goal achievement, willingness and ability to take responsibility, task-relevant experience, goal-related assertiveness, the ability to act independently, adaptability to change, flexibility, willingness to expand one's interests, capability of taking a long-term perspective, the ability to utilize resources on the basis of merit and task achievement rather than social or organizational status or position, and awareness of what is happening within self and institution.

Maturity can range from low to high. One overly simplified scale of maturity would include the following four levels: (1) not able, not willing, (2) willing, not able, (3) able, not willing, and (4) both able and willing. Thus, in a mental health center a staff person's maturity with respect to counseling may be much higher (both able and willing) than his or her maturity with respect to interacting with other community agencies (willing, not able).

Once there is agreement with a staff person on that person's objective, most managers allow him or her to "get on with it." That is, level-4 maturity is assumed, whether it exists or not.

> Vanessa C., the director of the clinic, commissions John T., a staff member who devotes most of his time to counseling, to contact other human-service agencies in the area with respect to establishing a mutually funded and staffed Rape Crisis Center. With respect to this task, John has

level-1 or perhaps level-2 maturity. He asks a couple of his fellow staff members how they think he should go about this task, but he feels that their responses do not give him enough direction. Because he feels inadequate, he keeps putting the task off. After a month, Vanessa asks him what progress he has made, and he is embarrassed to say none.

Managers frequently delegate a task to a person who is not ready for it. At the opposite extreme, people who are actually at level 4 are treated as if they were at level 1.

The four different levels constitute four different "situations" in managerial leadership. Hersey and Blanchard provide a model or formula for matching styles of leadership with levels of maturity. In this model, managerial style, kind of task, and maturity of staff person constitute the three interacting angles of the leadership process. The two elements of managerial style are (1) providing task-related direction and (2) providing socio-emotional support.

Situation 1: level-1 maturity. With an employee at level 1, managers need to focus on the task rather than the relationship and provide a high degree of structure. Thus managers devote most of their energy to the competence needs of staff members by providing direction—describing what needs to be done and how to do it. Without being unfriendly, managers spend little time providing socio-emotional support and reinforcement. The managers' task behavior is relatively high, while relationship behavior is relatively low.

Situation 2: level-2 maturity. With employees at level 2, managers still need to provide a relatively high degree of structure but also a relatively high degree of socio-emotional support. Managers spend a great deal of time providing direction for staff members, but since the latter are willing, managers also spend time in two-way communication, providing support. This is the style used by managers who are interested in developing staff members.

Situation 3: level-3 maturity. With level-3 employees, managers deal with the needs of staff members, especially the kinds of incentives they need to use their abilities to attain goals. At this level of maturity, there is a greater emphasis on the staff members' participation in decisions.

Situation 4: level-4 maturity. Level-4 employees are mature staff members. Managers can safely delegate responsibility to these employees. They need relatively little attention in terms of direction and socio-emotional support. These staff members are the competent self-starters that all managers would like to have on their teams.

This quick overview of situational leadership hardly does justice to the details of the model, but it illustrates the fact that leadership is a three-cornered interactional process and focuses on some important variables associated with the "followers" corner of the triangle. No model, however, describes the complexity of the leadership process. Although this model deals with some of the complexities of followers and some of the options of leaders, it does not actually deal with the complexities of the situations. Furthermore, the notion of staff member "maturity" is a complex and difficult one. A staff member might be unwilling to undertake a task because of obstacles in the system or because the system provides no incentives for taking on such tasks. In this case unwillingness is not a sign of immaturity but a result of the deficiencies of the system. As Blake and Mouton (1982) suggest, instead of adapting their style to the maturity level of staff members, many managers need to improve the system.

PARTICIPATIVE MANAGEMENT

Everybody is familiar with the pyramid organizational structure and "chain of command" (Figure 11-3). As Naisbitt (1982) notes, the "pyramid structure has been praised and blamed, but its detractors have never come up with a better or more successful framework for organizations, although many have tried" (p. 189). Peters and Waterman (1982) found that in the best organizations, the structure was kept "lean and trim"; there were relatively few layers between the top and the bottom of the organization. Moreover, the people at the top of the best organizations were quite accessible. Some even kept an open-door policy to *anyone* in the organization. Tichy (1983) reflects this kind of thinking by representing the pyramid as a "network" as well as a "chain of command" (Figure 11-4). Tichy calls his version a "human resources organic model" based on these assumptions: (1) Democratic leadership and supportive leaders are most efficient. (2) Employees are most productive when they can participate in decision making. (3) Openness, honesty, and trust facilitate the transfer of information (p. 44). Tichy espouses an organizational culture that is currently the exception rather than the rule.

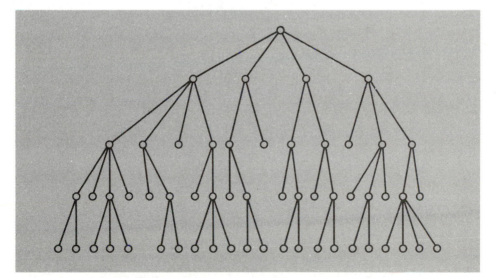

FIGURE 11-3. The classic pyramid organizational structure

Naisbitt, who sees networking as a major trend both in society as a whole and in organizations and institutions, suggests a "networking" approach to problem solving and decision making. Naisbitt's approach should certainly appeal to human-service practitioners, who grapple daily with social problems and seek to empower their clients. The main points made by Naisbitt deal with networking (a) in society as a whole and (b) in organizations and institutions (pp. 189–205).

In society as a whole: The failure of various kinds of hierarchies to solve social problems has given impetus to networking. An example in human services is the rapid growth of self-help groups. Networks provide what hierarchies cannot— horizontal links. Naisbitt points out, "Networks cut diagonally across the institutions that house information and put people in direct contact with the person or resource they seek" (p. 197). The network is egalitarian; each individual is at the center of a network.

"Causes" energize people and give rise to networking. Organizations and institutions that have lost their sense of "cause" can easily develop into rigid bureaucracies. I once tried to get some information on retirement homes for a friend. I contacted several agencies without learning much more than I already knew. However, I chanced on a person who was part of a network dealing with the elderly. She opened up a whole new world to me.

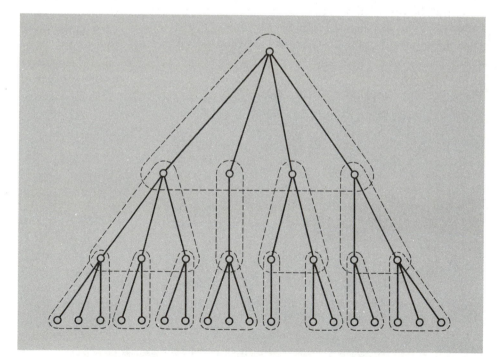

FIGURE 11-4.   Human resources organic model *(Tichy, 1983)*

In organizations: While the pyramid and other hierarchical forms that emphasize central decision making remain, many people are no longer convinced of their efficacy. Various studies show that Americans have lost faith in leaders. A Harris Poll reported in the *Washington Post National Weekly Edition* (1983) showed that the number of respondents who say they have "a great deal of confidence" in the leaders of medicine, organized religion, major companies, and organized labor has declined drastically since 1966. In 1966, 73% of respondents could make that statement about leaders in medicine. However, in 1983, only 35% could.

Hierarchies as they now exist have networks that are part of the informal system. All kinds of leadership—professional-technical, managerial, and transformational—include informal networks. As networking becomes more valued in the organization, a different *style* of management emerges, one that encourages autonomy and participative decision making. Naisbitt notes, "Small groups of talented people can govern their own work environment and produce spectacular results" (pp. 198–199). Naisbitt claims that "baby-boomers," more highly educated than their predecessors, are demanding more of a say in organizations. "Baby-boomers"—those born immediately after World War II—are now moving into managerial positions. It seems likely that organizations will eventually be restructured into smaller, more participatory units. Network-based approaches to authority, control, and decision making are not displacing the pyramid with its chain of command and control, but they are helping to humanize organizations and make them more effective and more efficient.

Should staff members participate in decisions made by managers? Some management experts say that is a meaningless question since followers invariably affect the decisions of leaders, as indicated by the leadership-process triangle. However, the triangle deals with *informal* impact on decision making. When it comes to *formal* participation in decision making, some people see disadvantages:

- Self-serving approaches on the part of management may be replaced by self-serving approaches on the part of staff members.
- "Least-common-denominatorism" may take over; trivial issues will be made to seem important.
- Staff members lack the knowledge and the overview of managers.
- Participative decision making is too emotional, too time consuming, too cumbersome, and too costly.
- Employee involvement may lead to a lot of compromises, which in turn will lead to mediocre work and outcomes.
- Employee participation is countercultural; most organizations are not ready for it. It is futile to try to move beyond traditional adversarial relationships between managers and employees.
- Many staff members will not be interested in participating in decision making for a number of reasons: It makes them nervous, it is not their job, it is not what they like to do or are used to doing, and so forth.

On the other hand, those that favor participative decision making claim that:

- Staff members will become more autonomous and more self-directed.
- If they "own" the enterprise more fully, they will give themselves more fully to its mission.
- They will learn more about the system and be able to participate in its functions in more enlightened ways; such learning will increase options both for staff members and for the organization.
- There will be a less adversarial relationship between staff and managers. As a result, staff will be able to listen to managers in less biased ways and more freely accept their good ideas.
- Participation provides staff members an opportunity to use the information they have. In many ways they are closer to the work of the system than managers are. Their information will fill in gaps that managers have.
- Creativity of members will be tapped.
- Managers will become more accountable; their assumptions and decisions will be open to disconfirmation.
- Participative management recognizes that staff members are important stakeholders in the organization or institution.

Tannenbaum and Schmidt have illustrated various degrees of participation (Figure 11-5). Participative management needs to be seen, understood, and judged from various points of view—productivity, quality of life, organizational culture, and what is happening in the environment; in other words, in the social setting in which the organization is found. Research cannot focus on just one of these variables. Tannenbaum and Schmidt's enhanced model (Figure 11-6) takes environment into consideration. Naisbitt (1982) reports that his research suggests a societal demand for more participation and that participation leads to greater productivity.

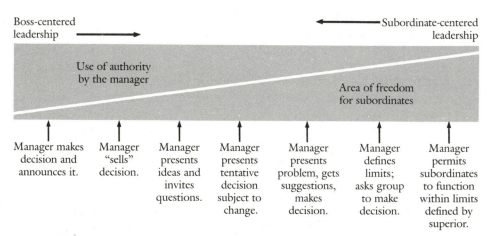

FIGURE 11-5.   Continuum of leadership behavior *(Tannenbaum and Schmidt, 1973)*

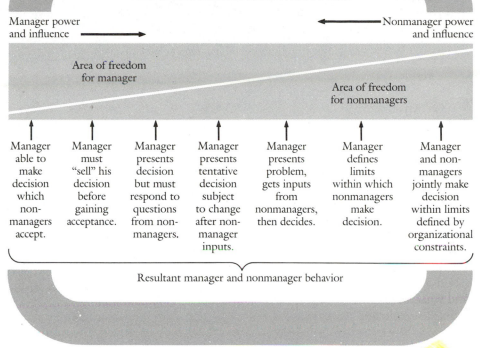

THE SOCIETAL ENVIRONMENT

THE ORGANIZATIONAL ENVIRONMENT

Manager power and influence ⟶   ⟵ Nonmanager power and influence

Area of freedom for manager

Area of freedom for nonmanagers

| Manager able to make decision which non-managers accept. | Manager must "sell" his decision before gaining acceptance. | Manager presents decision but must respond to questions from non-managers. | Manager presents tentative decision subject to change after non-manager inputs. | Manager presents problem, gets inputs from nonmanagers, then decides. | Manager defines limits within which nonmanagers make decision. | Manager and non-managers jointly make decision within limits defined by organizational constraints. |

Resultant manager and nonmanager behavior

FIGURE 11-6.   Enhanced continuum of leadership model *(Tannenbaum and Schmidt, 1973)*

The values held by human-service providers certainly support participative man-agement. Given their increased self-responsibility, their understanding of human nature, and their ability to interact with others even in difficult situations, human-service providers can make excellent consultants to organizations, institutions, and communities searching for ways to become less authoritarian.

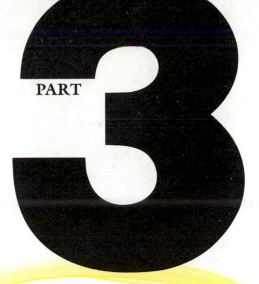

PART **3**

THE PERVASIVE
DIMENSIONS

Incentives, working conditions, interactions with the environment, and organizational culture can be managed to create institutions that serve the needs of both human-service providers and their clients. Consequently, the third section of Model A deals with four sets of factors that pervade or rinse through the system:

- *The reward system.* Do both human-service providers and their clients have the incentives to work toward and achieve goals? Chapter 12 is about the principles that govern behavior in the delivery of service.
- *Climate and quality of life.* Chapter 13 is concerned with the needs and wants of the providers themselves. What is it like to work here? What is it like to be a client here?
- *Interactions with the environment.* Human behavior is influenced by its context. Just as social settings affect clients and both create problems and provide resources for their management, so the environment affects human-service delivery systems and must be managed (Chapter 14). Environmental factors may be economic, political, ecological, demographic, legal, technological, or cultural.
- *Culture and other forms of arationality.* Culture—the culture of individuals, of systems, and of society—is the most pervasive of the environmental variables, forming the basis of much of the arational, whether enhancing or limiting. Chapter 15 asks, to what degree can organizational or institutional culture at any level be molded and managed?

213

12

The Reward System

Organizations, institutions, and communities are dynamic systems. Goals are pursued through transactions among individual members, among the subunits of the system, and between the systems themselves and their environments. The behavior of these systems and of their members can be analyzed in terms of the principles of behavior. Ideally, human-service practitioners understand these principles and help their individual clients apply them to their lives. But the practitioners often fail to examine how well they use these principles in their relationships among themselves, and in helper-client relationships, in their own organizations, and in the organizations, institutions, and communities with which they work.

The principles of behavior underlie and pervade the system (Figure 12-1). Organizations, institutions, and communities are poorly designed or become dysfunctional when those managing these systems fail to take these principles into consideration. From a more positive perspective, a working knowledge of these principles is a source of system-enhancing and individual-enhancing power for managers and members alike.

B. F. Skinner (1953) started a revolution (and a controversy) by systematically developing the principles underlying behavior and its modification. A great deal of research over the past quarter of a century has culminated in sophisticated compilations of these principles (for instance, Bandura, 1975) in the application of these principles to everyday behavior (for example, Malott, Tillema, and Glenn, 1978), to social learning and personality development (Bandura, 1977), to a variety of human settings (Kazdin, 1975), to abnormal behavior (Ullman and Krasner, 1975), to self-management (Watson and Tharp, 1981; Williams and Long, 1983), and finally to the behavior of people in organizations (Luthans and Kreitner, 1975; Miller, 1978). These principles are sometimes called the *principles of learning,* for

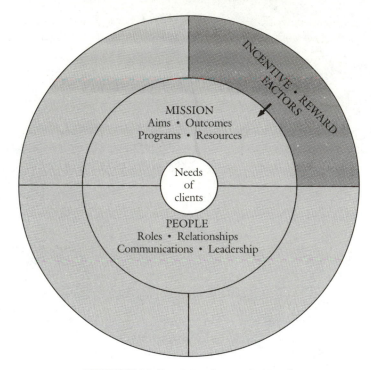

FIGURE 12-1.   Incentives and rewards

they underlie the ways in which people learn (and unlearn) to behave in both self-limiting and self-enhancing ways. Consider the following examples.

The small group. One of the members of a counseling group breaks the tension of a hostile interaction in the group with a humorous quip. All the members of the group laugh and feel relieved. As the group moves on, it becomes rather common for group members to interrupt activities they do not like with humor and, since people laugh, the humorists feel rewarded. It becomes an unstated norm in the group that humor can be used to interrupt activities that are disliked for whatever reason. Gradually group members begin complaining that the group is not getting anywhere.

The supervisor. A social worker supervisor diligently points out every mistake students make in their field work. He does so with almost surgical precision, pointing out that "there is nothing personal in this." He says little about what the interns do well. Sometimes students try to avoid these conferences, but over the years he has developed ways of "handling" students who try to do so.

In the first example there is a misuse of reward. In the second, there is a misuse of punishment. While most of us would use basic common sense to point out what is wrong in both examples, a review of the principles of behavior will provide a more systematic framework for determining how these principles might be used actively to encourage individual- and system-enhancing behavior.

ANTECEDENTS AND CONSEQUENCES

One of the primary tasks of change agents is to acquire a clear, behavioral understanding of what is happening in the human system with which they are working. Human behavior is always embedded in a context; that is, behavior and behavioral events have both antecedents and consequences, as the following ABC model shows:

Antecedents →	*Behavioral events* →	*Consequences*
A social work supervisor notices that an intern is handling a case incorrectly.	The supervisor points out what the intern is doing right, what he is doing wrong, and how he can correct what he is doing wrong.	The intern feels good about what he is doing right, corrects what he is doing wrong. The supervisor feels rewarded and continues to give confirmatory and corrective feedback to this and other interns.

From the supervisor's point of view, noticing the self-defeating behavior of the intern is an *antecedent* that acts as a stimulus to the *behavior* of giving feedback. Since the *consequence* of giving feedback is experienced by the supervisor as positive and rewarding, the supervisor continues to give feedback in the same manner. This simple schema is useful in analyzing the complexity of human behavior. Any behavioral event can be seen in terms of what takes place before an act, the act itself, and the consequences of the act.

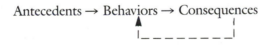

Antecedents → Behaviors → Consequences

Antecedents are conditions, states, behaviors, or events that signal, cue, or stimulate some kind of behavior. They cue a behavior by signaling the probability of some consequence of the behavior.

The behavior will probably lead to some reward. For instance, a consultant notices that her client, the director of a neighborhood organization, is in a self-reflective mood. He talks about himself openly and about some doubts about his leadership style. This stimulates her to give him some feedback on his style based on her interactions with him.

The behavior will probably lead to some kind of punishment or aversive consequence. For example, a volunteer worker in a rape crisis center is about to offer a suggestion at a staff meeting. But she remembers that a suggestion offered by another volunteer had been belittled at a previous meeting. She infers that offering a suggestion might well lead to some kind of punishing consequence, and she decides not to speak up.

Behavior will probably lead to mixed consequence—that is, in one way rewarding but in another way punishing. When asked to move into the position of director of human services for her state, Lisa imagines the long hours, the political haggling, and the stress that the new position will bring; but she also sees the opportunities to provide more effective services and the financial and career rewards associated with that position. Accepting the position will lead to both rewarding and punishing consequences.

Behavior will probably lead to neither a rewarding nor a punishing consequence. The director of a proposed halfway house for exconvicts attends several meetings of local clergy in an attempt to solicit their support for the house. He believes that they could improve public relations in the neighborhood where the house will be located. Each time he goes to a meeting, the clergy listen politely, compliment him for undertaking such valuable work, and even invite him to return for further discussions—but he never gets a firm commitment. He finally stops going to clergy meetings, believing that his time could be better spent.

Behaviors are the ways in which people act or fail to act. Assessing needs, elaborating mission, determining major aims, establishing goals, constructing and implementing programs, devising roles, collaborating with fellow workers on projects, giving and receiving information, giving and receiving feedback, dealing with conflict, coordinating work processes, managing the environment, and planning and managing change—or failing to do any of these—are the forms of organizational behavior stressed in this book. The question is: How can the principles of behavior raise the probability that system- and individual-enhancing behaviors will take place in this organization, institution, or community?

Consequences, as the term implies, are the rewards or punishments or the mixture of the two that follow some behavior. Consequences have a profound impact on subsequent behavior. If you take the time to write excellent proposals for the funding of projects for your agency only to meet refusal after refusal, you may begin to put off this necessary task. Consequences are the rewards, punishments, the mixture of the two, or the absence of either that lead to the increase in, the maintenance of, or the decrease in the frequency or intensity of the behaviors they follow.

If the principal cues for the supervisor's behavior are the mistakes the interns make, the supervisor's principal behavior is corrective feedback. The supervisor feels rewarded by a sense of accomplishment after telling the interns what they do wrong.

If the routine work and creative ideas of the interns are the principal cues for the supervisor's behavior, the supervisor's principal behavior is more positive: asking the interns to discuss what they did well, what needs to be improved, and how they plan to bring about improvement. The intern is encouraged to manage the feedback session, while the supervisor contributes creative ideas and helps to illuminate blind spots. By helping the interns become more responsible for their own growth and development, the supervisor improves services to clients. As relationships with the interns improve, the supervisor feels rewarded.

INCENTIVES: CRITICAL ANTECEDENTS

Perhaps the most critical antecedents for system functioning are incentives. An incentive may be either a promise that performance will be rewarded or a threat that nonperformance will be punished. Some organizations need to talk less about motivation and more about incentives. Motivation deals with internal states that are difficult to identify even with the cooperation of the people being studied. Incentives are much more manageable. Effective systems provide both extrinsic incentives such as decent wages and intrinsic incentives such as the satisfaction of a job well done.

> [T]he two causes of poor performance most commonly espoused are motives ("they don't care") and capacity ("they're too dumb"). But these are usually the last two places one should look for causes of incompetence, simply because they rarely are the substantial problem. . . . Except for a few strange individuals, people generally care a great deal about how they perform on the job, or in school. . . . Improvements in training can do wonders for most people we consider slow-witted; better incentives can usually obliterate all evidence of defective motivation [Gilbert, 1978, p. 89].

It is less painful for a manager to say, "The people who work here are not motivated" than to say, "I have not succeeded in discovering the kinds of incentives that appeal to them."

Gilbert (1978) lays down six principles for creating *incompetence* in an organization:

- Make sure that poor performers get paid as well as good ones.
- See that good performance gets punished in some way.
- Don't make use of nonmonetary incentives.
- Design the job so that it has no future.
- Avoid arranging working conditions that employees would find more pleasant.
- Give pep talks rather than incentives to promote performance in punishing situations (p. 87).

Since incentives are promises that rewards will be conferred, all promises must be fulfilled if a system is to maintain its integrity. In an effectively functioning system, the incentives are clear and abundant. Peters and Waterman (1982) found that the "excellent companies" abound in incentives. Common incentives are money and fringe benefits, the work itself, achievement, recognition, promotion, responsibility, education, training, personal growth, opportunities to choose preferred kinds of work, to work with congenial people, to choose one's own working hours (flextime), and to participate in decisions that affect one's life in the system.

THE POWER OF CONSEQUENCES

Behavior is a function of its consequences—that is, behaviors are strengthened, maintained, or weakened by events that follow them. Guards in a correctional facility are more likely to pass on information that their superiors need to make staffing decisions if information sharing is encouraged and praised rather than taken for granted. If most members of a neighborhood fail to show up for community council meetings, it is probably because they see little payoff in attending such meetings, or because they experience alternate behaviors (such as being with their families or watching television) as more rewarding.

Strengthening behavior: Reinforcement

The "strength" of a behavior is related to its probability or frequency. If a supervisor in a mental health center meets with interns and new counselors once or twice every week, then "meeting with supervisees" is a strong behavior for that supervisor. If this same supervisor has to be reminded to turn in late reports, then "turning in reports on time" is a weak behavior. "Strong" and "weak" are relative terms. If 50% of the families in a neighborhood join the local community council, this is a strong behavioral response; but if a supervisor shows up for only 50% of the supervisory conferences, this is a weak behavioral response.

If a consequence strengthens a behavior, it is called a *reinforcer*. For instance, if a volunteer in a mental hospital feels productive when she helps new patients become adjusted to hospital routine, she will want to continue volunteering. The positive consequences of her behavior tend to maintain the strength of the behavior. There are two different kinds of reinforcement, but each serves to maintain or increase the strength of a behavior.

Positive reinforcers. A positive reinforcer is a consequence that maintains or strengthens a behavior. A mental health clinic reorganizes itself in such a way that the director no longer makes all the decisions. The entire staff of eight counselors and three social workers now participates in the decision-making process. There is less absenteeism, more clients are seen in the same amount of time, fewer clients return with the same problems, and there is less bickering among the staff and between staff members and the director. All these strengthened behaviors are related to the system of participative decision making.

Fortunately, all the strengthened behaviors outlined above are desirable behaviors. It is also possible to provide positive reinforcement for *unwanted* behaviors and therefore strengthen them. If a mother rewards a child with attention only when the child makes a fuss, then it is likely that fussing behavior will be maintained or even increased.

Negative reinforcers. Negative reinforcement takes place when an unpleasant or noxious stimulus is removed. Since the removal is usually experienced as rewarding, it tends to strengthen the behavior it follows. For instance, Carl, a social worker, whines and pouts when he is asked to see a client after ordinary hours. If Carl complains long and loud, Angel, his supervisor, asks someone else; that is, she removes the threat of the unpleasant stimulus of working overtime. But this response can reinforce Carl's complaining behavior, because behaviors that are reinforced, either positively or negatively, tend to be repeated. Note, too, that Carl's complaining behavior is unpleasant to Angel. When she stops asking Carl to see clients outside regular hours, Carl's annoying complaining also stops. And so Angel's giving-in behavior is negatively reinforced and tends to be strengthened. Negative reinforcement is the basis of avoidance behavior.

Reinforcers versus rewards. Technically reinforcers and rewards are not the same, although the terms are often used interchangeably. What people believe to be a reward is actually a reinforcer only if in fact it maintains or strengthens behavior. Suppose the director of a mental health clinic tries to solve disagreements with members of the staff by giving them a pay increase. Pay raises could be seen as a reward. In this case, however, staff members see it as their due and don't relate it to their disagreements with the director.

What seems to be a reward is a reinforcer *only if it is experienced as a reward by the person for whom it is intended*. Neighborhood block parties will not be experienced as rewarding by residents who chose the neighborhood because they wanted anonymity. Luthans and Kreitner (1975) give an example of a company that "rewarded" its employees by putting on a big Christmas dinner at the local country club. The managers, most of whom were members of the club, were surprised when the employees asked for money instead of a party. It was not rewarding for most of them to go where they felt out of place.

Intrinsic versus extrinsic reinforcement. A group of friends get together for a party one weekend evening. During the evening the conversation turns to some of the more serious developmental issues they are facing in their lives. Since they find their interchange intrinsically rewarding, they decide to meet frequently.

Five consultants are invited to help a professional school of psychology design a new doctoral program. Each one is offered two hundred dollars plus expenses for the day. Of the five invited, one does not show up because the stipend is too small. At the end of the day the design has not been completed, and the consultants are invited to return the next day if they would like to. Since there are no further funds, however, the consultants will have to contribute their services. Only one consultant shows up the next day.

To explain the consultants' behavior there are at least three possibilities: (1) A consultant comes only because of the stipend. (2) A consultant comes because he or she enjoys this kind of work and feels productive doing it. The stipend is incidental and is not a factor in the consultant's coming. (3) A consultant comes both because of the stipend and because she or he enjoys that kind of work. If either factor were missing, he or she would not show up. In case (1) the reinforcement is extrinsic, in case (2) it is intrinsic, and in case (3) it is a mixture of the two.

Everyone works for some kind of reinforcement, whether intrinsic or extrinsic or a combination of both. Even altruistic behavior is intrinsically rewarding, and often deeply so, for the people who give themselves in service to others. The universality of the principle of reinforcement makes some people so uncomfortable that they try to ignore it—for instance, by expecting people to be loyal to systems in which there is no payoff or by working for causes in which they have no real investment. Most people operate on a combination of intrinsic and extrinsic reinforcers, and sometimes on either intrinsic or extrinsic reinforcers alone.

Community-living systems such as families, peer groups, and communes provide a high degree of intrinsic reinforcement by filling basic needs for security, companionship, mutual help, and intimacy. There may be something wrong in homes where children must be bribed to contribute to the common good of the family.

An overemphasis on extrinsic reinforcement has been dubbed "leaping for lollipops" because it represents a superficial approach to human motivation. Research on differences between intrinsic and extrinsic reinforcement should make us cautious in our use of extrinsic reinforcement (Benware and Deci, 1975; Deci, 1971, 1972, 1975; Condry, 1977; Uranowitz, 1975). Condry found that extrinsic reinforcements such as earning good grades and doing well in exams can actually block rather than stimulate learning. Einstein is reported to have said that after passing his final exams, he found working on scientific problems distasteful for an entire year (see Condry, p. 460). Benware and Deci found that adding extrinsic reinforcement for tasks that were intrinsically reinforcing actually reduced commitment to these tasks. These findings suggest that a moderate distrust of extrinsic reinforcement is preferable to an overreliance on it.

Many people find satisfaction simply in knowing that they are doing a job competently and that they are fulfilling their part of a contract. This is even true of some workers in very humdrum jobs. Extrinsic rewards may be used to make jobs less humdrum (for instance, to compensate for the paper work that most people in human-service professions must do). However, it is a mistake to assume that no one can experience intrinsic rewards in tedious jobs or that people who don't complain about such jobs don't know any better or can't do anything else. Human-service practitioners would do well to analyze carefully the intrinsic satisfactions available for both individual and organizational clients.

Nevertheless, it is a mistake to romanticize tedious work. Grinding work can grind up workers both physically and psychologically (Rubin, 1976; Terkel, 1974). Undoubtedly advances in technology, rearrangement and improvement of working conditions, and a more sensible and liberal use of extrinsic reinforcement can make work a more human experience. It is quite possible to exploit a worker's need to do a job competently or willingness to fulfill an unjust contract. Admittedly the principles of human behavior can be used to pursue evil as well as good ends.

Contingency. If a reinforcer is to influence behavior in a systematic way, it must be made *contingent* on the desired behavior. Contingency refers to an "if-then" relationship: If the patient in the rehabilitation ward of the hospital does her exercises, then she may watch a television program of her choice. A contingent reinforcer is one that is delivered after, and only after, a certain desirable behavior. The behavior leads to the reinforcer. Behaviors are maintained or strengthened only if the reinforcers associated with them are made contingent on performance.

If people receive a reinforcer whether they engage in a desired behavior or not, that reinforcer will not affect the behavior. If people receive their salaries every week whether they do their work or not, it cannot be expected that salary will act as a reinforcer. Luthans and Kreitner (1975) summarize the problems of the use of money as a reinforcer in work situations (see pp. 104–107). If behavior is to be maintained or strengthened, then it is the contingency relationship that is important, not the reinforcer alone.

The contingency problem is solved in the case of intrinsic reinforcement, for instance, when people do counseling because they like the work. When people get satisfaction from their work, feeling a sense of competence and accomplishment in what they do, the "if-then" relationship is built in and the need for contingent

extrinsic reinforcers is lessened. However, the "built-in" nature of intrinsic reinforcers can also cause serious problems. When an alcoholic takes a drink, the relief
from stress (reward) is immediate. The problem here is to break or lessen the "if-
then" relationship. If the man takes Antabuse (a drug that causes nausea when taken
with alcohol) and then gets nauseated when he takes a drink, the contingency
relationship (drink-pleasure) is broken up.

Uses of positive reinforcement. In many systems positive reinforcement is woefully
underused. Children hear few words of encouragement when they do their house-
hold chores and parents receive too little encouragement from one another or from
their children. Sometimes managers, directors, administrators, and supervisors are
embarrassed to give verbal reinforcement—"He was a difficult client, but you did
a fine job"—as if encouragement were cheap or silly. In many organizations and
institutions positive feedback seems to be countercultural. But positive reinforcement is like an oil that helps a system run more smoothly. If social-work interns
hear from their supervisors only when they make mistakes, supervisors become
noxious stimuli to be avoided. Reinforcement works best if it follows *closely* on a
behavior it is designed to support. Intrinsic reinforcement, of course, is ideal because
it accompanies the behavior.

If we want any given human system to work more effectively, then we must check
every element of its design and functioning—the needs it is to meet, its mission
statements and goals, its programs, its selection, education, and training processes,
its access to other program-related resources, its structure, the relationships that
follow from structure, its communication processes, its climate, and its relationship
to its environment—from the viewpoint of the use or abuse of the principles of
positive reinforcement. For instance, if the way work is divided up leaves most
members dissatisfied, then the principles of reinforcement have been ignored and
the system will probably suffer.

Questions about the use of reinforcement throughout the system are:

- Have the principles of reinforcement been taken into consideration in the design
  and functioning of the system?
- Are there enough incentives and are they strong enough?
- Is there an emphasis on positive rather than negative reinforcement?
- Is there too much reinforcement—that is, reinforcement that is too frequent
  or too easy to come by?
- Is there too little reinforcement—that is, reinforcement that is too infrequent
  or too hard to come by?
- Is reinforcement contingent on getting the tasks of the system done or is not
  getting these tasks done sometimes rewarded?
- Is there an emphasis on intrinsic motivation and a balance between intrinsic
  and extrinsic motivation, or are workers "leaping for lollipops"?
- Are reinforcements actually experienced as rewarding by those for whom they
  are intended?
- Are reinforcements timed appropriately or are they given too soon or too late?

Weakening behavior: Punishment and extinction

Punishment is a consequence that weakens behavior. There are two kinds of punishment, both involving some unpleasant consequence: (1) A person's behavior leads to an aversive event. You are caught not listening to a client and the client gets angry. (2) A person's behavior leads to the loss of something pleasant. A guard in a correctional facility is occasionally late and takes too many breaks. He fails to get the promotion he expected.

Notice the difference between punishment and negative reinforcement. First of all, negative reinforcement maintains or strengthens the behavior it follows, while punishment by definition weakens the behavior it follows. Negative reinforcement means that a person escapes or avoids some impending unpleasant event, while punishment plunges the person into an unpleasant event.

People who manage human-service systems—including parents, teachers, ministers, administrators, doctors, project directors, supervisors, and the like—often fail to recognize the punitive side effects of their decisions, policies, and behaviors. When system members react like punished people, the managers don't understand their reactions. If a manager could say, "I wonder in what way they feel punished, even though I have not intended to punish them," he or she would be using the principles of behavior creatively.

Punishment.   Punishment is especially effective if it is contingent on a certain behavior or a failure to behave in a certain way. For instance, if the chief psychologist at a state hospital suspends an intern for two weeks for coming to work late and missing too many days of work, the intern no longer comes late or misses work. However, the mere *effectiveness* of punishment is not the only issue. The overall *efficiency* of punishment can be low and the price the punisher pays can be quite high. Here are some of the unwanted side effects of punishment:

Temporary effects.   Often the desired decrease in unwanted behavior is only temporary. The unwanted behavior pops up again when the punished person forgets about the punishment or supervision decreases. When the chief psychologist goes on vacation, the intern starts coming in late again.

No new learning.   Even when punishment successfully inhibits unwanted behavior, it does not in and of itself suggest any new behavior. It creates a kind of behavioral vacuum. For instance, if the members of a self-help group use different kinds of punishment such as hostility, ridicule, threats of expulsion, and heavy-handed advice to influence one of their members to stop drinking, they may be successful, but their success may be short-lived unless they help him or her replace drinking with more constructive patterns of living.

Deviousness.   One kind of new learning is often associated with punishment: The person punished learns how to avoid punishment by becoming sneaky or by avoiding the punisher. Staff members invent excuses for not seeing clients or leave early when they know the supervisor is going to be away. If staff members are avoiding work, there is probably something wrong with the system and the rewards it offers. Instituting punitive controls is probably not a very constructive response to the problem.

Emotional disruption. Punishment has unpleasant emotional consequences of two forms: (1) The punished person loses self-esteem, seeing himself or herself as bad or incompetent. (2) The punished person sees the punisher as bad and learns to fear and dislike the supervisor. Whenever punishment is used, it can lead to disruption in the relationship between the person being punished and the punisher. A supervisor and the interns in her charge live in an uncertain truce. The climate is not one that encourages learning.

The suppression of wanted behavior. While it inhibits unwanted behavior, punishment can also inhibit desirable behavior that is related to the punished behavior. Consider the following example:

> Two consultants were hired by the administrator of a large state psychiatric hospital. They started by interviewing him and some of the members of his executive team. They also interviewed a few psychiatrists and psychologists. The administrator did not know that they were going to interview staff members. He called them in and accused them of going beyond their mandate. They quickly became wary of him, tended not to talk to people without explicit permission, and tended not to discuss with the administrator what they observed as they moved around the hospital. The administrator, at least for a while, lost a valuable source of information.

Punishment in this case was "successful"—that is, it inhibited certain forms of behavior. But it also suppressed useful forms of behavior on the part of the consultants. The consultants and the administrator eventually worked out their problems and developed a climate of trust, but punitive behavior had retarded the whole consultation process.

The overuse and abuse of punishment. Given the potentially negative side effects of punishment, why do those with the responsibility for the management of systems so often resort to negative control? Luthans and Kreitner (1975) suggest many philosophical, sociological, and cultural reasons for the popularity of negative control, but they also offer a behavioral explanation: punishment reinforces its user. The director of nursing in a psychiatric hospital reprimands the nurses' aides for standing around and talking with one another instead of working. The short-term effect is less time spent in talking and a more expeditious carrying out of tasks. This consequence is reinforcing for the director of nursing.

> The seemingly overwhelming use of punishment is not completely hopeless. As human resource managers come to recognize the questionable side effects and long range implications of punitive control, they can begin to put themselves under the control of different contingencies. Specifically, the short-run negative reinforcement associated with the use of punishment may be passed up in favor of long-run positive reinforcement derived from working in a nonpunitive and self-controlling, supportive environment. Although tempting, punishment's immediate payoffs should most often be resisted [Luthans and Kreitner, 1975, p. 117].

If in your system you see people avoiding certain tasks, ask yourself what punishers may be at work.

Is there a case for some punishment?   To suggest that punishment is never necessary or useful would be overstating the case. However, effectively operating systems *minimize* the use of punishment. Punishment is used only if necessary and even then it is combined with positive reinforcement. When some unwanted behavior is punished, some desired behavior that is incompatible with the unwanted behavior is reinforced. For instance, if the members of a peer group punish one of the members for her sarcastic remarks by being cold to her or lecturing her, they also reward her with attention and other forms of social reinforcement when her conversation is devoid of sarcasm. There is little use in punishing unwanted behavior unless wanted behavior is substituted.

Reducing the need for punishment through effective management.   Good management reduces the need for rules and discipline and therefore reduces the amount of punishment in a system. Ground rules and disciplinary procedures set the *limits* within which people operate, but they don't provide incentives for doing well. For instance, correctional facilities have ground rules and disciplinary procedures to set the limits within which inmates and staff are expected to operate. However, it is reinforcement that helps inmates and staff operate constructively within these limits. If punishment for violating rules and regulations is central, then the system is poorly managed.

After all, disciplinary policies set the limits on how *poor* performance can be and still be tolerated. Good management, which includes the intelligent use of incentives and rewards, confirmatory and corrective feedback, and the effective use of system design, tries to bring performance above absolute minimums so that disciplinary actions need not be used. Enforcing rules in order to get minimally acceptable performance on the part of the members of a system might well be part of the managing package, but it is hardly the most important part. Stimulating and reinforcing good performance minimizes the need to be an enforcer (see Brethower, 1972).

Extinction.   Extinction means that some behavior that was once reinforced is now no longer reinforced. Ordinarily the behavior begins to weaken and occurs less frequently. Sometimes at the beginning of the extinction process there is a "frustration" effect that may include emotional reactions such as crying, passive resistance, aggression, pouting, withdrawal, depression, and the like, and a temporary *increase* in the previously reinforced behavior.

> Ivan and Ramona have been having problems in their marriage. Ivan has been getting his way much of the time by passive-aggressive behavior. When Ramona doesn't want to do something he does, he withdraws and pouts. She has been giving in and therefore has been reinforcing his pouting behavior. She now decides that she will ignore his pouting, wait until he is civil again, and then try to make bilateral decisions with him in an adult-to-adult fashion. When she ignores his pouting behavior, he becomes very angry and screams and yells at her (the frustration effect). She refuses to play the game of "uproar" and ignores his screaming and yelling also. His passive aggressive behavior gradually begins to lessen.

Extinction is one of the processes by which we adjust our behavior to the chang-ing world around us. It is not the same as punishment, though it might seem similar. Ivan feels punished (frustrated) because Ramona no longer rewards his pouting by giving in. However, in extinction no unpleasant consequence is added.

Extinction works best when the unwanted behavior is no longer reinforced and some alternate, incompatible, but desired behavior is reinforced. In this way good behavior forces bad behavior out of the system. In the weekly meetings of a self-help group, the members stop laughing at Bill's jokes, which they have come to see as his way of avoiding the work of the group. When he makes a serious contribution, they respond with attention and empathy. Bill's disruptive humor decreases with a concomitant increase in the time he spends dealing with serious issues.

Schedules of reinforcement affect both learning and extinction. If reinforcement follows every instance of behavior, it is said to be *continuous*. For instance, if Ramona gives in every time Ivan pouts, she is providing continuous reinforcement. But behaviors are seldom reinforced 100% of the time. If they are sometimes reinforced and sometimes not, reinforcement is called *intermittent*.

Continuous reinforcement helps promote rapid new learning. Intermittent rein-forcement (the usual reinforcement of everyday life) can make behavior extremely resistant to extinction. Let us say that in the past Ramona reinforced Ivan's pouting by giving in just about every time (continuous reinforcement). Under such a sched-ule of reinforcement Ivan quickly learned to use pouting as a means of getting his way. Now Ramona ignores his pouting and his pouting behavior begins to decrease, but it does not disappear. Ramona makes the mistake of giving in once in a while—that is, she provides intermittent reinforcement for Ivan's pouting behavior. His pouting behavior persists and, if anything, even gets stronger. She finally realizes her mistake and never gives in when Ivan resorts to pouting. But now the extinction process takes much longer, for Ivan hopes that his passive-aggressive behavior might work at least some of the time. (See Miller, 1978, pp. 157–182, for a more extended discussion of intermittent reinforcement.)

AVOIDANCE BEHAVIOR

Avoidance behavior insidiously affects our participation in all the systems of our lives and is highly resistant to extinction. It is my conviction that avoidance behavior is central to the "psychopathology of the average" and underlies the failed potential of both individuals and human systems.

Some of the residents in a neighborhood in a large city were becoming alarmed because of the number of nursing homes being built in their area. Apartment buildings were being bulldozed and residents were being dis-placed as a disproportionate number of these profitable businesses opened. The entire character of the neighborhood was changing.

The director of the local community organization and his immediate staff were slow to act for a variety of reasons: First, they thought that some people would see the stance of the community council as antihu-manitarian. Second, many of the most active members of the organization were not affected by the nursing home boom. Third, and perhaps most influential, they disliked the prospect of the political battles that might take place. Their avoidance behavior characterized the general style of that particular community council. The members thought that overly bold initiatives would only alienate people.

The director sent the matter to committee, but the residents being affected were not satisfied. Working with the local alderman, and on their own initiative, they filed a law suit to prevent further building. The people in that area of the community eventually formed a splinter group that acted as a gadfly for the community organization. For the director and his immediate staff, the second state was worse than the first. By not acting, the director avoided immediate political hassles, but in the long run his avoidance behavior led to punitive consequences.

Avoidance behavior is immediately rewarded. For instance, if a supervisor puts off giving feedback to a troublesome intern, the reward is the immediate relief of avoiding an unpleasant situation. The immediacy of the reward raises the probability that this kind of behavior will be repeated in the future.

Watson and Tharp (1981) indicate why avoidance, like punishment, has a deadly impact on learning.

> Avoidance learning is highly resistant to extinction, because the antecedent stimulus evokes the avoidance behavior and the person who has learned the avoidance response will not have an opportunity to learn that the old unpleasant outcome is no longer there [p. 95].

Once a pattern of avoidance becomes *habitual,* it becomes even more impervious to management. It "goes underground" and is no longer recognized as avoidance behavior.

Avoidance behavior is very common in the systems of our lives:

- Many parents avoid discussing sexuality with their children because the subject is embarrassing or because it arouses their own unresolved sexual feelings.
- The administration and faculties of schools avoid setting new behavioral goals that meet the learning needs of students more effectively rather than face and work out their practical and ideological differences.
- Managers and administrators avoid involving staff members in goal setting because they fear giving their power away.
- A minister gives up attempts to persuade the members of the congregation to minister to one another because his attempts have disturbed some of the "pillars" of the church.
- A mental health clinic avoids reorganizing its delivery of services because the press of work is too great.

Avoidance behavior is one of the primary sources of individual- and system-limiting arationality. Effectively functioning systems are not immune to avoidance behavior; their members realize that avoidance will be common, insidious, and difficult to deal with. Wise managers, administrators, and consultants help their organizations and institutions deal with its most debilitating forms. For instance, they build an assessment of avoidance behaviors into their periodic reviews by asking, "What are we currently avoiding and what negative impact is this avoidance having on the system?" Such systems are eager for new learning that creates more options for the system, its members, and the people it serves.

In effectively functioning systems, avoidance and failure are not rewarded. Employees are not rewarded for not working, students for not learning, supervisors for not giving feedback, marriage partners for not facing issues that divide them, counselors for not helping, or churches for not fostering community. One criticism of social welfare is that it rewards failure.

> We create all sorts of potentially useful programs for the needy among us—public housing, financial assistance, job training, special education projects. But instead of using these programs to reinforce and encourage good things, we do just the opposite.
>
> The one overriding criterion for access to any of these programs is: failure. . . .
>
> In general, we reward those things we wish to see repeated. But in social welfare, we reward those things that most distress us, and we are endlessly surprised when people react negatively to the things we offer as rewards for their negative attributes. . . . We never seem to understand that by rewarding failure we encourage failure. . . . I have a feeling we'd all be better off if we turned the thing on its head. Suppose, for instance, that in addition to sheer need—a negative criterion—we established positive criteria for, say, public housing eligibility (Raspberry, 1977, p. 34).

A working knowledge of the principles of human behavior and the ability to apply them to issues such as social welfare will not make these seemingly intractable problems go away, but it will certainly help us to manage them.

SHAPING BEHAVIOR

Shaping refers to the process of reinforcing successive approximations to an objective or goal. Shaping includes reinforcement of each approximation to the goal and the extinction of behaviors that do not lead to the goal. Effective shaping includes the control of such antecedents as goal-setting, giving instructions, and modeling goal-related behaviors. The paunchy middle-aged man who wheezes when he walks and envies the trim jogger has yet to learn the power of shaping. Certainly running a mile in seven minutes is beyond his grasp today, but he can walk two blocks without harming himself. And he can commit himself to a gradual program of exercise and diet that could change his envy to exaltation. No magic is involved. Just a common-sense combination of successive approximations, positive reinforcement, and extinction.

As it applies to behavior in organizations, institutions, and communities, shaping means that groups of people move step by step toward well-defined goals and that they are reinforced along the way for successfully completing each step.

> The old adage, "A thousand-mile journey begins with a single step," can be applied to the shaping process. Most complex organizational behavior must begin with a single step and then build [Luthans and Kreitner, 1975, p. 131].

Miller (1978) defines shaping as "breaking a large or difficult task down into 'bits and pieces' until the complete task is performed" (p. 395). In a broader sense shaping refers to proper sequencing. In designing a system, for example, identifying the needs and wants of the receiving system should take place before programs are elaborated. Each program should be a properly sequenced step-by-step process leading to the accomplishment of clear and specific goals. Proper sequencing of behaviors accompanied by adequate reinforcement has a great many applications to human systems.

Watson and Tharp (1981) suggest two simple rules for shaping: (1) you can never begin too low, and (2) the steps upward can never be too small (p. 134). In the beginning shaping may seem like a waste of time. The middle-aged man newly embarked upon an exercise program says to himself, "Instead of walking a quarter of a mile and then jogging a quarter of a mile, I'll run the whole mile." But if he exercises too much too soon, he risks doing violence to his body and giving up the program because of aching muscles and discouragement. Shaping helps assure that progress is real and lasting.

The process by which people learn to perform well according to their roles within a given system can be called *system socialization* (see Luthans and Kreitner, 1975, p. 131). A counselor, a minister, an administrator, a supervisor, a parent, a social worker, a spouse, a teacher, a consultant, a student—all learn to play roles that lead to goal attainment. Shaping is an important part of this learning process: "It seems likely that much of what we call socialization is achieved by various methods of *behavior shaping*—that is, selective reinforcement of performances that approach some socially acceptable standard" (McGinnies, 1970, p. 97).

At first glance, shaping can be seen as an overly manipulative process. If *I* understand shaping and know how to use it and *you* do not, then I am in a position to manipulate and control your behavior. But you can prevent manipulation by learning how to use these principles yourself. Once we both know the principles, we can use them collaboratively to shape both our own behavior and the behavior of the systems to which we belong. Thus a common understanding of the principles of behavior is one basis for intelligent collaboration.

Shaping goes on constantly in the systems of our lives whether we advert to it or not. If a supervisor says nothing when a staff member is delinquent, that omission shapes the worker's behavior just as much as a reprimand or a conference between the supervisor and the worker on mutual understanding of responsibilities. Children's behavior is being shaped constantly by school, friends, television, popular music, and the like. Therefore, using the principles of behavior directly, especially in a collaborative process, is really a step toward freedom. For the person who "shapes" his or her body through a common-sense program of exercise and dieting, shaping can mean new energy and new freedom.

Shaping has been described as a process of building on strengths (Brethower, 1972). Challenging strengths is much more productive than confronting weaknesses (Berenson and Mitchell, 1974; Egan, 1976). Brethower suggests the following principles:

Search out the strengths of people in the system. Find out what people do well. You can always find strengths if you look for them. Since we are conditioned to notice weaknesses rather than strengths, searching for strengths might be somewhat difficult at first. In extreme cases any improvement is a strength. For instance, a counselor trainee is less inaccurate in the use of empathy today than he or she was yesterday.

Select behavioral approximations. Identify the behaviors people are good at and which are similar to the desired performance. If people are good observers in a self-help group, note how this ability relates to the tasks and goals of the group.

Build on present goal performance. Once strengths have been identified and those behaviors that are similar to goal-related behavior have been selected, then people can be helped to build on what they already do well. Show them how to apply skills they already have.

Emphasize progress toward a goal rather than distance from it. If you overemphasize what is still to be done, the people who are trying to shape their behavior may become disheartened. If too much is asked of them, the effect is the same as emphasizing weaknesses instead of strengths. Brethower suggests that pointing out a weakness can be practical if the weakness is small and can be overcome easily, but in most cases emphasizing progress is better.

Provide ample reinforcement. As people begin to move toward a goal, support them. Failures can be noted, but they need not be stressed. People are already under pressure to build on their strengths; overemphasis on failures only adds to this pressure.

Do not impose elaborate and rigid systems. If you set up programs that are rigid and complicated, you emphasize weaknesses.

> There is usually more than one way of doing something. . . . The manager . . . who looks for weaknesses tends to fix upon a particular way of doing something (his way). . . . If the performer doesn't do it that particular way, a weakness is identified. On the other hand, the manager . . . who looks for strengths is more likely to find a way of doing it . . . which is similar to what the performer already . . . does. For example, if you want supervisors to give better feedback on performance, you will find it easier and more effective to begin by finding out what feedback they already give and encouraging them to give more of it. As it pays off, they will become more receptive to giving more elaborate feedback systems. If you begin by designing an elaborate system and viewing anything less as a weakness on their part, you will meet more resistance (Brethower, 1972, p. 9–2).

Rigidity and overcomplexity are, from the viewpoint of shaping, ultimately self-defeating. We have already seen that autonomy is an extremely important reinforcer for many people. The best organizations provide their members with a great deal of autonomy (Peters and Waterman, 1982).

MODELING/IMITATION

One definition of a model is "an example for imitation or emulation." Good organizations provide good models of effective organizational behavior. Effective organizations and communities are aware of the power of modeling and its impact on the behavior of their members. Modeling, when used constructively, can increase both the quantity and quality of goal-directed behaviors. Human-service trainees learn new behaviors as they observe effective counselors, social workers, and other human-service providers in action.

Modeling can help strengthen inhibitions to undesirable behavior. For example, a father of a family gives up smoking and explains to his children the negative effects he has experienced from this habit. His example can strengthen his children's inhibitions to smoking. Modeling can also weaken inhibitions to desirable behavior. For instance, the trainer in a human-relations training group begins, caringly and responsibly, to give the members feedback on goal-related behavior and to challenge them to live up to the group contract. The trainees experience feedback and challenge as positive behaviors and their reluctance to use them diminishes.

Finally, modeling can help increase the frequency, intensity, and duration of goal-related behaviors. For example, during the weekly staff meeting, the director of a mental health center listens carefully to what the other members have to say about each project and lets them know that he or she understands their point of view. This example raises the probability that other team members will listen and respond to one another with empathy. In this case, modeling helps strengthen behaviors that are already in the repertoire of the members of the team.

Miller (1978) believes that those in authority in human systems need to understand and use the modeling/imitation process.

> The behavior of other persons in the workplace exerts a powerful influence over the behavior of employees. The behavior of managers and the consequences to the manager's behavior exert an especially powerful control over the employees directly under the manager. The employee perceives the manager to be more highly reinforced than the employee. . . . It is both folk wisdom and empirically based psychology that the manager must manage by example. . . . The manager who behaves in one way and expects his employees to behave in another is creating an incongruity that produces poor performance and job dissatisfaction [p. 227].

THE COMPLEXITY OF BEHAVIOR

The principles of behavior are presented here as a set of tools and as *one* of the significant elements of Model A. An overemphasis on these principles, however, is a possible source of arationality. Skinner and the principles he has elaborated are not without their critics (for example, see Gilbert, 1978; Sarason, 1972). Our use of the principles of behavior should be tempered by our understanding of the complexity of social life. Sarason makes a distinction between behavior principles and social principles.

> Their generality [the principles of behavior espoused by Skinner] . . . is gained at the expense of an analysis of the structure of human society, and what he tells us about human society is obviously not derived from his principles. . . . Proposals for action require a unified conception of principles and society, of man in society. Action based in behavioral principles unrelated to social principles is a guarantee of failure [p. 270].

For Sarason there is something too pat about these principles and their application. In his mind, behaviorists do not come to grips with social principles and values:

Skinner seems to believe that his principles of behavior represent a sharp break with the substantive traditions of American psychology, if not with all past thinking in Western civilization. Unfortunately for him, he is but the latest example of a tradition in which isolated organisms are studied in contrived and unnatural settings. This is not an inherently bad tradition, except when it purports to serve as a basis for understanding and controlling behavior in complicated social settings [p. 260].

*   *   *   *

As soon as the individual (or group) takes, or is given, the role of leader, his surrounding environment changes in terms of strength and types of stimulation and reinforcement and the leader is not always aware, indeed can never be completely aware, of these changes. . . . Even if leaders had the keenest understanding of Skinnerian principles, the nature and requirements of action would prevent them from being able to know and assess the complexities impinging on them [pp. 264–265].

Others are not as severe as Sarason in their criticisms. They expect neither too much nor too little from the principles of behavior. Gilbert's main objection is that preoccupation with behavior distracts people's attention from *outcomes*. Hackman and Oldham (1980) emphasize, as does Model A, that these principles constitute only *one* of the sets of tools needed by managers.

In sum, contingent rewards, when well selected and administered in appropriate organizational circumstances, can often enhance employee motivation and help people gain valued personal outcomes in return for their contribution to the attainment of organizational objectives. Yet the efficacy of contingent rewards . . . appears to depend substantially on how the work itself is designed. When jobs [programs, tasks, roles, and responsibilities] are poorly structured, then the use of performance-contingent rewards may result in a motivational "backlash." When, however, jobs are designed so that they provide built-in incentives for good performance, then performance-contingent rewards sometimes can help make an already decent motivational situation even better [p. 41].

While the principles of behavior should be kept in mind when designing, facilitating, or assessing any of the elements of Model A, this focus should not inhibit the use of other filters, models, viewpoints, and frameworks by change agents working with organizations, institutions, and communities.

13

Climate and Quality of Life

Olga, an aide in a psychiatric hospital, says, "Once my shifts ends, I can't wait to get out of here. I like being an aide. I like working with the patients, but I can't stand it in this place." Pablo, when asked how he feels about where he's living, says, "It's an awful neighborhood. I don't feel safe there; it's one of those neighborhoods the city abandoned." Eunice, a teenager involved in a number of extracurricular activities at her high school, says, "To tell the truth, I stay at school as much as I can. There is so much tension at home between my mother and father and between my father and my older brother, I get out whenever I can. I don't like being at home."

These three people have something in common: They live or work in social settings in which the *climate* is poor and therefore their *quality of life* suffers. They are complaining because some of their legitimate needs and wants are not being satisfied within these social settings. For instance, when questioned further, Olga says that the unit she works on is managed so poorly that she has to live with unnecessary chaos. Pablo's need for safety and minimum city services such as garbage removal are not being met. Eunice's need for peace and harmony are not being met at home.

Various terms are used to describe the social setting itself and the impact the social setting has on people who work or live in it:

Climate. "Technically stated, climate is a set of properties of a given environment, based on the collective perceptions of the people who live and work in that environment, and demonstrated to influence their motivation and behavior. Simply stated, climate is a way of measuring people's perceptions of what it is like to [live or] work in a given environment" (Litwin, Humphrey, and Wilson, 1978, pp. 187–188). People describe the climate of the system as good, poor, creative, neutral, challenging, relaxed, tense, and so forth.

Internal environment. Just as the system itself is affected by what happens in the external environment, so the members of the system are affected by the internal environment—that is, by what is going on around them in the system. The organization and the people in it impinge on each member in many different ways.

Morale. Webster's dictionary defines morale as "the mental and emotional attitudes of individuals to the function or tasks expected of them by their group and loyalty to it." Caplow (1976) elaborates:

> The morale of an organization should not be confused with the happiness of the individuals who belong to it. Morale is *satisfaction with an organization,* not with life in general. An organization has high morale when most of its members: (1) accept its goals; (2) obey its important rules; and (3) continue to participate in its programs. . . .
>
> Under normal circumstances, being part of a high-morale group is a much more pleasant experience than being a part of a low-morale group engaged in the same activity, so that in general high morale contributes to individual happiness. . . .
>
> The most important distinction between morale and happiness, from the manager's standpoint, is that while he has no way of keeping all the people in his organization happy, he has, or can acquire, the means to sustain a high level of morale.
>
> These means consist of policies about recruiting, training, and evaluating people; policies about rewarding and punishing people; decisions taken under these policies; and procedures for the peaceful settlement of the conflicts they inevitably provoke [pp. 128–129].

The members, too, and not just the manager, are responsible for the morale of the system.

Quality of life. Quality of life refers to the satisfaction of a broad range of human needs, but it can be broken down into more specific categories such as quality of work life, quality of institutional life, quality of community life, quality of family life, or quality of personal life. Lawler (1982) defines quality of work life (QWL) in terms of both its causes and its effects.

> The definitions that have been offered so far for QWL fall into one of two broad categories. The first equates a high QWL with the existence of *a certain set of organizational conditions and practices.* For example, it is argued that a high QWL exists when jobs are enriched, democratic supervision is practiced, employees are involved in their work, and safe working conditions exist. The second approach to defining QWL equates a good quality of work life with the *demonstrated effects* that the working conditions have on individual employee well-being. This definition equates a good QWL with a workplace in which individuals are safe, express satisfaction, and are able to grow and develop as human beings. In short, it relates QWL to the degree to which the full range of human needs is met [p. 487].

Quality of life, then, relates to the *satisfaction of the legitimate needs and wants of the members of any given system.* "Legitimate" means those needs and wants that are commonly expected to be satisfied in that system. For instance, the satisfaction of some, but not all, social needs can be expected in the work place.

As illustrated in Figure 13-1, climate/quality of life is the second of the four pervasive variables affecting organizations, institutions, and communities. Quality-of-life issues are central to the lives of human-service providers. In fact, the very

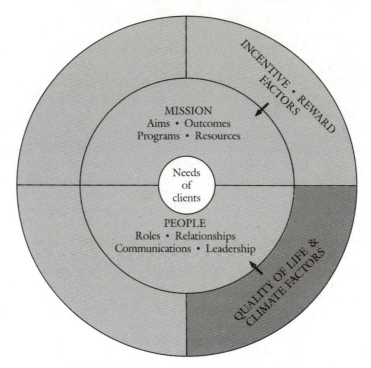

FIGURE 13-1.   Climate and quality of life

mission of human-service agencies is to help people improve the quality of their lives. Human-service providers are working more and more with groups, organizations, and institutions and therefore encounter both climate and quality-of-life issues. Since most human-service providers work in some organization, institution, or agency, they also are affected by the climate of that system and the quality of their own work lives.

Model A can be used to analyze the quality-of-life needs of the members of the system. Carlson (1980) sees quality of work life as a philosophy, a goal or outcome, and an ongoing process. In terms of Model A it is (1) a mission—which includes philosophy, values, and policies—(2) a set of outcomes or goals, and (3) an ongoing set of programs to achieve these goals.

Mission. The quality-of-life mission of an organization is to satisfy the legitimate needs and wants of its members. For instance, human-service providers need work schedules that enable them to participate fully in the lives of their own families. Carlson (1980) sees human dignity as the central philosophical issue: "We must encourage and foster a climate in which the fundamental *human dignity* of all members of the organization is recognized—not only because they are entitled to it, but because people are the most critical assets to an organization and its future" (p. 83).

Quality of life is a set of values about people, about the ways they live in communities and institutions, and about the nature of work. These concrete values flow from a social philosophy of human beings and their interactions with one another. Advocates of quality-of-life programs do not all have the same values because they do not all espouse the same philosophy. For instance, not all would include "democracy in the work place" (Zwerdling, 1980) as an essential quality-of-work-life value, and even those who include it espouse different forms of democracy.

Quality of life is a set of policies—stated "ways of doing things" in the organization, institution, or community—that stem from the overriding philosophy and values. These policies act as a bridge between philosophy/values and the pattern of behavior and accomplishments in the organization that relate to quality of life.

Goals or outcomes. The concrete manifestation of quality-of-life mission, philosophy, values, and policies takes place when "more involving, satisfying, and effective jobs and work environments for people at all levels of the organization" are created (Carlson, 1980, p. 83). Quality of life means that certain patterns of behavior are *in place* in the organization, institution, or community. For instance, supervisors are habitually treating workers with respect. Or in a marriage both husband and wife are habitually involved in the decisions that affect their lives.

Ongoing process. Programs have a beginning, a middle, and an end. On the other hand, effective quality-of-work-life endeavors, Carlson points out, are "long-range, ongoing, and even never-ending" processes (p. 84). Quality of life, as a form of happiness, is not real if it is ephemeral. Fordyce (1983), emphasizing that happiness is much more than a temporary mood state, describes it as "a longer-term overall felt sense of emotional well-being and contentment with life—a global index of life satisfaction" (p. 484). All human endeavors are subject to entropy, the tendency to decay over time. This includes quality of life in organizations, institutions, and communities. There is no free lunch. A couple must constantly work at a marriage if quality of married life is to remain high. Otherwise it will decay. Quality-of-working-life processes cannot be instituted and then forgotten. They must be embedded in the organization and then constantly reviewed and reworked.

COMPONENTS OF QUALITY OF LIFE

Aristotle suggested that, while happiness is the ultimate goal of life, it cannot be pursued directly. It is a state created when things are done well. In the same way, quality of life cannot be pursued directly. It is a by-product of things done well by organizations, institutions, and communities and their members.

The discussion that follows emphasizes components of quality of work life because most of the literature deals with work rather than community or institutional living. This emphasis on the work place provides human-service practitioners an opportunity to review quality-of-life issues in their own organizations and agencies. It will soon be evident, however, that much of what is said applies to quality of life in many different settings. The quality-of-life components are:

- Interpersonal relations and social life.
- The physical and psychological dimensions of the work place, including physical and psychological safety, job security, and comfort.
- Organizational clarity.

- Access to the resources needed to be an effective system member.
- Good job design.
- Reasonable autonomy and opportunity to influence others.
- An adequate and fair reward system.
- Equitable financial rewards, including wages and other financial benefits.
- Achievement and recognition.
- Opportunities to learn.
- Opportunities for promotion.
- Challenge.

Quality of life becomes a reality only when these components are translated into accomplishments—that is, *patterns* of behavior that are in place in the organization, institution, or community. The following descriptions show how the quality-of-life components are manifested in the best systems.

Interpersonal relations. The best systems foster healthy interpersonal relationships. The dignity of each member of the system is recognized by everyone else and becomes the basis for interpersonal relations. Because of their basic dignity, people are treated with respect. Sincere attempts are made to minimize and eliminate bias and prejudice; people are friendly and courteous to one another, and fairness is prized.

In effective systems conflict is seen as a normal part of relating and prized as a possible source of creativity. In conflict situations people learn how to "fight fair." People in authority, such as managers, supervisors, teachers, parents, pastors, and the like, are especially careful not to use their power to dominate those with less power. Human-service providers understand the nature of their power with clients and are especially careful how they use their influence. The rights of system members are clear, and these rights are respected both by those in authority and by fellow members. When members feel that their rights have been violated, there is a forum to which they can bring their grievances (Ewing, 1977a, 1977b).

Social relations, including social relations in the work place, are seen as fitting and important. Of course, work, not social relating, is central. No one is forced into an undesirable type of social relating; for instance, an unwelcome sexual relationship. Members of the system have a sense of *belonging* to the system or to some social unit within the system. They feel that they are a part of a group, are meaningfully related to other members of the group, and have something in common with them. In work settings teamwork is encouraged: "Teamwork involves the feeling of belonging to an organization; it is characterized by cohesion, mutual warmth and support, trust, and pride" (Litwin, Humphrey, and Wilson, 1978, p. 191). Neither work nor the environment is so designed that meaningful human contact during the work day is made impossible. Work breaks provide the opportunity for brief socializing by those who want it.

Argyris (1982) discusses how most organizations and institutions overplay the rational and deemphasize the emotional—especially negative emotions. In the best systems, however, feelings and emotions are recognized and not forbidden by some unstated cultural policy. Since system members are not asked to leave their emotions, either positive or negative, at the door, they are not surprised when they see expressions of genuine and appropriate emotion. However, the system does not become a forum for emotional self-indulgence. System members are expected to manage their emotions so that they contribute rather than detract from both quality of life and productivity.

The physical and psychological demands of the system. In the best systems the physical and psychological demands of the work environment and of the work itself are reasonable. Members are protected from physical harm. The organization introduces safety measures not merely because some government agency demands it, but because the welfare of its members is important. In work settings the long-range effects of the work environment (for instance, sitting for long hours in front of a computer terminal) are studied, and no one is exposed unnecessarily to risks that are not understood.

Members are protected from the psychological (and sometimes physical) harm that comes from excessive *stress*. (See Adams, 1981; Burchfield, 1979; Corlett and Richardson, 1982; French and others, 1976; House, 1982; Kyriacou and Sutcliffe, 1978; Levi, 1982; McLean, 1982; Moracco and McFadden, 1982; Moss, 1982; Selye, 1976; Shostak, 1980; and Warshaw, 1982.) Debilitating stress in organizations, institutions, and communities is no respecter of persons. Researchers have shown that a certain amount of anxiety or stress can be helpful insofar as it motivates people to deal with problems and accomplish goals. Indeed, too little pressure can lead to low productivity. There comes a point, however, varying from person to person, where anxiety and stress become dysfunctional.

In well functioning systems people are aware that excessive stress interferes with both productivity and quality of life. While crises are seen as a normal part of life, care is taken not to contribute to them by the mismanagement of the system. Human-service providers are likely to experience burnout because they are constantly dealing with people in crisis and because they receive relatively little support from the institutions and agencies in which they work. When these agencies are managed, they contribute to the stress of practitioners instead of helping them cope with it. Good organizations review their members periodically in order to identify people under stress. Ways of handling stress—support, counseling, time off, and so forth—are provided.

Rosow considers job security a key quality-of-life issue in the 1980s (Rosow, 1981; Kerr and Rosow, 1979):

> The great majority of American employees (excluding those in education, civil service, the military, and the church) have a minimum degree of job security. Although union members are often protected by labor contracts that provide seniority protection, most American workers can literally be dismissed on a moment's notice with little, if any, recourse.

* * * *

> Employment without security places the burden of survival on the individual worker instead of on the enterprise or on society. This is an unequal burden. It cannot be borne lightly. . . . Concerned about an insecure and uncertain future, the employee is less

likely to produce at the optimum level in day-to-day employment [Rosow, 1981, p. 41].

Finally, there is the issue of comfort—not to be confused with luxury—which varies from one system to another. Comfort for the coal miner is different from comfort for the executive secretary. In the best human-service organizations, the physical setting is warm, clean, equipped with the ordinary amenities and, if possible, aesthetic. The number of hours worked, the amount of travel to and from work, the difficulty of the work, and the amount of work expected during and after regular hours are reasonable. Employees have adequate time to meet personal needs— bathroom, rest periods, personal emergencies, and so forth. (On the other hand, all of us know human-service providers who ignore adverse work conditions because of their dedication to a cause.)

Organizational clarity. The lives of members of organizations, institutions, and communities can be miserable if they don't know what the system is about and what is expected of them. In the best system, there is clarity in mission, goals, programs, roles, relationships, information, and feedback. As new goals, programs, roles, and relationships emerge, they are reviewed and explained to whoever is affected. Factors that make systems productive are also factors that contribute to the quality of life of their members. People like working in well-run organizations and living in well-run communities.

Access to resources. System members have ready access to the resources needed to accomplish their goals. They do not have to beg, fight, or compete for these resources. They can mobilize whatever resources they need with a reasonable amount of effort. If resources are limited, some fair system for allocating these resources is devised and organization members understand this system.

Members have ready access to the people whose aid is necessary in carrying out projects and solving problems. People in managerial positions have the working knowledge and skills (competence) to be resources for those who seek their help. The information needed to accomplish goals and manage problem situations is readily available. Information is not hoarded or used as a political tool. Equipment needed to get the work done is available and in good repair; supplies are available when needed. People are hired because they have the working knowledge and skills to do the job effectively and efficiently, or they are trained to do so. Thus they are resources rather than liabilities for their fellow workers.

Job design. In the best systems jobs and programs are designed and developed with a view to both the needs of workers and the needs of the system. Organizations are seen as "socio-technical systems" (Cummings and Srivastva, 1977; Pasmore and Sherwood, 1978). Technology is integrated into the social system; the needs and wants of people are taken into consideration when new technology is adopted. Jobs are not mindless: They offer an opportunity for variety and learning; their organizational meaning and their relevance to organizational goals are clear; tasks are not so small or so circumscribed as to appear meaningless. Work schedules and program implementation are flexible. The interests of workers are taken into consideration when job responsibilities are assigned. Once jobs have been designed, the design is continually updated and fine-tuned. The initial design eliminates most of the obstacles that could stand in the way of workers as they pursue their goals. Fine tuning helps eliminate further obstacles as they arise.

Reasonable autonomy and influence. Drucker (1968) has pointed out that responsibility and authority are correlative terms. People in systems can be expected to carry out responsibilities effectively and efficiently only insofar as they have the authority to do so. Stein (1980) insists that authority to make decisions is essential in a world that becomes more and more complex.

> In technology we have moved from a world in which most tasks (digging a ditch, hammering nails, shoveling coal) were simple and visible to one in which tasks are complex and private. Modern organizations at almost every level require people's commitment and will. We depend on people not merely to take directions, but to interpret them and apply them to particular situations. In a world where people's commitment is necessary for productivity itself, quality of work life issues become critical [p. 9].

In other words, in complex systems implicit delegations of authority are not just a luxury. They are unavoidable. Failure on the part of management to understand this leads to misunderstandings with workers. Manager: "Who told you you could do that?" Staff member: "Good grief! My common sense told me."

In effective organizations those who are to carry out decisions are able to influence the people who make these decisions in reasonable ways. Inquiries and suggestions are encouraged and objections are treated seriously. People in the system are given as much control over their activities as possible. Control refers to the ability to affect one's own environment. Generally, decisions are made at the level where needed information is readily available. In some cases both managers and workers must contribute information. In other cases, however, workers have the information necessary to make the decision without further recourse to management. In fact, continual recourse to management with respect to decisions for which management is uninformed could have a significant negative impact on productivity. Managers delegate enough authority so that workers are not impeded in carrying out their work.

Principles relating to the reward system. In the best systems rewards and not punishment are central to the motivational system. Rewards are made contingent on the accomplishment of realistic goals for which members have adequate resources and support. If rewards are given out randomly or by whim, morale soon drops. To keep morale high, emphasis is placed on incentives rather than on motivation. Managers assume that the ordinary member of the system is motivated to pursue the goals of the system when the proper incentives are available. Rewards are adequate to meet the needs of system members; their distribution is fair; there is flexibility of rewards so that the different needs of various members can be met.

Financial rewards. Financial rewards include both wages and other benefits. Rosow (1981) cites a survey in which 77% of workers said that "good wages" was the most important aspect of the job. Medical benefits, ranked second, were cited by only 43%.

Wages are basic; if wages are considered poor, other quality-of-life components are blocked. On the other hand, if wages are considered good, further raises may not increase motivation. Raising wages from a good to a very good level will not necessarily increase productivity, but may increase expectations for further raises.

Benefits other than wages are another form of pay, often lightly disguised. Today workers feel entitled to benefits that once were considered "extras": health care, longer vacations, sick time, and pension plans. Of these the most important are health care and pension plans. Employees expect a "good package of benefits," just as they expect good wages. Without these benefits, they feel shortchanged.

In the best systems pay and benefits are certainly adequate, but they are not considered the principal incentives. Herzberg (1968) suggests that pay and other quality-of-life components, such as good physical working conditions, adequate supervision, good relationships with managers, and the like, are not really incentives but factors that must be present in order to avoid *dissatisfaction* in the system. If they are not present, workers are dissatisfied, but their presence in and of themselves does not contribute significantly to increased worker *satisfaction* and increased worker productivity. Herzberg calls adequate wages, good supervisory relationships, a clean work place, adequate resources, and the like, "hygienic" factors. They contribute to quality of life insofar as they make the system "clean" in both a literal and a metaphorical sense. On the other hand, what he calls "motivating" factors, including a sense of achievement, recognition, increased responsibility, and opportunities to grow, contribute significantly to both quality of life and productivity.

According to Kanter (1977), a number of both productivity and quality-of-life factors deal with *opportunity* and *power* (see also Goodmeasure, 1979a, 1979b; Kanter, 1983; Stein and Kanter, 1980).

> Behaviorally, the most relevant aspects of a position within the organization are: (a) the level of opportunity, and (b) the amount of power available to the person occupying that position. Opportunity, in addition to its standard definition as "access to advancement," means challenge and the chance to grow (increase competence and skills) and contribute to the central goals of the organization. Power means access to resources, the capacity to mobilize them, and the tools to accomplish tasks efficiently [Stein and Kanter, 1980, p. 373].

Power and opportunity are "higher-level" incentives that do not appeal to everyone in the same way or to the same degree.

Achievement and recognition. People who contribute to the goals of the system can take pride in their own achievements. While self-recognition like self-feedback has a kind of primacy, recognition by others also is important. People at all levels of the organization can "make a difference," whether that difference relates to the cleanliness of the building, to a successful intervention in a troubled family, or to the adroit management of the organization's finances. A sense of personal achievement and recognition for a job well done are significant rewards in themselves. In many organizations, institutions, and communities people are noticed only when they fail or deviate from a standard. In the best systems, "catching people doing a good job" is much more important than confronting people at moments of failure.

Opportunities to learn. The best organizations give their members many different opportunities to learn. By learning to do a number of different tasks, for example, employees fend off boredom and become more versatile and potentially better contributors to the organization. Human-service providers can be involved in preventive, not just remedial, programs. They can learn to become consultants. Educational and training opportunities, both within the organization and outside, can be offered to employees. Additional education prepares them to do their jobs more effectively, readies them for promotion, and contributes to their overall career objectives. Opportunities to learn may be both formal and informal.

Promotion. In the best organizations there are chances for promotion and career development. Promotion is achieved through talent and accomplishment rather than through organizational politics. Since only a limited number of managerial positions are available, it is difficult to avoid competition and politics.

> The labor force will gradually age over the next twenty years. As one consequence, people will spend more time in certain kinds of jobs, rather than advancing rapidly, because the slots above will already be filled with relatively young people. Therefore, much more will have to be done to enhance the challenge, influence, recognition, and reward available in the jobs that they will occupy [Kanter and Stein, 1980].

There are forms of promotion or career development that do not necessarily entail ascending the organizational ladder (Kaye, 1982): merit increases in wages, membership in an employee council, being consulted more frequently on decisions that affect the work place, and being given more opportunities to learn. Ouchi (1981) believes that the time has come to devise what he calls "nonpromotional" job changes—job changes that are meaningful both to workers and to the organization but do not needlessly swell the ranks of managers and supervisors.

Challenge. Some workers are satisfied only if they feel some kind of challenge:

- These workers do not merely want well-designed jobs, they want a hand in the design process itself.
- Autonomy and control are prime incentives for them.
- They are willing to work hard and put in long hours, but they expect that accomplishments will be rewarded financially.
- They see themselves as talented and expect opportunities to demonstrate their talent.
- They are not only interested in being well-supervised and managed but they have ambitions to supervise and manage well.
- They see themselves as willing learners and look for ample opportunities to learn both on and off the job.
- In general, they are eager to participate in the decisions that affect their work and their careers.
- Quality of work life is intimately related to the productivity of the organization. They want to work for the most productive organizations.
- They are eager for feedback and seek it out when it is not forthcoming.
- They see themselves as "insiders" or at least aspire to become "insiders."

Many managers react favorably to the relatively elite group of workers who rise to the challenge. They see similarities between themselves and this elite and know that future managers are to be chosen from among this group.

Since the mission of human-service organizations and institutions is to help clients improve the quality of their lives, the quality of life within human-service systems themselves should reflect this mission. A nursing home with unhappy workers will do little to improve the quality of life of its residents. On the other hand, a hospice with staff members who are committed to its mission and belong to a caring and enthusiastic team will do a great deal to improve the quality of life of the terminally ill. As human-service providers learn to improve the quality of life of their own organizations and the helping relationship itself, they become better prepared to be both helpers to individuals and quality-of-life consultants to systems.

14

Managing the Environment

Every organization, institution, and community is surrounded by other organizations, institutions, and communities and affected by economic, social, and political conditions and events. Managing "externalities"—the relationship between the focal system and the individuals, systems, and events with which it interacts and by which it is affected—is a major task. Figure 14-1 adds the environment and the ecological perspective to Model A.

> The administrator of a boys' reformatory wanted desperately to change the school for the better, but he did not know where to turn for help. He finally happened on a group of consultants who helped him change the school totally. A new mission was developed in which rehabilitation was central, and clear goals were established for administrators, guards, teachers, and inmates. The best guards were trained in helping and human relationship skills and they in turn trained other guards. Within a year one of the major outcomes, a significant drop in recidivism, was achieved. But the project was abandoned!
>
> The administrator and the consultants had not monitored the political environment carefully. First, in the course of the change project some of the administrative team and some of the guards had been alienated. They complained to friends who were in a position to talk to people in power. Second, people higher up in the correctional system had not been brought on board so that they could take some of the credit for the results. The venture ended with a futile encounter between the principal consultant and the governor. Politics won.

In many systems, members become aware of environmental threats only when it is too late to do anything about them. If the environment is a highly politicized

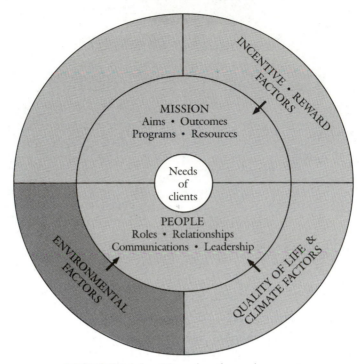

FIGURE 14-1.   Managing the environment

one, it must be factored into the planning stage. As Kanter (1983) notes, "Management of critical boundary-spanning issues is the task of the top: developing strategies, tactics, and structural mechanisms for functioning and triumphing in a turbulent and highly politicized environment" (p. 49).

There are threats, limitations, and opportunities "out there," and it is important for those who manage systems to identify and deal with all three.

> Many of the residents in an inner-city neighborhood in a large midwestern city felt that they were being ignored by city government. The building that housed a makeshift boys' club in the neighborhood was condemned by a city inspector and ordered vacated. That same week, however, a new youth center was opened in one of the parks in a much more affluent part of the city. Some local leaders saw an opportunity in the coincidence of these two events. They contacted the media, pointed out the contrast, and asked reporters to do a story on it. The contrast was played up both in the newspapers and on television. This publicity did not lead to a major change in city government priorities, but it did provide some political leverage for the residents of this inner-city neighborhood.

When the 1980 election ushered in a new administration in Washington, people in human services expected profound changes in federal government support. But the time to begin managing the threats, limitations, and opportunities created by a new administration is before the polls close.

Managing the environment means both taking advantage of opportunities and fending off or coping with barbs, especially those that threaten the very life or well-being of the system. For a down-and-out family in times of high unemployment, it might mean protecting itself from the violence of a drug-ridden ghetto neighborhood, while trying to satisfy basic needs through federal food stamp programs, city housing programs, and neighborhood outreach programs.

ANALYZING THE ENVIRONMENT

Environment is difficult to define because it includes so many variables. Social scientists have analyzed these variables and adopted various terms to categorize them. Hall (1972) distinguishes between general and specific organizational environments.

The *general environment* includes conditions that affect many different kinds of organizations, institutions, and communities: (1) economic conditions, (2) cultural conditions, (3) political conditions, (4) ecological conditions, (5) demographic conditions, (6) legal conditions, and (7) technological conditions.

> General environmental conditions may be thought of as those that are "potentially" relevant for the focal organization. Moreover, the organization is not typically "in touch" with these elements on a day-to-day basis, but must create special environmental scanning and monitoring activities to deal with them [Miles, 1980, p. 195].

Members of the focal organization may not even be aware of how it is being affected by these conditions, even though they permeate the system and control it in various ways.

As important as general environmental conditions are, they are hard to get at.

> While the roles of technology, legal patterns, culture, and so on have been demonstrated to be important, we cannot even assign a ranking to the various factors to indicate their relative importance. The situation is further complicated by the fact that these general environmental factors themselves interact, so that it is difficult to isolate any one thing for analysis [Hall, 1972, p. 312].

Many systems become aware of threats in the environment only when it is too late to do anything about them.

The general environment includes what Roeber (1973) calls "emergent systems," which could also be called emergent environmental conditions, many of them social, political, and cultural: urban decay, demographic changes, changing sexual mores, radical politics, the antinuclear movement, the women's movement, anti-industry sentiment, the decline of confidence in professionals, the drug culture, the gay movement, declining productivity, proliferating international "hot spots," the end of easy money for mortgages, and the proliferation and power of political interest groups. When such trends first emerge, they are often dismissed as environmental "noise." The fact that such movements have profoundly affected society points to the necessity of developing ways to distinguish between social trends and mere fads.

The specific environment of an organization, institution, or community includes those other organizations, institutions, and communities that influence it through direct contact. Any given system can draw up a chart that indicates not only the organizations, institutions, and communities that constitute its specific environment, but also the frequency of these contacts. Figure 14-2 charts the specific environment for a police department. The chart could be expanded to include various sections of the town and the frequency of incidents demanding police attention in each neighborhood. By using the expanded chart, members of the department could see at a glance the distribution of the demands placed on its services.

Emery and Trist (1965) have divided environment into four categories: (1) the internal environment or internal interdependencies, (2) the input-related external environment, (3) the output-related external environment, and (4) external environmental interdependencies (see also Adams, 1975, 1976; Miles, 1980).

Internal environment or interdependencies. The term "internal environment," sometimes used as a synonym for climate, refers here to "the other units in the same

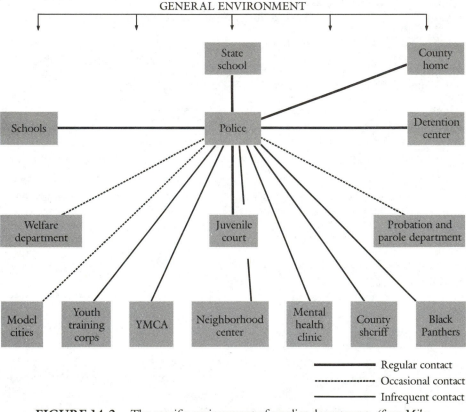

FIGURE 14-2.   The specific environment of a police department   *(from Miles, 1980; adapted from Hall, 1972).*

system." In a psychiatric hospital, for instance, the human resource development department is one unit. Its internal environment consists of the other units of the hospital for which it provides services, its "customer" units, and any other unit that can affect it. In a residential neighborhood other householders constitute a householder's internal environment, while adjacent neighborhoods are part of the external environment.

The external environment. The external environment, divided into three categories, includes everything not within the focal system, but especially those individuals and systems that provide resources for or pose threats or limitations to the system. For a clinical psychology program, the accreditation unit of the American Psychological Association is an important environmental system. For a rape crisis center, the police and the courts are important environmental systems.

The *input-related external environment* refers to individuals and systems that provide different kinds of input for the focal system. For instance, the schools that provide psychiatric and clinical psychology interns for a psychiatric hospital are part of the input-related environment for that hospital. The clinical sites that provide placement and training for clinical psychology students constitute part of the input-related environment for graduate programs. External consultants are part of the input-related external environment of the organizations for which they work.

The *output-related external environment* refers to the individuals and systems that are affected by the output of the focal system. For instance, the quality of counselors produced by a graduate program affects the organizations and institutions in which these counselors are employed. Psychiatric hospitals affect the families of their patients by the kinds of care they provide. Schools affect the societies in which they exist.

The influence process is bidirectional. If System B is part of the environment of System A, then the converse is also true. There is action and reaction on both sides. Staff members in clinical sites sometimes complain that students who come from graduate clinical psychology programs are not well prepared to deliver services. The faculty members of psychology departments sometimes complain that clinical sites are too conservative and that they impose unnecessary limitations on clinical interns.

Finally, *external environmental interdependencies,* that is, interactions between systems in the external environment, can affect the focal system. For instance, the ways in which the President and Congress interact affect human-service systems in terms of funding and regulation. A downturn in the economy forces organizations to cut back their training budgets; as a result, external consultants lose their contracts and fewer students apply for admission to a university-based organizational development program. It is clear, then, that the interconnectedness of systems and events "out there" can dramatically affect what is happening "in here."

Meyer and his associates (1978) assert that organizations, institutions, and communities do not merely interact with their environments, but are permeated throughout by their environments. Through their influence, outside systems construct and control the system under discussion. Educational institutions, for example, are not isolated from the society, but are permeated and influenced by it.

The connection between education and the workplace, school and industry, is not in doubt. The design of curricula and scope of examinations are influenced by perceptions of future occupational or professional requirements. Leaders of industry and commerce are represented on the governing bodies of the institutions responsible for promoting educational research and teacher training. There is a constant pressure for education at all levels to be relevant to the needs of the workplace as defined by management [Reynolds, 1982, p. 30].

Government and industry support of research in universities opens channels of both direct and indirect influence—not necessarily pernicious, but seldom publicly acknowledged. The permeation of systems by their *cultural* environments is especially significant (see Chapter 16).

MANAGING THE ENVIRONMENT

By developing an "ecological" perspective, human-service practitioners can help individual clients manage their lives and problem situations better, manage their own organizations, institutions, and agencies more effectively, and become consultants to other human-service systems.

Clients and their environments

Many individual clients have problems that stem from the social settings of their lives (Egan and Cowan, 1979), and human-service practitioners need to be sensitive to this complexity. Murrell (1973), who sees individuals as "linking pins" between systems, believes that people should think about themselves as members of systems as an antidote to an individual-oriented conception of the world.

It is not easy to "get into" the idea that as individuals we are as we are partly because of the forces in our social systems. Our culture constantly emphasizes the individual dominating his environment. Our television heroes conquer all through direct (often violent) independent action. . . . We boast of our frontier forebears who "conquered" the wilderness. . . . We have "conquered" space by going to the moon. . . .

This cultural emphasis on the individual is good to the degree that we value each and every person. . . . The idealization of independent individual action is fictional if it ignores individual-system *interaction* [p. 25].

Human-service providers can be sensitive to person-environment interactions and help clients develop an awareness of "externalities" that affect their lives with a view to changing or coping with them.

There are four levels of systems or environments in society that require attention in the delivery of human services:

Personal settings such as the family, friends, and the work place constitute the immediate context of life. At different times and in different ways people either grow and flourish or stagnate and regress in these systems. Some systems provide a great deal of support, some very little. Dealing with the battered wife without dealing with the family setting itself can be fruitless. On the other hand, an adolescent with leukemia who goes home to a supportive family has increased chances for survival.

The network of personal settings, illustrated in Figure 14-3, refers to the ways in which personal systems interact with and influence one another. The student who is drained by fighting between his parents at home has special problems in school. The human-service provider who goes home to her family after a trying day drags some of the work place along with her. The work place "lives within her family" and affects it.

The larger systems of society, illustrated in Figure 14-4, and the ways in which they directly or indirectly affect one another and individuals and their personal systems constitute the third level of systems. The economy, the media, government, the professions, and the like are included here. Human-service providers cannot always help people deal with these systems directly—though sometimes even that is possible—but they can help clients examine their lives and their problem situations in the light of "significant externalities" with a view to coping with threats and exploiting opportunities.

Culture is the fourth level. As Figure 14-5 indicates, culture is the largest and most pervasive of the systems. Culture deserves separate attention in the final chapter of this book.

Systems and their environments

Human-service providers need to manage the externalities of their own systems well and, as consultants, help other systems do the same. If those who exercise leadership positions in organizations, institutions, and communities are to manage the relationships between their system and the environment well—that is, take ad-

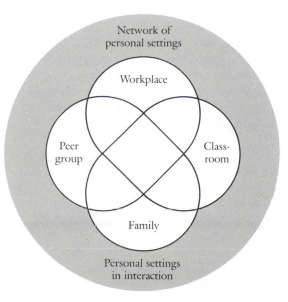

FIGURE 14-3. Personal settings

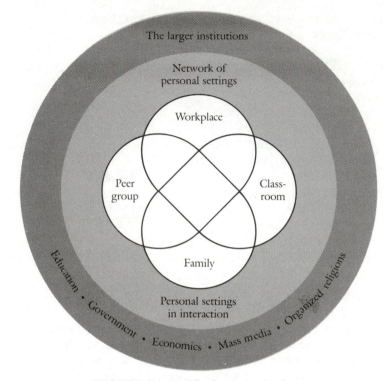

FIGURE 14-4.   The larger institutions

vantage of environmental opportunities and cope with environmental threats and limitations—then they must take three steps: (1) chart the principal systems and trends in the environment that pertain to the focal system, (2) identify critical externalities and assess their possible impact, and (3) develop and implement strategies for coping with threats and exploiting opportunities. In their role as consultants to organizations, institutions, or communities, human-service practitioners can help these systems "scan" the environment for both threats and opportunities, and help them cope with the former and exploit the latter.

   Scanning the environment.   Like salesmen in *The Music Man*, "Ya gotta know the territory." The territory includes significant externalities in both the general and specific environments. *Environmental scanning* is a process by which the focal system reviews other systems and events in the environment to maximize the use of environmental resources and minimize environmental risks. Metcalf, Riffle, and Seabury (1981) define environmental scanning as "an iterative process to monitor events external to the [system]—a threat/opportunity screen to provide timely detection of changes significant to the [system]" (p. 4). Miles (1980) defines scanning as "primarily a search for major discontinuities in the external environment that might provide opportunities or constraints to the organization" (p. 322).
   Environmental charting. The first question is: What individuals, systems, or trends in the environment are significant for us? An environmental chart helps us to answer

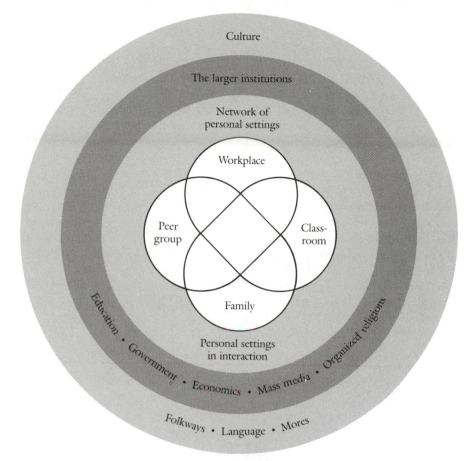

FIGURE 14-5.   Culture: The largest of the systems

this question. Such a chart, like the one in Figure 14-2, includes a preliminary overview of the systems with which the focal system has contact in both the internal and external environment and some estimation of the frequency of the contact. It produces a picture of the environmental "geography." This kind of chart can be drawn up for both the internal and the external environments of any system or any subunit of a system. Figure 14-6 charts some of the environmental systems and trends that could prove significant for the Master's Degree Program in Organization Development (OD) of a large urban university. Note that systems and trends both within the university (the internal environment) and outside (the external environment) are included.

In making this chart the director of the program and his assistant asked themselves: What systems and trends in both the internal and external environment are actually or potentially meaningful for us in terms of either threats or opportunities? To this list they added a brief note to explain why each item was included. The *internal environment* list follows:

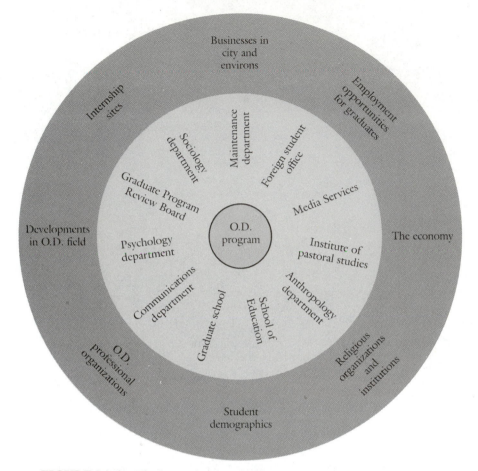

FIGURE 14-6.   The internal and external environments of a master's degree program in Organization Development

- Foreign student office: Some foreign students have trouble with credentials.
- Media Services: They make great professional tapes of possible use in our advertising program.
- Institute of Pastoral Studies: We might cooperate with them on a summer program directed to religious institutions.
- Anthropology Department: One of their faculty members teaches our course on organizational culture.
- School of Education: They resisted establishment of our program because they wanted to do it themselves.
- Graduate School: We report directly to them.
- Communications Department: They have an organization communications track.
- Psychology Department: Both the director of the OD program and the assistant director are from this department.

- Graduate Program Review Board: They appraise us; we might want a new Ph.D. program.
- Sociology Department: One of their faculty members teaches for us.
- Maintenance Department: Their services are critical, especially for the half-dozen workshops we put on during the year.

The *external environment* list includes the following:

- Business in city and environs: They are one of the main sources of students and of possible employment opportunities for graduates.
- City and county government agencies: They are a source of students, possible internship sites, and "OD in politics" possibilities.
- The economy: A downturn means fewer students apply to the program.
- Religious organizations and institutions: They are an untapped source of students and internship sites.
- Student demographics: Are students entering these programs across the country? What kind of program is most popular? What are the trends?
- Professional organizations in OD: These are sources of trends, networking, national workshops, recruiting possibilities.
- Developments in the OD field: We need to stay current with what OD professionals are doing, innovative training programs, trends, new models, best books.
- Internship sites: Developing good internship placements—places where things are happening, where interns are really welcomed, and where supervision is good—is an ongoing concern.

Once potentially critical systems and trends have been charted, they can be evaluated and priorities can be established.

The impact of environment.   After key environmental systems and trends have been identified, the next step is to determine which are the *critical* externalities—that is, which are most threatening and which are sources of the greatest opportunities. Any given externality may be critical in a tactical, operational, or strategic sense. In a *tactical* sense, it should be dealt with immediately. In an *operational* sense, it should be dealt with in the relatively short term, perhaps over the next year or two. In a *strategic* sense, it has long-term significance and should be taken into consideration in the system's strategic planning. Questions to be asked are:

- What individuals, systems, or trends are important or critical?
- In what ways are they important?
- How important are they? How rich are the opportunities and how serious are the threats? Minimal threats and low-grade opportunities may well be ignored or merely monitored.
- How time-sensitive are these externalities? How quickly do we have to act if we are to take advantage of a significant opportunity or fend off a significant threat?

In the example that follows, environmental threats and opportunities were assessed by the director and assistant director of a graduate program in organizational development:

Threats. One threat that needed immediate attention came from the Office of Foreign Students. A significant number of applications to the program came from other countries. Though highly qualified, these applicants were having trouble with admission because the Office of Foreign Students had not developed realistic procedures for assessing their qualifications or coordinated its efforts with the Graduate School or Office of Credentials. Since a number of these students had already applied for admission, immediate action was necessary.

A mixture of threat and possibility was found in the Graduate Program Review Board. The OD director wanted to expand the OD program into a small, tightly controlled Ph.D. program, which would give the best students an opportunity for advancement and involve them in the training and development of the M.A. students through internal internship programs. Since the Graduate Review Board had put a strict moratorium on new Ph.D. programs, this obstacle seemed to be a strategic issue. And although the goal was about four or five years away, it was not too soon to start groundwork with the members of the board.

Opportunities. A significant number of students in the Organization Development Program were from religious organizations and institutions. Since the university had an Institute of Pastoral Studies, the OD program and the IPS might benefit from some kind of cooperation, perhaps a summer M.A. program for people from religious settings. This proposal was seen as an operational issue. It would be ideal if the program could begin within a year. Consequently, it was not too soon to approach the religious organizations and institutions in the city and environs about student recruitment and possible internship sites.

A further opportunity lay with Media Services. One of the faculty members of the OD program had taped a series on counseling, which demonstrated the efficiency and professionalism of the members of this department. One way of recruiting good students was to send similar tapes to various organizations and institutions—one for business settings and one for church settings—illustrating the content and the advantages of the OD program. Recruiting was another operational issue, but the tape should be completed as soon as possible.

The program director and his associates identified and evaluated all the critical externalities, labeled them as tactical, operational, or strategic, and set up priorities for action.

Developing action plans.   Environmental scanning in organizations, institutions, and communities is often implicit and reactive rather than explicit and proactive. Ideally, scanning is an ordinary tool of an ongoing strategic planning process. But strategic planning, whether of the systematic or emergent variety, tends to be underused even in the business world. The environment is not scrutinized unless some catastrophe takes place. Environmental stability, while highly desirable, may foster a false sense of security and prevent adequate vigilance.

Once significant environmental systems and trends have been identified and their impact or potential impact has been assessed, it is possible to plan strategies to take advantage of opportunities and manage or cope with threats.

A contingency approach to managing the environment seems most useful. In developing coping mechanisms, planners need to adapt their coping strategies to current environmental conditions, taking into consideration the importance of the decision, the degree of turbulence in the environment, and the degree of uncertainty that remains even after careful monitoring and scanning.

"Placid" environments. Terreberry (1968) describes two important attributes of "placid" environments: (1) the environment itself is not formally organized, and (2) transactions are largely initiated and controlled by the focal organization (p. 600). If applicants to clinical psychology programs approved by the American Psychological Association far outnumber places available, then these programs are in control of this aspect of their environment.

In such cases organizations, institutions, and communities can formulate what Aldrich (1979) calls "proprietary" strategies. They can "go it alone," devising tactics to meet environmental threats as they appear. One proprietary strategy is to reorganize internally so that the organization is stronger and more capable of withstanding random attacks from the environment. "Internal structural modifications are often sufficient to close off unwanted external influence and so organizational change occurs without an increase in interorganizational dependence" (Aldrich, 1979, p. 293). Religious schools, for example, can organize themselves and their student bodies so as to exclude many "secular" influences.

In summary, if the environment is placid enough, the system is able to handle opportunities and threats by mobilizing its own resources. Obviously the cost of this mobilization (for instance, internal reorganization) should be taken into account.

Placid but organized environments. If the systems in the environment are organized, then it is risky to try to cope with them tactically as they arise. Tactics should be replaced with long-term strategies. Aldrich (1979) suggests "dyadic" strategies.

> After proprietary strategies, the next most preferred strategies are those requiring cooperation or negotiation with isolated or small numbers of organizations. Dyadic strategies require giving up some autonomy to win a greater measure of control over essential resources or an environmental contingency. This strategy is more problem-laden than the proprietary strategy because it involves negotiation and bargaining with other organizations, which are also attempting to preserve their independence and exploit their bargaining positions. Whether a focal organization will play a dominant, equal, or subordinate role depends on whether it has access to the conditions promoting independence . . . [p. 295].

If people who want to start a halfway house for ex-convicts realize that there will be opposition from various sources in the community, then they might start by building a coalition, for instance, among churches and other service-oriented community groups. Trying to take on, one at a time, each individual or group that is opposed might prove to be an impossible task.

Disturbed and turbulent environments. Disturbed and turbulent environments drain the resources of systems. For instance, since information is at a premium in turbulent environments, for instance, a great deal of energy must be spent in intelligence operations. Consider the Organizational Development program in a disturbed environment. If university enrollments drop, if a downturn in the economy limits funding from business and industry, if government funding dries up, and if the university is cutting budgets, the OD program finds itself in a competitive environment and the atmosphere of the entire university becomes politicized. Since there are too many snouts at the trough, a certain amount of political pushing and shoving can be expected. An organization or unit in such a situation may resort to a set of strategies that Emery and Trist (1965) call "operations." An operation "consists of a campaign involving a planned series of tactical initiatives, calculated reactions of others, and counteractions" (p. 7). For instance, when the new interdisciplinary M.A. program in organizational development was proposed, some of the "tactical initiatives" included publishing the favorable results of a needs survey; consulting the dean of the graduate school on the design, since he strongly favored interdisciplinary programs; choosing the chairperson of another department as principal spokesperson for the program, a person who was also a member of the religious order that operated the university; and asking the advice of the chairpersons of all social-science and human-service departments. The "calculated reactions of others" included opposition from some of the members of the school of education, who wanted to have such a program themselves, from the dean of the school of nursing who seemed to hate all new programs, and from the dean of the business school, who saw the new program as an invasion of his territory. Some of the "counteractions" included private conferences (rather than public meetings) with the two opposing deans, the circulation of statements of support from key figures in the university, and stonewalling the objections of the members of the school of education. These and other measures worked. The meetings with the various university review committees were difficult and two of the committees asked for second meetings, but the program was finally approved by the board of trustees. Of course, all of this is highly political. Chapter 15 deals with politics as one of the principal forms of system arationality.

Loose environmental coupling

To say that the environment often lives within and constructs the reality of any given system is not the same as saying that "everything is intimately related to everything else."

> Is it then plausible to assert that "everything is related to everything else?" If someone in New York sneezes, does someone in Peoria catch cold? Does the failure of the ABC Laundry in Boston affect the unemployment rate in Hartford? If the sociology department at Ivy University declines in prestige, does the chemistry department cease to attract qualified post-doctoral students? . . . There are countless examples, but the central point should be clear: Many situations in everyday life are only loosely related to one another, if at all, even within the same organization or group [Aldrich, 1979, p. 76].

It is foolish to imagine environmental relationships where none exist and futile to try to identify everything in the internal or external environment that has an impact on the system. Environmental scanning is difficult and time-consuming but essential to strategic planning. Strategies must be tailored to environmental realities and to the values espoused by the system. Such strategies make it possible for the system to deal with environmental threats and take advantage of environmental opportunities as they arise.

15

Managing Arationality

Many people talk about the limitations of rational models in designing, managing, and changing organizations, but until recently, few people offered solutions. Today, however, social scientists are aware that the arational dimensions of organizations present the greatest challenges to both managers and consultants. Peters and Waterman's book *In Search of Excellence* (1982) is about the ability of an organization to cope with system-limiting forms of the arational and to develop system-enhancing forms. Figure 15-1 shows why understanding and dealing with the arational in organizations is critical. Although the percentages in the diagram are mythic, they show that in the actual operation of an organization, arationality has the edge. The percentages change. Some managers swear that in times of crisis the percentages look more like 20% and 80% respectively. In chaotic families, they might be 10% and 90%. The models used by those who design and run organizations are not as rational, linear, and systematic as they first seem because all rational models are in practice permeated by the various forms of the arational.

The term *arational* need not have the negative connotations that the term *irrational* has. If the administrator of a mental health center were to shoot an incompetent staff member, everyone would recognize the act as irrational. However, when an administrator keeps an incompetent staff member over a considerable period of time, people can recognize one of the more common arationalities of organizational life. The term *arational* does not attempt to place blame. When the director and assistant director of a correctional facility enter an expressed or implied contract in good faith and then both, in different ways, fail to live up to this contract, the failure is one of the normal arationalities of life. A strictly rational view of contracts would demand that each party live up to the letter of the contract. On the other hand, it would be both irrational and unethical for parties to enter a contract that they have no intention of keeping.

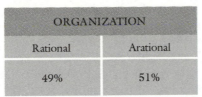

ORGANIZATION	
Rational	Arational
49%	51%

FIGURE 15-1.   The arational edge in organizations and institutions

Emotions, by definition, are arational, but this does not make them irrational or unreasonable. In fact, it is quite reasonable that people feel and express emotions. Emotions add depth and color to human interactions. However, if a project director constantly uses anger as a way of exercising warranted control over the members of the project team, then her *use* of emotions becomes irrational or unreasonable.

The rational is what might be expected in the world if everyone were to follow reason all the time; the arational refers to such categories as the following:

- Phenomena such as emotions and intuition which, by definition, fall outside the rational
- Phenomena that, because of their complexity, are presently beyond the scope of reason; for instance, assembling and fully understanding all the data relating to a complex decision
- Phenomena that are presently unpredictable, including many of the actions of individuals and many of the events in the environment
- The deviations from reason that are so common among human beings that they do not merit being called irrational; for instance, failure to live up to some of the provisions of a complex contract

Smart managers and consultants understand and can use the rational organizational models, methods, and skills that underlie common management practice. On the other hand, *wise* managers and consultants, while understanding and using rational models and methods, also understand both system-limiting and system-enhancing forms of the arational. They understand that rational models do not always work, even though they might not understand why. They are not surprised by, but rather expect and even befriend, the various quirks in the system. They learn how to manage the negative forms of arationality that rinse through the system. They know how to promote system-enhancing forms of the arational; for instance, arrangements in the informal system that help both people and productivity.

It would be impossible to establish a complete list of all the kinds of arationality with which managers and consultants must contend. A few examples of the arational will demonstrate that in the best organizations, system-enhancing forms of the arational are supported and cultivated and system-limiting forms are coped with and managed. Now that the arational has been defined as a practical field for study on the part of managers, Model A can be used as a framework for organizing some of the categories of the arational. In Model A, the rational filters through which we view and understand the world, especially the world of human services, are complemented by a useful set of arational filters. People who work in human-service settings, unlike their counterparts in business settings, are specifically trained to help people grapple with the arational within themselves and in the world around them. Of course, there are obvious risks in the paradox of trying to create a rational overview of arationality.

People have written about enhancing forms of the arational (Peters and Waterman, 1982) and limiting forms of the arational (Gall, 1975) without creating a taxonomy of individual- and system-enhancing and individual- and system-limiting forms of arationality relevant to managerial practice. The categories in Table 15-1 constitute a start toward a taxonomy and can be used by the reader to learn to recognize enhancing and limiting forms of the arational. In the list, system-enhanc-

TABLE 15-1.   Arational elements that affect organizations

Individual Behavior	
emotions	inertia
individual differences	caring
face saving	resistance
champions	commitment
laggards	reluctance
motivation	selflessness
incentives	persistence
unpredictability	cowardice
self-interest	bravery, heroism
defense mechanisms	reluctance
excuse making	interior life

Cognitive	*Emotional*
intuition	upside emotions
complexity	downside emotions
faith	enthusiasm
blind spots	fanaticism
imagination	endurance
unclear data	need for security
values	spirit
data overload	boredom, despair
creativity	hoopla
standards	conflict
vision	patience
ignorance	repression
ambiguity	hope

System-related Behavior	
slack resources	"loose coupling"
unpredictable environments	culture
preoccupation with the mundane	informal system
politics	vested interests
"arrangements"	stagnation
quest	hidden agendas

ing and system-limiting forms are mixed together because they are mixed together in daily living and because many forms of the arational can, in different circumstances or from different points of view, be either enhancing or limiting. For instance, the use of intuition in decision making can lead to amazing creativity or to disaster.

POLITICS AND ARATIONALITY

Now that we have a working description of arationality, let us turn our attention to one of its principal forms. Tichy (1983) believes that politics as a form of arationality in organizations, institutions, and communities deserves special attention.

> All organizations face the problem of allocating power and resources. The uses to which the organization will be put, as well as who will reap the benefits of the organization, must be determined. Decisions around these issues get reflected in compensation programs, career decisions, budget decisions, and the internal power structure of the organization. Unlike the technical area, in which there are formalized tools such as strategic planning and organization design, in the political area, the concepts and language are less formal and often less obvious. Nonetheless, a great deal of management time and attention are given to strategic political issues . . . [p. 10].

Tichy goes on to demonstrate how politics, woven as it is into the fabric of systems, needs to be taken into account by those who are instituting and managing change. Figure 15-2 adds politics to the other pervasive variables that affect the functioning

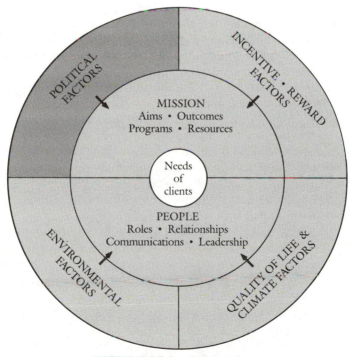

FIGURE 15-2. Political factors

of systems. Because of its importance, it deserves a special slot in Model A. Politics is understandable, but in our sense arational, because it nowhere appears on formal organizational and institutional charts.

The world of organizational politics is a morass of arationality. Politics deals with such phenomena as interest groups, coalitions, power, influence, conflict, and bargaining (Bacharach and Lawler, 1981). Politics implies at least two types of inter-related competition: People compete for power, influence, and control, and they compete for scarce resources.

Prestige, power, influence, and control. Some people find setting norms for and controlling the behavior of others rewarding. Tucker (1981) suggests that politics "is in essence the pursuit and exercise of power—in the interest of those who pursue and exercise it" (p. 1).

> If a person seeks power only for instrumental purposes, we can predict that his search will be bounded; he wishes to control other people only insofar as that control will contribute to the attainment of other goals. If, on the other hand, he finds the experience of controlling others intrinsically rewarding [or extrinsically in terms of payoffs, I would add], there may be few limitations on the number of people over whom he will strive for power, the magnitude of power to which he will aspire, or the kinds of activity over which power will be sought [Kahn, 1964, pp. 5–6].

The Sophists claimed that politics was about prestige and the exercise of power. Plato believed that politics was leadership at the service of the public good. For most, perhaps, it is some combination, however one-sided, of power and service.

Scarce resources and control over their allocation. Politics is about the "pork barrel." For instance, being elected mayor of a city brings with it a great deal of power in the form of patronage. Members of the Senate and House of Representatives make sure that their states and districts get their piece of the pie.

Politics is about *vested interests.* Webster's dictionary defines vested interest as "an interest, as in an existing political, economic, or social arrangement, to which the holder has a strong commitment." Unions were founded to protect their members from companies that pursued their profits at the expense of the workers. The stakes were justice and human decency. Later some of these same unions began using their power to protect the economic gains of their members, not against the onslaught of management, but against relatively disadvantaged individuals or groups who were looking for their fair share of the economic pie. Some unions did the same kinds of things that they had been formed to fight against.

While some systems are less political than others, all systems have some kind of politics. This observation includes business organizations, but it also includes insti-tutions like correctional facilities and community systems like churches and families. In a reformatory or a penitentiary politics becomes a stark and even terrifying reality. The politics of systems and their accompanying rules are not written down and posted. Rather they are acted out. Not to know them can lead to the danger of being ground up by them.

Since some people are more political than others, individual differences can lead to inequities in any kind of system. Some people grow up thinking that politics is basically "dirty," a kind of necessary evil that will disappear when Utopia arrives. By leaving politics to others, they give those who are more political even wider latitude to gain power and exercise influence.

A frequently asked question is, "My organization is so political—how do I cope with its politics?" Often this question means, "I feel powerless. I don't know the rules; I don't know how to play the political game. What can I do to exercise more influence in this system?" The first step is to identify what people who are politically successful do. Who are the political exemplars in the system? In a school this group might include the principal, a coach, and some of the teachers. In the family it might be father or mother or even one of the children (politics is no respecter of age). In a penitentiary it might be a group of trusties. Political success calls for skills that can be learned and practiced.

Understanding the political environment. Politicians do not see social systems in isolation. They see systems as power networks.

Learning the informal system. Good politicians have a feeling for the arational, including an understanding of what is happening in the informal system.

Organizing. People who are politically astute are good at organizing other people, enlisting them in the service of a cause. They know that there is power in numbers.

Forming coalitions. Politicians know when it is time to get together with other individuals or groups that possess power to pursue common goals.

Addressing self-interest. The politically astute appeal to the self-interest of those they are organizing. "Do it my way and you will get what you want." Politicians are forever listening to polls and even taking them, formally or informally. They know which way the political winds are blowing and they know how to set sail with the wind.

Communications. Politicians know how to talk to people or, if they are not good at these skills, they gather around themselves people who are adept at communicating. Politicians are good at persuading and selling. They are assertive; they are not hesitant to sell their ideas, opinions, values, goals, and programs.

Using conspiracy. Effective politicians know when to work in public and when to work behind the scenes. If they cannot organize people openly, they do so quietly. They know when and how to use a conspiratorial approach to power.

Making friends. One way to gain power is to make friends with those in power. This may mean swallowing one's pride, but loss of pride may be a small enough price to pay for the cause. Of course, political friendships differ qualitatively from ordinary human friendships. Since a strong element of self-interest is never lacking, political friendships can be discarded when they are no longer useful. If a President's policies are embarrassing, members of his own party feel little compunction in distancing themselves from him at election time.

Identifying with causes. People who are politically astute know how to "work" causes. They find parades, get in front of them, and then lead them where they want to go. Or they create issues around which people can rally. They know that, historically, the ideas or ideals that have inflamed people are basically simple. Therefore, public discussions about the cause are simple and exhortatory. The more complex issues associated with the cause are dealt with privately.

The utilitarian nature of political skills and strategies is distasteful to some, and with good reason. The values they hold urge them to depoliticize systems, not to learn how to play the game. On the other hand, politicians are not in and of themselves unprincipled. Some very effective human-service providers accept the fact that life is political and that the systems for which they work are political. They learn how to manage political processes. Even highly principled politicians use some of the means outlined above to further causes that they believe will benefit people. Without becoming cynical, they go about the daily task of managing what at first sight seem to be rational systems but which are permeated through and through with rich and infuriating forms of arationality.

THE ARATIONALITY OF INDIVIDUALS AND SYSTEMS

Figure 15-3 depicts arationality as like the connecting tissue in organisms and, like connecting tissue, it gets little direct attention; bones and organs are on center stage. But without connecting tissue, there would be no organism. One reason people despair of rational models like performance planning is that the arational is not "factored in"; that is, the connecting tissue is missing and the models seem unrealistic. Arationality is characteristic of both individuals and systems. What follows is a sampling of the kinds of arationality that beguile both individuals and the systems they are in.

The arationality of individuals

A great deal of the arationality of organizations, institutions, and communities stems from the arationality, complexity, and unpredictability of the individual members of these systems. The complexity of human beings is both charming and infuriating. Wise individuals in positions of responsibility—parents, managers, supervisors, teachers, ministers, judges, legislators, doctors, lawyers, and probation officers— "know what is in men and women." Without becoming cynical, they are seldom surprised by eruptions of irrationality in human behavior. Taking an organic rather than a mechanistic view of systems, they make allowances for individual differences, emotions, erratic behavior, defense mechanisms, excuse making, and the like. They realize that even in totalitarian systems individuals exercise their freedom in a variety of unpredictable ways, and they are not surprised even when individuals seem to use their freedom against their own interests. Encounters with what is best in people encourage wise leaders without making them unwarrantedly optimistic, and encounters with human venality do not discourage them or erode their basic optimism. They meet people where they are instead of where they wish they were.

Human beings as excuse makers. When reality becomes too intrusive, threatening, or painful, people develop strategies for warding off threats. These strategies have been called defense mechanisms. Because that term is rooted in psychoanalytic theory, however, it is often associated with psychopathological distortions of reality. Although the names of defense mechanisms such as *rationalization, denial,* and *projection* are common enough in everyday speech, Snyder, Higgins, and Stucky

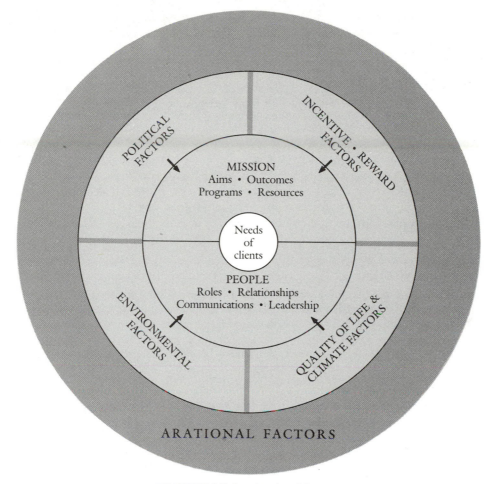

FIGURE 15-3. Arational factors

(1983) prefer the term *excuse making* to describe the ordinary person's daily attempts to escape reality.

Face-saving behavior, as Goffman (1967) illustrates so well, is not a form of exotic behavior found only in Mideastern and Far Eastern societies. It is alive and well in the West as well. People want their "performances" reviewed favorably, whether these reviews come from self or others. Failures and performances that fall short of some standard must be explained. "Excuses," say Snyder, Higgins, and Stucky, "are explanations or actions that lessen the negative implications of an actor's performance, thereby maintaining a positive image for oneself and others" (p. 45).

The premise that we have adopted throughout this chapter is that actors are concerned with maintaining their positive self-images; further, these positive self-images are assumed to be, in most instances, as much for the actor as they are for the audience. When "bad reviews" enter, as they seem to for most of us, the actor is painfully aware of the link to an activity that threatens his or her positive self-image. In such circumstances excuses diminish one's responsibility for the negative activity, as well as lessen the perceived negativeness of the act. If successful, the excuse masquerade maintains one's positive image. Perhaps "the show goes on" precisely because excuses enable the cast of actors to preserve their positive self-images for future performances [pp. 59–60].

Furthermore, since excuse making is rewarded, it tends to be repeated. In fact, it can become so instinctive and habitual that individuals are not even aware of their excuse-making behavior. Snyder, Higgins, and Stucky catalogue different kinds of excuses under two major categories: retrospective excuses or "masquerades for the past," and anticipatory excuses or "masquerades for the future." It is embarrassing to find oneself unmasked on almost every page of their book.

Since organizations are also "actors," they are not only makers of excuses, but also vendors. Snyder, Higgins, and Stucky see such institutions as mental-health systems and the courts as excuse vendors.

Mental health institutions have been criticized for providing individuals with ready-made ways of avoiding responsibility for their behavior. Central to this alleviation of individual responsibility is the use of diagnostic labels implying that individuals have diseases. . . . Although mental health professionals are not, as a group, oblivious to the long-term detrimental effects of psychiatric diagnoses, the mental health system is constructed in such a way as to make it difficult for the individual professional to avoid dispensing them. . . . Mental health institutions, then, can be seen as vendors of excuses both to individuals and to society more generally [pp. 298–299].

And yet alcoholics are sometimes relieved to learn that they have a disease, but one they can control. The diagnostic label wipes the slate clean and saves face, allowing them to marshal their forces to cope successfully with the disease.

Most of us are familiar with the comedy of organizational excuse making.

The "self" of a system is physically and conceptually elusive so that, when a system is called on to take responsibility for itself, what often results is a massive game of finger pointing, better known as "passing the buck." Responsibility in systems often resembles a hot potato being passed around a circle of players; no one person can ever be said to "have" it. The board of directors blames government policies or top-level management, who blame middle management, who blame line workers, who blame middle management, and so on. "Administrative hassles," often experienced as being switched from one department to another (none of whom will actually deliver the necessary goods, services, information, or explanation), are common experiences for individuals in our society [Snyder et al., 1983, p. 301].

The head of an important agency of the federal government recently came under fire because the agency had showed favoritism in hiring the sons and daughters of the well-connected in Washington. Instead of engaging in the usual excuse-making game, the director admitted what had happened, said that it was wrong, and outlined how it would be corrected. The issue dropped out of the press almost instantly.

Excuse making is here to stay. Snyder, Higgins, and Stucky suggest that a world devoid of excuse making would be a bleak one resembling the society described in

Orwell's *1984*. Or it would be a world of such selflessness as to negate the self altogether. These authors say that if excuse making helps us preserve our positive self-images for future performances, then let there be excuse making, at least in moderation. While excuses can be dysfunctional for both individuals and systems, they are not all bad. They can be tools for helping people recognize their own limits and the limitations of the social settings in which they live and work and they can help social interactions run more smoothly. In a sort of backhanded way, they can even help people become better risk takers because they can always be called upon if risk results in failure.

Human beings as searchers. On the other hand, there is a rich humanistic and religious literature, backed up by countless examples, that suggests even ordinary people are capable of achieving extraordinary goals. While people in the human-potential movement from William James on have contended that unused human potential is among the most serious problems that humankind faces and have pointed out that most individuals use but a fraction of their potential, their very complaints bear witness to the belief that men and women are capable of at least relative greatness. Peters and Waterman (1982) talk about product and system champions, Carkhuff (1983) and Gilbert (1978) talk about exemplars, and Burns (1978) talks about transformational leaders who can ignite the spark that sets fire to the best in people. Mediocre students can be transformed into excellent learners when given tasks that meet their needs. This is the paradox: People, including ourselves, who are capable of exemplary achievements, nevertheless are inveterate excuse makers.

The arationality of systems

I am sure that each reader has his or her own set of stories about the arationalities of human organizations, institutions, and communities. This sampling deals with the informal system, slack resources, inertia, and entropy.

The informal system.   Much of Model A describes the "formal" system, that set of arrangements that is publicly and officially acknowledged. Meyer and his associates (1978) suggest that the formal structure of many organizations is primarily a myth or public account that may have little connection with the actual activities of the organization's members, but that it serves the crucial function of legitimating the organization as an institution with society. These authors contend that organizational survival demands not simply that a system engage in rational exchange with its environment, but that it have the confidence of its environment (and of its own members) in order to gain the political and social resources that provide for success and stability. In other words, the formal system, which at first glance seems so rational, is not what it seems to be. It is a response to complex environmental demands.

Parallel to this public and official set of arrangements, however mythic they might be, is the "informal" system. The informal system refers to the arrangements that actually exist within the system without official public endorsement. Arationality is not synonymous with ineffectiveness and inefficiency. This second set of arrangements may either contribute to or interfere with productivity and quality of life.

The course catalogues of universities, for example, are often so imposing that prospective students are frightened by course descriptions that seem to demand too much. They read the outline of a course and say to themselves, "I couldn't possibly fulfill all those requirements." And yet students just like themselves are actually taking and passing these formidable courses. The demanding language of the catalogue speaks of the set of arrangements publicly endorsed by the university, but the actual accomplishments of the course do not always meet the published standards. There is an unwritten principle that states, "Here is the ideal, but it is left to each instructor to translate this ideal as he or she sees fit for both the students and the institution." Sometimes the course as it is actually conducted bears little resemblance to the course described in the catalogue.

A graduate student in clinical psychology had put off taking his final statistics course because he heard from other students that it was very dull. He finally had to take it the last semester before he was to get his doctorate. There were five other students in the class. Even though the title of the course in the catalogue suggested that the course related to the statistical bases of intelligence testing, it was announced in class that the course would cover advanced probability theory. After the first three classes, the graduate student said to one of the other members in the class: "I haven't understood a word this man has said." The reply was: "Don't let it bother you, no one does." The student pressed: "I see others writing things down." The reply: "Write down whatever he puts in blocks." The student said: "His putting things in blocks seems to me like random behavior." The reply: "The exam is based on the blocks. In the final exam he lets you use your notes and more or less indicates what blocks he wants."

The student said to himself that he simply could not at this time in his life write down meaningless blocks of material with a view to taking a meaningless final exam. He attended most classes because it seemed to be the political thing to do, but he skipped the final exam. The day after the exam he ran into the professor as he walked across the campus. The professor indicated that the student had missed the final exam and said that he would have to make it up. The student nodded and then put the whole affair out of his head. He knew that he had taken twenty-six *required* courses in a program that was supposed to have only twenty-four courses in all. The student received his grades the day after he received his doctorate. The "required" course in advanced probability theory had been marked "I" (incomplete). He said to himself: "I seem to have a Ph.D./I."

In this case the student had thrown himself on the mercy of the arationality of the informal system and had won. He could well have lost.

The person talking about the informal system says something like this: "I know what's written down, but *this* is the way we do it." The administration and the guards are supposed to run a prison, but it is not uncommon for inmates to seize a great deal of authority in correctional institutions. A guard once testified before a committee, "We do what they [the inmates] let us do." When new members of correctional facilities have "learned the ropes," they know both the formal and the informal system. The formal system relates to the rules and regulations set down by the administration. The informal system relates to such things as recognizing the inmate power hierarchy and knowing how to survive.

Sometimes the members of a system are unaware of its informal aspects. For instance, the members of an organization know the formal procedures to follow in order to be promoted, but they are not sure just how the final decisions are made. Sometimes the leaders of a system are unsure about some of its informal aspects. For instance, managers are not sure of the "arrangements" made among staff members. In both cases, there is some knowledge that an informal system exists.

There are advantages of maintaining both systems. If there is both a formal and an informal system, the total system remains "loosely coupled" (Weick, 1979) and therefore potentially more flexible. The rules and regulations that are not enforced are still "on the books" and can be used as a backup if the informal system of rules and regulations fails. The informal system at its best tempers the rigidities of the formal system, takes into consideration the idiosyncrasies of people, spreads both authority and responsibility more widely throughout the system, blends justice with equity, is sensitive to quality-of-life issues such as the need for slack resources, manages roadblocks to productivity quietly and efficiently, and generally deals creatively with the tensions that are common in the struggle to balance productivity with quality of life. From a manager's point of view, the price of such advantages may be some loss of formal control—but there are trade-offs in every system.

Managing the informal system. Wise managers know that most, if not all, systems are "loosely coupled" and that the formal system is usually complemented by informal forms and processes. In Peters and Waterman's (1982) terms, they know how to celebrate informality.

> Analyze, plan, tell, specify, and check are the verbs of the rational process. Interact, test, try, fail, stay in touch, learn, shift direction, adapt, modify, and see are the verbs of the informal managing processes [p. 50].

Wise managers also know when the informal system is dysfunctional. For instance, wise parents understand that their teenage children will find a variety of ways of distancing themselves from the injunctions of their elders in their search for independence. Such parents may well ignore certain violations of rules and regulations provided that the security of both the family unit and of individual members is protected. On the other hand, prison officials may ignore the actions of the informal system—such as assaults—because they don't want to know, they don't care, they feel powerless, or they feel that it is part of the punishment inmates must suffer. They are living with, rather than managing, the informal system.

Slack resources.   The concept of slack (March and Simon, 1958; Cyert and March, 1963) was originally associated with the problem of cognitive complexity in organizations. For instance, when Pounds (1963) investigated those responsible for making impossible scheduling decisions in manufacturing companies—"impossible" because more data were involved in the scheduling process than either humans or computers could handle—he found that most people had no difficulty with scheduling. "What scheduling problem?" they asked.

Researchers found that a kind of conspiracy emerges in such situations to protect schedulers from being overwhelmed by impossible decisions. Central to the conspiracy is the notion of *slack resources*. If a supervisor needs eight people to operate a work unit at peak times, for instance, he or she might hire nine. Slack is introduced into the system. When a sales representative makes a sale, knowing that delivery can be made in four weeks, he or she quotes a delivery of six weeks. More slack is introduced into the system. If eight machines are needed to handle peak loads, ten are purchased. Even more slack is introduced into the system. The conspiracy introduces enough slack to ensure that the scheduler need not suffer from decision overload.

Clearly manufacturing concerns are not the only kind of systems subject to slack, nor is protection from decision overload the only reason for slack. Slack evolves in most systems for a variety of reasons, some of them related to quality of life. Even people who like to work hard need a bit of elbow room now and again.

> A large airline asked a consultant to do some "human relations training" as a way of handling a "personnel" problem at a major airport. Baggage handlers and ticket sellers had begun to argue with one another, sometimes in front of the customers. The manager wanted the consultant to solve the problem through human relations work in small groups with both baggage handlers and ticket sellers.
>
> The consultant learned that the airline had increased its business 30% the previous year without hiring any new employees, and that the immediate supervisors of both the ticket sellers and baggage handlers tended to ignore the situation and spend more time in their offices.
>
> The consultant saw the problem as a lack of slack resources. The system had become too taut. With workers under greater stress and rubbing elbows with one another more frequently, it was not surprising that there was friction. Furthermore, the supervisors were not used to handling a taut system. Thus their response was to withdraw into their offices and ask higher management for help.

This example demonstrates clearly that it does not always make sense for consultants to do what they are asked to do. The answer to the problem did not lie in training line personnel in human relations skills.

The problem with managing slack resources is that they are part of the informal rather than the formal system. Managers do not sit around asking themselves how they might introduce slack into the system. If anything, they are trying to get rid of dysfunctional slack. Since slack does not appear in any formal way on the rational charts of the organization, it is difficult to define a problem as a lack of useful slack or as a failure to manage a taut system.

Rational managers try to eliminate as much slack as possible. Wise managers understand the common conspiracy to introduce slack in order to solve the problem of cognitive complexity or to meet some other legitimate organizational or individual need. They realize that they themselves at times introduce slack and, up to a point, they know where it is. Further, they learn how to manage trade-offs between tightening up the system for the sake of effectiveness and efficiency and the stress and dissatisfaction created when a system is too tight.

Beginnings, enthusiasm, and inertia. Both upbeat and downbeat forms of arationality are found at the beginning of enterprises, projects, and programs. Beginnings can be fragile. For some people they take on an almost mystic significance. At the beginning of an enterprise it is not uncommon to find enthusiasm, inertia, or even a combination of both.

Peters and Waterman (1982) point out over and over again that the best organizations are good at generating and maintaining enthusiasm. Sarason (1972) says that what people find so attractive at the beginning of an enterprise is that it introduces welcome novelty and challenge into their lives. Boredom, one of the most insidious forms of arationality, is the enemy.

> The feeling that one is locked into a particular job or line of work, that one will never have the opportunity to test one's self in diverse kinds of tasks, is one consequence of pyramidally, hierarchically organized settings, but not limited to them. Many professional people outside such settings also feel trapped by circumstances that they perceive as preventing them from exploring new roles and untested interests and capacities. . . . A fair reading of *Walden Two* should leave the impression that Skinner believes that boredom is one of the most destructive feelings in our society and that one of the major accomplishments of his utopia is that it is organized in a way that permits an individual the time and support to lead a diversified existence in which boredom is the exception rather than the rule. . . . Skinner believes that the happiness of an individual depends on an environment that permits him to remain curious about himself and his world and supports his efforts to move in new directions [pp. 267–268].

But initial enthusiasm sometimes creates false hopes and leads to the failure of projects or organizations. "My experience leaves no doubt that the failure of most new settings is contained in simplistic notions compounded of unbridled hope, the best intentions, and the denial of present or future conflict" (Sarason, 1972, p. 266). While initial excitement drives people and helps them overcome inertia and initial obstacles, it also creates blind spots. If a project has only a fifty-fifty chance of succeeding, then excessive enthusiasm can lead to debilitating depression if the enterprise does not succeed. Therefore, a manager needs to encourage enthusiasm—create it even—and at the same time foresee and try to control its potentially limiting side effects.

Sarason, in commenting on Frazier, the leader of the community in Skinner's *Walden Two,* suggests ways to counteract false hopes.

> The model of how to talk and act is its founder, Frazier, who never seems to let himself or others forget what the community is about, the necessity for confronting and not avoiding problems, that a rosy view of the future is no substitute for vigilance in the present, that courteous talk is too frequently a cover for straight talk and that the primacy of group values is a necessary condition to permit individuals to live creative and diversified lives [1972, p. 267].

What Sarason implies is not the kind of caution that puts a damper on everything. There is a difference between caution at the service of creativity and caution at the service of inertia. Beginnings can bring out the "playful" in people in the creative sense of that term. Ellis (1973) discusses play in terms of "optimal arousal theory," the hypothesis that people try to strike a balance between boredom and terror in their lives: "Play is that behavior motivated by the need to elevate the level of arousal towards the optimal" (Ellis, 1973, p. 110). The best managers don't kill a sense of play in staff members; the best staff members don't kill a sense of play either in themselves or in others.

Inertia. A body at rest tends to remain at rest; a body in motion tends to remain in motion in the same direction. These physical laws have their psychological and organizational counterparts. Individuals have always complained about how difficult it is to get started: "I did a hundred things, everything but the work I was supposed to do." Organizations, like individuals, experience two kinds of inertia.

> The total system has *high inertia.* Anything that requires a coordinated effort of the organization in order to start is unlikely to be started. Anything that requires a coordinated effort of the organization to be stopped is unlikely to be stopped [Cohen and March, 1974, p. 207].

Many organizations have trouble starting performance planning and appraisal systems—something that certainly requires a coordinated effort. Nothing seems to happen on schedule. The first year, plans are not in on time, feedback meetings do not take place, and appraisals are characteristically late. Inertia is part of the "expected messiness of beginnings." However, once it is recognized that both organizational and individual inertia are a normal part of human experience and that inertia does not necessarily imply ill will, it is easier to deal with.

Managing inertia is mainly a question of managing *incentives* and the other antecedents to human behavior:

- Are there enough incentives to get people started on a task?
- Are these incentives clear?
- Are they incentives that can motivate *this* person or *this* unit?
- Are there competing incentives—incentives for doing something else besides the required task?
- What else is distracting the individual or the unit from the task?
- What can be done to increase the power of task-related incentives?
- What can be done to decrease the power of task-detracting incentives?
- What can be done to minimize distractions?

These questions could be used, for example, to help doctoral students overcome the tendency to postpone dissertation research as they become more and more involved in the delivery of clinical services. Procrastination leads to hurried and sometimes careless research in order to meet deadlines established by the psychology department and the graduate school. In extreme cases, students fail to get their degrees. To manage this situation better, the faculty can meet with students and devise both individual and system solutions. More probable behaviors (in this case, clinical work) can be used as incentives for less probable behaviors (in this case dissertation research). Students can be allowed to begin clinical work only after they have finished their dissertation proposals. In this and in most other cases, overcoming inertia can be solved by a combination of individual and system efforts.

The second form of inertia—a body in motion tends to stay in motion in the same direction—accounts for resistance to change. Organizational and personal cultures establish a kind of "trajectory" over time. These trajectories are difficult to alter, especially if assumptions, values, and norms are covert. Wise managers do not try to impose change overnight. A sailing metaphor is useful. Organizational culture is like a wind. Those wanting to innovate can expend a great deal of energy trying to sail (or row) against the wind. On the other hand, they can abdicate and move with the wind. Or they can befriend the wind and use it to get where they want to go. The third option, of course, demands patience and a longer-term perspective.

Entropy.   In human-service settings, entropy affects both individuals and relationships. First, the relationship between providers and clients can decay over time if providers take it for granted and fail to work at it. Second, entropy is one of the major restraining forces in the lives of clients. Wise practitioners understand this and help clients develop the kinds of "rachets" they need to keep programs for improvement moving forward.

There are two major ways of managing entropy—prevention, and maintenance or follow-up.

Prevention. The kinds of "rachets" (Stein, 1980) that help to prevent backsliding differ from system to system and from program to program. For instance, a youth officer found that his charges did well as long as he had contact with them, but if the contacts stopped or became spaced too far apart, they got into trouble again. He found some rachets by cooperating with a community organization that worked with the young people of the neighborhood. He began meeting his charges at the youth center, which provided the kinds of supplementary contacts and programs that served as rachets. Keeping in touch is important. Members of Alcoholics Anonymous give new members their telephone numbers. When recovering alcoholics need help or just want to talk to someone, there is always someone available. These contacts are rachets that help to prevent many alcoholics, especially in the beginning of the rehabilitation process, from falling back.

At the beginning of every project or program, managers need to step back and ask themselves, "In what ways is this venture likely to decay over time?" Once they understand the kinds of entropy that are likely to be operative in this program, they can develop the needed rachets from the start.

Follow-up. Webster's dictionary defines *follow-up* as "a system or instance of pursuing an initial effort by supplementary action." The word *system* is key. Most people will admit that follow-up is important and involve themselves in follow-up occasionally, but few build it into the program systematically.

Of course, follow-up is not the work of the consultant. However, part of the consultation process should be to see to it that the members of the system elaborate their own follow-up procedures. Follow-up gets a lot of lip service in organizations but not much action. No one kind of follow-up is applicable to all organizations. Imagination must uncover novel forms of follow-up and ways of tailoring them to the specific system.

These, then, are but a few of the forms of arationality that both enrich and limit organizations and institutions, and the projects and programs within them. One major form of arationality, organizational or institutional *culture*, merits special attention.

16

Understanding and Managing
Organizational Culture

Culture, the largest and most controlling of the arational factors, rinses through the system, giving it individuality and color. In a very real sense, the culture of the system *is* the system. As a major source of both system-enhancing and system-limiting arationality, it is receiving more and more theoretical and practical attention (Deal and Kennedy, 1982; Allen and Kraft, 1982; Kanter, 1983; Peters and Waterman, 1982; Tichy, 1983). As indicated in Figure 16-1, organizational culture pervades and affects every element of Model A, including the other pervasive elements.

Culture can be understood through the following five overlapping and interactive categories: (1) tradition, (2) beliefs, (3) values, (4) standards, and (5) patterns of behavior.

Tradition. The past lives on in the organization's present. History includes the stories, the critical historical incidents, the myths, the founders, the heroes and heroines, the exploits, and the folklore, still alive and affecting the system. People celebrate certain events in the system's past and forget others. In one university the picture of the founder of the children's clinic is displayed prominently in the foyer, and his name and visions are still mentioned frequently. That he ruled with an iron hand, made unilateral decisions that adversely affected the life of the staff, and had an explosive temper—these facts have been forgotten. From time to time historical perceptions are officially revised for political and ideological reasons. Stalin and Mao may be presented as heroes in one decade or generation and as misguided villains in the next.

History lives on in the oral tradition, the stories and myths that are told and retold. More significantly, it lives on because it is embedded in the beliefs, values, and norms of the system.

Beliefs. Beliefs, assumptions, understandings, and dogmas relate to the system, the work it does, the people in the system, and the environment. Churches state

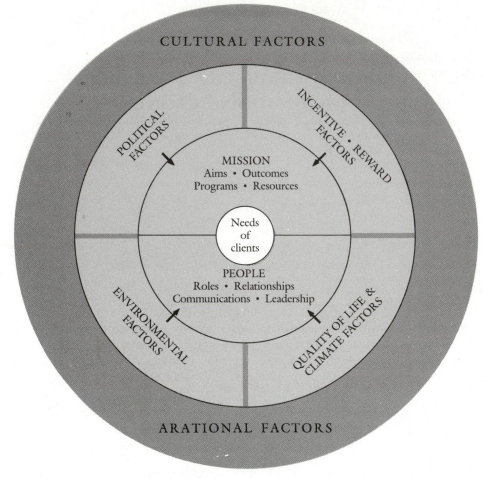

FIGURE 16-1.   Cultural factors

their beliefs explicitly. Human-service systems espouse many beliefs; for instance, a belief in the dignity and worth of each individual human being, but only a few organizations state their beliefs. As indicated in Chapter 5, however, the trend is changing; the Johnson and Johnson Company, for example, has an elaborate "credo" that begins, "We believe that our first responsibility is to our customers . . ." This company's principal espoused beliefs are spelled out in this statement of philosophy.

The faculty members of a graduate program in organizational development expressed the belief that students learn best when they take responsibility for their learning by setting learning goals and drawing up learning contracts with instructors.

Values. Values are whatever the organization prizes. Staff members of a mental health center might prize such things as self-responsibility, honesty, openness, caring, "tough love," team work, neighborhood development, personal freedom, and fairness in transactions among themselves and in their dealings with clients. Peters and Waterman's research (1982) suggests that the best organizations are "values driven."

The faculty members of the OD program value feedback from students. They express that value by asking the students in the program evaluation course to evaluate some dimension of the program each year.

Norms and standards. These are the "oughts," "shoulds," "musts," "dos," "don'ts," norms, standards, policies, rules, principles, regulations, laws, and taboos that govern the behavior of the system as a whole, of the subunits within the system, and of individual members of the system.

Ethical standards for professional practice published by such organizations as the American Psychological Association establish norms and policies for dealing with clients. Norms and standards spell out the kinds of behaviors that will be rewarded in the system and set limits to the kinds of behavior that will be tolerated.

The faculty members of the OD program decided that the students in the program must take a supervised practicum experience in which they use skills learned in experiential classroom settings, hone these skills, and learn new models, techniques, and skills.

Patterns of behavior. In the system, specific patterns of behavior, habits, rites, rituals, ceremonies, and folkways are prevalent. Just as history and tradition help mold an organization's present beliefs, values, and standards, so beliefs, values, and standards generate the patterns of behavior prevalent in the organization. Conservative organizations, for example, prize stability and discourage risk-taking behaviors.

The director and faculty members of the OD program believe that feedback is essential for learning and prize the free sharing of both confirmatory and corrective feedback. They habitually give one another feedback, provide students with feedback, and solicit it from students and others who might be in a position to evaluate their goals and programs.

In practice, the development of culture is not a simple unidirectional process— from history to beliefs to values to norms to patterns of behavior. Changing beliefs can lead to changes in the ways in which system members understand the system's history. Or new behaviors are tried that lead to revisions in the "oughts" of the system. Or values are rearranged to provide a foundation for de facto behavior. Despite the linearity of the framework just presented, culture itself is an arational phenomenon and there is a great deal of arationality involved in the creation and maintenance of an organizational culture.

The impact of internal culture

Human-service providers use various models and filters to understand the people with whom they work. For instance, they study personality theory and abnormal psychology in order to develop practical frameworks to help them assess and interact with clients. Since culture, in the sense outlined here, can be predicated of *individuals* as well as systems, it is a useful framework for understanding and helping people.

History. Clients have been shaped by their histories. The past lives on in their internal and external behavior in both self-enhancing and self-limiting ways. Human-service providers help people handle the past insofar as it has generated beliefs, values, norms, and patterns of behavior that are limiting the present.

Beliefs. Clients have their "assumptive worlds." Often they need help to challenge self-limiting assumptions and develop beliefs to live by. For instance, some clients believe that they are "no good." They degrade themselves, feel that they should be punished, and actually engage in patterns of self-punishing behavior.

Values. Clients have what Argyris (1982) calls "values-in-use" even though they might not be able to name them. Counselors often help clients clarify the values they are acting on and deal with value conflicts that emerge in the clarification process.

Norms. Clients have both self-limiting and self-enhancing standards. Sometimes their normative lives are too controlling; "I want to" is translated into "I must" so frequently that their options are limited.

Patterns of behavior. In this model, patterns of behavior emerge from history, beliefs, values, and norms. Practitioners can help clients deal with self-limiting patterns of behavior both directly and indirectly—that is, through history, beliefs, values, and norms. Conversely, new patterns of behavior can help create new beliefs, values, and standards. This approach is called acting one's way into a new way of thinking instead of trying to think or reason one's way to a new way of acting.

In sum, then, both in organizations and in individuals: past experiences and behaviors give rise to beliefs, values, and norms, which become expressed in enhancing and limiting patterns of behavior. The ways in which these five interactive categories are patterned constitute the culture of the system.

Overt and covert cultures

Every system has its culture, but the people inside the system are never fully conscious of that culture as a whole or of its parts. There are individual differences in awareness: One citizen takes pride in understanding the historical roots of patriotism, while another citizen who is not particularly patriotic is indifferent to the idealistic beliefs and aspirations rooted in the nation's history. Staff members in a psychiatric hospital might dislike working there without ascribing their discomfort to a conflict between their values and those of the system. Differences in cultural awareness suggest the notions of overt and covert culture.

Overt culture refers to the degree to which the five elements of culture are written down in public documents, discussed in a public forum, celebrated publicly, and open to challenge, at least within the organization. Although the members of an organization may talk privately to one another about the company's policies, often there is no public forum within the organization. For instance, staff members in a social-service agency may complain to a consultant that their views are not heard at higher managerial levels (upward communication is not valued; there are covert injunctions against upward communication), but they are afraid to express this complaint in meetings with their supervisors or with the director of the agency.

Some organizations have an official history and honor the birthday of their founder; in their mission statements they outline their beliefs and values; they publish policies and rules; they have public rituals such as award dinners, the Christmas party, and the company picnic. All of these are dimensions of the overt culture of the organization.

Culture, if overt, is reflected in the mission of the organization. A full statement of mission includes an expression of organizational identity (history), a statement of philosophy (beliefs), a statement of values, and an indication of the major policies (standards, preferred behaviors) that stem from organizational philosophy and values—all as bases for the accomplishment, and quality of life of the system.

Covert culture refers to the degree that any of the five elements of culture: are not written down, tend toward the unawareness end of the continuum, are only partially understood, and remain for the most part undiscussed in the public forums of the organization.

In some families, for example, sex is never discussed and references to sex are never found in the language used at home. There is an unacknowledged rule: "We don't talk about sex here." That rule is not written down or discussed, however, and some members of the family may be unaware of it. After the children have grown up and left home, one may say to another, "Not only did we not talk about sex at home, but the word *sex* itself never even came up in our conversations."

Hall (1966, 1977) refers to culture as the "hidden dimension." There are various degrees of the cultural covertness in systems.

Undiscussed. The undiscussed in an organization, institution, or community may well be what is taken for granted. Tiger (1983) stresses the importance of the undiscussed: "Anthropologists have a useful little rule when they go out to study a culture which is different from theirs: The most important thing to know about a culture is what it takes for granted" (p. 93).

Undiscussable. Some dimensions of culture may be so sensitive that they are seen as undiscussable in a public forum. For instance, the fact that one of the more prominent members of the faculty of a psychology department was an alcoholic and that his alcoholism affected his teaching and relationships with clients was discussed only between individual faculty members. This situation went on for more than two years. Department heads in a hospital saw themselves as relatively impotent with respect to a senior vice-president. They discussed their feelings freely with consultants, yet, given the opportunity, they would not discuss their concerns in a retreat with higher management.

Undiscussability as undiscussable. Some dimensions of culture may be so sensitive that they cannot even be *alluded* to in a public forum. For instance, in one organization the possibility that the president was both incompetent and vindictive was a completely forbidden topic. It was unthinkable to put such an item even indirectly on any agenda in any public forum within the organization. People were hesitant or afraid to allude to this possibility even in private.

Unconscious. The impact of history and tradition, current beliefs, values, and standards, and patterns of organizational behavior may be so hidden that most of the people in the organization are unaware of them. This "underground" culture is part of the informal system. It is a powerful regulator of behavior and much of its power is drawn from the fact that it is out of sight.

We often see what happens when the organizational unconscious is not understood and dealt with. When a program is imposed upon an organization without dealing with its "unconscious," at first the change may appear to succeed, but gradually unseen forces take over until finally the change is no longer visible. The organization, like a giant, soft, resilient pillow, accepts the changes laid upon it, then gradually puffs out again as if nothing had happened. Results are only temporary—they cannot be permanent results until the organizational unconscious is dealt with effectively and the "soft pillow" is remolded into a shape that will support the desired innovations [Allen and Kraft, 1982, p. 4].

Human-service providers need to ask themselves some pointed questions about the covert dimensions of cultures:

- What are the covert cultural dimensions of my own organization? In what ways are they individual-enhancing? System-enhancing? Individual-limiting? System-limiting?
- What are the covert cultural dimensions of the systems I am working with? For instance, what is taken for granted in the family with which I am working?
- What are the undiscussable issues in my own organization and in the institutions to which I am a consultant?
- What is taken for granted in my own organization? With what effect?

Change efforts in organizations and institutions can be stymied by the overt culture of the system, but the underground culture is a far more potent restraining force.

Espoused culture versus culture-in-use. The fact that an organization states its beliefs, values, and standards in some public way does not prove that it acts on them. The actual patterns of behavior found in an organization tell us what the organization actually believes, prizes, encourages, and sanctions. For instance, many organizations state that their workers are their most important resource, but demonstrate the opposite through their behavior. For instance, quality-of-work-life considerations are easily brushed aside at times of economic downturn.

Strong versus weak cultures.   All organizations have traditions, beliefs, values, and standards, but organizations differ to the degree that these elements actually influence patterns of behavior. If these elements, whether overt or covert, have a strong impact on behavior, then we can say that the organization has a *strong* culture. For instance, if a mental-health organization says that prevention is important and then establishes a variety of prevention programs in the community based on a meaningful needs assessment, then we can say that their belief in prevention, which is part of the overt culture, is strong.

On the other hand, if history, tradition, beliefs, values, and standards, whether overt or covert, have little impact on behavior, then we can say that an organization has a weak culture. For instance, if an organization claims that two-way communication is important but rarely encourages upward communication, and if subordinates seldom make the effort at upward communication, then the overtly stated belief in the importance of two-way communication is weak. Or if a social-service center says that its staff members constitute its most importance resource, but provides little positive feedback, resists innovative ideas that come from staff, and has a covert expectation that staff members will put in more hours than they are paid for, then this espoused value is not a value-in-use; it has little impact on managerial behavior. It is obvious that an organization may well have a mixed culture, strong in some ways and weak in others.

The interplay between the strong/weak and overt/covert dimensions of culture is outlined in the grid in Figure 16-2. Organizations with weak cultures, whether overt or covert, tend to be aimless. They don't know what they believe in, what they want, or where they are going.

In their book *In Search of Excellence* (1982), Peters and Waterman imply that the best companies have strong, overt cultures. These companies celebrate the best in their traditions, publicly promote strong beliefs, values, and standards, and generate patterns of behavior that are both system- and individual-enhancing. They found that the most successful companies:

- Have a bias toward action instead of getting lost in planning
- Stick close to customers
- Encourage autonomy and entrepreneurship; let the exemplars experiment
- Believe in people and develop them as the most important resource
- Are driven by clearly espoused values that are also values in use
- Stick to their knitting; do what they do best
- Develop a simple structural form and a lean staff
- Let everyone know what needs to be tight, such as quality of services, and
  what can be loose, such as ways of getting things done

Peters and Waterman make these injunctions overt. But, whether overt or covert, these rules can help drive organizations, including human-service organizations, toward excellence. If you walk into a human-service agency with a strong, overt, upbeat culture, it doesn't take long to discover that something good is happening here. The converse also is true.

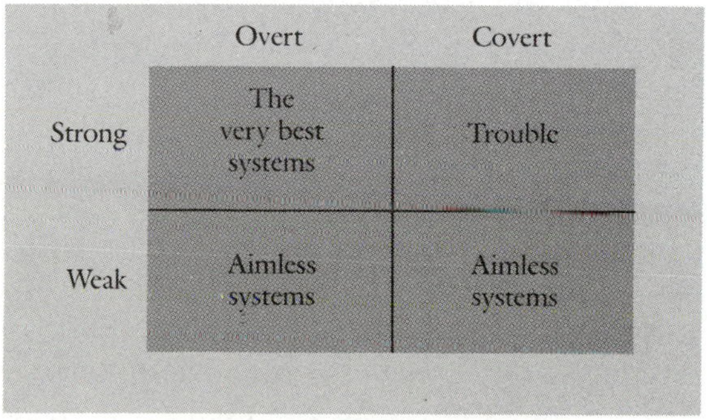

	Overt	Covert
Strong	The very best systems	Trouble
Weak	Aimless systems	Aimless systems

FIGURE 16-2.   A culture grid

The impact of external culture

Up to this point we have been considering the *internal* culture of organizations, institutions, and communities. These cultures, however, are constantly influenced by the culture of the societies in which they reside—the *external* culture. According to Bronfenbrenner (1977), culture in this sense includes

> general prototypes, existing in the culture or subculture, that set the pattern for the structures and activities occurring at the concrete level. Thus, within a given society, one school classroom looks and functions like another. The same holds true for other settings and institutions, both formal and informal. It is as if they were all constructed from the same blueprints. These "blueprints" are the macrosystem. Some actually exist in explicit form as recorded laws, regulations, and rules. But most macrosystems are informal and implicit—carried, often unwittingly, in the minds of the society's members as ideology made manifest through custom and practice in everyday life [p. 515].

And so history, tradition, beliefs, assumptions, values, norms, and standards are also operative in society at large.

Berger and Neuhaus (1977) give an example of how teachers and administrators are "carriers" of the values of the cultural environment from which they come.

> By birth or social mobility, the personnel of the education establishment are upper middle class and this is reflected in the norms, the procedures, and the very cultural climate of that establishment. This means the child who is not of an upper-middle-class family is confronted by an alien milieu from his or her first day at school. In part this may be inevitable. The modern world is bourgeois and to succeed in a bourgeois world means acquiring bourgeois skills and behavior patterns. We do not suggest, as some do, that the lower-class child is being raped when taught correct English, but there are many other, sometimes unconscious, ways in which the education establishment systematically disparages ways of life other than those of the upper middle class. Yet these disparaged ways of life are precisely the ways in which millions of American children live. Thus schools teach contempt for the parents and, ultimately, self-contempt [pp. 21–22].

The "hidden curriculum" of classrooms—"those unstated norms, values, and beliefs that are transmitted to students through the underlying structure of classrooms as opposed to the formally recognized and sanctioned dimensions of classroom experience" (Giroux and Penna, 1977, p. 40)—are not just inventions of the schools themselves. They are fashioned by the society of which the schools are a part.

If schools were completely rational systems, they would continually assess the needs and wants of students together with the needs and wants of the society. They would be sensitive to cultural differences and, in light of this sensitivity, they would create and revise curricula that would prepare students to pursue their own developmental tasks and to provide both support and challenge for the society in which they live. But this is not the case. As Meyer and his associates (1978) note, viewed rationally as producing systems, educational systems are often extremely inefficient. This observation is not surprising since enculturation is an important, though unstated, part of the school's mission. The formal organizational structure of schools may reflect more the demands of the environment for the standardization and categorization of both teachers and students than the needs of students to learn. For instance, when publicly recognized credentials become more important than competence, learning may get lost in the shuffle.

People who look at all of this from a completely rational point of view—that is, from the viewpoint of educational efficiency—will throw up their hands in despair. The present system is illogical when evaluated from the perspective of technical output. But the needs of the bureaucratic social environment for standardization and categorization also are pressing. Therefore, what happens in schools is understandable from a sociological perspective. The often uncritiqued beliefs, assumptions, values, norms, and standards of society are alive and well in the educational system. This observation is true in different ways and to different degrees of all organizations, institutions, and communities, including, of course, human-service delivery systems.

And so we see three layers of culture: the culture of each individual interacting with the cultures of each of the social settings of which he or she is a member, and both sets of culture "nested in" and interacting with the predominant culture and subcultures of society.

MANAGING CULTURE-RELATED ARATIONALITY

Dysfunctional traditions, beliefs, assumptions, "musts," taboos, aspirations, and rituals constitute cultures that inhibit the development of both people and systems. Why do people tolerate the dysfunctional dimensions of system cultures? What are the mechanisms that keep the dysfunctional dimensions of cultures in place? Some of the answers lie in adaptation, lowered awareness, inertia, and the need for security. Managing the dysfunctional dimensions of culture, then, means managing these variables.

Adaptation. As Galbraith (1979) points out, part of the power of culture comes from *adaptation.* He suggests that one reason (but certainly not the only reason) the poor remain locked into their poverty is that they adapt to the culture of poverty. They learn to live with it in the sense that, even though they continue to feel the effects of poverty, they no longer reflect upon themselves as poor. When children are born into poverty, adaptation to poverty is part of their inheritance. Adaptation, however, is not reserved just for the poor. Cultural adaptation affects everyone. Middle-class people adapt to the mores and rituals of the middle class.

Hackman and Oldham (1980) claim that millions of well-educated people in North America are *underemployed.* Since they adapt, however, job dissatisfaction remains a relatively invisible phenomenon. Self-reports of job satisfaction are suspect since, because of adaptation, unless the work situation is intolerable, people will say that they are satisfied. Moreover, once dissatisfied workers have adapted to their surroundings, they resist change, even changes that would provide more satisfying jobs. Change means that they will have to learn new methods at a time when their zest for learning has waned.

Given the fact of cultural adaptation, organizations need consciousness raising with respect to both the general notion of organizational culture and the dimensions of the culture currently in place.

Lack of awareness. Most people do not reflect explicitly on culture. Adaptation means cultural unawareness. Argyris (1982) reports that even people who were explicitly aware of the differences between enhancing and limiting cultures, and had committed themselves to move toward a more enhancing culture, were often unaware that the strategies they were using were contrary to the new culture they espoused. Therefore, a vital step in the process of managing a culture is simply becoming aware of it. Both system managers and members could benefit from the skills of what anthropologists call *ethnography,* the work of describing and understanding a culture (see Spradley, 1979, 1980).

> Although we can easily see behavior and artifacts, they represent only the thin surface of a deep lake. Beneath the surface, hidden from view, lies a vast reservoir of *cultural knowledge.* . . . Although cultural knowledge is hidden from view, it is of fundamental importance because we all use it constantly to generate behavior and interpret our experience. Cultural knowledge is so important that I will frequently use the broader term *culture* when speaking about it. Indeed, I will define culture as *the acquired knowledge people use to interpret experience and generate behavior.* . . . *Explicit* culture makes up part of what we know, a level of knowledge people can communicate about with relative ease. . . . At the same time, a large portion of our cultural knowledge remains *tacit,* outside our awareness [Spradley, 1978, pp. 6–7].

Helping people to get in touch with the dysfunctional dimensions of culture can be a thankless job. If you realize that your system practices covert forms of racism, you will meet with a great deal of denial if you merely announce this realization as a fact and provide evidence for it. Rather you would do better to help the members of the system to come to this realization themselves. People are not always eager to examine their behavior, its meaning, and the premises on which it is based. Plato said that the unexamined life is not worth living, but most people throughout history have failed to adopt his point of view.

Paolo Freire (1970) has made the term "consciousness raising" part of our contemporary vocabulary. Unless people get in touch with their oppression and its causes, they remain victims of both themselves and others. However, consciousness raising is not something that one person or one group does to another. The term implies, first of all, that self-search has become part of the educator's style. For Freire the term also implies that "free and informed choice" is a value. Helping people recognize how they have been victimized by their culture can become another form of oppression—like dragging slaves kicking and screaming to their freedom.

Inertia. The interactive web of traditions, beliefs, values, norms, behaviors, and language that constitute culture is not readily changed. The way we have been and the way we are tend to anchor us to the way we are, rather than speeding us on to the way we could be. If inertia is to be managed, its managers must find incentives to lure people beyond where they are. Imagination is extremely important in this process. Managing cultural inertia means tapping into the imaginal resources of the members of the system. If the present scenario inhibits personal and system

growth and development, more attractive scenarios should be written. "What if
. . ." can be a powerful tool: "What if 'maximizing win-win situations' were to take
the place of 'maximizing winning, minimizing losing' as a central governing variable in this organization [institution, community, family, relationship]?"

Security. Everyone has security needs. As long as these needs are filled, we rarely
reflect on them. But threat soon mobilizes our "fight or flight" tendencies. Maintaining the cultural status quo represents security to many people. For instance,
some people choose poverty over emigrating to an unfamiliar place with an unfamiliar culture. Present evils, however bad they are, sometimes seem pale in comparison with unknown ones.

The quest for security causes people to engage in self-defeating behavior. Even
when people are poorly served by government, schools, the helping and human-
service professions, and the church, they are slow to side with those who call for
reformation. These institutions deal with basic needs: the need for order instead of
chaos, knowledge rather than ignorance, health rather than sickness, and good
rather than evil. Therefore, even when people half realize that they are being poorly
served by these institutions, they do not want anyone to tamper with them too
much. They are willing to continue funding them, even when accountability is
poor, because they serve such critical functions.

In Argyris's earlier writings (see Argyris, 1976; Argyris and Schon, 1974) he
thought that cultural reeducation could be done relatively quickly. He has come to
realize, however, that facilitating changes in the culture of individuals and systems
is a long, arduous process and that some ideal forms of cultural change are still
beyond the capability of human beings. Cultural reeducation can lead to greater
freedom as all meaningful learning does; that is, it can help increase viable options
for individuals and organizations. However, those interested in facilitating cultural
reeducation must remember that a "working anthropology" of systems, especially
one's own set of systems, is not common (Egan and Cowan, 1979). People who
say they want to be free do not automatically do things that make them free. In the
long run, freedom must be seized; it cannot be conferred.

References

Abrams, R. M. The modern corporation. *Society,* 1979, *16* (3), 44–51.

Ackland, L. Guarding for hazards on the rise. *Chicago Tribune,* Wednesday, 8 July 1981.

Adams, J. D. *Understanding and managing stress: A book of readings.* San Diego, Calif.: University Associates, 1980a.

Adams, J. D. *Understanding and managing stress: Facilitator's guide.* San Diego, Calif.: University Associates, 1980b.

Adams, J. D. *Health, stress, and the manager's life style.* Amherst, Mass.: Human Resource Development, 1981.

Adams, J. S. The environmental context of negotiations between human systems. Paper presented at The Negotiation Conference, Center for Creative Leadership, Greensboro, N.C., July 1975.

Adams, J. S. The structure and dynamics of behavior in organization boundary roles. In M. D. Durnette (Ed.), *Handbook of industrial and organizational psychology.* Chicago: Rand McNally, 1976.

Alderfer, C. P., & Brown, L. D. Questionnaire design in organizational research. *Journal of Applied Psychology,* 1972, *56,* 456–460.

Alderfer, C. P., & Holbrook, J. A new design for survey feedback. *Education and Urban Society,* 1973, *5,* 437–464.

Aldrich, H. E. *Organizations and environments.* Englewood Cliffs, N.J.: Prentice-Hall, 1979.

Alexander, H. E. Corporate political behavior. In T. Bradshaw and D. Vogel (Eds.), *Corporations and their critics: Issues and answers on the problems of corporate social responsibilities.* New York: McGraw-Hill, 1981.

Allen, R. F., & Kraft, C. *The organizational unconscious: How to create the corporate culture you want and need.* Englewood Cliffs, N.J.: Prentice-Hall, 1982.

Alpert, J. L. (Ed.) *Psychological consultation in educational settings.* San Francisco: Jossey-Bass, 1982.

Ammons, R. B. Effects of knowledge of performance: A survey and tentative theoretical formulation. *Journal of General Psychology,* 1956, *54,* 279–299.

Annett, J. *Feedback and human behavior: The effects of knowledge of results, incentives, and reinforcement on learning and performance.* Baltimore: Penguin Books, 1969.

Anthony, W. A., Pierce, R. M., & Cohen, M. R. *The skills of rehabilitation programming.* Amherst, Mass.: Carkhuff Institute of Human Technology, 1979.

Argyris, C. *Increasing leadership effectiveness.* New York: Wiley, 1976a.

Argyris, C. Theories of action that inhibit individual learning. *American Psychologist,* 1976b, *31,* 638–654.

Argyris, C. Leadership, learning, and changing the status quo. *Organizational Dynamics,* 1976c, *4* (3), 29–43.

Argyris, C. *Reasoning, learning, and action: Individual and organizational*. San Francisco: Jossey-Bass, 1982.

Argyris, C., & Schon, D. A. *Theory in practice*. San Francisco: Jossey-Bass, 1974.

Ausubel, D. *Cognitive psychology*. New York: Holt, Rinehart, & Winston, 1968.

Bacharach, S. B., & Lawler, E. J. *Power and politics in organizations*. San Francisco: Jossey-Bass, 1981.

Bandura, A. *Psychological modeling: Conflicting theories*. Chicago: Aldine-Atherton, 1971.

Bandura, A. *Principles of behavior modification*. 2nd ed. New York: Holt, Rinehart, & Winston, 1975.

Bandura, A. Self-efficacy: Toward a unifying theory of behavioral change. *Psychological Review*, 1977, *84*, 191–215.

Bandura, A. Gauging the relationship between self-efficacy judgment and action. *Cognitive Therapy and Research*, 1980, *4*, 263–268.

Bandura, A. Self-efficacy mechanism in human agency. *American Psychologist*, 1982, *37*, 122–147.

Bass, B. M. *Stogdill's handbook of leadership*. New York: Free Press, 1981.

Baumhart, R. President sets university goals for 1981–1982. *We* (President's Newsletter), 1981, *6* (2), 1.

Benware, C., & Deci, E. L. Attitude change as a function of the inducement for espousing a proattitudinal communication. *Journal of Experimental Social Psychology*, 1975, *11*, 271–278.

Berenson, B. G., & Mitchell, K. M. *Confrontation: For better or worse*. Amherst, Mass.: Human Resource Development, 1974.

Berger, P. L. *Pyramids of sacrifice: Political ethics and social change*. New York: Basic Books, 1974.

Berger, P. L., & Neuhaus, R. J. *To empower people: The role of mediating structures in public policy*. Washington, D.C.: American Enterprise Institute for Public Policy Research, 1977.

Bergin, A. E. Negative effects revisited: A reply. *Professional Psychology*, 1980, *11*, 93–100.

Blake, R. R., & Mouton, J. S. *Consultation*. Reading, Mass.: Addison-Wesley, 1976.

Blake, R. R., & Mouton, J. S. Theory and research for developing a science of leadership. *Journal of Applied Behavioral Science*, 1982, *18*, 257–273.

Bledstein, B. J. *The culture of professionalism: The middle class and the development of higher education in America*. New York: Norton, 1976.

Blocher, D. H. A systematic eclectic approach to consultation. In C. A. Parker (Ed.), *Psychological consultation: Helping teachers meet special needs*. Minneapolis, Minn.: Leadership Training Institute/Special Education, University of Minnesota, 1975.

Block, P. *Flawless consulting: A guide to getting your expertise used*. Austin, Texas: Learning Concepts, 1981.

Blood, M. R. Intergroup comparisons of intraperson differences: Reward from the job. *Personnel Psychology*, 1973, *26*, 1–9.

Boris, E. T. Private enterprise and public values. *Society*, 1979, *16* (3), 18–19.

Bouchard, T. J., Jr. Field research methods: Interviewing, questionnaires, participant observation, unobtrusive measures. In M. D. Dunnette (Ed.), *Handbook of industrial and organizational psychology*. Chicago: Rand McNally, 1976, pp. 363–413.

Bowers, D. G., & Franklin, J. L. Survey-guided development: Using human resources measurement in organizational change. *Journal of Contemporary Business*, 1972, *1*, 43–55.

Bowers, D. G., & Franklin, J. L. *Survey-guided development: Data-based organizational change*. Ann Arbor: Institute for Social Research, 1976.

Bowers, D. G., & Franklin, J. L. *Survey-guided development I: Data-based organizational change*. La Jolla, Calif.: University Associates, 1977.

Bradshaw, J. The concept of social need. *New Society*, 1972, *30*, 640–643.

Bray, D. W., Campbell, R. J., & Grant, D. L. *Formative years in business: A long-term study of managerial lives*. New York: Wiley, 1974.

Brethower, D. M. *Behavioral analysis in business and industry: A total performance system*. Kalamazoo, Mich.: Behaviordelia, 1972.

Brokes, A. A process model of consultation. In C. A. Parker (Ed.), *Psychological consultation: Helping teachers meet special needs*. Minneapolis, Minn.: Leadership Training Institute/Special Education, University of Minnesota, 1975.

Bronfenbrenner, U. Toward an experimental ecology of human development. *American Psychologist*, 1977, 513–531.

Brown, P. L., & Presbie, R. J. *Behavior modification in business, industry, and government: A behavior modification resource guide for managers, foremen, executives, training directors, and other supervisory personnel*. Champaign, Ill.: Research Press, 1976.

Burchfield, S. R. The stress response: A new perspective. *Psychosomatic Medicine*, 1979, *41*, 661–672.

Burges, B. *Facts and figures: A layman's guide to conducting surveys.* Boston: Institute for Responsive Education, 1976a.

Burges, B. *You can look it up: Finding educational documents.* Boston: Institute for Responsive Education, 1976b.

Burges, B. Citizen action-research: A tool for change. *Voluntary Action Leadership,* 1978, Winter, 15–20.

Burns, J. M. *Leadership.* New York: Harper & Row, 1978.

Campbell, A., Converse, P. E., & Rodgers, W. L. *The quality of American life.* New York: Russell Sage Foundation, 1976.

Caplan, G. *Principles of preventive psychiatry.* New York: Basic Books, 1964.

Caplan, G. *The theory and practice of mental health consultation.* New York: Basic Books, 1970.

Caplan, N., & Nelson, S. D. The nature and consequences of psychological research on social problems. *American Psychologist,* 1973, *28,* 199–211.

Caplow, T. *How to run any organization: A manual of practical sociology.* Hinsdale, Ill.: Dryden, 1976.

Carkhuff, R. R. *Helping and human relations.* Vols. 1 and 2. New York: Holt, Rinehart, & Winston, 1969.

Carkhuff, R. R. *The development of human resources.* New York: Holt, Rinehart, & Winston, 1971.

Carkhuff, R. R. *The art of problem solving.* Amherst, Mass.: Human Resource Development, 1973.

Carkhuff, R. R. (Ed.) *Cry twice: From custody to treatment: The story of institutional change.* Amherst, Mass.: Human Resource Development, 1974.

Carkhuff, R. R. *How to help yourself: The art of program development.* Amherst, Mass.: Human Resource Development, 1974.

Carkhuff, R. R. *Sources of human productivity.* Amherst, Mass.: Human Resource Development, 1983.

Carkhuff, R. R., & Anthony, W. A. *The skills of helping: An introduction to counseling.* Amherst, Mass.: Human Resource Development, 1979.

Carkhuff, R. R., & Berenson, B. G. *Teaching as treatment: An introduction to counseling and psychotherapy.* Amherst, Mass.: Human Resource Development, 1976.

Carlson, B. C. A model of quality of work life as a developmental process. In W. W. Burke & L. D. Goodstein (Eds.), *Trends and issues in OD: Current theory and practice.* San Diego: University Associates, 1980.

Catalanello, R. F., & Kirkpatrick, D. L. Evaluating training programs—The state of the art. *Training and Development Journal,* 1968, *22,* 2–9.

Caulfield, T. J., & Perosa, L. M. Counselor education—Quo vadis? *Counselor Education and Supervision,* 1983, *22,* 178–184.

Chavis, D. M., Stucky, E., & Wandersman, A. Returning basic research to the community: A relationship between scientist and citizen. *American Psychologist,* 1983, *38,* 424–434.

Cherniss, C. Creating new consultation programs in community mental health centers. *Community Mental Health Journal,* 1977, *13,* 133–141.

Cherns, A. The principles of sociotechnical design. *Human Relations,* 1976, *29,* 783–792.

Churchman, C. W. *The systems approach.* New York: Dell, 1968.

Claiborn, W., Biskin, B., & Friedman, L. CHAMPUS and quality assurance. *Professional Psychology,* 1982, *13,* 40–49.

Clapp, N. W. Work group norms: Leverage for organizational changes I: theory, II: application. *Organization development series* (No. 2). Olamfield, N.J.: Block Petrella Associates, 1974.

Clausen, A. W. Listening and responding to employees' concerns. *Harvard Business Review,* 1980, *58* (1), 101–114.

Clifford, D. K. Building a strategic capability. Talk presented at the McGraw-Hill/*Business Week* Strategic Planning and Management Conference, Chicago, May 28-29, 1981.

Cochran, D. J. Organizational consultation: A planning group approach. *Personnel and Guidance Journal,* 1982, *60,* 314–318.

Cohen, L. H. Document-based peer review in a psychology training clinic: A preliminary report of a statewide program. *Professional Psychology,* 1983, *14,* 362–367.

Cohen, M. D., & March, J. G. Leadership in an organized anarchy. In W. R. Lassey & M. Sashkin (Eds.), *Leadership and social change.* Third edition. San Diego: University Associates, 1983. Excerpted from M. D. Cohen & J. G. March, *Leadership and ambiguity.* New York: McGraw-Hill, 1974.

Condry, J. Enemies of exploration: Self-initiated versus other-initiated learning. *Journal of Personality and Social Psychology,* 1977, *35,* 459–477.

Conyne, R. K. Models for conducting student organization development. *Personnel and Guidance Journal,* 1983, *61,* 394–397.

Corlett, E. H., & Richardson, J. *Stress, work design, and productivity.* New York: Wiley & Sons, 1982.

Cotton, C. C., Brown, P. J., & Golembiewski, R. T. Marginality and the OD practitioner. *The Journal of Applied Behavioral Science,* 1977, *13,* 493–506.

Cummings, T. G., & Srivastva, S. *Management of work: A sociotechnical systems approach.* San Diego, Calif.: University Associates, 1977.

Cyert, R., & March, J. G. *A behavioral theory of the firm.* Englewood Cliffs, N.J.: Prentice-Hall, 1963.

Deal, T. E., & Kennedy, A. A. *Corporate cultures: The rites and rituals of corporate life.* Reading, Mass.: Addison-Wesley, 1982.

Deci, E. L. Effects of externally mediated rewards on intrinsic motivation. *Journal of Personality and Social Psychology,* 1971, *18,* 105–115.

Deci, E. L. Intrinsic motivation, extrinsic reinforcement, and inequity. *Journal of Personality and Social Psychology,* 1972, *22,* 113–120.

Deci, E. L. *Intrinsic motivation.* New York: Plenum, 1975.

Deci, E. L. *The psychology of self-determination.* Lexington, Mass.: Lexington Books, 1980.

Delbecq, A. L., Van de Ben, A. H., & Gustafson, D. H. *Group techniques for program planning: A guide to nominal group and delphi processes.* Glenview, Ill.: Scott, Foresman, 1975.

De Meuse, K. P., & Liebowitz, S. J. An empirical analysis of team-building research. *Group and Organization Studies,* 1981, *6,* 357–378.

Dessler, G. *Organization and management.* Englewood Cliffs, N.J.: Prentice-Hall, 1976.

Diesing, P. *Reason in our society.* Westport, Conn.: Greenwood, 1962.

Drucker, P. F. *The age of discontinuity: Guidelines to our changing society.* New York: Harper & Row, 1968.

Dunnette, M. D., & Borman, W. C. Personnel selection and classification systems. In M. R. Rosenweig & L. W. Porter (Eds.), *Annual Review of Psychology,* 1979, *30,* 477–525.

Dyer, W. G. *Team building: Issues and alternatives.* Reading, Mass.: Addison-Wesley, 1977.

Egan, G. *Interpersonal living: A skill/contract approach to interpersonal relating in groups.* Monterey, Calif.: Brooks/Cole, 1976.

Egan, G. *You and me: The skills of communicating and relating to others.* Monterey, Calif.: Brooks/Cole, 1977.

Egan, G. Model A: The logic of systems as OD instrument. In W. W. Burke (Ed.), *The cutting edge: Current theory and practice in organization development.* San Diego: University Associates, 1978a.

Egan, G. The parish: Ministering community and community of ministers. In E. E. Whitehead (Ed.), *The parish: Community and ministry.* Paramus, N.J.: Paulist Press, 1978b.

Egan, G. Integrative problem solving. In E. K. Marshall & P. D. Kurtz (Eds.), *Interpersonal helping skills.* San Francisco: Jossey-Bass, 1982a.

Egan, G. *The skilled helper: Model, skills, and methods for effective helping.* 2nd ed. Monterey, Calif.: Brooks/Cole, 1982b.

Egan, G., & Cowan, M. A. *People in systems: A model for development in the human-service professions and education.* Monterey, Calif.: Brooks/Cole, 1979.

Ellin, L. R. Strategic planning and implementation: Pitfalls and potential. Talk presented at the McGraw-Hill/*Business Week* Strategic Planning and Management Conference, Chicago, May 1981.

Ellis, M. J. *Why people play.* Englewood Cliffs, N.J.: Prentice-Hall, 1973.

Emery, F. E., & Trist, E. L. The causal texture of organizational environments. *Human Relations,* 1965, *18,* 21–32.

Engelberg, S. Open systems consultation: Some lessons learned from case experience. *Professional Psychology,* 1980, *11,* 972–979.

English, F. W., & Kaufman, R. *Needs assessment: A focus for curriculum development.* Washington, D.C.: Association for Supervision and Curriculum Development, 1975.

Erikson, E. H. *Insight and responsibility.* New York: Norton, 1964.

Ewing, D. W. Employees' rights. *Society,* 1977a, *15* (1) 104–111.

Ewing, D. W. *Freedom inside the organization.* New York: Dutton, 1977b.

Faust, V. Developmental consultation in school settings. In C. A. Parker (Ed.), *Psychological consultation: Helping teachers meet special needs.* Minneapolis, Minn.: Leadership Training Institute/Special Education, University of Minnesota, 1975.

Fayol, H. *General and industrial management.* London: Pitman, 1949.

Fein, M. Job enrichment: A re-evaluation. *Sloane Management Review,* 1974, *15,* 69–88.

Fenhagen, J. C. *Mutual ministry: New vitality for the local church.* New York: Seabury, 1977.

Ferreira, J., & Burges, B. *Collecting evidence: A layman's guide to participant observation.* Boston: Institute for Responsive Education, 1975. This is presently available from ERIC on microfiche.

Fiedler, F. E. *A theory of leadership effectiveness.* New York: McGraw-Hill, 1974.

Fiedler, F. E., & Chemers, M. M. *Leadership and effective management.* Glenview, Ill.: Scott, Foresman, 1974.

Filley, A. *Interpersonal conflict resolution.* Glenview, Ill.: Scott, Foresman, 1975.

Finkle, R. B. Managerial assessment centers. In M. D. Dunnette (Ed.), *Handbook of industrial and organizational psychology.* Chicago: Rand McNally, 1976.

Fisher, C. D., & Gitelson, R. A meta-analysis of the correlates of role conflict and ambiguity. *Journal of Applied Psychology,* 1983, *68,* 320–333.

Fisher, D. *Communication in organizations.* St. Paul, Minn.: West, 1981.

Fisher, R., & Ury, W. *Getting to yes: Negotiating agreement without giving in.* Boston, Mass.: Houghton Mifflin, 1981.

Flanagan, J. C. A research approach to improving our quality of life. *American Psychologist,* 1978, *33,* 138–147.

Flanagan, J. C. Identifying opportunities for improving the quality of life of older age groups. Unpublished paper. American Institute for Research, Palo Alto, Calif., June 1979.

Fordyce, J. K., & Weil, R. *Managing with people: A manager's handbook of organization development methods.* Reading, Mass.: Addison-Wesley, 1971.

Fordyce, M. W. A program to increase happiness: Further studies. *Journal of Counseling Psychology,* 1983, *4,* 483–498.

Franklin, J. L., Wissler, A. L., & Spencer, G. J. *Survey-guided development III: A manual for concepts training.* La Jolla, Calif.: University Associates Press, 1977.

Frederiksen, L. W. Behavioral reorganization of a professional service system. *Journal of Organizational Behavior Management,* 1978, *2,* 1–9.

Freire, P. *Pedagogy of the oppressed.* New York: Herder & Herder, 1970.

French, J. R. R., Caplan, R. D., Van Harrison, R., & Pinneau, S. R. *Effects of social support on occupational stresses and strains.* Washington, D.C., 1976. (ERIC Document Reproduction Service No. ED 138859.)

Fuehrer, A. E., & Keys, C. B. Law enforcement in the court: Role identity and interpersonal relations training of deputy sheriffs. Paper presented at the Academy of Criminal Justice Sciences Annual Meeting, New Orleans, March 1978.

Galbraith, J. K. *The nature of mass poverty.* Cambridge, Mass.: Harvard University Press, 1979.

Galbraith, J. R. *Designing complex organizations.* Reading, Mass.: Addison-Wesley, 1973.

Galbraith, J. R. *Organization design.* Reading, Mass.: Addison-Wesley, 1977.

Gall, J. *Systemantics: How systems work and especially how they fail.* New York: Quadrangle, 1975.

Gallessich, J. *The profession and practice of consultation.* San Francisco: Jossey-Bass, 1982.

Gartner, A., & Riessman, F. *Self-help in the human services.* San Francisco: Jossey-Bass, 1977.

Gazda, G. M. Life skills training. In E. K. Marshall & P. D. Kurtz (Eds.), *Interpersonal helping skills.* San Francisco: Jossey-Bass, 1982.

Gazda, G. M. Multiple impact training: A life skills approach. In D. Larson (Ed.), *Teaching psychological skills: Models for giving psychology away.* Monterey, Calif.: Brooks/Cole, 1984.

Gibb, J. R. *Trust: A new view of personal and organizational development.* Los Angeles: Guild of Tutors Press, 1978.

Gilbert, T. F. *Human competence: Engineering worthy performance.* New York: McGraw-Hill, 1978.

Giroux, H., & Penna, A. Social relations in the classroom: The dialectic of the hidden curriculum. *Edcentric,* 1977, *40–41* (Spring-Summer), 39–46.

Gluckstern, N. B., & Packard, R. W. The internal-external change-agent team: Bringing change to a "closed institution." *Journal of Applied Behavioral Science,* 1977, *13,* 41–52.

Goffman, E. *Interaction ritual: Essays on face-to-face behavior.* New York: Anchor Books, 1967.

Goldstein, I. L. Training and organizational psychology. *Professional Psychology,* 1980, *11,* 421–427.

Goodmeasure. *Survey: Conditions for work effectiveness.* Cambridge, Mass.: 1979a.

Goodmeasure. *Instrument: Power dimensions in your job.* Cambridge, Mass.: 1979b.

Goodstein, L. D. *Consulting with human service systems.* Reading, Mass.: Addison-Wesley, 1978.

Gould, R. *The Matsushita phenomenon.* Tokyo: Diamond Sha, 1970.

Graber, J. M. Conceptualization and measurement of quality of working life. Unpublished paper. Chicago, 1981.

Grant, D. L. Issues in personnel selection. *Professional Psychology,* 1980, *11,* 369–384.

Grant, G. (Ed.) *On competence: A critical analysis of competence-based reforms in higher education.* San Francisco: Jossey-Bass, 1979.

Gray, F., & Burns, M. L. Does "management by objectives" work in education? *Educational Leadership,* 1979, *36,* 414–417.

Guion, R. M. Recruiting, selection, and job placement. In M. D. Dunnette (Ed.), *Handbook of industrial and organizational psychology*. Chicago, 1976.

Hackman, J. R., & Oldham, G. R. *Work redesign*. Reading, Mass.: Addison-Wesley, 1980.

Hall, E. T. *The hidden dimension*. New York: Doubleday, 1966.

Hall, E. T. *Beyond culture*. New York: Anchor Press, 1977.

Hall, R. H. *Organizations: Structures and processes*. Englewood Cliffs, N.J.: Prentice-Hall, 1972.

Hannafin, M. J., & Witt, J. C. System intervention and the school psychologist: Maximizing interplay among roles and functions. *Professional Psychology*, 1983, *14*, 128–136.

Harschnek, R. A., Jr., Petersen, D. J., & Malone, R. L. Which personnel department is right for you? *Personnel Administrator*, 1978, *23*, April, 58–66.

Harwood, E. The entrepreneurial renaissance and its promoters. *Society*, 1979, *16* (3) 27–31.

Hasenfeld, Y., & English, R. A. Introduction. In Y. Hasenfeld & R. A. English (Eds.), *Human service organizations*. Ann Arbor: University of Michigan Press, 1975.

Haskell, T. L. Power to the experts. *New York Review of Books*, 1977, *24* (16) 28–33.

Hausser, D. L., Pecorella, P. A., & Wissler, A. L. *Survey-guided development II: A manual for consultants*. La Jolla, Calif.: University Associates Press, 1977.

Havelock, R. G. *The change agent guide to innovation in education*. Englewood Cliffs, N.J.: Education Technology Publications, 1973.

Hersey, P., & Blanchard, K. H. *Management of organization behavior*. Englewood Cliffs, N.J.: Prentice-Hall, 1982.

Hersey, P., Blanchard, K. H., & Hambleton, R. K. Contracting for leadership style: A process and instrumentation for building effective work relationships. In W. W. Burke (Ed.), *The cutting edge: Current theory and practice in organization development*. San Diego: University Associates, 1978.

Herzberg, F. One more time: How do you motivate employees? *Harvard Business Review*, 1968, *46* (1), 115–124.

Hicks, H. G., & Gullett, C. R. *The management of organizations*. 3rd ed. New York: McGraw-Hill, 1976.

Hickson, D. J., Heninges, C. R., Lee, C. A., Schneck, R. E., & Penninges, J. M. A strategic contingencies theory of intraorganizational power. *Administrative Science Quarterly*, 1971, *16*, 216–227.

Hirschhorn, L. *Cutting back*. San Francisco: Jossey-Bass, 1983.

Hoffman, J. R., & Pool, R. A. Part-time faculty: Their own needs assessment. *Lifelong learning: The adult years*. 1979 (April), 26–27.

Holahan, C. J. Consultation in environmental psychology: A case study and a new counseling role. *Journal of Counseling Psychology*, 1977, *24*, 251–254.

Hollander, E. P. Conformity, status, and idiosyncrasy credit. *Psychological Review*, 1958, *65*, 117–127.

Hollander, E. P. *Leaders, groups, and influence*. New York: Oxford University Press, 1964.

Hollander, E. P. *Leadership dynamics: A practical guide to effective relationships*. New York: Free Press, 1978.

Hollander, E. P., & Julian, J. W. Contemporary trends in the analysis of leadership processes. *Psychological Bulletin*, 1969, *71*, 387–397.

House, J. S. *Work stress and social support*. Reading, Mass.: Addison-Wesley, 1982.

Huck, J. R. The research base. In J. L. Moses & W. C. Byham (Eds.), *Applying the assessment center method*. New York: Pergamon, 1977.

Hulin, C. L., & Blood, M. R. Job enlargement, individual differences, and worker responses. *Psychological Bulletin*, 1968, *70*, 41–55.

International Business Machines. *Manager's guide: The opinion survey*. (Internal company publication.) Armonk, New York: IBM, 1974.

James, B. Can "needs" define educational goals? *Adult Education*, 1956, *6*, 95–100.

Janis, I. L. *Victims of groupthink*. Boston: Houghton Mifflin, 1972.

Janis, I. L., & Mann, L. *Decision making: A psychological analysis of conflict, choice, and commitment*. New York: The Free Press, 1977.

Janowitz, M. Content analysis and the study of sociopolitical change. *Journal of Communication*, 1976, *26* (4).

Jay, A. *Corporation man*. New York: Random House, 1971.

Jenkins, G. D., Nadler, D. A., Lawler, E. E., & Cammann, C. Standardized observations: An approach to measuring the nature of jobs. *Journal of Applied Psychology*, 1975, *60*, 171–181.

Johnston, J. M. Punishment of human behavior. *American Psychologist*, 1972, *27*, 1033–1054.

Jones, J. E. The sensing interview. In J. W. Pfeiffer & J. E. Jones (Eds.), *The 1973 annual handbook for group facilitators*. San Diego: University Associates, 1973.

Journal of Applied Behavioral Science. Special edition on leadership/followership, 1982, *18*(3).

Kahn, R. L. Field studies of power in organizations. In R. L. Kahn & E. Boulding (Eds.), *Power and conflict in organizations.* New York: Basic Books, 1964.

Kahn, R. L., & Cannell, C. F. *The dynamics of interviewing.* New York: Wiley, 1967.

Kahneman, D., Slovic, P., & Tversky, A. *Judgment under uncertainty: Heuristics and biases.* Cambridge, England: Cambridge University Press, 1982.

Kanter, R. M. *Men and women of the corporation.* New York: Basic Books, 1977.

Kanter, R. M. *Change masters: Innovation for productivity in the American corporation.* New York: Simon & Schuster, 1983.

Kanter, R. M., & Stein, B. A. Foreword. In D. Zwerdling, *Workplace democracy.* New York: Harper & Row, 1980.

Katzell, R., Yankelovich, D., Fein, M., Ornati, O., & Nash, A. *Work, productivity, and job satisfaction: An evaluation of policy-related research.* New York: The Psychological Corporation, 1975.

Kaufman, R. A. *Educational systems planning.* Englewood Cliffs, N.J.: Prentice-Hall, 1972.

Kaufman, R. *Identifying and solving problems: A system approach.* La Jolla, Calif.: University Associates, 1976.

Kauffman, D. L., Jr. *Systems 1: An introduction to systems thinking.* St. Paul, Minn.: Future Systems/TLH Associates, 1980.

Kauffman, D. L., Jr. *Systems 2: Human systems.* St. Paul, Minn.: Future Systems/TLH Associates, 1981.

Kaye, B. L. *Up is not the only way.* Englewood Cliffs, N.J.: Prentice-Hall, 1982.

Kazdin, A. E. *Behavior modification in applied settings.* Homewood, Ill.: Dorsey Press, 1975.

Kellog, M. S., & Burstiner, I. *Putting management theories to work.* Englewood Cliffs, N.J.: Prentice-Hall, 1979.

Kerr, C., & Rosow, J. M. *Work in America: The decade ahead.* New York: Van Nostrand Reinhold, 1979.

Kilburg, R. Consumer survey as needs assessment method: A case study. *Evaluation and Program Planning,* 1978, *1*, 285–292.

Kimbrough, R. B. Power structures and educational change. In E. L. Morphet and C. O. Ryan (Eds.), *Planning and effecting needed changes in education.* New York: Citation Press, 1967.

Kindler, H. S. Two planning strategies: Incremental change and transformational change. *Group and Organization Studies,* 1979, *4*, 476–484.

Kleinfield, N. R. A human resource at Allied Corporation. *New York Times,* 6 June 1982.

Koontz, H. The management theory jungle revisited. *Academy of Management Review,* 1980, 5 (2), 175–187.

Kotter, J. *Organizational dynamics: Diagnosis and intervention.* Reading, Mass.: Addison-Wesley, 1978.

Kuhn, T. S. *The structure of scientific revolutions.* 2nd ed. Chicago: University of Chicago Press, 1970.

Kyriacou, C., & Sutcliffe, J. A model of teacher stress. *Educational Studies,* 1978, *4*, 1–6.

Landen, D. L. *Evolution of QWL as a movement within society, government, and General Motors.* Detroit: General Motors Corp., 1977.

Larson, D. (Ed.). *Teaching psychological skills: Models for giving psychology away.* Monterey, Calif.: Brooks/Cole, 1984.

Lassey, W. R., & Sashkin, M. *Leadership and social change.* 3rd ed. San Diego: University Associates, 1983.

LaVan, H., Welsch, H. P., & Full, J. M. A contingency approach to organization development based on differentiated roles. *Group and Organization Studies,* 1981, *6*, 176–189.

Lawler, E. E., III. For a more effective organization—Match the job to the man. *Organization Dynamics,* 1974, *2*, 19–29.

Lawler, E. E., III. Strategies for improving quality of work life. *American Psychologist,* 1982, *37*, 486–493.

Lawrence, P. R., & Lorsch, H. W. *Organization and environment.* Boston: Division of Research, Harvard Business School, 1967.

Lawrence, P. R., & Lorsch, J. W. *Developing organizations: Diagnosis and action.* Reading, Mass.: Addison-Wesley, 1969.

Lawrence, P. R., Weisbord, M. R., & Charns, M. P. *Academic medical center self-study guide.* Washington, D.C.: Report of Physicians Assistance Branch, Bureau of Health, Manpower Education, National Institute of Health, 1973.

Leonard, M. M. The counseling psychologist as an organizational consultant. *Counseling Psychologist,* 1977, *7* (2), 73–77.

Levi, L. *Preventing work stress.* Reading, Mass.: Addison-Wesley, 1982.

Levinson, H. *Organizational diagnosis.* Cambridge, Mass.: Harvard University Press, 1972.

Lewin, K. Quasi-stationary social equilibria and the problem of permanent change. In W. G. Bennis, K. D. Benne, & R. Chin (Eds.), *The planning of change.* New York: Holt, Rinehart, & Winston, 1969.

Likert, R. *New patterns of management.* McGraw-Hill, 1961.

Likert, R. *The human organization.* New York: McGraw-Hill, 1967.

Lindblom, C. E. *The intelligence of a democracy.* New York: The Free Press, 1965.

Lippitt, G. L. *Visualizing change: Model building and the change process.* Fairfax, Va.: NTL Learning Resources Corporation, 1973.

Lippitt, R. Dimensions of the consultant's job. *Journal of Social Issues,* 1959, *15* (2), 5–12.

Lippitt, R. A human energy issue: The temporary mobilization and use of human resources. *Group and Organization Studies,* 1979, *4,* 309–315.

Litwin, G. H., Humphrey, J. W., & Wilson, T. B. Organizational climate: A proven tool for improving performance. In W. W. Burke (Ed.), *This cutting edge.* San Diego: University Associates, 1978.

Lorsch, J., & Morse, J. *Organizations and their members: A contingency approach.* New York: Harper & Row, 1974.

Lundberg, C. C. On teaching organizational development: Some core instructional issues. *Exchange: The Organizational Behavior Teaching Journal,* 1980, *5* (2), 21–24.

Luthans, F., & Kreitner, R. *Organizational behavior modification.* Glenview, Ill.: Scott, Foresman, 1975.

Macy, B. A., & Mirvis, P. H. A methodology for assessment of quality of work life and organizational effectiveness in behavioral economic terms. *Administrative Science Quarterly,* 1976, *21,* 212–226.

Malone, R. L., & Petersen, D. L. Personnel effectiveness: Its dimensions and development. *Personnel Journal,* 1977, *56* (October), 498–501.

Malott, R., Tillema, M., & Glenn, S. *Behavior analysis and behavior modification: An introduction.* Kalamazoo, Mich.: Behaviordelia, 1978.

March, J. G., & Simon, H. A. *Organizations.* New York: Wiley, 1958.

Margulies, N., & Wallace, J. *Organizational change: Techniques and applications.* Glenview, Ill.: Scott, Foresman, 1973.

Marshall, E. K., & Kurtz, P. D. *Interpersonal helping skills.* San Francisco: Jossey-Bass, 1982.

Maslow, A. *Towards a psychology of being.* 2nd ed. New York: Van Nostrand Reinhold, 1968.

McCall, G., & Simmons, J. *Issues in participant observation.* Reading, Mass.: Addison-Wesley, 1969.

McGehee, W., & Thayer, P. W. *Training in business and industry.* New York: Wiley, 1961.

McGinnies, E. *Social behavior: A functional analysis.* Boston: Houghton Mifflin, 1970.

McHale, J. Resource availability and growth. *Society,* 1979, *16* (3), 78–83.

McKie, J. W. Advertising and social responsibility. *Society,* 1979, *16* (3), 39–43.

McLean, A. A. *Work stress.* Reading, Mass.: Addison-Wesley, 1982.

McMahon, J. P. The maturity factor: Add insight to your conflict training. *Training,* 1983, *20* (11), 55–60.

Metcalf, E. I., Riffle, L. V., & Seabury, F., III. Environmental scanning: What is it—Who needs it—How to use it. Workshop presented by *Business Week* on Strategic Planning, Chicago, May 1981.

Meyer, M. W. (Ed.). *Environments and organizations.* San Francisco: Jossey-Bass, 1978.

Miles, R. H. *Macro organizational behavior.* Santa Monica, Calif.: Goodyear, 1980.

Miller, G. A. Psychology as a means of promoting human welfare. *American Psychologist,* 1969, *24,* 1063–1075.

Miller, G. A. Giving away psychology in the '80s: George A. Miller interviewed by Elizabeth Hall. *Psychology Today,* 1980, *13* (8), 38–50, 97–98.

Miller, L. M. *Behavior management: The new science of managing people at work.* New York: Wiley, 1978.

Monette, M. L. The concept of educational need: An analysis of selected literature. *Adult Education,* 1977, *27,* 116–127.

Monette, M. L. Need assessment: A critique of philosophical assumptions. *Adult Education,* 1979, 83–95.

Moore, L. I. The FMI: Dimensions of follower maturity. *Group and Organization Studies,* 1976, *1,* 203–222.

Moos, R. H. *Evaluating educational environments: Procedures, measures, findings, and policy implications.* San Francisco: Jossey-Bass, 1979.

Moracco, J. C., & McFadden, H. The counselor's role in reducing teacher stress. *Personnel and Guidance Journal,* 1982, *60,* 549–552.

Moses, J. L., & Byham, W. C. *Applying the assessment center method.* New York: Pergamon Press, 1977.

Moss, L. *Management stress.* Reading, Mass.: Addison-Wesley, 1982.

Murrell, S. *Community psychology and social systems.* New York: Behavioral Publications, 1973.

Myers, M. S. *Every employee a manager.* New York: McGraw-Hill, 1970.

Nadler, D. A. *Feedback and organization development: Using data-based methods*. Reading, Mass.: Addison-Wesley, 1977.

Nadler, D. A., & Tushman, M. L. A diagnostic model for organizational behavior. In J. R. Hackman, E. E. Lawler, & L. W. Porter (Eds.), *Perspectives on behavior in organizations*. New York: McGraw-Hill, 1977.

Nagel, S. S. Determining when data is worth gathering. *Society,* 1978, *16* (1), 20–23.

Naisbitt, J. *Megatrends: Ten new directions transforming our lives*. New York: Warner, 1982.

National Industrial Conference Board. *Perspectives for the '20s and '80s: Tomorrow's problems confronting today's managers*. New York: National Industrial Conference Board, Special Report, 1970.

Neff, F. Survey research: A tool for problem diagnosis and improvement in organizations. In A. W. Gouldner & S. M. Miller (Eds.), *Applied Sociology*. New York: Free Press, 1965.

Nicholls, H. G. Instituting a strategic management capability. Paper and workshop presented at the McGraw-Hill/*Business Week* Strategic Planning and Management Conference, Chicago, May 1981.

Nilson, L. B., & Edelman, M. The symbolic evocation of occupational prestige. *Society,* 1979, *16* (3), 57–64.

Nisbett, R., & Ross, L. *Human inference: Strategies and shortcomings of social judgment*. Englewood Cliffs, N.J.: Prentice-Hall, 1980.

Nord, W. Beyond the teaching machine: The neglected area of operant conditioning in the theory and practice of management. *Organizational Behavior and Human Performance,* 1969, *4,* 375–401.

Norris, W. C. *New frontiers for business leadership*. Minneapolis, Minn.: Dorn Books, 1983.

O'Brien, R. T. The many faces of the four-style grid. *Training, HRD,* 1982, *19* (11), 37.

O'Neill, P., & Trickett, E. J. *Community consultation: Strategies for facilitating change in schools, hospitals, prisons, social service programs, and other community settings*. San Francisco: Jossey-Bass, 1982.

Ouchi, W. *Theory Z: How American business can meet the Japanese challenge*. Reading, Mass.: Addison-Wesley, 1981.

Owens, W. A. Background data. In M. D. Dunnette (Ed.), *Handbook of industrial and organizational psychology*. Chicago: Rand McNally, 1976.

Pancoast, D. L., Parker, P., & Froland, C. *Rediscovering self-help: Its role in social care*. Beverly Hills, Calif.: Sage, 1983.

Parker, C. A. (Ed.) *Psychological consultation: Helping teachers meet special needs*. Minneapolis, Minn.: Leadership Training Institute/Special Education, University of Minnesota, 1975.

Parkinson, C. N. *Parkinson's law and other studies in administration*. Boston: Houghton Mifflin, 1957.

Parsons, H. M. What happened at Hawthorne? *Science,* 1974, *183,* 922–932.

Pascale, R. T., & Athos, A. G. *The art of Japanese management*. New York: Simon & Schuster, 1981.

Pasmore, W. A., & Sherwood, J. J. *Sociotechnical systems: A sourcebook*. San Diego, Calif.: University Associates, 1978.

Personnel and Guidance Journal. Consultation I: Definition, models, programs. February, 1978, *56*.

Personnel and Guidance Journal. Consultation II: Dimensions, training, bibliography. March 1978, *56*.

Peter, L. J., & Hull, R. *The Peter principle*. New York: Bantam, 1970.

Peters, T. J., & Waterman, R. H. *In search of excellence: Lessons from America's best-run companies*. New York: Harper & Row, 1982.

Petersen, D. J., & Malone, R. L. The personnel effectiveness grid: A new tool for estimating personnel department effectiveness. *Human Resource Management,* 1975, *14* (Winter), 10–21.

Pettigrew, A. Information control as a power resource. *Sociology,* 1972, *6,* 187–204.

Pfeiffer, J. W., & Jones, J. E. OD readiness. In W. W. Burke (Ed.), *The cutting edge: Current theory and practice in organization development*. San Diego: University Associates, 1978.

Pondy, L. R. Organizational conflict: Concepts and models. *Administrative Science Quarterly,* 1976, *12,* 296–320.

Porter, L., Lawler, E., III, & Hackman, K. *Behavior in organizations*. New York: McGraw-Hill, 1975.

Pounds, W. F. The scheduling environment. In J. F. Muth & G. Thompson (Eds.), *Industrial scheduling*. Englewood Cliffs, N.J.: Prentice-Hall, 1963.

President's Commission on National Goals. *Goals for Americans*. New York: Columbia University, 1960.

Prue, D. M., Frederiksen, L. W., & Bacon, A. Organizational behavior management: An annotated bibliography. *Journal of Organizational Behavior Management,* 1978, *1,* 216–257.

Quinn, J. B. *Strategies for change: Logical incrementalism*. Homewood, Ill.: Dow Jones-Irwin, 1980.

Quinn, J. B. Managing strategic change. Paper presented at the McGraw-Hill/*Business Week* Strategic Planning and Management Conference, Chicago, May 1981.

Quinn, R., & Staines, G. *1977 quality of employment survey*. Ann Arbor, Mich.: Institute for Social Research, 1979.

Raia, A. P. *Managing by objectives*. Glenview, Ill.: Scott, Foresman, 1974.

Ranson, S., Hinings, B., & Greenwood, R. The structuring of organizational structures. *Administrative Science Quarterly*, 1980, *25*, 1–17.

Rappaport, J. In praise of paradox: A social policy of enpowerment over prevention. *American Journal of Community Psychology*, 1981, *9*, 1–26.

Raspberry, B. Why reward failure? *Chicago Sun-Times*, 21 February 1978.

Reynolds, M. Learning the ropes. *Society*, 1982, *19* (6), 30–33.

Rickard, H. C., & Clements, C. B. Administrative training for psychologists in APA-approved clinical programs. *Professional Psychology*, 1981, *12*, 349–355.

Rizzo, J., House, R., & Lirtzman, S. Role conflict and ambiguity in complex organizations. *Administrative Science Quarterly*, 1970, *15*, 150–163.

Robbins, S. P. *Managing organizational conflict: A nontraditional approach*. Englewood Cliffs, N.J.: Prentice-Hall, 1974.

Robert, M. *Managing conflict from the inside out*. Austin, Tex.: Learning Concepts, 1982.

Roeber, R. J. C. *The organization in a changing environment*. Reading, Mass.: Addison-Wesley, 1973.

Rose-Ackerman, S. *Corruption: A study in political economy*. New York: Academic Press, 1978.

Rosen, S., Tesser, A. On the reluctance to communicate undesirable information: The MUM effect. *Sociometry*, 1970, *33*, 253–263.

Rosen, S., Tesser, A. Fear of negative evaluation and the reluctance to transmit bad news. *Proceedings of the 79th Annual Convention of the American Psychological Association*, 1971, *6*, 301–302.

Rosow, J. M. Quality of work life issues for the 1980s. *Training and Development Journal*, 1981 (March), 33–52.

Rubin, L. B. *Worlds of pain: Life in the working-class family*. New York: Basic Books, 1976.

Ryan, W. *Blaming the victim*. New York: Pantheon, 1971.

St. Charles Hospital statement of mission and philosophy. Oregon, Ohio: 4 February 1983.

Sarason, S. B. *The creation of settings and the future societies*. San Francisco: Jossey-Bass, 1972.

Schachte, H. B., & Powers, C. W. Business responsibility and the public policy process. In T. Bradshaw & D. Vogel (Eds.), *Corporations and their critics*. New York: McGraw-Hill, 1981.

Schatzman, L., & Strauss, A. *Field methods*. Englewood Cliffs, N.J.: Prentice-Hall, 1972.

Schein, E. H. *Process consultation: Its role in organization development*. Reading, Mass.: Addison-Wesley, 1969.

Schein, E. H. *Career dynamics: Matching individual and organizational needs*. Reading, Mass.: Addison-Wesley, 1978a.

Schein, E. H. Human resource planning and development: A total system. In W. W. Burke (Ed.), *The cutting edge: Current theory and practice in organization development*. San Diego: University Associates, 1978b.

Schmitt, N. Social and situational determinants of interview decisions: Implications for the employment interview. *Personnel Psychology*, 1976, *29*, 70–101.

Schochet, G. J. Social responsibility, profits, and the public interest. *Society*, 1979, *16* (3), 20–26.

Scriven, M., & Roth, J. Needs assessment: Concept and practice. *New Directions for Program Evaluation*, 1978, *1* (1), 1–11.

Sechrest, L., & Hoffman, P. The philosophical underpinnings of peer review. *Professional Psychology*, 1982, *13*, 14–18.

Selye, H. *The stress of life*. Hightstown, N.J.: McGraw-Hill, 1976.

Selznick, P. *Leadership in administration*. New York: Harper & Row, 1957.

Shellow, R. Reinforcing police neutrality in civil rights confrontations. *Journal of Applied Behavioral Science*, 1965, *1*, 243–254.

Sherwood, J. J. A workshop on action research. Chicago: Loyola University, October 1981.

Sherwood, J. J., & Glidewell, J. C. Planned renegotiation. In J. E. Jones & J. W. Pfeiffer (Eds.), *The 1973 annual handbook for group facilitators*. San Diego, Calif.: University Associates, 1973.

Sherwood, J. J., & Scherer, J. J. A model for couples: How two can grow together. *Small Group Behavior*, 1975, *6*.

Shostak, A. *Blue collar stress*. Reading, Mass.: Addison-Wesley, 1980.

Shueman, S. A model of peer review. *Professional Psychology*, 1982, *12*, 639–646.

Skinner, B. F. *Science and human behavior*. New York: Macmillan, 1953.

Skinner, B. F. Why don't we use the behavioral sciences? *Human Nature*, 1978, *1* (3), 86–92.

Smith, A. *The wealth of nations*. New York: Random House, 1937.

Snyder, C. R., Higgins, R. L., & Stucky, R. J. *Excuses: Masquerades in search of grace*. New York: Wiley, 1983.

Snyder, M., & Swann, W. B. Hypothesis testing processes in social interaction. *Journal of Personality and Social Psychology*, 1978, *36*, 1202–1212.

Spier, M. S. Kurt Lewin's "force-field analysis." In J. W. Pfeiffer & J. E. Jones (Eds.), *The 1973 annual handbook for group facilitators*. San Diego, Calif.: University Associates, 1973.

Splete, H., & Bernstein, B. A survey of consultation training as a part of counselor education programs. *Personnel and Guidance Journal*, 1981, *59*, 470–472.

Spradley, J. P. *The ethnographic interview*. New York: Holt, Rinehart, & Winston, 1979.

Spradley, J. P. *Participant observation*. New York: Holt, Rinehart, & Winston, 1980.

Stahler, G., & Tash, W. (Eds.) *Innovative approaches to mental health evaluation*. New York: Academic Press, 1982.

Steers, R. M., & Porter, L. W. *The role of task goal attributes in employee performance*. Report No. TR–24. Washington, D.C.: Office of Naval Research, 1974.

Stein, B. A. Quality of work life in context: What every practitioner should know. Unpublished manuscript. Cambridge, Mass.: Goodmeasure, Inc., 1980.

Stein, B. A., & Kanter, R. M. Building the parallel organization: Creating mechanisms for permanent quality of work life. *Journal of Applied Behavioral Science*, 1980, *16*, 371–386.

Stogdill, R. M. *Handbook of leadership: A survey of theory and research*. New York: Free Press, 1974.

Strube, M. J., & Garcia, J. E. A meta-analytic investigation of Fiedler's contingency model of leadership effectiveness. *Psychological Bulletin*, 1981, *90*, 307–321.

Stum, D. L. DIRECT—A consultation skills training model. *Personnel and Guidance Journal*, 1982, *60*, 296–301.

Summers, C. W. Protecting *all* employees against unjust dismissal. *Harvard Business Review*, 1980, *58* (1), 132–139.

Tannenbaum, A. S. *Control in organizations*. New York: McGraw-Hill, 1968.

Tannenbaum, R. Some matters of life and death. UCLA Human Systems Development Study Center Working Paper 76–2. Unpublished manuscript, University of California at Los Angeles, 1976.

Tannenbaum, R., & Schmidt, W. H. How to choose a leadership pattern. *Harvard Business Review*, 1973 (May-June), 115–124.

Task Force on Development of Assessment Center Standards. Standards and ethical considerations for assessment center operations: May 1975. In J. L. Moses & W. C. Byham, *Applying the assessment center method*. New York: Pergamon Press, 1977.

Task Force on Assessment Center Standards. Standards and ethical considerations for assessment center operations: December 1978. *Journal of Assessment Center Technology*, 1979, *2* (2), 19–23.

Taylor, F. W. *The principles of scientific management*. New York: Harper & Row, 1911.

Taylor, J., & Bowers, D. G. *The survey of organizations: A machine-scored standardized questionnaire instrument*. Ann Arbor, Mich.: Institute of Social Research, 1972.

Terkel, S. *Working*. New York: Pantheon, 1974.

Terreberry, S. The evolution of organizational environments. *Administrative Science Quarterly*, 1968, *12*, 590–613.

Tesser, A., & Rosen, S. Similarity of objective fate as a determinant of the reluctance to transmit unpleasant information: The MUM effect. *Journal of Personality and Social Psychology*, 1972, *23*, 46–53.

Tesser, A., Rosen, S., & Batchelor, T. On the reluctance to communicate bad news (the MUM effect): A role play extension. *Journal of Personality*, 1972, *40*, 88–103.

Tesser, A., Rosen, S., & Tesser, M. On the reluctance to communicate undesirable messages (the MUM effect): A field study. *Psychological Reports*, 1971, *29*, 651–654.

Tharp, R. G. The triadic model of consultation: Current considerations. In C. A. Parker (Ed.), *Psychological consultation: Helping teachers meet special needs*. Minneapolis, Minn.: Leadership Training Institute/Special Education, University of Minnesota, 1975.

Tharp, R. G., & Wetzel, R. *Behavior modification in the natural environment*. New York: Academic Press, 1969.

Thayer, R. Measuring need in the social services. *Social and Economic Administration*, 1973, *7*, 91–105.

Thomas, K. W. Conflict and conflict management. In M. D. Dunnette (Ed.), *Handbook of industrial and organizational psychology*. Chicago: Rand McNally, 1976.

Thomas, K. W., & Kilmann, R. H. *The Thomas-Kilmann conflict mode instrument*. Tuxedo, N.Y.: Xicom, 1974.

Thomas, K. W., & Schmidt, W. H. A survey of managerial interests with respect to conflict. *Academy of Management Journal*, 1976, *19*, 315–318.

Thompson, J. *Organizations in action*. New York: McGraw-Hill, 1967.

Thorsrud, E. Policy making as a learning process. In A. B. Cherns, R. Sinclair, & W. I. Jenkins (Eds.), *Social science and government: Policies and problems*. London: Tavistock Publications, 1972.

Tichy, N. M. *Managing strategic change: Technical, political, and cultural dynamics*. New York: Wiley, 1983.

Tiger, L. Theatre and the human animal. *Society*, 1983, *20* (4), 93–95.

Tilles, S. The manager's job: A systems approach. *Harvard Business Review*, 1963, *41* (1), 73–81.

Tsongas, P. *The road from here: Liberalism and realities in the 1980s*. New York: Knopf, 1981.

Tucker, R. C. *Politics as leadership*. Columbia, Mo.: University of Missouri Press, 1981.

Tyler, F. B., Pargament, K. I., & Gatz, M. The resource collaborator role: A model for interactions involving psychologists. *American Psychologist*, 1983, *38,* 388–398.

Ullman, L. P. & Krasner, L. Psychological approaches to abnormal behavior. 2nd ed. Englewood Cliffs, N.J.: Prentice-Hall, 1975.

Uranowitz, S. W. Helping and self-attributions: A field experiment. *Journal of Personality and Social Psychology*, 1975, *31,* 852–854.

Vaill, P. B. Commentary on Lundberg's "Teaching organizational development: Some core instructional issues." *Exchange: The Organizational Behavior Teaching Journal*, 1980, *5* (2), 25–30.

Van Kaam, A. *Existential foundations of psychology*. Pittsburgh: Dusquesne University Press, 1966.

Vogel, D. The responsibilities of multinational corporations. *Society*, 1979, *16* (3), 52–56.

Wagner, J. The organizational double bind: Toward an understanding of rationality and its components. *Academy of Management Review*, 1978, *3,* 786–795.

Walton, R. *Interpersonal peacemaking: Confrontations and third party consultation*. Reading, Mass.: Addison-Wesley, 1969.

Walton, R. E. Work innovations in the United States. *Harvard Business Review*, 1979, *57* (4), 88–98.

Wanous, J. P. Realistic job previews for organizational recruitment. *Personnel*, 1975, *52,* 50–60.

Wanous, J. P. Organizational entry: Newcomers moving from outside to inside. *Psychological Bulletin*, 1977, *84,* 601–618.

Wanous, J. P. *Organizational entry*. Reading, Mass.: Addison-Wesley, 1980.

Warheit, G. J., Bell, R. A., & Schwab, J. J. *Needs assessment approaches: Methods and techniques*. Washington, D.C.: U.S. Government Printing Office, 1977.

Warheit, G. J., Buhl, J. M., & Bell, R. A. A critique of social indicators analysis and key informants surveys as needs assessments methods. *Evaluation and Program Planning*, 1978, *1,* 239–247.

Warshaw, L. J. *Stress management*. Reading, Mass.: Addison-Wesley, 1982.

Washington Post National Weekly Edition. Harris Poll: Confidence in institutional leadership. 5 December 1983.

Watson, D., & Tharp, R. *Self-directed behavior*. 3rd ed. Monterey, Calif.: Brooks/Cole, 1981.

Webb, E. J., Campbell, D. T., Schwartz, R. D., & Sechrest, L. *Unobtrusive measures: Nonreactive research in social sciences*. Chicago: Rand McNally, 1966.

Weick, K. E. *The social psychology of organizing*. Reading, Mass.: Addison-Wesley, 1969.

Weick, K. E. *The social psychology of organizing*. 2nd ed. Reading, Mass.: Addison-Wesley, 1979.

Weick, K. E. Administering education in loosely coupled schools. *Phi Delta Kappan*, 1982, *63,* 673–676.

Weisbord, M. R. Organizational diagnosis: Six places to look for trouble with or without a theory. *Group and Organizational Studies*, 1976, *1,* 430–447.

White, R. Motivation reconsidered: The concept of competence. *Psychological Review*, 1956, *66,* 297–334.

Whyte, W. F. *Money and motivation: An analysis of incentives in industry*. New York: Harper, 1955.

Williams, L. K., Seybolt, J. W., & Pinder, C. C. On administering questionnaires in organizational settings. *Personnel Psychology*, 1975, *28,* 93–103.

Williams, R. L., & Long, J. D. *Toward a self-managed life style*. 3rd ed. Boston: Houghton Mifflin, 1983.

Wills, T. A. Perceptions of clients by professional helpers. *Psychological Bulletin*, 1978, *85,* 968–1000.

Wilson, S. R., Flanagan, J. C., & Uhlaner, J. E. *Quality of life as perceived by 30 year old Army veterans*. Arlington: U.S. Army Research Institute for the Behavioral and Social Sciences, 1975.

Wolin, S. The rise of private man. *New York Review of Books*, 1977, *24* (6), 19–20, 25–26.

Woodman, R. W., & Sherwood, J. J. The role of team development in organization effectiveness: A critical review. *Psychological Bulletin*, 1980, *88,* 166–186.

Yukl, G. A. *Leadership in organizations*. Englewood Cliffs, N.J.: Prentice-Hall, 1981.

Zawacki, J. A system of unofficial rules of a bureaucracy: A study of hospitals. Doctoral Dissertation, University of Pittsburgh, 1963.

Zwerdling, D. *Workplace democracy*. New York: Harper & Row, 1980.

Name Index

Subject Index